BERND SIEFERT

SWEET

Gold

PRALINEN / CHOCOLATES

MARZIPAN

EIS / ICE CREAM

2

MATTHAES VERLAG GMBH

FOREWORD

After the sweeping success of "Sweet Gold 1", the decision to publish a second volume was not a hard one. Initially I thought that it would become easier after having written a book before, but I think I was mistaken: it was just the same as with my seminars – a new challenge every time because you don't want to rest on your laurels and offer something new. I don't want to exaggerate, but I think we have succeeded in that.

Originally we had planned that everything should go much faster than with the first volume but since then we have built our own seminar centre, have made alterations to our café and the profile of my activities has changed considerably so that "Sweet Gold 2" took a bit longer than anticipated. Please forgive me for that. But the wait was worth it. As one of my old teachers used to say: "Rome wasn't built in a day".

When choosing the subjects for "Sweet Gold 2" I opted for three distinct branches of patisserie that I am particularly fond of. Unfortunately they are often neglected but when done well one can be very successful with them. Ice-cream is one of my strong passions. When my father opened up his patisserie, he made the ice-cream himself. But due to lack of time he stopped doing that and for a long time we had the ice-cream delivered to us. After I finished my training, I bought a small sorbetière and tried out all kinds of sorbets and ice-creams. I volunteered in those nations that are big on ice-cream, extracted the best and created my own ideas. Then I took my first big step and we bought a small five-litre ice-cream maker; at the time it was a dinosaur but success proved me right. Bit by bit I replaced the industrial ice-creams and made my first ice-cream gateaux for weddings. Today this sector accounts for more than 50 % of our special orders. The crowning success came when I was appointed consultant at one of the largest ice-cream suppliers – Pregel – a position I held for 10 years. It is likely that my love for Italy stems from that time.

My other two strong passions are chocolate and chocolate candies. Chocolate is one of the most mysterious ingredients we know in our trade. Many years ago, chocolate used to be either white, light brown or almost black. Today all chocolates are not the same: bars often fetch more than 5 Euro, and if you ask me what is my favourite type I would not be able to tell whether it is bitter chocolate or Porcelana. Customers are open to new things: for example I have just launched a perfume collection as well as an oil collection for the "Salon du Chocolat" in Tokyo and not to forget the "Hessenpralinen", a range of chocolate candies containing green sauce, amongst other ingredients, for the State of Hessia in Germany. This is the first official range of chocolates that I had the privilege to create for one of the Federal States of Germany. Green sauce is a speciality which is more usually found in savoury recipe compositions, as is cheese or extreme spices such as chilli. It is true, chilli has been around for a long time with the ancient inhabitants of South America, but it was not until the film "Chocolat" came out that people began to be open for things that not long ago would have been considered a joke.

Likewise, marzipan has become a passion of mine over the years. Even back in my days at school I loved modelling figures from various raw materials. As a child I did not like marzipan; but when I was allowed to taste a really good piece of marzipan during a stay in Italy, I changed my mind and have been passionate about it ever since. I like to model marzipan figures at all kinds of events, especially when children are present. It simply is a fantastic material and with very little effort one can produce the most attractive figures. I made the conscious decision not to cultivate a designer style because I feel that, as a priority, my figures should be fun for children.

Whatever your preference, I hope you will enjoy exploring the recipes offered here. And always remember: practice makes perfect.

Yours

BERND SIEFERT

Nach dem großen Erfolg von „Sweet Gold 1" fiel mir die Entscheidung nicht schwer, auch einen zweiten Band zu veröffentlichen. Anfangs dachte ich, dass dies bestimmt leichter wird, wenn man schon einmal ein Buch geschrieben hat, aber ich glaube, da habe ich mich getäuscht: Es war genauso wie bei meinen Seminaren – es ist jedes Mal etwas Neues und man möchte sich nicht auf dem alten Erfolg ausruhen, sondern immer noch nachlegen. Ohne übertreiben zu wollen, ich glaube das ist uns gelungen.

Ursprünglich war geplant, dass alles viel schneller läuft als beim ersten Band, da wir aber in der Zwischenzeit ein eigenes Seminarzentrum aufgebaut haben, das Café umgebaut wurde und sich auch mein Aufgabenbereich stark verändert hat, brauchte „Sweet Gold 2" doch etwas länger als gedacht. Bitte verzeihen Sie mir. Aber das Warten hat sich gelohnt. Wie sagte einer meiner alten Meister so schön: „Gut Ding will Weile haben."

Bei den Themen von „Sweet Gold 2" habe ich mir drei Sparten der Konditorei ausgesucht, die mir sehr am Herzen liegen. Sie werden leider oft vernachlässigt, aber man kann mit ihnen, wenn man es richtig macht, sehr erfolgreich sein. Eis ist eine meiner großen Leidenschaften. Mein Vater hat, als er mit seiner Konditorei anfing, das Eis selbst hergestellt. Aufgrund von Zeitmangel wurde das rasch wieder eingestellt und wir wurden jahrelang beliefert. Während meiner Gesellenzeit habe ich mir dann eine kleine Sorbetière gekauft und alle möglichen Eissorten ausprobiert. Ich volontierte bei den großen Eisnationen, zog das Beste davon heraus und entwickelte meine eigenen Ideen. Dann machte ich den ersten großen Schritt und wir kauften eine kleine Fünf-Liter-Eismaschine, damals ein Dinosaurier, aber die Erfolge gaben mir Recht. Ich ersetzte nach und nach die Industrieeissorten und machte meine ersten Hochzeitseistorten. Heute machen sie bereits mehr als 50 % der Sonderbestellungen aus. Als krönender Erfolg des Ganzen war ich 10 Jahre lang als Berater bei einem der größten Eiszulieferer – Pregel – tätig. Wahrscheinlich kommt daher auch meine Liebe zu Italien.

Pralinen und Schokolade sind meine beiden anderen großen Leidenschaften. Schokolade ist eine der geheimnisvollsten Zutaten, die wir in unserem Handwerk kennen. Vor Jahrzehnten war Schokolade einfach nur weiß, hellbraun oder fast schwarz. Heute gibt es eine richtige Schokoladenkultur. Die Tafeln erzielen oft Preise von über 5 Euro, und wenn Sie mich nach meiner Lieblingssorte fragen, fällt es mir schwer, mich zu entscheiden. Die Kunden sind offen für Neues: Zum Beispiel habe ich gerade für den „Salon du Chocolat" in Tokio eine Parfumcollection und eine Oilcollection herausgebracht, nicht zu vergessen die Hessenpraline, die ich als erster Konditor offiziell für ein Bundesland entwickeln durfte – sie enthält unter anderem „Grüne Soße". Dies ist eine Spezialität, die sonst eher in herzhaften Kompositionen Verwendung findet. Ebenso wie Käse oder extreme Gewürze wie Chili. Gut, Chili gab es schon bei den Ureinwohnern Südamerikas, aber erst der Film „Chocolat" hat den Menschen die Augen für Dinge geöffnet, die noch vor nicht allzu langer Zeit eher ein Faschingsscherz gewesen wären.

Auch Marzipan ist für mich im Laufe der Jahre zu einer Leidenschaft geworden. Schon in der Schule habe ich es geliebt, aus verschiedenen Rohstoffen Figuren zu modellieren. Als Kind mochte ich kein Marzipan, bis ich in Italien zum ersten Mal richtig gutes Marzipan kosten durfte – ab diesem Zeitpunkt war es um mich geschehen. Bei allen möglichen Events, besonders wenn Kinder dabei sind, modelliere ich gerne Marzipanfiguren. Es ist einfach ein tolles Material und vor allem kann man mit wenig Aufwand die schönsten Figuren herstellen. Ich habe ganz bewusst auf einen Designerstil verzichtet, denn ich denke, meine Figuren sollen vor allem Kindern eine Freude machen.

Ich wünsche Ihnen jedenfalls viel Spaß beim Nachmachen der Rezepte. Und denken Sie wie immer daran: Es ist noch kein Meister vom Himmel gefallen.

Ihr

BERND SIEFERT

GRUSSWORTE

Ich hatte bereits mehrfach Gelegenheit Bernd Siefert bei Semi-naren im Hause Pfersich in Neu-Ulm mit seinem Können und all seiner Kreativität zu erleben. Seine freundschaftliche und professionelle Weise Fachkenntnisse weiterzugeben, aber auch seine Fachbuchreihe „Sweet Gold" – die ein Schatz für alle ist, die süße Kreationen lieben und sich dieser Kunst verschrieben haben – machen ihn zu dem großen Mann, der er heute ist. Hinzu kommt nicht zuletzt die Tatsache, dass er trotz allem Erfolg mit beiden Beinen am Boden und vor allem Mensch ge-blieben ist.

Mach weiter so, Bernd!

REINHARD LACKNER
Executive Pastry Chef
InterContinental Singapore

On several occasions I had the good fortune of meeting Bernd Siefert with all his skills and creativity during seminars at Pfer-sich in Neu-Ulm. His friendly and professional way of teaching specialist knowledge as well as his book series "Sweet Gold" – which is a treasure for all who love sweet creations and are work-ing in this field – make him into the personality he is today. In addition, there is the fact that in spite of all his success he remains firmly rooted on the ground.

Keep it up Bernd!

REINHARD LACKNER
Executive Pastry Chef
InterContinental Singapore

Ich habe das große Glück gehabt, Bernd Siefert bei einer der größten kulinarischen Veranstaltungen der Welt kennenzulernen. Ich war immer sehr gespannt auf unsere Treffen, einfach weil ich die Entwicklung seiner Arbeit beobachten wollte. Er hat das Talent, das nur die größten seines Faches besitzen: Er schafft es immer wieder, aus allen gastronomischen Bereichen Inspirationen auf-zunehmen und sie in seine Arbeit zu integrieren. Deshalb kom-men seine Kreationen sowohl im Restaurant und im Eiscafé als auch in der reinen Konditorei so hervorragend an. Man denke nur an die Lorbeerblätter, die seinem Cassissorbet so eine ganz besondere Note verleihen. Bernd, vielen Dank für dieses Buch, es ist eine große Bereicherung für die Gastronomie.

SERGIO DONDOLI
Eisweltmeister, San Giminiano Italien

I had the great good fortune of getting to know Bernd Siefert at one of the world's largest culinary events. I have always looked forward to meeting him, simply because I wanted to follow the develop-ment of his work. He has a talent that only the most gifted in his profession have: time and again he manages to draw inspirations from all types of gastronomic branches and incorporate them in his work. That is the reason why his creations are so successful in restaurants as well as ice-cream parlours and patisseries. Just think of the bay leaves that provide a very special flavour to his cassis sorbet. Bernd, many thanks for this book – it is a true enrichment for all who work in this field.

SERGIO DONDOLI
World champion ice-cream maker, San Giminiano, Italy

GREETINGS

I hope that Bernd Siefert's new book project will be a big success because with his enthusiastic commitment he really deserves it. I would like to take this opportunity to express my gratitude for the professional support in training young people for the German section of "Jeunes Restaurateurs", of which I was president between 2000 and 2006. During that time he has supported our work as patron of the patisserie competition, as member of the jury and as lecturer in our elite class as well as our latest "baby", the pastry class. All professions need role models who motivate and inspire with their work. Dear Bernd Siefert, I wish you every success for all your activities, especially for your own patisserie shop and your family.

HARALD RÜSSEL AND RÜSSEL's LANDHAUS ST. URBAN
European Representative of "Jeunes Restaurateur"

Ich wünsche Bernd Siefert für sein neues Buchprojekt, dass es ein großer Erfolg wird, denn bei seinem Engagement hat er dies wirklich verdient. An dieser Stelle möchte ich ihm Dank sagen für die fachliche Unterstützung bei der Nachwuchsarbeit der Jeunes Restaurateurs, Sektion Deutschland, deren Präsident ich von 2000 bis 2006 war. Während dieser Zeit hat er, als Schirmherr unseres Pattiseriewettbewerbes, als Jurymitglied oder als Dozent unsere Arbeit unterstützt. Ebenso unsere Elite-Klasse und unser neuestes „Baby" – die „Pastry-Class". Jeder Berufsstand braucht Vorbilder, die durch ihre Arbeit motivieren und inspirieren. Ihnen, lieber Bernd Siefert, wünsche ich für alle Ihre Aktivitäten viel Erfolg, besonders aber für Ihren eigenen Betrieb und Ihre Familie.

HARALD RÜSSEL UND RÜSSEL's LANDHAUS ST. URBAN
„Jeunes Restaurateur" Europaabgeordneter

What I share with Bernd Siefert is the passion for our wonderful profession. I can't think of any other trade that offers so many opportunities for creativity. Because of the complexity of our profession there are few pastry chefs whose competence extends to all the different branches. Bernd is such a universal confectioner who is familiar with all aspects of our profession and is also very accomplished in passing his knowledge on.
I am just fascinated by the way in which he uses tried and tested confectionery methods as a basis for modern and unusual patisserie products.
After "Sweet Gold 1" the expectations are obviously high, but I am sure that with his new book Bernd will add to his already impressive standing.

Best wishes,

LEO FORSTHOFER
several times winner of the Pastry Oscar, Vienna, Café Oberlaa

Mit Bernd Siefert verbindet mich die Leidenschaft für unseren großartigen Beruf. Welches Handwerk sonst bietet so viele Möglichkeiten sich kreativ zu betätigen. Bei der Vielfalt die unser Beruf bietet, gibt es nur wenige Fachleute, die in jeder Sparte kompetent sind. Bernd ist ein so universeller Konditor, der mit allem was unsere Profession zu bieten hat, vertraut ist und dies auch gekonnt weitervermittelt.
Mich begeistert, wie er fundiertes, traditionelles Konditorenwissen in moderne und zeitgemäße Patisserieprodukte umsetzt.
Nach „Sweet Gold 1" sind die Erwartungen natürlich groß, aber ich bin mir sicher, dass Bernd sich mit seinem neuen Buch erneut ein Denkmal setzen wird.

Mit besten Wünschen,

LEO FORSTHOFER
mehrfacher Patisserie-Oskar-Gewinner, Wien, Cafe Oberlaa

GRUSSWORTE

Im Jahre 1997 bekam ich die Gelegenheit, gemeinsam mit namhaften Kollegen, bei der Konditorenweltmeisterschaft in Stuttgart die Arbeiten der Teilnehmer zu beurteilen. Als Weltmeister wurden Bernd Siefert und Manfred Bacher gekürt. Seit dieser Zeit kenne ich Bernd Siefert. Es gehört zu meinen Aufgaben als Leiter des Bereichs Konditorei der renommierten Richemont Fachschule, die Entwicklungen in unserem Beruf aufmerksam zu verfolgen. So wurde ich immer wieder durch Publikationen, Ausstellungen und Zeitschriften auf Bernd Siefert und seine enorme Schaffenskraft aufmerksam. Auch für mich persönlich konnte ich immer wieder Inspirationen sammeln. Dieser Mann hat Leidenschaft, Berufsstolz und -freude und gerade deshalb ist es wichtig, sein angesammeltes und selbst entwickeltes Wissen in Kursen und Büchern als Anregung für den Berufsnachwuchs weiterzugeben. Ich wünsche Bernd mit seinem neuen Buch viel Erfolg. Ich bin überzeugt, es wird nicht seine letzte Publikation sein. Für mich ist er schon lange nicht mehr der Weltmeister von damals, sondern der eigenständige Bernd Siefert.

FREDY EGGENSCHWILER

Leiter Konditorei, Richemont Fachschule Schweiz

In 1997 I had the opportunity, together with well-known colleagues, to assess the entries of contestants at the Confectioner's World Championship in Stuttgart. The champion's title was awarded jointly to Bernd Siefert and Manfred Bacher. So that is the first time I met Bernd Siefert. As Head of Confectionery at the renowned Richemont College, one of my tasks is to closely monitor the development in our profession. In that capacity my attention has often been drawn to Bernd Siefert and his enormous creativity through publications, exhibitions, journals etc. I personally have also been able to find inspiration from his work on many occasions. This man has passion, pride in his profession and enjoys his work, which is why it is so important that he passes on his accumulated skills and knowledge in courses and books as an inspiration for the young people taking up the profession. I wish Bernd and his new book every success. I am convinced that it will not be his last publication. For me Bernd Siefert no longer is the World Champion of years gone by but has become a personality in his own right.

FREDY EGGENSCHWILER

Head of Confectionery, Richemont College, Switzerland

Bernd Siefert's Kreativität und seine unübertroffenen technischen Fähigkeiten machen ihn zu einem herausragenden Profi seines Fachs. Diese Qualitäten spiegeln sich erneut in diesem wundervollen Buch wieder, in dem Bernd eine ganz neue Seite seines magischen Könnens aufschlägt.

SÉBASTIEN CANONNE, M.O.F. AND JACQUY PFEIFFER
Mitbegründer/Miteigentümer/Ausbildungsleiter Konditorei
The French Pastry School in Chicago, IL, Vereinigte Staaten von Amerika

Bernd Siefert's creativity combined with his unsurpassed technical skills makes him a tremendous professional. Theses qualities are reflected once again in this magnificent book where Bernd takes his magic to a new level.

SÉBASTIEN CANONNE, M.O.F. AND JACQUY PFEIFFER
Co-founders/Co-owners/Pastry Chef Instructors
The French Pastry School in Chicago, IL United States of America

GREETINGS

Tasteful, handsome, gracious, precise, perfect, creative, surprising, extraordinary, funny, mischievous, first-class, highly professional, a role model, cheeky, audacious, caring, modest, with an open heart, expansive, successful, affable, attractive, unique, unforgettable, spectacular, lasting, informative, interesting, on top of his game, passionate, important, masterful, impressive.

That's how he is, my friend Bernd. Why should his book be different?

OTTO KOCH
Celebrity and television chef

Geschmackvoll, schön, anmutig, präzise, perfekt, kreativ, überraschend, außergewöhnlich, lustig, verschmitzt, erstklassig, hochprofessionell, vorbildlich, frech, mutig, liebevoll, bescheiden, herzlich, aufwendig, erfolgreich, sympathisch, attraktiv, unverwechselbar, unvergesslich, beeindruckend, nachhaltig, bildend, interessant, zukunftsweisend, leidenschaftlich, bedeutend, meisterlich, eindrucksvoll.

So ist er, mein Bernd. Warum sollte sein Buch anders sein?

OTTO KOCH
Sterne-und Fernsehkoch

Bernd's non-stop pursuit of pastry excellence has afforded him a unique international perspective in the culinary arts. Even if this book is not written in your native tongue, Chef Siefert's elegant compositions and harmonious use of color transcends language. I am sure, if there were an international museum of modern art for pastry, Bernd's work would be among the most collectable.

MICHAEL JOY
Founder of Chicago School of Mold Making

Mit seinem unaufhaltsamen Streben nach Perfektion hat Bernd Siefert internationales Ansehen im Bereich moderner Kochkunst errungen. Auch wenn dieses Buch nicht in Ihrer Muttersprache geschrieben sein sollte, so werden die eleganten Kompositionen und die harmonische Verwendung von Farben auch ohne Worte für sich sprechen. Gäbe es ein internationales Museum für moderne Konditoreikunst, so gehörten die Werke von Bernd mit Sicherheit zu den begehrtesten Sammelobjekten.

MICHAEL JOY
Gründer der Chicago School of Mold Making

GRUSSWORTE

GREETINGS

Bernd Siefert's Produkte sehen aus wie Kunstwerke und seine Ideen kommen aus aller Welt. Handgeschöpfte Schokolade, frisches Konditoreneis und leckeres Marzipan sind wieder stark nachgefragte Erzeugnisse beim Konditor.

„Sweet Gold 2" erscheint deshalb gerade zur rechten Zeit und wird sicherlich nahtlos an den Erfolg seines ersten Buches anknüpfen. Rezepte, Fotos und Ideen tragen wieder die unverwechselbare Handschrift eines ganz Großen seiner Branche.

Das Feuerwerk an Ideen wird Lehrling, Gesellen und Meister begeistern.

Ich wünsche dem zweiten Meisterwerk von Bernd Siefert viel Erfolg.

ROBERT WIDMANN

Generalsekretär der UIPCG

Weltverband der Konditoren, Patissiers,

Confiseure und Eishersteller

Bernd Siefert's products look like works of art and his ideas come from all over the world. Hand-made chocolate, ice-cream made on the premises and tasty marzipan are again highly in demand in patisseries and cafés.

For this reason "Sweet Gold 2" is published at just the right time and is sure to repeat the success of the first book. His recipes, photographs and ideas yet again carry the signature of one of the greats in is profession.

For apprentices, qualified and master confectioners there is a firework of ideas to look forward to.

I wish Bernd Siefert's second masterpiece every success.

ROBERT WIDMANN

General Secretary of UIPCG

World Organisation of Pastry Cooks, Patissiers, Confisiers and Ice-Cream Makers

Klare, inspirierende, herausragende Eleganz! Dieses Buch basiert auf den, in den beiden vorhergehenden Werken von Bernd Siefert gesammelten Erfahrungen und stellt eine weitere Steigerung dar. Es zeigt eine Mischung aus traditionellen und modernen Techniken und Fähigkeiten und wie diese von einem Visionär wie Bernd umgesetzt werden. Die Herzstücke sind praxistauglich und verständlich. Die Rezepte sind eine vergnügliche, erfrischende Mischung aus verschiedenartigen Aromen und Konsistenzen.

GILLES RENUSSON

Ehemaliger Trainer des „US World Pastry Cup"-Teams und des „US Pastry Olympic"-Teams

Pure, inspiring, sophisticated elegance! This book builds on the knowledge shared in Chef Bernd Siefert two previous masterpieces, and continues to expend the horizon of pastries and sweets. It is a blend of traditional and modern techniques and skills, as practiced by the visionary that Bernd is. The centerpieces are practical and accessible. The recipes are a fun, refreshing blend of flavors and textures.

GILLES RENUSSON

Former Coach of the US World Pastry Cup team and of the US Pastry Olympic team

GREETINGS

For many years, Bernd has been a great craftsman who is always passionate about his work. He has developed his hobby into his professional career. Even though patisserie, chocolate and ice-cream have inspired the world for many, many years, Bernd is still surprising us with a book, which is full of new ideas. He has tackled the task with limitless creativity and drive. I am sure that this book will be loved by many people who are interested in more than just recipes when they read a book. Due to its thorough details as well as its versatility, this book is very suitable for all pastry chefs, cooks, ice-cream makers and chocolatiers. This is one of the books that will have a fixed place on my desk.

Congratulations to the author!

JEAN PIERRE WYBAUW
Book author and renowned juror of international championships (e.g. of the World Pastry Championships)

Bernd ist ein großer Künstler, der sich seit vielen Jahren hingebungsvoll seiner Arbeit widmet. Sein Hobby wurde zur Profession. Obwohl Gebäck, Schokolade und Eiscreme die Welt seit vielen Jahren begeistern, überrascht uns Bernd wieder einmal mit einem Buch, das voller anregender Ideen steckt. Seine Kreativität und seine Begeisterung kennen keine Grenzen. Ich bin sicher, dass alle, die von einem Buch mehr als nur Rezepte erwarten, dieses Buch lieben werden. Aufgrund der fundierten Detailkenntnisse und der Vielfältigkeit eignet sich dieses Buch bestens für Konditormeister, Köche, Eiskreateure und Chocolatiers.

Meine Glückwünsche an den Autor!

JEAN PIERRE WYBAUW
Buchautor und anerkannter Juror internationaler Wettbewerbe (z. B. der World Pastry Championships)

Dear Bernd,

What shall I say?
It is the end of the meal that stays in the guests' memories.
What a delight to have a teacher like you who is so skillful at orchestrating the ending of that symphony of tastes.
The day of our first meeting was magical and has remained firmly in my memory throughout my long working life. I have met some truly great patissiers in my life, but your gentleness, your knowledge and skills, your humility and your willingness to always lend a helping hand is rare these days.
Many thanks for your friendship, Bernd.

JEAN MARIE MEULIER
19,5 points Gault Millau, 3 stars Guide Michelin

Lieber Bernd,

Was soll ich sagen?
Das Ende einer Mahlzeit verbleibt in der Erinnerung eines jeden Gastes.
Es ist ein reines Vergnügen, einen Lehrmeister wie Dich zu haben. Du verstehst es, aufgrund Deines Fachwissens, mit dem Dessert einen fulminanten Schlusspunkt an das Ende eines Menüs zu setzen.
Der Tag unserer ersten Begegnung war ein magischer Tag, den ich im Laufe meines Berufslebens nie vergessen habe. Ich habe viele große Konditoren getroffen, aber Deine Freundlichkeit, Dein Fachwissen, Deine Demut und Deine stets helfend ausgestreckte Hand sind in der heutigen Zeit äußerst seltene Eigenschaften. Danke für Deine Freundschaft, lieber Bernd.

JEAN MARIE MEULIER
19,5 Punkte Gault Millau, 3 Sterne Guide Michelin

GRUSSWORTE

GREETINGS

Bernd Siefert ist ein passionierter Künstler in der neuen Welt der Patisserie. Er verbindet klassisches Handwerk mit praktischer Kunst und Kreativität. Das Buch lässt uns Bernd's Hingabe, seine Philosophie und die Liebe für sein Handwerk deutlich spüren.

STANTON HO

ACF Konditormeister des Jahres

Bernd Siefert is passionate craftsman in the new world of pastry profession. He has formulated his wisdom based on the classical pastry production and formulated practical artistry and creativity of modern desserts. Bernd is truly inspiring to his passion, philosophy, and love for his craft.

STANTON HO

ACF Pastry Chef of the year

Man begegnet im Leben wenigen Menschen, die ganz speziell sind, die wegweisend sind, die mit ihrer Art und ihrem Können begeistern, mitreißen und zugleich Freund sind – Bernd Siefert ist so ein Mensch.

Es gibt wenige Menschen, die beruflich die Gabe besitzen, überschäumende Kreativität mit fundiertem Wissen zu paaren, immer wieder offen für Neues zu sein und sich stetig zu verbessern und andere an ihrem Wissen teilhaben zu lassen.

In seinem neuen Werk kommen all diese Attribute zusammen: „Sweet Gold 2" illustriert Weitsicht, Professionalität und natürlich seine sprudelnde Fantasie, die ihn geschmacklich immer wieder neue Wege gehen lässt.

Ich wünsche meinem guten Freund Bernd viel Erfolg mit seinem neuen Buch, ich bin mir sicher, dass es wieder jedermann begeistern wird.

RALF WELLAUER

Konditor des Jahres

You don't meet many people in your life who are very special, who can show you the way and are able to inspire you with their art and skills, and at the same time can be your friend – Bernd Siefert is such a person.

There are few people who have the gift of being able to combine exuberant creativity with in-depth knowledge, who keep an open mind to absorb new things and improve their skills and who are willing to share that knowledge with others.

All these attributes come together in Bernd Siefert's new book: Sweet Gold II demonstrates his vision, his professional approach and, of course, his abundant imagination that always leads him to explore new avenues of taste.

I hope Bernd, my good friend, that this new book will be very successful – I am sure that everybody will love it, just like the last one.

RALF WELLAUER

Confectioner of the Year

GREETINGS

Patisserie creates a bond between people, even across different continents. Bernd Siefert is a cosmopolitan who is living proof of this – he draws the inspiration for his extraordinary creations from his travels around the globe. He is the ultimate confectioner, his skills reach the top level of perfection. With his skills he uses the technical basis to focus on what matters: the enjoyment of culinary highlights for the senses.

SYLVIE DOUCE AND FRANÇOIS JEANTET
Organisateurs du Salon du Chocolat.
Founders and Producers of the Salon du Chocolat

The most beneficial of all arts is the art of living well, said Cicero. You are one of those who is skilled in that art.

Congratulations!

JEAN-PAUL HÉVIN
Meilleur Ouvrier de France

The world of confectionery can count itself lucky: Bernd shows us once again that there is still much to say in this profession. This book is the work of a person who offers an inspiring modern perspective without losing sight of traditional values. Perfection, technique, philosophy, purity and above all a very individual and refined artistry entice the reader throughout this book. Sweet Gold II is a special gift for each confectioner.

ALBERT AND FERRAN ADRIÀ

Patisserie verbindet Menschen verschiedener Kontinente. Dies beweist der Kosmopolit Bernd Siefert aufs Vortrefflichste, der die Inspiration zu seinen außergewöhnlichen Kreationen aus seinen Reisen rund um die Welt schöpft. Er ist der Patissier, sein Können erreicht absolute Perfektion. Sie erlaubt es ihm, die Technik als Basis zu nutzen, den Fokus aber auf das Wesentliche zu legen: Die Freude an kulinarischen Highlights für alle Sinne.

SYLVIE DOUCE UND FRANÇOIS JEANTET
Organisateurs du Salon du Chocolat.
Founders and Producers of the Salon du Chocolat

Die fruchtbringendste aller Künste ist die Kunst, gut zu leben, sagt Cicero. Sie verstehen es meisterhaft, dieses Wissen umzusetzen.

Glückwunsch!

JEAN-PAUL HÉVIN
Meilleur Ouvrier de France

Die Welt der Konditorei kann sich gratulieren. Bernd beweist uns wieder einmal, dass in diesem Beruf noch lange nicht alles gesagt ist. Dieses Werk vereint innovative und moderne Aspekte mit traditionellen Werten und Techniken. Perfektion, Technik, Philosophie, Klarheit und eine sehr persönliche Sichtweise hinsichtlich ästhetischer Schönheit, bestimmen dieses Werk. Sweet Gold II ist ein Geschenk für jeden Konditor.

ALBERT UND FERRAN ADRIÀ

INHALT

CONTENT

INHALT

CONTENT

PRALINEN
CHOCOLATES

QUITTENTRÜFFEL CÄCILIE

QUINCE TRUFFLE "CÄCILIE"

Quitten sind für mich die Früchte, die mich an meine Grossmutter und ihre Kunst des Marmeladekochens erinnern. Ich liebe Quittengelee zum Frühstück. Und da mein Vater wundervolle Odenwalder Brände macht, ist in unseren Quittentrüffeln neben hausgemachtem Quittengelee auch ein exzellenter Quittenbrand. Hochwertige Zutaten sind das A und O der Pralinenherstellung.

Quinces are fruits that remind me of my grandmother and her marmalade-making skills. I love quince jelly for breakfast. And since my father makes wonderful Odenwälder brandy, you will not only find homemade quince jelly in our quince truffles but excellent quince brandy as well. Excellent ingredients are essential for making chocolates.

INGREDIENTS FOR 140 CHOCOLATES

FILLING

200 g	quince jelly
250 g	cream, 32 % fat
525 g	white couverture
100 g	unsalted butter
100 g	quince brandy 40 % vol.

white hollow spheres

COATING
white couverture

DECORATION
silver leaf

ZUTATEN FÜR 140 PRALINEN

FÜLLUNG

200 g	Quittengelee
250 g	Sahne, 32 % Fett
525 g	weiße Kuvertüre
100 g	Butter
100 g	Quittenbrand, 40 %-vol.

weiße Hohlkugel

ÜBERZUG
weiße Kuvertüre

DEKORATION
Blattsilber

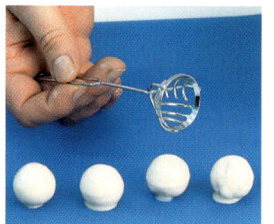

*Quittentrüffel mit temperierter weißer Kuvertüre
überziehen*

*Cover the quince truffle with tempered white
couverture*

1

*Spezialdekorstempel in der temperierten
Kuvertüre anwärmen*

*Heat the special decoration stamp in tempered
white couverture*

2

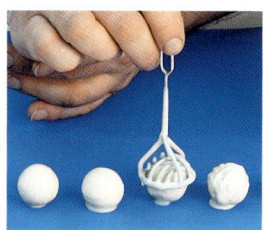

Pralinen stempeln

Mold the praline

3

HERSTELLUNG

Quittengelee mit Sahne aufmixen, dann
aufkochen und über die gehackte weiße
Kuvertüre geben. Mit einem Spatel zu einer
glatten Masse rühren, ohne Luft einzuar-
beiten, dann die Butter unterarbeiten.
Masse etwas abkühlen lassen, um den
Quittenbrand einzurühren. Die Masse bei
30 °C in die weiße Hohlkugeln abfüllen.
Über Nacht auskristallisieren lassen, dann
mit weißer Kuvertüre verschließen und
überziehen. So bald die Kuvertüre anzieht,
mit einem Dekorstempel verzieren und
mit Blattsilber dekorieren.

MAKING THE PARTS

Mix the quince jelly with cream, bring to
boil and pour over the chopped white couverture. Use a spatula to stir to a smooth
mixture without incorporating air then
add the butter. Leave to cool so that you
can add the quince spirit. When the mixture is 30 °C, pour it into the white hollow
spheres. Let them crystallize overnight
then seal the balls with the white couverture. As soon as the couverture chocolate begins to harden, garnish with the
decoration stamp and decorate with the
silver leaf.

WALNUSSWEICHKROKANT

SOFT WALNUT CROQUANT

Für dieses Weichkrokantrezept habe ich mir eine Variation mit Walnüssen, Zimt und Honig ausgedacht. Das Wappentier Michelstadts ist die Biene, deshalb versteht es sich von selbst, dass der Odenwald wunderbare Honigvarianten zu bieten hat. Den Buchweizenhonig habe ich allerdings auf einem Seminar in Polen kennen gelernt. Trauen sie sich mit den Zutaten zu experimentieren, es lohnt sich!

For this soft croquant recipe, I have thought up a variation with walnuts, cinnamon and honey. The bee is the heraldic animal of Michelstadt town. It therefore goes without saying that Odenwald has fantastic variety of honey to offer. However, the first time I got to know about the buckwheat honey was at a seminar in Poland. Dare to experiment with your ingredients - it is worth it!

Zutaten für 130 Pralinen

Füllung

250 g	Zucker
250 g	Sahne, 32 % Fett
10 g	gemahlene Zimtblüten
75 g	Buchweizenhonig
75 g	Wiesenhonig
350 g	Walnussgrieß, leicht im Ofen geröstet

Überzug

Bitterkuvertüre

Dekoration

Foliendekor

Ingredients for 130 chocolates

Filling

250 g	sugar
250 g	cream, 32 % fat
10 g	ground cinnamon flowers
75 g	buckwheat honey
75 g	meadow honey
350 g	walnut semolina, slightly roasted in the oven

Coating

bitter couverture

Decoration

foil decoration

Praline mit Bitterkuvertüre überziehen

Coat the chocolate with bitter couverture

1

*Foliendekor vorsichtig knicken,
damit das Muster nicht verwischt*

**Carefully fold the foil decoration
so that the design does not get smudged**

2

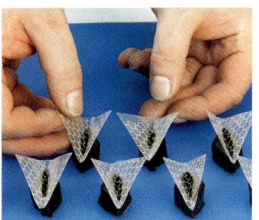

*Dekor auflegen, anziehen lassen,
dann Folie vorsichtig abnehmen*

**Apply the decoration, leave to harden
then carefully remove the foil.**

3

MAKING THE PARTS

Melt the sugar to caramel. Heat the cream with the cinnamon flowers then use the mixture to deglaze the caramel. Boil the mixture to 112 °C, add the honeys the boil to 117 °C. Add the slightly roasted walnut semolina and stir until smooth. Pour the mixture onto a silicone baking mat, shape into a square and roll out. As soon as the mixture cools, brush the bottom side with a thin layer of temperate couverture chocolate then use a cutting roller to cut out diamond shapes. Coat the diamond shapes with bitter couverture then decorate with the foil decoration.

HERSTELLUNG

Zucker zu einem Karamell schmelzen, die Sahne mit den Zimtblüten erhitzen und den Karamell damit ablöschen. Die Masse auf 112 °C kochen, die Honige zugeben, dann auf 117 °C kochen. Den leicht gerösteten Walnussgrieß zugeben und glatt rühren. Masse auf eine Silikon-Backmatte gießen, gleichmäßig quadratisch formen und ausrollen. Sobald die Masse ausgekühlt ist, die Unterseite mit temperierter Kuvertüre dünn bestreichen und mit der Schneidewalze in Rauten schneiden. Dann Rauten mit Bitterkuvertüre überziehen und den Foliendekor aufbringen.

APRIKOSENBLÄTTERNOUGAT

APRICOT NOUGAT BRITTLE

Trockenfrüchte sind etwas Wunderbares. Denken Sie nur an Datteln, gefüllt mit Marzipan oder an Dörrpflaumen in Bitterganache mit Zwetschgenwasser – einfach herrlich! Die Variante mit Trockenaprikosen ist eine Leckerei, die besonders Kindern schmeckt und zudem noch sehr lange haltbar ist.

Dry fruits are something special. Just think of dates filled with marzipan or prunes in bitter ganache with plum brandy – simply exquisite! The alternative with dried apricots is a treat for children and it can be stored for very long.

Ingredients for 90 chocolates		**Zutaten für 90 Pralinen**	
500 g	dried apricots	500 g	Trockenaprikosen
	Filling		**Füllung**
45 g	milk couverture	45 g	Vollmilchkuvertüre
450 g	bitter almond nougat	450 g	Mandelbitternougat
80 g	feuilletine (crushed waffles)	80 g	Feuilletine (Waffelbruch)
	Coating		**Überzug**
	bitter couverture		Bitterkuvertüre
	icing sugar		Puderzucker

Trockenaprikosen längs aufschneiden

Slice the dried apricots lengthwise

1 ——————————————

Aprikosen wie einen Schmetterling aufklappen

Open the apricots like a butterfly

2 ——————————————

HERSTELLUNG

Trockenaprikosen längs aufschneiden und wie einen Schmetterling aufklappen. Die Vollmilchkuvertüre auflösen, dann den Mandelbitternougat zugeben und ebenfalls auflösen. Die Masse temperieren, die Feuilletine zugeben, untermischen, dann in kleine Silikon-Halbkugelformen geben, glatt streichen und erstarren lassen. Den Feuilletinenougat ausformen und die Aprikosen damit füllen. Die Handinnenflächen mit Bitterkuvertüre bestreichen, dann die Aprikosen in den Händen rollen bis sie vollkommen mit der Kuvertüre überzogen sind. Sofort in Puderzucker wälzen, leicht anziehen lassen und anschließend in einem Sieb abpudern.

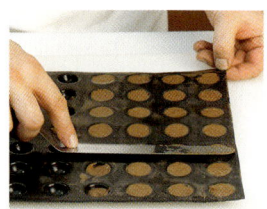

Feuilletinenougat in Silikon-Halbkugelformen geben, glatt streichen und erstarren lassen

Fill the feuilletine-nougat in silicone hemisphere molds, level the surface and leave to set

3 ——————————————

Feuilletinenougat ausformen

Take out the feuilletine-nougat

4 ——————————————

MAKING THE PARTS

Slice the dried apricots lengthwise and open them up like a butterfly. Melt the milk couverture, add the bitter almond nougat and stir until it melts. Temper the mixture; add the feuilletine and mix. Fill the mixture in small silicone hemisphere molds, level the surface and leave to set. Take out the feuilletine-nougat and fill the apricots with it. Smear your palms with bitter couverture chocolate and roll the apricot between your palms until it is fully covered with couverture. Quickly roll it in icing sugar, let it harden and apply the icing sugar in a sieve.

Aprikosen mit Feuilletinenougat füllen

Fill the apricots with feuilletine-nougat

5 ——————————————

Mit Bitterkuvertüre überzogene Pralinen in Puderzucker wälzen

Roll the bitter couverture coated chocolates in icing sugar

6 ——————————————

BLÄTTERKROKANT

LEAF CROQUANT

EIN KLASSIKER DER PRALINENKUNST: EINFACH UND SCHNELL HERZUSTELLEN! DABEI SO LECKER, DASS ICH MIT DEM NASCHEN NICHT MEHR AUFHÖREN KANN, WENN ICH MAL ANGEFANGEN HABE. WIE BEI VIELEN ANDEREN REZEPTEN KANN MAN AUCH HIER VARIIEREN — EINE ANDERE NOUGATSORTE VERWENDEN, DEN KARAMELL HELLER ODER DUNKLER HERSTELLEN ODER DEN NOUGAT MIT GE-WÜRZEN KOMBINIEREN. UNSCHLAGBAR.

A PRALINE CLASSIC: EASY AND QUICK TO MAKE! SO DELICIOUS THAT I CAN'T CONTROL MY SWEET TOOTH ONCE I HAVE HAD ONE. LIKE SEVERAL OTHER RECIPES THERE ARE VARIATIONS TO THIS ONE TOO — USE ANOTHER TYPE OF NOUGAT, MAKE THE CARAMEL LIGHTER OR DARKER OR EVEN COMBINE THE NOUGAT WITH SPICES. UNBEATABLE.

ZUTATEN FÜR 90 PRALINEN

FÜLLUNG
500 g	Nussnougat
50 g	Kakaobutter
500 g	Zucker
100 g	Butter

ÜBERZUG
Bitterkuvertüre

DEKORATION
Bitterkuvertüre zum Filieren
Blattgold

INGREDIENTS FOR 90 CHOCOLATES

FILLING
500 g	nut-nougat
50 g	cocoa butter
500 g	sugar
100 g	unsalted butter

COATING
bitter couverture

DECORATION
bitter couverture for netting
gold leaf

MAKING THE PARTS

Heat the nut-nougat, melt the cocoa butter, mix and stir until smooth. Pour the mixture onto a silicone baking mat and spread equally.

Melt the sugar to caramel, add the butter and stir until the caramel absorbs the butter. Spread the caramel butter evenly over the nougat and mix – the more you mix the smoother the texture of the nougat will get. Quickly shape the mixture evenly, cover it with another silicone baking mat and roll to 1 cm thick. Remove the baking mat and cut into diamond shapes with the cutting roller.

As soon as the chocolates have cooled, coat and decorate with bitter couverture, then garnish with the gold leaf.

HERSTELLUNG

Nussnougat erwärmen, Kakaobutter auflösen, mischen und zu einer glatten Masse rühren. Diese auf eine Silikon-Backmatte ausgießen und gleichmäßig verteilen.

Den Zucker zu einem Karamell schmelzen, die Butter zugeben und so lange rühren, bis der Karamell die Butter aufgenommen hat. Karamellbutter gleichmäßig auf dem Nougat verteilen und tablierend mischen – je mehr gemischt wird, desto feiner wird die Struktur des Nougats. Masse schnell gleichmäßig formen, mit einer zweiten Silikon-Backmatte abdecken, einen Zentimeter dick ausrollen, die Backmatten entfernen und dann mit der Schneidewalze zu Rauten schneiden.

Sobald die Pralinen ausgekühlt sind, mit Bitterkuvertüre überziehen, filieren und mit Blattgold verzieren.

Fertig überzogene Pralinen mit einem Garniertütchen filieren

Decorating the coated chocolates with a decorating bag

1

Fertige Pralinen

Finished chocolates

2

PISTACHIO MARZIPAN

Ich liebe Pistazienmarzipan – egal ob zum Frühstück oder als Betthupferl. In Deutschland stellen Konditoren leider nur noch ganz selten Marzipan selbst her, da von den Zulieferern sehr gute Grundmassen angeboten werden. Wichtig ist es, Marzipan der höchsten Qualitätsstufe zu kaufen, denn man schmeckt den Unterschied.

I love pistachio marzipan – it does not matter if I have them for breakfast or as a bedtime snack. In Germany, it is unfortunately rare for confectioners to make their own marzipan because the suppliers offer them with high quality basic mixtures. It is important to buy the best quality because it is possible to taste the difference.

INGREDIENTS FOR 80 CHOCOLATES

MARZIPAN
500 g	marzipan raw mixture from Mediterranean almonds
100 g	pistachio paste, 100 %
100 g	pistachio-semolina
25 g	Kirschwasser (cherry brandy), 40 % vol.
25 g	Acacia honey

COATING
bitter couverture

DECORATION
foil decorations

halved pistachios

ZUTATEN FÜR 80 PRALINEN

MARZIPAN
500 g	Marzipanrohmasse aus Mittelmeermandeln
100 g	Pistazienpaste, 100 %
100 g	Pistaziengrieß
25 g	Kirschwasser, 40 %-vol.
25 g	Akazienhonig

ÜBERZUG
Bitterkuvertüre

DEKORATION
Foliendekor

halbe Pistazien

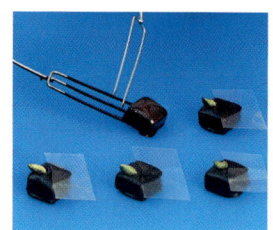

Überzogene Praline mit der Überziehgabel absetzen

Position the coated chocolate with a dipping fork

1 _____

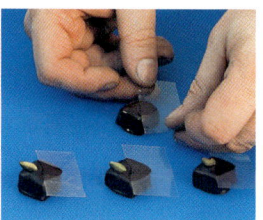

Dekorfolie auflegen

Apply the foil decoration

2 _____

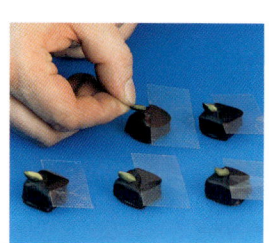

Mit einer halben Pistazie dekorieren

Decorate with half a pistachio

3 _____

HERSTELLUNG

Die Marzipanrohmasse mit den anderen Zutaten verkneten, zwischen zwei Backmatten einen Zentimeter dick quadratisch ausrollen. Die Unterseite mit temperierter Bitterkuvertüre bestreichen und mit der Schneidegeige in Quadrate schneiden. Die Quadrate auseinander setzen und über Nacht trocknen lassen. Pralinen mit Bitterkuvertüre überziehen. Die Dekorfolie in Streifen schneiden und diagonal auf die Pralinen auflegen. Die andere Hälfte mit einer halben Pistazie dekorieren. Wenn die Kuvertüre fest ist und sich löst, Folie vorsichtig abziehen.

MAKING THE PARTS

Knead the marzipan raw mixture with the other ingredients. Place the mixture between two baking mats and roll to 1 cm thick. Apply bitter couverture on the bottom side and use a confectionary cutting guitar to cut out squares. Separate the squares and leave to dry overnight. Coat the chocolates with bitter couverture. Cut the foil decorations in strips and place them diagonally across the chocolates. Decorate the other half with a halved pistachio. When the couverture chocolate has hardened, carefully pull off the foil.

DORNFELDER TRÜFFELSCHNECKEN

DORNFELDER TRUFFLE SWIRLS

DER ODENWALD IST EINES DER KLEINSTEN WEINANBAUGEBIETE DEUTSCHLANDS, DAS HERVORRAGENDE ROTWEINE PRODUZIERT. DIE KOMBINATION VON ROTWEIN UND BITTERSCHOKOLADE IST WUNDERBAR. ALLERDINGS SOLLTE MAN VORHER GENAU PRÜFEN, OB DER GESCHMACK DES WEINES MIT DER SCHOKOLADENSORTE AUCH WIRKLICH HARMONIERT.

ODENWALD IS ONE OF GERMANY'S SMALLEST WINE-GROWING REGIONS THAT PRODUCES EXQUISITE RED WINES. THE COMBINATION OF RED WINE AND BITTER CHOCOLATE IS FANTASTIC. IT IS HOWEVER IMPORTANT TO ENSURE THAT THE TASTE OF THE WINE HARMONIZES WITH THE TYPE OF CHOCOLATE.

ZUTATEN FÜR 100 PRALINEN

Bitterkuvertüre

GANACHE

20 g	*Glukosesirup*
70 g	*Sahne, 32 % Fett*
210 g	*Dornfelder (Rotwein)*
70 g	*Banyuls (Dessertwein)*
140 g	*Bitterkuvertüre*
210 g	*Vollmilchkuvertüre*
35 g	*Butter*
70 g	*Rotwein-Tresterbrand, 40 %-vol. (möglichst vom Dornfelder)*

DEKORATION
rote Kakaobutterfarbe

INGREDIENTS FOR 100 CHOCOLATES

bitter couverture

GANACHE

20 g	*glucose syrup*
70 g	*cream, 32 % fat*
210 g	*Dornfelder (red wine)*
70 g	*Banyuls (dessert wine)*
140 g	*bitter couverture*
210 g	*milk couverture*
35 g	*unsalted butter*
70 g	*red wine-Pomace Brandy, 40 % vol. (if possible one from Dornfelder)*

DECORATION
red cocoa butter color

HERSTELLUNG

Die Schneckenformen mit temperierter Bitterkuvertüre ausgießen und dann zum Füllen vorbereiten.

Für die Ganacheherstellung (temperierte Methode) den Glukosesirup mit der Sahne aufkochen und mit den Weinen mischen. Kuvertüren temperieren und untermischen, so dass eine homogene Masse entsteht. Erst weiche Butter und zum Schluss den Tresterbrand untermischen, bis die Ganache alles gebunden hat. Ganache in die vorbereiteten Schneckenformen füllen, über Nacht ziehen lassen, dann mit temperierter Kuvertüre verschließen. So bald sich die Pralinen aus den Formen lösen lassen, diese ausformen und leicht anfrieren. Rote Kakaobutterfarbe auf 38 °C temperieren und die Pralinen von einer Seite samtig ansprühen.

MAKING THE PARTS

Dip the swirl molds in tempered bitter couverture chocolate and prepare them for the filling.

To make the ganache (tempering method), boil the glucose syrup with the cream and mix it with the wines. Temper and stir in the couverture to form a consistent mixture. Add the softened butter then stir in the pomace brandy until the ganache has absorbed all ingredients. Fill the ganache in the swirl molds, allow a crust to form overnight then seal with the tempered couverture. As soon as chocolates can be loosened from their forms, take them out and freeze them shortly. Temper the red cocoa butter color to 38 °C then gently spray the chocolates on one side.

Leicht angefrorene Praline von einer Seite mit roter Kakaobutter ansprühen

Spray the slightly frozen chocolate on one side with red cocoa butter

1

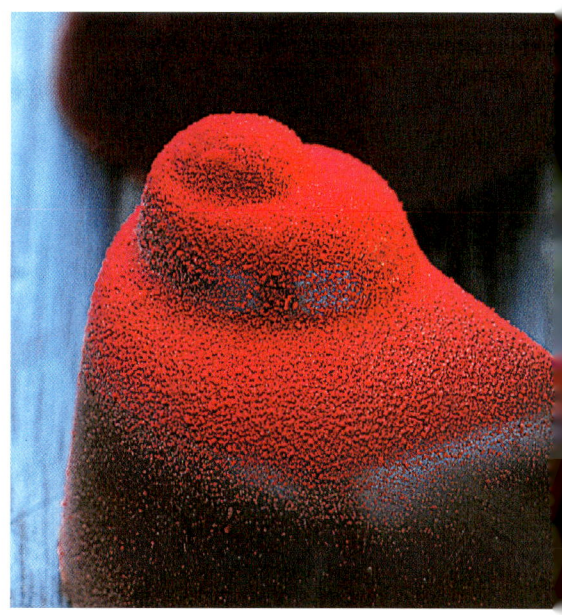

STIELKIRSCHEN

STEMMED CHERRIES

EINES DER GRÖSSTEN KIRSCHANBAUGEBIETE DEUTSCHLANDS LIEGT IN HESSEN, BEI WITZENHAUSEN. STIELKIRSCHEN SIND WOHL EINE DER ÄLTESTEN PRALINEN-SPEZIALITÄTEN ÜBERHAUPT UND FÜR MICH EINE GANZ BESONDERE LECKEREI. SIE SIND NATÜRLICH SEHR AUFWENDIG IN DER ZUBEREITUNG, ABER DER GENUSS ENTSCHÄDIGT FÜR ALLE MÜHE.

ONE OF GERMANY'S LARGEST CHERRY-GROWING REGIONS IS IN WITZENHAUSEN IN THE FEDERAL STATE OF HESSE. STEMMED CHERRIES ARE ONE OF THE OLDEST CHOCOLATE SPECIALTIES AND A VERY SPECIAL TREAT FOR ME. THEY ARE OF COURSE COMPLEX TO PREPARE BUT THEY ARE WORTH THE TROUBLE.

INGREDIENTS FOR 100 CHOCOLATES		ZUTATEN FÜR 100 PRALINEN	
1 kg	*sour cherries with stem*	1 kg	*Sauerkirschen mit Stiel*
1 l	*cognac*	1 l	*Cognac*
500 g	*fudge*	500 g	*Fondant*

COATING	**ÜBERZUG**
bitter couverture	*Bitterkuvertüre*

39

1

Stielkirschen auf Küchenpapier abtrocknen lassen

Dry the stemmed cherries on kitchen paper towels

Stielkirschen bis kurz vor dem Stiel in heißen Fondant tauchen und auf einer Backmatte abkühlen lassen

Dip the cherries in fudge making sure they are covered in fudge up to the point just before the beginning of the stem then let them dry on a baking mat

2

3

4

5

40

Kleine Tupfen Bitterkuvertüre auf eine Backmatte dressieren und leicht anziehen lassen

Put drops of bitter couverture on the baking mat then leave to set lightly

Stielkirschen aufsetzen

Place the stemmed cherries on the couverture drops

Absetzen der mit Kuvertüre überzogenen Stielkirschen

Let the couverture coated stemmed cherries dry

MAKING THE PARTS

Poke the fresh sour cherries several times with a needle and shorten the stems to two thirds of their length. Put the cherries in a large, airproof, closable jar. Pour the cognac into the jar until all the cherries are fully covered and store them in a cool and dark place for at least two months. Take the cherries out of the jar and leave to dry on kitchen paper towels.

Heat the fudge to 70 °C, dip the cherries in the hot fudge (make sure they are covered in fudge up to the point just before the beginning of the stem) and leave to cool on a baking mat. Use a decorating bag to put small drops of bitter couverture on the baking mat then leave to set lightly. Put the stemmed cherries on the couverture drops so that the cherries get a small base then dip them again in tempered couverture until a third of each cherry is covered in couverture.

HERSTELLUNG

Frische Sauerkirschen mit einer Nadel mehrmals pikieren (anstechen) und Stiele auf zwei Drittel Länge kürzen. Kirschen in ein großes, luftdicht verschließbares Glas füllen. Mit Cognac übergießen bis die Kirschen vollständig bedeckt sind und mindestens zwei Monate an einem kühlen und dunklen Ort lagern. Kirschen aus dem Cognac nehmen und auf Küchenpapier abtrocknen lassen.

Fondant auf 70 °C erwärmen, Stielkirschen bis kurz vor dem Stiel in heißen Fondant tauchen und dann auf einer Backmatte abkühlen lassen. Mit einer Garniertüte kleine Tupfen Bitterkuvertüre auf eine Backmatte dressieren und leicht anziehen lassen. Stielkirschen aufsetzen, damit die Kirschen einen kleinen Fuß bekommen, dann nochmals ganz bis zum ersten Drittel des Stiels in temperierte Kuvertüre tauchen.

KIRSCHWASSER-MONTBLANCS

KIRSCHWASSER-MONT BLANC

Der Buttertrüffel reiht sich problemlos in die Liste der absoluten Klassiker ein: Er ist eine etwas leichtere Variante der Ganache-Trüffel. Auch hier sind der Fantasie bei der Variation keine Grenzen gesetzt. Egal, ob man die Kuvertüre oder den Alkohol austauscht, Nusspasten oder Konfitüre zugibt, das Geschmackserlebnis wird immer wunderbar sein.

The butter truffle is with no doubt an absolute classic: It is the lighter version of the ganache truffle. Also here, there are no limitations to your fantasy. Whether you change the couverture or the alcohol, add nut pastes or the jam, the taste will always be fantastic.

INGREDIENTS FOR 100 CHOCOLATES		ZUTATEN FÜR 100 PRALINEN	
CROQUANT (FRENCH FOR CRUNCHY)		**KROKANT**	
50 g	glucose	50 g	Glukose
500 g	sugar	500 g	Zucker
200 g	sliced almonds	200 g	gehobelte Mandeln
BUTTER GANACHE		**BUTTERGANACHE**	
200 g	unsalted butter	200 g	Butter
100 g	fudge	100 g	Fondant
600 g	milk couverture, at least 40 % cocoa	600 g	Milchkuvertüre, mind. 40 % Kakaoanteil
100 g	Kirschwasser (cherry brandy) 40 % vol.	100 g	Kirschwasser 40 %-vol.
COATING		**ÜBERZUG**	
	milk couverture		Vollmilchkuvertüre
DECORATION		**DEKORATION**	
	silver dust		Silberstaub

Kakaobutter mit einem Pinsel auf Backpapier auftragen

Using a brush, smear the cocoa butter onto baking paper

1

Krokantplättchen auflegen und leicht andrücken

Put the croquant discs on the smeared baking paper and press lightly

2

HERSTELLUNG

Glukose schmelzen, den Zucker nach und nach zugeben und ebenfalls schmelzen. Achtung: Den Karamell so hell wie möglich halten, dabei aber alle Zuckerkristalle auflösen, sonst kristallisiert der Krokant vorzeitig aus und ist nicht mehr zu verarbeiten. Die gehobelten Mandeln unterrühren, dann Krokant sofort auf eine Backmatte geben, mit einer zweiten Backmatte abdecken und dünn ausrollen. Falls der Krokant zu schnell auskühlt, im Ofen wieder erwärmen. Mit einem Metallausstecher Kreise ausstechen und auskühlen lassen. Die Krokantplättchen auf ein mit Kakaobutter bepinseltes Papier legen. So bald die Kakaobutter fest ist haften die Plättchen und man kann problemlos die Butterganache aufdressieren.

Für die Butterganache Butter mit Fondant aufschlagen, erst die temperierte Kuvertüre, dann den Alkohol zugeben.

Die Butterganache mit einer Sterntülle zu kleinen Spitzen auf die Krokantplättchen dressieren. Fest werden lassen, dann mit der Vollmilchkuvertüre überziehen. Sobald die Kuvertüre anzieht, mit Silberstaub dekorieren.

MAKING THE PARTS

Melt the glucose and gradually add the sugar so that it melts. Attention: Keep the caramel as light as possible but make sure that all sugar crystals dissolve otherwise the croquant will crystallize prematurely rendering it useless. Add the sliced almonds, then immediately place the croquant on a baking mat. Cover the croquant with a second baking mat and roll into a thin layer. Incase the croquant cools too quickly warm it again in the oven. Using a metal cutter cut out in discs and leave to cool. Place the small croquant discs on a paper that has been brushed with cocoa butter. As soon as the cocoa butter hardens, the discs are stuck to the paper. You can now decorate with the butter ganache.

For the butter ganache; beat the butter with the fudge then add the tempered couverture then the alcohol.

Using a star nozzle, decorate the butter ganache in small spikes on the croquant disc. Let it harden then coat with the milk couverture. As soon as the couverture has set, decorate with silver dust.

ERDBEER-JOGHURT-TRÜFFEL

STRAWBERRY YOGHURT TRUFFLE

Dieses bunte und leckere „Stückchen" macht besonders Kindern Freude. Die Farbe kann selbstverständlich nach Belieben durch Kakaobutter oder Fruchtpulver variiert werden. Achtung: Diese Praline hat durch den verwendeten Joghurt sowie den hohen Flüssigkeitsgehalt nur eine begrenzte Haltbarkeit.

This bright and tasty treat is a joy especially for children. The color can be varied according to your taste using cocoa butter and fruit powder. Attention: This chocolate can only be stored for a limited period of time because of the yoghurt and the high liquid content.

Zutaten für 100 Pralinen	Ingredients for 100 chocolates
Kakaobohnenformen	**Cocoa bean forms**
rote und gelbe Kakaobutter	red and yellow cocoa butter
Bitterkuvertüre	bitter couverture
weiße Kuvertüre	white couverture

Erdbeer-Joghurt-Füllung		Strawberry yoghurt filling	
50 g	Sahne, 32 % Fett	50 g	cream, 32 % fat
150 g	Erdbeerpüree	150 g	strawberry puree
25 g	gefriergetrocknetes Erdbeerpulver	25 g	freeze-dried strawberry powder
1 g	Joghurtkulturen (aus dem Naturkostladen)	1 g	yoghurt culture (from the organic food store)
200 g	Naturjoghurt	200 g	natural yoghurt
375 g	weiße Kuvertüre	375 g	white couverture
25 g	Butter	25 g	unsalted butter

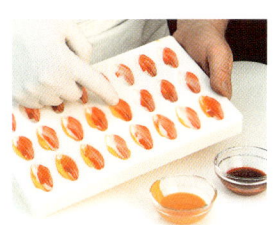

Pralinenformen mit temperierter roter Kakaobutter auswischen, dann mit gelber Kakaobutter

Wipe the chocolate forms with tempered red cocoa butter then with yellow cocoa butter

1

Übergang zwischen roter und gelber Kakaobutter mit temperierter Kuvertüre bestreichen. Anziehen lassen und mit weißer Kuvertüre ausgießen

Cover the transition from red cocoa butter to yellow cocoa butter with tempered white couverture. Let the couverture harden then pour white couverture over

2

MAKING THE PARTS

Wipe the cocoa bean forms with red cocoa butter tempered to 38 °C, then with the yellow cocoa butter. Temper the bitter couverture and apply it above the middle of the red/yellow cocoa butter. As soon as the bitter couverture has hardened, pour the white couverture over.

Mix the cream with the strawberry puree and boil for a short time. Add the strawberry powder and the yoghurt cultures and mix with the yoghurt until smooth. Melt the white couverture and temper as you add it to the mixture. At 30 °C stir in the soft butter, pour the filling in the prepared forms and leave until a crust forms. Cover with tempered white couverture and take out as soon as the chocolate loosens from its form.

HERSTELLUNG

Kakaobohnenformen mit auf 38 °C temperierter roter Kakaobutter auswischen, dann mit gelber Kakaobutter. Bitterkuvertüre temperieren und über der Mitte der rot/gelben Kakaobutter auftragen. Sobald die Bitterkuvertüre angezogen hat, mit weißer Kuvertüre ausgießen.

Sahne mit dem Erdbeerpüree mischen und kurz aufkochen. Erdbeerpulver und die Joghurtkulturen zugeben und mit Joghurt glatt mixen. Die weiße Kuvertüre auflösen und temperiert zugeben. Dann bei 30 °C die weiche Butter untermixen, die Füllung in die vorbereiteten Formen füllen und verhauten lassen. Mit temperierter weißer Kuvertüre abdeckeln und sobald sich die Pralinen aus der Form lösen, ausformen.

WILLIAMS-KRUSTENLIKÖR-PRALINE
WILLIAMS SUGAR CRUST PRALINE

KRUSTENLIKÖR-PRALINEN FINDET MAN LEIDER IMMER SELTENER IN DEN KONDITOREIEN UND CONFISERIEN. VIELLEICHT LIEGT ES DARAN, DASS MAN SICH MEISTENS BEKLECKERT, WENN MAN HERZHAFT HINEINBEISST. MITTLERWEILE GIBT ES SOGAR UNTERSUCHUNGEN, DIE ANHAND DER ART WIE JEMAND EINE PRALINE ISST, RÜCKSCHLÜSSE AUF DESSEN CHARAKTER ZIEHEN LASSEN. KRUSTENLIKÖR-PRALINEN STECKE ICH IMMER GANZ IN DEN MUND.

IT IS UNFORTUNATELY VERY RARE TO FIND WILLIAMS SUGAR CRUST CHOCOLATES AT THE CONFECTIONERS. MAY BE IT IS BECAUSE WE USUALLY SPILL THE LIQUOR ON OURSELVES WHEN WE TAKE A HEARTY BITE INTO THE CHOCOLATE. MEANWHILE, RESEARCH IS BEING DONE ON IF IT IS POSSIBLE TO DETERMINE ONE'S CHARACTER BY THE WAY YOU EAT A PRALINE. I ALWAYS PUT THE WHOLE WILLIAMS SUGAR CRUST CHOCOLATE IN MY MOUTH.

INGREDIENTS FOR 80 CHOCOLATES		ZUTATEN FÜR 80 PRALINEN	
	starch mixture		*Pudergemisch*
	cake powder		*Weizenpuder*
	cornstarch		*Maisstärke*
	SYRUP		**SIRUP**
500 g	*sugar*	500 g	*Zucker*
150 g	*cold water*	150 g	*kaltes Wasser*
180 g	*Williams (peer brandy) 40 % vol.*	180 g	*Williams 40 %-vol.*
35 g	*spirit of Wine 96 % vol.*	35 g	*Weingeist 96 %-vol.*
	COATING		**ÜBERZUG**
	dark liquid couverture spray		*dunkle Sprühkuvertüre*
	broken cocoa beans		*Kakaobohnenbruch*
	bitter couverture		*Bitterkuvertüre*

Fertige Krusten mit Sprühkuvertüre absprühen

Spray the finished crusts with dark liquid couverture

1

Kakaobohnenbruch aufstreuen

Scatter the broken cocoa beans

2

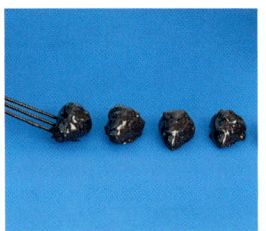

Praline mit temperierter Bitterkuvertüre überziehen

Coat the chocolate with tempered bitter couverture

3

MAKING THE PARTS

To make the starch mixture, mix two portions of cake powder to one portion of cornstarch. Sieve the dry starch mixture twice, compress it in starch trays then use the plaster mold to press it into the liquor praline molds. Leave some starch mixture aside for sifting the chocolates.

Mix the sugar with the water and quickly bring to boil to 120 °C. Then take it off the cooker and add the Williams and the Spirit of Wine. Cover and lightly sway the alcohol. Pour the hot syrup into the prepared chocolate forms using a filling funnel. Using a sieve, powder the chocolates with the remaining starch mixture and leave overnight. Carefully turn the liquor forms and once again leave them overnight so that a fine sugar crust can build around it.

Powder the liquor forms with a fine brush, spray with the dark liquid couverture; scatter the broken cocoa beans over as soon as the couverture hardens. Coat the praline with tempered bitter couverture.

HERSTELLUNG

Ein Pudergemisch aus zwei Teilen Weizenpuder und einem Teil Maisstärke herstellen. Das gut trockene Pudergemisch 2 Mal sieben, in Puderkästen verdichten, dann mit Gipsstempeln die Likörpralinenformen eindrücken. Etwas Pudergemisch für das Absieben der Pralinen beiseite lassen.

Den Zucker mit dem Wasser mischen und schnell auf 120 °C kochen. Dann vom Herd nehmen, Williams und Weingeist zugeben, zudecken und den Alkohol leicht unterschwenken. Den noch heißen Sirup in einen Fülltrichter geben und in die vorbereiteten Pralinenformen füllen. Pralinen mit einem Sieb und dem vorbereiteten Pudergemisch abpudern und über Nacht stehen lassen. Den Likörkörper vorsichtig wenden und nochmals über Nacht stehen lassen, so dass sich rundum eine feine Zuckerkruste bildet.

Die Likörkörper mit einem feinen Pinsel abpudern, mit Sprühkuvertüre absprühen; Kakaobohnenbruch aufstreuen und sobald die Sprühkuvertüre fest ist, Praline vollständig mit temperierter Bitterkuvertüre überziehen.

KÖNIGSBERGER MARZIPANKONFEKT

KÖNIGSBERGER MARZIPAN SWEETS

Die Marzipanstadt Königsberg liegt heute in Russland, aber die Tradition der Marzipan-Herstellung hat sich in Deutschland erhalten. Königsberger Marzipan wird abgeflämmt und mit Rosenwasser verfeinert. Ansonsten sind der Phantasie keine Grenzen mehr gesetzt.

Although Königsberg, the legendary marzipan city is in Russia, the tradition of making marzipan has remained strong in Germany. This marzipan is always singed then perfected with rose water. Otherwise fantasy knows no limits.

Zutaten für 100 Pralinen		Ingredients for 100 chocolates	
Königsberger Marzipan		**Königsberger Marzipan**	
700 g	Marzipanrohmasse	700 g	marzipan raw mixture
35 g	Rosenwasser	35 g	rose water
	Gummi Arabicum		Gum Arabic
Zwetschgenwasser-Ganache		**Plum brandy ganache**	
10 g	Glukosesirup	10 g	glucose syrup
100 g	Sahne, 32 % Fett	100 g	cream, 32 % fat
200 g	Bitterkuvertüre	200 g	bitter couverture
20 g	Butter	20 g	unsalted butter
40 g	Zwetschgenwasser	40 g	plum brandy
Odenwälder Pflaumenmus		**Odenwälder plum jam**	
250 g	Pflaumen	250 g	plums
125 g	Zucker	125 g	sugar
2,5 g	Sternanis	2.5 g	star-anise
2,5 g	Zimtstangen	2.5 g	cinnamon sticks
$1/2$	Vanilleschote	$1/2$	vanilla pod
25 g	Balsamico	25 g	balsamic vinegar

MAKING THE PARTS

Knead the marzipan raw mixture with very high quality rose water. Make sure that the water content of the rose water is not too high because it is hard to stamp out damp marzipan. Using a special cookie cutter, stamp out marzipan shapes and leave to dry overnight. Singe them with a gas burner or in a "Salamander" then bring them to sparkle with dissolved Gum Arabic.

Boil the glucose syrup with the cream, add finely chopped bitter couverture and stir to a smooth ganache. Stir in the butter and the plum brandy. Fill the marzipan shapes to three quarters with the warm ganache.

For the plum jam, mix the plums with the remaining ingredients and leave overnight in the oven at 160 °C. The mixture will reduce to half its original size. Leave to cool, filter through a sieve and decorate the top of the ganache with it using a decorating bag. You can now garnish the chocolate with chocolate fans and a gold leaf for example.

HERSTELLUNG

Marzipanrohmasse mit dem sehr hochwertigen Rosenwasser verkneten. Achtung, der Wassergehalt des Rosenwassers darf nicht zu hoch sein, denn sehr feuchter Marzipan lässt sich schlecht ausstechen. Mit einem Spezialausstecher Marzipankörper ausstechen und über Nacht trocknen lassen. Marzipankörper mit einem Gasbrenner oder im Salamander abflämmen, danach mit aufgelöstem Gummi Arabicum abglänzen.

Glukosesirup mit der Sahne aufkochen, fein gehackte Bitterkuvertüre zugeben und eine glatte Ganache herstellen. Butter und Zwetschgenwasser einrühren. Marzipankörper zu drei Viertel mit der noch warmen Ganache füllen.

Für das Pflaumenmus die Pflaumen mit den restlichen Zutaten mischen und über Nacht im Ofen bei 160 °C auf die Hälfte reduzieren. Abkühlen lassen, durch ein Sieb passieren und mit einem Garniertütchen auf die Ganache geben. Die fertige Praline kann nun ausdekoriert werden, z. B. mit einem Schokoladenfächer und etwas Blattgold.

IRISH-COFFEE-WATTLESEED

IRISH COFFEE-WATTLESEED

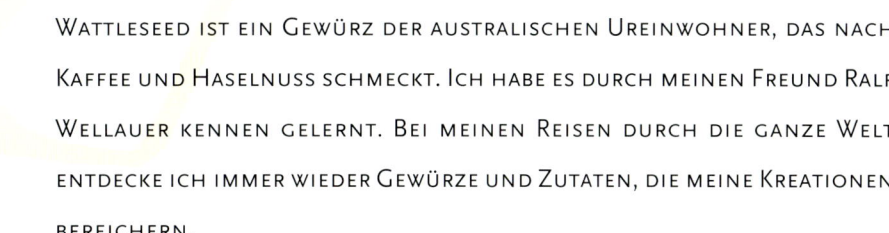

Wattleseed ist ein Gewürz der australischen Ureinwohner, das nach Kaffee und Haselnuss schmeckt. Ich habe es durch meinen Freund Ralf Wellauer kennen gelernt. Bei meinen Reisen durch die ganze Welt entdecke ich immer wieder Gewürze und Zutaten, die meine Kreationen bereichern.

The wattle seed is a spice from the Australian aboriginals that tastes like coffee and hazelnut. I got to know about this spice from my friend Ralf Wellauer. During my trips to various countries, I keep discovering spices and ingredients that enrich my creations.

Ingredients for 100 chocolates		**Zutaten für 100 Pralinen**	
	bitter couverture		Bitterkuvertüre
	Wattle seed croquant		**Wattleseedkrokant**
15 g	glucose	15 g	Glukose
125 g	sugar	125 g	Zucker
60 g	ground wattle seed (Acacia seeds)	60 g	gemahlene Wattleseedsamen (Akaziensamen)
	Irish coffee fudge		**Irish Coffee Fondant**
500 g	fudge	500 g	Fondant
70 g	glucose	70 g	Glukose
70 g	unsalted butter	70 g	Butter
150 g	egg liquor	150 g	Eierlikör
60 g	mocha paste	60 g	Mokkapaste
50 g	milk couverture	50 g	Vollmilchkuvertüre
	Decoration		**Dekoration**
	white couverture		weiße Kuvertüre

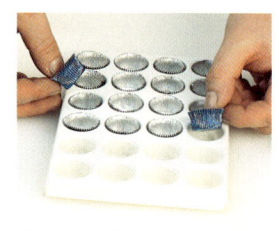

1

2

3

Herstellung

Alukapseln in Spezialformen einlegen, temperierte Bitterkuvertüre eindressieren, mit einem Spezialgitter bedecken und die überflüssige Kuvertüre durch Stürzen ausgießen. Die dünn ausgegossenen Alukapseln abkühlen lassen.

Glukosesirup schmelzen, den Zucker nach und nach zugeben. Achtung: unbedingt darauf achten, dass der Karamell möglichst hell bleibt, aber alle Zuckerkristalle geschmolzen sind, sonst kristallisiert der Krokant vorzeitig aus und ist dann nicht mehr zu verarbeiten. Die gemahlenen Wattleseedsamen zugeben und unterrühren. Krokant auf eine Backmatte geben, ausstreichen und abkühlen lassen. Den Krokant hacken und in die vorbereiteten ausgekühlten Alukapseln geben.

Making the parts

Place the foil capsules in special molds, decorate them with tempered bitter couverture, cover with a special rack and turn them over to pour out the extra couverture. Let the thin layer of couverture in the foil capsules cool.

Melt the glucose syrup and gradually add the sugar. Attention: Keep the caramel as light as possible but make sure that all sugar crystals dissolve otherwise the croquant will crystallize prematurely rendering it useless. Add the ground wattle seeds and stir. Spread out the croquant on a baking mat and leave to cool. Chop up the croquant and place the chopped croquants in the cooled foil capsules.

Alukapseln in Spezialformen einlegen

Place the foil capsules in special molds

Eindressieren von temperierter Bitterkuvertüre in die Alukapseln

Fill the tempered bitter couverture in the foil capsules

4

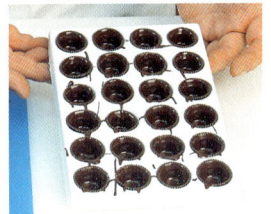

Ausgießen der Bitterkuvertüre durch Stürzen

Pour out the bitter couverture by overturning the foil capsules

Alukapseln mit einem Spezialgitter bedecken

Cover the foil capsules with a special rack

5

Dünn ausgegossene Alukapseln für die weitere Verwendung

Leave the thin-layered foil capsules to cool

Carefully heat the fudge and the glucose, mix with the butter, egg liquor and the mocha paste and stir until smooth. Melt the couverture and add it to the mixture then fill the cool mixture in the small chocolate molds. As soon as a crust forms decorate with a drop of white couverture and impress a frozen stamp while the couverture is still soft. Individual name-stamps make a good impression when used here.

Fondant und Glukose vorsichtig erwärmen, mit der Butter, dem Eierlikör und der Mokkapaste glatt rühren. Die Kuvertüre auflösen, zugeben und anschließend die leicht abgekühlte Masse in die Pralinen-förmchen füllen. Sobald sich eine Haut gebildet hat, mit einem Tropfen weißer Kuvertüre dekorieren und solange die Kuvertüre noch flüssig ist, einen gefrorenen Stempel eindrücken. Hierzu eignen sich sehr gut Namensstempel.

JASMINTEE-INGWER-PRALINE „CHINESE GIRLS"

JASMINE TEA-GINGER-PRALINE "CHINESE GIRLS"

DIESE AUSSERGEWÖHNLICHE PRALINE FASZINIERT ZUERST DURCH IHR OUTFIT. DIE „CHINESE-GIRLS" HABE ICH BEI MEINER LETZTEN PEKINGREISE ENTDECKT UND FINDE DIE „DAMEN" PASSEN ALS AUFLEGER HERVORRAGEND ZU DIESER KREATION. ÜBRIGENS SIND TEETRÜFFEL EBENSO VARIANTENREICH WIE DIE TEESORTEN SELBST.

THIS FIRST FASCINATING THING ABOUT THIS CHOCOLATE IS ITS OUTFIT. I DISCOVERED THE "CHINESE GIRLS" DURING MY LAST TRIP TO PEKING AND I FIND THE "LADIES" ARE A PERFECT ACCESSORY TO THIS CREATION. BY THE WAY, THERE ARE AS MANY TYPES OF TEA TRUFFLE AS THERE ARE TEA ASSORTMENTS.

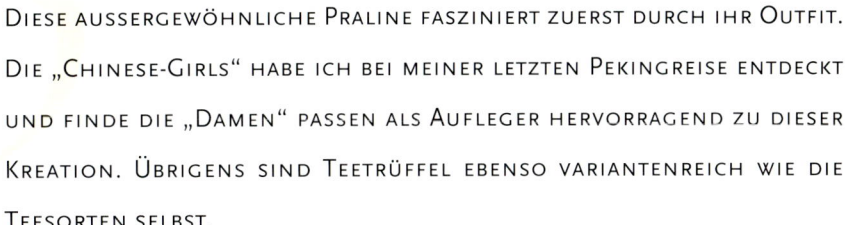

INGREDIENTS FOR 130 CHOCOLATES

JASMINE TEA-GINGER-GANACHE

200 g	whole milk
30 g	Jasmine tea
	up to
200 g	cream, 32 % fat
700 g	milk couverture, at least 40 % cocoa content
100 g	unsalted butter
100 g	fine chopped, candied ginger

COATING
white couverture

ZUTATEN FÜR 130 PRALINEN

JASMINTEE-INGWER-GANACHE

200 g	Vollmilch
30 g	Jasmintee
	bis zu
200 g	Sahne, 32 % Fett
700 g	Vollmilchkuvertüre, mind. 40 % Kakaoanteil
100 g	Butter
100 g	fein gehackter, kandierter Ingwer

ÜBERZUG
weiße Kuvertüre

1

2

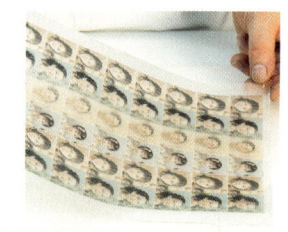

3

## Herstellung	## Making the parts
Die Vollmilch aufkochen und über den Tee gießen (je nach Teequalität Milch vor dem Aufgießen etwas abkühlen lassen). Maximal 5 Minuten ziehen lassen, dann durch ein Passiertuch pressen. Mit Sahne aufgießen, so dass 300 g Teefond entstehen. Diesen nochmals aufkochen, über die feingehackte Kuvertüre gießen und daraus eine glatte Ganache rühren. Die Butter bei etwa 30 °C einrühren, zuletzt den gehackten Ingwer zugeben.	Boil the whole milk and pour it over the tea (let the milk cool a little before pouring – depending on the quality of the tea). Steep for not more than 5 minutes then press through a cloth strainer. Pour cream over until you have 300 g of tea stock. Boil this mixture again and pour it over the fine chopped couverture then stir until you have a smooth ganache. Stir in the butter at about 30 °C then add the chopped ginger.
Ganache in einen vorbereiteten Rahmen gießen, ausstreichen und kristallisieren lassen. Mit temperierter weißer Kuvertüre von einer Seite dünn bestreichen, mit der Schneidenadel schneiden, dann rundum mit weißer Kuvertüre überziehen und mit den vorbereiteten Chinese-Girls-Auflegern belegen.	Pour the ganache in the prepared molds, spread it and leave to crystallize. Brush a thin layer of tempered white couverture chocolate on one side, cut with a confectionary cutting guitar then coat the whole chocolate with white couverture. Decorate with the "Chinese girls".

Speiseöl auf eine Acrylglasplatte aufgießen

Pour cooking oil on a plexi-glass plate

Öl mit einem Küchenpapier gleichmäßig dünn verteilen

Spread the oil in an even thin layer with a kitchen paper towel

---

Foliendekor auflegen

Put on the foil decoration

4 —

Foliendekor leicht andrücken

Lightly press the foil decoration down

5 —

Temperierte weiße Kuvertüre aufgießen

Pour the tempered white couverture chocolate over

6 —

Kuvertüre ausstreichen

Spread out the couverture

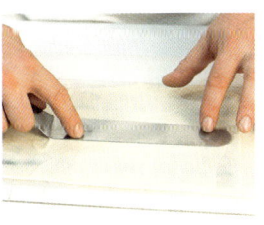

7 —

Wenn Kuvertüre gleichmäßig dünn ausgestrichen ist, aushärten lassen

After the couverture has been evenly spread, leave to harden

8 —

Pralinendekore mit der Schneidenadel präzise ausschneiden

Accurately cut out the praline decorations with the cutting needle

---

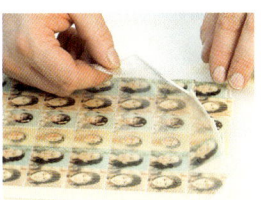

9 —

Dekor von der Folie abziehen

Pull the foil off the decoration

MANGOGELEE MIT PFEFFERGANACHE

MANGO JELLY WITH PEPPER GANACHE

NACH EINER REISE DURCH BRASILIEN HABE ICH MIR AUF DEM FLUGHAFEN VON SÃO PAULO EIN PAAR PRALINEN GEGÖNNT, UND WAR ÜBERRASCHT, DASS SIE SCHLICHT AUS MANGO-GELEE MIT SCHOKOLADE BESTANDEN. FÜR DIESES REZEPT HABE ICH EIN FRANZÖSISCHES GELEE MIT PEKTIN GEWÄHLT. NATÜRLICH DARF DER RUM BEI EINER BRASILIANISCH INSPIRIERTEN PRALINE NICHT FEHLEN.

AFTER TRAVELING THROUGH BRAZIL, I TREATED MYSELF TO A FEW CHOCOLATES AT THE AIRPORT IN SÃO PAULO. I MUST SAY I WAS AMAZED THAT THE CHOCOLATES WERE ONLY MADE OF MANGO JELLY AND CHOCOLATE. I HAVE CHOSEN A FRENCH JELLY WITH PECTIN FOR THIS RECIPE. OF COURSE RUM IS AN IMPORTANT INGREDIENT FOR A CHOCOLATE INSPIRED BY BRAZIL.

INGREDIENTS FOR 150 CHOCOLATES		ZUTATEN FUR 150 PRALINEN	
MANGO JELLY		**MANGOGELEE**	
470 g	mango puree	470 g	Mangopüree
12 g	pectin	12 g	Pektin
550 g	sugar	550 g	Zucker
70 g	glucose	70 g	Glukose
60 g	rum	60 g	Rum
3 g	citric acid	3 g	Zitronensäure
GANACHE		**GANACHE**	
40 g	glucose	40 g	Glukose
150 g	cream, 32 % fat	150 g	Sahne, 32 % Fett
6 g	green pepper from a tin	6 g	grüner Pfeffer aus dem Glas
1 g	salt	1 g	Salz
300 g	milk couverture, at least 40 % cocoa content	300 g	Vollmilchkuvertüre, mind. 40 % Kakaoanteil
COATING		**ÜBERZUG**	
	bitter couverture		Bitterkuvertüre

1

Folie abziehen

Pull off the foil

2

Geleeseite mit Zucker bestreuen

Sprinkle the jelly-side with sugar

3

Zucker gleichmäßig verteilen

Spread the sugar evenly

4

Überflüssigen Zucker abpinseln

Brush off extra sugar

5

Pralinen mit der Scheidegeige schneiden

Cut the chocolateswith a confectionary cutting guitar

6

Metallplatte unterschieben und Pralinen um 90 Grad drehen

Push the metal plate underneath and turn the praline 90 degrees

7

8

9

Zweite Seite der Pralinen schneiden

Cut the second side of the chocolate

Pralinen bis zum Zuckerrand in Bitterkuvertüre tauchen

Dip the chocolate up to the sugar brim in bitter couverture

Pralinen mit der Überziehgabel herausnehmen, an der Drahtkante abstreifen und absetzen

Take the chocolate out with the dipping fork, level off on the edge and put down

MAKING THE PARTS

Heat the mango puree to 50 °C. Mix the pectin with 50 g sugar and stir into the mango puree with a whisk. Boil the mixture, add the remaining sugar and glucose. Boil to 110 °C then immediately add the rum and the citric acid that has been dissolved in little water. Pour the jelly in a foiled-silicone mold and spread it evenly. Leave to cool.

Boil the glucose with the cream, the finely chopped pepper and the salt. Pour over the finely chopped couverture and stir until smooth. Pour the mixture over the jelly. Leave overnight to crystallize. Brush the ganache-side with a thin layer of tempered bitter couverture, turn it over and sprinkle sugar over the jelly-side. Cut the chocolate with the confectionary cutting guitar and dip in bitter couverture until the upper brim of the jelly.

HERSTELLUNG

Das Mangopüree auf 50 °C erwärmen. Das Pektin mit 50 g Zucker mischen und mit einem Schneebesen in das Mangopüree einrühren. Mischung aufkochen, den restlichen Zucker und die Glukose zugeben. Auf 110 °C kochen, dann sofort den Rum und die in wenig Wasser aufgelöste Zitronensaure zugeben. Das Gelee schnell in eine mit Folie ausgelegte Silikonform gießen und gleichmäßig verteilen. Auskühlen lassen.

Glukose mit der Sahne, dem fein gehackten Pfeffer und dem Salz aufkochen. Über die fein gehackte Kuvertüre gießen, Masse glatt rühren und auf das Gelee geben. Über Nacht auskristallisieren lassen. Ganacheseite dünn mit temperierter Bitterkuvertüre bestreichen, umdrehen und die Geleeseite mit Zucker bestreuen. Die Pralinen mit der Schneidegeige schneiden und in Bitterkuvertüre bis zum oberen Rand des Gelees absetzten.

ROSMARIN-PFIRSICH-TRÜFFEL

ROSEMARY-PEACH-TRUFFLE

Rosmarin ist ein tolles Kraut. Der Name Rosmarin kommt übrigens aus dem Lateinischen und bedeutet so viel wie „Rose des Meeres", denn die Seefahrer im antiken Mittelmeerraum konnten den Duft schon riechen, ehe sie an Land gegangen waren. Ich liebe die Kombination von Kräutern und Schokolade!

Rosemary is a fantastic herb. By the way, the name Rosemary is derived from Latin and it literally means "dew of the sea" because the seamen in the antique Mediterranean could smell it long before they reached land. I love the combination of herbs and chocolate!

Ingredients for 140 chocolates		**Zutaten für 140 Pralinen**	
Peach jam		**Pfirsichkonfitüre**	
150 g	peach puree from Weinberg	150 g	Weinbergpfirsichpüree
75 g	sugar	75 g	Zucker
1,5 g	pectin	1,5 g	Pektin
1	drops of bitter almond oil	1	Tropfen Bittermandelöl
Rosemary ganache		**Rosmaringanache**	
75 g	cognac	75 g	Cognac
7 g	dried rosemary	7 g	getrockneter Rosmarin
300 g	cream, 32 % fat	300 g	Sahne, 32 % Fett
450 g	milk couverture, at least 40 % cocoa content	450 g	Vollmilchkuvertüre, mind. 40 % Kakaoanteil
Coating		**Überzug**	
	milk couverture		Vollmilchkuvertüre
Decoration		**Dekoration**	
	candied rosemary needles		kandierte Rosmarinnadeln
	decoration foil		Dekorfolie

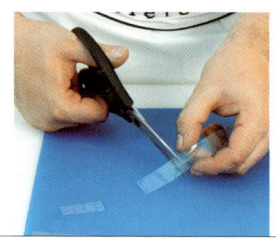

Matt glänzende Dekorfolie in Streifen schneiden

Cut the matt glossy decoration foil in strips

1

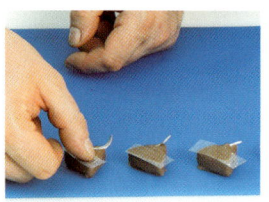

Kandierte Rosmarinnadeln sowie Dekorfolien-streifen auf die Praline auflegen

Place the candied rosemary needles and the decoration foil strips on the chocolate

2

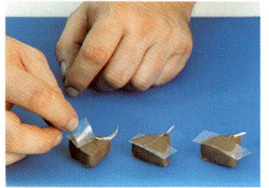

Sobald die Kuvertüre fest ist und sich die Folie abziehen lässt, diese entfernen

Pull the foil off as soon as the couverture hardens.

3

HERSTELLUNG

Das Pfirsichpüree erwärmen, Zucker mit Pektin mischen, zugeben und aufkochen. Etwa 3 Minuten weiterkochen lassen, das Bittermandelöl zugeben, dann die Pfirsich-konfitüre. Den Fruchtaufstrich auskühlen lassen, durch ein Sieb passieren und je-weils etwa 3 g in vorbereitete Formen fül-len, hier z. B. Coldstone Schalen.

Cognac auf 70 °C erwärmen, den Rosma-rin zugeben, mit Frischhaltefolie abgedeckt etwa 30 Minuten ziehen lassen, dann ab-passieren. In der Zwischenzeit die Sahne aufkochen, über die fein gehackte Kuver-türe gießen, zu einer glatten Masse rühren und sobald die Masse auf 30 °C abgekühlt ist, den Rosmarinsud unterrühren. Ros-maringanache in die mit Fruchtaufstrich befüllten Formen füllen und auskristalli-sieren lassen.

Pralinen mit Vollmilchkuvertüre überzie-hen und mit kandierten Rosmarinnadeln sowie Dekorfolienstreifen belegen. (Ich nenne diese Folie „Schattenfolie", weil nur ein Schatten des Dekors auf der Praline zu sehen ist.)

MAKING THE PARTS

Heat the peach puree, mix the sugar with the pectin then add and boil. Leave to boil for about 3 minutes then add the bitter almond oil. Leave the fruit spread to cool then sieve and fill approximately 3 g of it in the prepared molds – in this case Cold Stone dishes for example.

Heat the Cognac to 70 °C, add the rose-mary, cover with saran wrap and leave to brew for about 30 minutes then sieve. In the mean time boil the cream, pour it over the finely chopped couverture and stir until smooth. As soon as the mixture cools down to 30 °C, stir in the rosemary brew. Fill the rosemary ganache in the molds that contain the fruit spread and leave to crystallize.

Coat the chocolates with milk couverture and decorate with the candied rosemary needles and the decoration foil strips. (I call this foil "shadow foil" because the shadow of the decoration can be seen on the chocolate.)

MARACUJATRÜFFEL

PASSION FRUIT TRUFFLE

Dieser Maracujatrüffel passt perfekt in jede Sommerkollektion. Er ist exotisch und sehr erfrischend. Wichtig ist, bei einem eventuellen Transport auf ausreichende Kühlung zu achten.

This passion fruit truffle is perfect for the any summer collection. It is exotic and very refreshing. It is important to make sure you have adequate cooling equipment if you intend to transport it.

Zutaten für 100 Pralinen		Ingredients for 100 chocolates	
Halbkugelformen		**Hemisphere molds**	
	Bitterkuvertüre		bitter couverture
	orangefarbene Kakaobutter		orange-colored cocoa butter
	weiße Kuvertüre		white couverture
	dunkle Sprühkuvertüre		bitter liquid couverture spray
Maracujaganache		**Passion fruit ganache**	
200 g	Zucker	200 g	sugar
50 g	Dextrose	50 g	dextrose
250 g	Maracujapüree	250 g	passion fruit puree
1	Vanilleschote	1	vanilla bean
100 g	Kakaobutter	100 g	cocoa butter
200 g	Vollmilchkuvertüre	200 g	milk couverture
75 g	Butter	75 g	unsalted butter

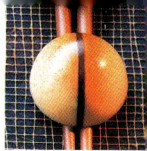

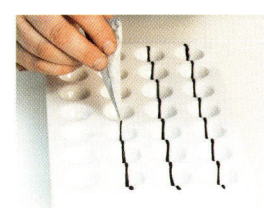

Temperierte Bitterkuvertüre mit einer Garniertüte in die Pralinenhalbkugelformen eingarnieren

Using a decorating bag, garnish the chocolate hemispheres with tempered bitter couverture

1

Linie mit orange gefärbter, auf 38 °C temperierter Kakaobutter mit einem Thermoairbrush nachziehen

Using a thermo airbrush, streak the line with orange-colored cocoa butter tempered to 38 °C

2

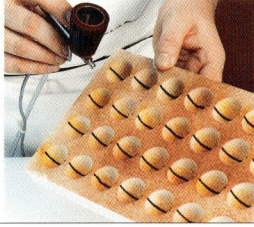

Formen mit dunkler, verdünnter Sprühkuvertüre aussprühen

Spray the forms with dark diluted couverture spray

3

MAKING THE PARTS

Garnish a line in the chocolate hemisphere molds with tempered bitter couverture. Use a thermo airbrush to streak along the line with orange-colored cocoa butter (tempered to 38 °C) then spray with diluted couverture spray. As soon as the decoration hardens pour white couverture over.

Melt the sugar with the dextrose, heat the passion fruit puree and add. Cut the vanilla bean lengthwise and scratch out the vanilla bean paste. Add the vanilla pod and the paste and leave to boil. Remove the vanilla pod. Pour the passion fruit mixture over the finely chopped cocoa butter and let it dissolve, then pour this mixture over the couverture chocolate and stir to a smooth ganache. Leave the ganache to cool, fill it in the prepared molds, let a crust form and coat with tempered white couverture. Take out of the forms as soon as the chocolate loosens itself from the form.

HERSTELLUNG

Aus temperierter Bitterkuvertüre eine Linie in Pralinenhalbkugelformen eingarnieren. Mit einem Thermoairbrush die Linie mit orange gefärbter, auf 38 °C temperierter Kakaobutter nachziehen und mit dunkler, verdünnter Sprühkuvertüre aussprühen. So bald der Dekor fest ist, die Formen mit weißer Kuvertüre ausgießen.

Den Zucker mit Dextrose schmelzen, das Maracujapüree erhitzen und zugeben. Die Vanilleschote längs aufschneiden, Mark auskratzen, Vanilleschote und Mark zugeben und aufkochen lassen. Vanilleschote entnehmen. Maracujamasse über die fein gehackte Kakaobutter gießen und diese auflösen lassen, dann über die Kuvertüre geben und eine glatte Ganache herstellen. Die Ganache abkühlen lassen, in die vorbereiteten Formen füllen, verhauten lassen und mit temperierter weißer Kuvertüre abdeckeln. So bald sich die Pralinen lösen, ausformen.

HIMBEERTRÜFFEL NUMBER ONE

RASPBERRY TRUFFLE NUMBER ONE

Dies ist und bleibt eines meiner Lieblingsrezepte. Der Himbeergeschmack passt hervorragend zu dem herben Aroma der Schokolade und zu Hause, im Odenwald, stehen mir für meine Arbeit, dank dem reichhaltigen Garten meines Vaters, beste Früchte zur Verfügung.

This is and remains my favorite recipe. The taste of raspberries harmonizes with the brut chocolate aroma. Thanks to my father's rich garden back home in Odenwald, I have the best fruits at my disposal.

INGREDIENTS FOR 120 CHOCOLATES

80 g	glucose
300 g	raspberry puree
400 g	milk couverture, at least 40 % cocoa content
200 g	bitter couverture, at least 66 % cocoa content
100 g	unsalted butter
60 g	wild raspberry brandy, 40 % vol.

COATING
bitter couverture

ZUTATEN FÜR 120 PRALINEN

80 g	Glukose
300 g	Himbeerpüree
400 g	Vollmilchkuvertüre, mind. 40 % Kakaoanteil
200 g	Bitterkuvertüre, mind. 66 % Kakaoanteil
100 g	Butter
60 g	Waldhimbeerbrand, 40 %-vol.

ÜBERZUG
Bitterkuvertüre

Mit Bitterkuvertüre überzogene Praline absetzen

Put down the chocolate coated with bitter couverture

1

Stempel muss gefrostet sein, um ein schönes Ergebnis zu erhalten

The stamp must be frozen in order to have good results

2

Praline mit dem gefrosteten Stempel stempeln

Stamp the chocolate with the frozen stamp

3

HERSTELLUNG

Die Glukose mit dem Himbeerpüree aufkochen, mit dem Mixstab gut durchmixen, die Vollmilch- und die Bitterkuvertüre fein gehackt unterrühren und zu einer glatten Ganache verarbeiten. Bei 30 °C die Butter untermixen, dann den Waldhimbeerbrand.

Die Ganache einen Zentimeter hoch in vorbereitete Rahmen eingießen, über Nacht auskristallisieren lassen, dann die Unterseite dünn mit Bitterkuvertüre bestreichen. Pralinen mit einer Schneidegeige in die gewünschte Größe schneiden, mit Bitterkuvertüre überziehen und mit einem gefrosteten Briefsiegel stempeln. Pralinen in Kakaopulver wälzen, damit sie eine antike Optik erhalten.

MAKING THE PARTS

Bring the glucose with the raspberry puree to boil, stir well with the hand blender, stir in the finely chopped milk and bitter couverture and stir to a smooth couverture. Mix in the butter at 30 °C then the wild raspberry brandy.

Pour the ganache in prepared forms to a thickness of 1 cm, leave to crystallize overnight then brush a thin layer or bitter couverture on the bottom side. Cut the chocolates into sizes of your choice using a confectionary cutting guitar, coat with bitter couverture then stamp with a frozen letter seal. Roll the chocolates in cocoa powder to give it an antique look.

ANANASWEICHKROKANT

SOFT PINEAPPLE CROQUANT

TONKABOHNEN SIND, WIE VIELE ANDERE GEWÜRZE AUCH, NICHT UNGEFÄHR-
LICH. SOWOHL BEI IHNEN ALS AUCH BEI ZIMT, MUSKATNUSS UND WALDMEISTER
SOLLTE MAN MIT DER DOSIERUNG SEHR VORSICHTIG SEIN. DIE GELTENDEN
RICHTLINIEN SIND IM INTERNET ABRUFBAR. TONKABOHNE KANN ABER AUCH
DURCH VANILLE ERSETZT WERDEN.

TONKA BEANS, LIKE OTHER SPICES, ARE NOT HARMLESS. AS IS THE CASE WITH
CINNAMON, NUTMEG AND WOODRUFF YOU HAVE TO BE CAREFUL WITH THE
DOSAGE OF TONKA BEANS. YOU CAN FIND THE APPLICABLE GUIDELINES IN THE
INTERNET. VANILLA CAN SUBSTITUTE TONKA BEANS.

ZUTATEN FÜR 130 PRALINEN		INGREDIENTS FOR 130 CHOCOLATES	
WEICHKROKANT		**SOFT CROQUANT**	
40 g	Glukosesirup	40 g	glucose syrup
375 g	Zucker	375 g	sugar
40 g	Butter	40 g	unsalted butter
40 g	Honig	40 g	honey
	(Leatherwood aus Tasmanien)		(Leatherwood from Tasmania)
100 g	Sahne, 32 % Fett	100 g	cream, 32 % fat
330 g	Marzipanrohmasse	330 g	marzipan raw mixture
225 g	fein geriebene,	225 g	finely grated and slightly
	leicht geröstete Mandeln		roasted almonds
150 g	kandierte, fein gehackte Ananas	150 g	candied, finely chopped pineapples
1 g	Tonkabohne oder Vanille	1 g	Tonka beans or vanilla
ÜBERZUG		**COATING**	
	Bitterkuvertüre		bitter couverture
DEKORATION		**DECORATION**	
	flüssige Kakaobutter		liquid cocoa butter
	Bitterkuvertüre		bitter couverture
	Schokoladenplättchen		chocolate paillets

Karamellmasse auf eine Silikon-Backmatte geben

Spread the caramel mass onto a silicone baking mat

1

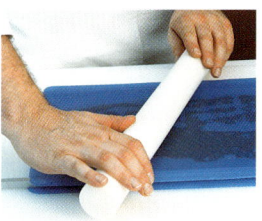

Mit einer zweiten Silikon-Backmatte abdecken und gleichmäßig dick ausrollen.

Cover with a second silicone baking mat and roll out evenly.

2

Nach dem Erkalten eine Seite dünn mit temperierter Bitterkuvertüre bestreichen

Leave to cool then brush one side with tempered bitter couverture

3

MAKING THE PARTS

Melt the glucose in a pan. Gradually add the sugar to make a light caramel. Add the butter and honey, knead the cream with the marzipan raw mixture and add to the other ingredients then stir to a smooth mixture. Place the soft caramel between two silicone baking mats and roll out until it is 1 cm thick then leave to cool. Brush one side of the caramel with bitter couverture and leave to harden. Spread the liquid cocoa butter over the top surface so that the caramel glazes, cut into desired sizes using the cutting roller and place in tempered bitter couverture. Decorate with a couverture chocolate line and the chocolate paillets.

HERSTELLUNG

Die Glukose in einem Topf schmelzen. Nach und nach den Zucker dazugeben und einen hellen Karamell herstellen. Butter und Honig zugeben, die Sahne mit der Marzipanrohmasse verkneten und zusammen mit den restlichen Zutaten zugeben und zu einer glatten Masse rühren. Den Weichkaramell zwischen zwei Silikon-Backmatten einen Zentimeter dick ausrollen und auskühlen lassen. Eine Seite des Karamells mit Bitterkuvertüre bestreichen und dann fest werden lassen. Anschließend die Oberfläche mit flüssiger Kakaobutter abglänzen, mit der Schneidewalze in die gewünschte Größe schneiden und in temperierter Bitterkuvertüre absetzen. Mit einer Kuvertürelinie und Schokoladendekorplättchen dekorieren.

CHAMPAGNER-KARAMELL-TRÜFFEL

CHAMPAGNE-CARAMEL-TRUFFLE

Champagnertrüffel sind etwas ganz Besonderes. Dummerweise haben Champagnertrüffel einen Nachteil: das Prickeln des Champagners bleibt nur ein paar Tage erhalten. Deshalb immer ganz frisch anbieten!

Champagne truffles are something really special. Unfortunately champagne truffles have a disadvantage: the tingling sensation of the champagne only lasts a few days. Always serve the truffles fresh!

INGREDIENTS FOR 120 CHOCOLATES		ZUTATEN FÜR 120 PRALINEN	
	whole milk hollow spheres		Vollmilchhohlkugeln
CARAMEL		**KARAMELL**	
20 g	glucose	20 g	Glukose
200 g	sugar	200 g	Zucker
40 g	cream, 32 % fat	40 g	Sahne, 32 % Fett
120 g	unsalted butter	120 g	Butter
60 g	Marc de Champagne	60 g	Marc de Champagne
GANACHE		**GANACHE**	
100 g	cream, 32 % fat	100 g	Sahne, 32 % Fett
30 g	glucose	30 g	Glukose
200 g	milk couverture	200 g	Vollmilchkuvertüre
20 g	unsalted butter	20 g	Butter
100 g	Champagne	100 g	Champagner
25 g	Marc de Champagne	25 g	Marc de Champagne
COATING		**ÜBERZUG**	
	milk couverture		Vollmilchkuvertüre
	icing sugar		Puderzucker
DECORATION		**DEKORATION**	
	gold leaf		Blattgold

*Temperierte Vollmilchkuvertüre auf
die Handflächen aufstreichen*

*Spread tempered milk couverture on
the hand surface*

1

HERSTELLUNG

Die Glukose in einem Topf schmelzen.
Nach und nach den Zucker zugeben und
dann einen hellen Karamell herstellen.
Die Sahne erwärmen und den Karamell
damit ablöschen. Die Butter nach und nach
untermixen und zu einer glatten Karamellmasse rühren. Karamell leicht abkühlen
und Marc de Champagne unterrühren,
dann die Vollmilchhohlkugeln zur Hälfte
damit füllen.

Sahne mit Glukose aufkochen, über die
fein gehackte Vollmilchkuvertüre gießen
und zu einer glatten Ganache verarbeiten.
Die Butter bei 30 °C untermixen, dann den
Champagner und den Marc de Champagne vorsichtig unterrühren. Halb gefüllte
Hohlkugeln mit der Ganache auffüllen,
über Nacht verhauten lassen und mit Vollmilchkuvertüre verschließen. Trüffel in
den Händen mit Vollmilchkuvertüre rollen, in Puderzucker wälzen, abpudern und
mit einem Vollmilchpunkt sowie einem
Blattgoldtupfen dekorieren.

Mehrere Trüffel gleichzeitig in den Händen rollen
Roll several truffles in the hands at a go

2

Trüffel sofort in Puderzucker wälzen
Immediately roll in icing sugar

3

*Überflüssigen Puderzucker in einem Sieb
abpudern*
Powder with the extra icing sugar in a sieve

4

MAKING THE PARTS

Melt the glucose in a pan. Gradually add
the sugar to make a light caramel. Heat
the cream and deglaze the caramel with it.
Gradually stir in the butter until it forms
a smooth caramel mixture. Leave to cool,
add the Marc de Champagne and then
half-fill the whole milk hollow spheres.

Boil the cream with the glucose and pour
it over the finely chopped milk couverture
and stir to a smooth ganache. Stir in the
butter at 30 °C then carefully stir in the
champagne and the Marc de Champagne.

Fill the half-filled hollow spheres with the
ganache, let a crust form overnight and
cover with the milk couverture. Roll the
truffle in your hands with milk couverture,
then roll them in icing sugar and decorate
with a milk point and a drop of gold leaf.

SCHWARZER SESAMNOUGAT

BLACK SESAME NOUGAT

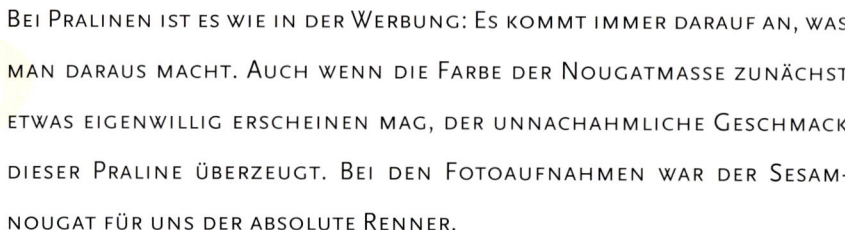

BEI PRALINEN IST ES WIE IN DER WERBUNG: ES KOMMT IMMER DARAUF AN, WAS MAN DARAUS MACHT. AUCH WENN DIE FARBE DER NOUGATMASSE ZUNÄCHST ETWAS EIGENWILLIG ERSCHEINEN MAG, DER UNNACHAHMLICHE GESCHMACK DIESER PRALINE ÜBERZEUGT. BEI DEN FOTOAUFNAHMEN WAR DER SESAMNOUGAT FÜR UNS DER ABSOLUTE RENNER.

CHOCOLATES ARE LIKE ADVERTISEMENTS: IT ALL DEPENDS ON WHAT YOU MAKE OF THEM. EVEN THOUGH NOUGAT PASTE APPEARS TO HAVE AN UNCONVENTIONAL COLOR, THE INIMITABLE TASTE OF THIS CHOCOLATE IS VERY TEMPTING. DURING THE PHOTO SHOOTS THE SESAME NOUGAT WAS A BIG HIT.

ZUTATEN FÜR 120 PRALINEN		INGREDIENTS FOR 120 CHOCOLATES	
75 g	Zucker	75 g	sugar
150 g	schwarzer Sesam	150 g	black sesame
750 g	Sahnenougat extra hell	750 g	cream nougat extra light
75 g	Kakaobutter	75 g	cocoa butter
	Bitterkuvertüre		bitter couverture

DEKORATION	DECORATION
Bitterkuvertüre	bitter couverture
Blattgoldtupfen	gold leaf drops
Bitterkuvertüredreiecke	triangular bitter couverture

Kuvertürepunkt mit der Garniertüte aufbringen

Place the couverture point on the praline with the decorating bag

Blattgold mit einem speziellen Stempel auf die Kuvertüre aufbringen

Use a special mold to put the gold leaf on the couverture

1

2

MAKING THE PARTS

Melt the sugar, stir in the sesame then pour the mixture onto a baking mat and leave to cool. Crush the sesame caramel into coarse pieces and grind to a smooth crispy mass in a cutter or a rolling mill. Dissolve the nougat and the cocoa butter and mix them in the crispy mass. Pour the sesame nougat into a 0.5 cm-high foil-covered mold and leave to solidify. Brush the bitter couverture from the bottom side and use a confectionary cutting guitar to cut out square pieces. Place the chocolates in the bitter couverture. Use the decorating bag to put a bitter couverture point in one of the corners. As soon as it sets, decorate with the gold leaf and complete the chocolate with a bitter couverture triangle.

HERSTELLUNG

Zucker schmelzen, den Sesam einrühren, dann die Masse auf eine Backmatte gießen und auskühlen lassen. Den Sesamkaramell grob zerkleinern und im Kutter oder Walzwerk zu einer feinen Knuspermasse verarbeiten. Den Nougat und die Kakaobutter aufgelöst und temperiert unter die Knuspermasse mischen. Sesamnougat in einen 0,5 cm hohen, mit Folie ausgelegten, Rahmen gießen, erstarren lassen, von der Unterseite mit Bitterkuvertüre bestreichen und mit der Schneidegeige rechteckig schneiden. Die Pralinen in Bitterkuvertüre absetzen. Den Bitterkuvertürepunkt mit der Garniertüte in einer Ecke aufbringen. Sobald er anzieht mit Blattgold dekorieren. Mit einem Bitterkuvertüredreieck fertigstellen.

PASSIONSFRUCHT-BLÄTTERKROKANT
PASSION FRUIT-LEAF CROQUANT

SCHON IM ERSTEN BAND VON „SWEET GOLD" HABE ICH EIN REZEPT MEINER FRAU VERÖFFENTLICHT. DIESMAL IST ES IHR PASSIONSFRUCHT-BLÄTTERKROKANT. AUCH WENN WIR DAS REZEPT GEMEINSAM ENTWICKELT HABEN, IST ES TROTZDEM „IHR" REZEPT, DENN DAMIT HAT SIE DEN WETTBEWERB „KONDITOR DES JAHRES" GEWONNEN. GEKLAUT IST GEKLAUT.

I HAVE ALREADY PUBLISHED ONE OF MY WIFE'S RECIPES IN THE "SWEET GOLD", THE FIRST VOLUME. THIS TIME IT IS HER PASSION FRUIT-LEAF CROQUANT. ALTHOUGH WE DEVELOPED THIS RECIPE TOGETHER IT IS STILL "HER" RECIPE BECAUSE SHE WAS CROWNED "CONFECTIONER OF THE YEAR" BECAUSE OF IT. STOLEN IS STOLEN.

INGREDIENTS FOR 100 CHOCOLATES

PASSION FRUIT-LEAF CROQUANT

500 g	sugar
50 g	Passoa passion fruit liquor concentrate 40 % vol.
500 g	cream nougat
20 g	freeze-dried passion fruit powder

COATING
white couverture

ZUTATEN FÜR 100 PRALINEN

PASSIONSFRUCHT-BLÄTTERKROKANT

500 g	Zucker
50 g	Passoa Passionsfrucht-likörkonzentrat, 40 %-vol.
500 g	Sahnenougat
20 g	gefriergetrocknetes Maracuja-fruchtpulver

ÜBERZUG
weiße Kuvertüre

Maracujafruchtpulver in den aufgelösten Sahnenougat einrühren

Stir the passion fruit powder in the cream nougat

1

Maracuja-Sahnenougat auf eine Silikon-Backmatte gießen und gleichmäßig ausstreichen

Pour the passion fruit cream nougat on a silicone baking mat and spread evenly

2

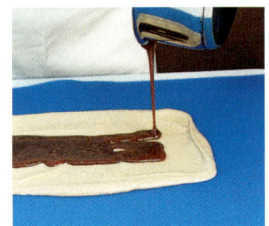

Karamell auf den Sahnenougat aufgießen und verteilen

Pour the caramel on the cream nougat and spread

3

4

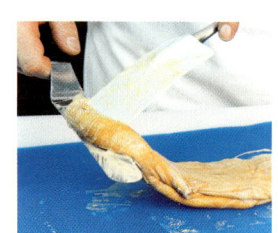

5

6

Massen mit einer Winkelpalette schnell vermischen

Quickly mix the mixtures with an angular spatula

Weitermischen bis sich die Massen eben gerade verbunden haben

Continue mixing until the mixtures have bonded

Fertigen Blätterkrokant mit der Schneidewalze rechteckig schneiden

Use a cutting roller to cut the finished leaf croquants in rectangles

MAKING THE PARTS

Gradually melt the sugar to a light caramel. Add the Passoa and stir until smooth. Melt the cream nougat and then stir in the passion fruit powder. Pour the passion fruit cream nougat on a silicone baking mat and spread evenly. Daub a thin layer of the caramel over. Mix both mixtures until they bond. Quickly cover with the second baking mat and roll out until it is 1 cm thick. Cut the croquant into rectangular chocolates using a cutting roller. If necessary re-cut the lines made by the cutting roller with a large knife. Leave to cool, coat with white couverture and decorate with fork decorations.

HERSTELLUNG

Den Zucker nach und nach zu einem hellen Karamell schmelzen. Passoa zugeben und glatt rühren. Sahnenougat auflösen, dann das Maracujafruchtpulver unterrühren. Den Maracuja-Sahnenougat auf eine Silikon-Backmatte gießen und gleichmäßig ausstreichen. Den Karamell dünn darauf verteilen. Beide Massen übereinander schlagen (tourieren) bis sie sich verbunden haben. Schnell mit einer zweiten Backmatte abdecken und einen Zentimeter dick ausrollen. Krokant mit einer Schneidewalze in rechteckige Pralinen schneiden. Die von der Schneidewalze vorgezeichneten Linien, wenn nötig, mit einem großen Messer nachschneiden. Die Pralinen auskühlen lassen, mit weißer Kuvertüre überziehen und mit einem Gabeldekor fertig stellen.

SESAMKROKANT-TÜTCHEN MIT ORANGENGANACHE

SESAME BRITTLE CONES WITH ORANGE GANACHE

Die Auswahl an Rezepten mit Orangen ist vielfältig. Sesam ist eine perfekte Ergänzung zu diesen Früchten. Die leichte Lavendelnote macht für mich diese Kreation zum perfekten Genuss, auch wegen meiner Leidenschaft für die mediterranen Gefilde.

There is a great choice of recipes that use oranges. Sesame is a perfect complement to this kind of fruit. For me the slight hint of lavender makes this creation particularly delightful, partly because of my passion for everything Mediterranean.

INGREDIENTS FOR 100 CHOCOLATES		ZUTATEN FÜR 100 PRALINEN	
SESAME BRITTLE CONES		**SESAMKROKANT-TÜTCHEN**	
60 g	glucose	60 g	Glukose
500 g	sugar	500 g	Zucker
100 g	unsalted butter	100 g	Butter
260 g	sesame seeds	260 g	Sesam
	lavender oil		Lavendelöl
ORANGE GANACHE		**ORANGENGANACHE**	
30 g	glucose	30 g	Glukose
140 g	cream, 32 % fat	140 g	Sahne, 32 % Fett
600 g	orange milk couverture	600 g	Orangen-Milchkuvertüre
140 g	softened unsalted butter	140 g	weiche Butter
40 g	Grand Marnier liqueur	40 g	Grand-Marnier-Likör
DECORATION		**DEKORATION**	
	bitter couverture		Bitterkuvertüre
	white couverture		weiße Kuvertüre
	lavender flowers		Lavendelblüten

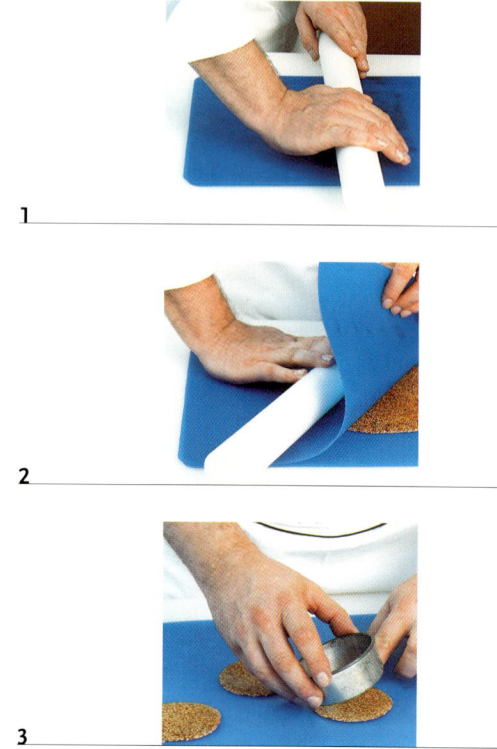

1

2

3

SESAMKROKANT-TÜTCHEN

Die Glukose in einem Topf schmelzen.
Nach und nach den Zucker zugeben und
einen hellen Karamell herstellen. Die Butter, dann den Sesam unterrühren und zuletzt das Lavendelöl (je nach Qualität und
Intensität sparsam dosiert) zugeben und
sofort zwischen zwei Silikon-Backmatten
dünn ausrollen. Kreise ausstechen, dritteln
und aus jedem Drittel ein Tütchen formen.
Trocken zwischenlagern.

SESAME BRITTLE CONES

Melt the glucose in a pan. Add the sugar
gradually to produce a light coloured caramel. Stir in the butter followed by the
sesame seeds and the lavender oil (use the
oil sparingly, depending on its quality/
intensity) and immediately roll out the mixture between two silicone baking mats.
Cut out circles, divide into three equal segments and use these to form the cones.
Store in a dry place.

Sesamkrokant heiß zwischen zwei Silikon-Back-matten dünn ausrollen. Falls der Sesamkrokant zu schnell auskühlt, im Backofen nochmals erwärmen

Roll out the sesame brittle thinly between two silicone baking mats while still hot. If the sesame brittle cools down too quickly it can be reheated in the oven.

Obere Backmatte abnehmen

Remove upper baking sheet

Mit einer Schere die Kreise dritteln

Use scissors to cut the circles in three

4

Kreise ausstechen

Cut out circular shapes

Aus den entstandenen Dreiecken Tütchen formen

Use the segments to form cones

5

ORANGENGANACHE

Bring the glucose and cream to the boil, allow to cool down to 32 °C and then stir in the tempered orange milk couverture. Add the softened butter and the Grand Marnier and blend into a smooth ganache.

Fill the cones with ganache and place down with the point upwards. Leave to crystallise overnight, then apply some bitter couverture to the open side of the cone. Decorate the point of the cone with some white couverture and a lavender flower.

ORANGENGANACHE

Die Glukose mit der Sahne aufkochen, auf 32 °C abkühlen lassen, dann die temperierte Orangen-Milchkuvertüre unter-rühren. Mit der weichen Butter und dem Grand Marnier zu einer glatten Ganache mischen.

Ganache in die Tütchen füllen und auf der Öffnung absetzen. Über Nacht auskristal-lisieren lassen, dann die Öffnung in Bitter-kuvertüre absetzen. Spitze der Tütchen mit einem heruntergezogenen weißen Kuvertürepunkt und einer Lavendelblüte dekorieren.

OLIVE TRUFFLES

ZUM ERSTEN MAL HABE ICH GESÜSSTE OLIVEN IN SHANGHAI GEGESSEN. IMMER, WENN ICH DIESES REZEPT BEI SEMINAREN IN ITALIEN VORSTELLE, GIBT ES GROSSE DISKUSSIONEN UNTER DEN TEILNEHMERN, WELCHE OLIVENSORTE SICH WOHL AM BESTEN DAFÜR EIGNET. WIE IMMER IST ES GESCHMACKSSACHE – ICH PERSÖNLICH BEVORZUGE LIGURISCHE OLIVEN, DA DEREN GESCHMACK NICHT SO HART UND GRASIG IST.

THE FIRST TIME I CAME ACROSS SWEETENED OLIVES WAS IN SHANGHAI. WHENEVER I INTRODUCE THIS RECIPE IN MY SEMINARS IN ITALY, IT SPARKS LENGTHY DISCUSSIONS AMONGST THE PARTICIPANTS ABOUT WHICH KIND OF OLIVE IS BEST SUITED FOR IT. AS ALWAYS, IT IS A QUESTION OF TASTE; I PERSONALLY PREFER OLIVES FROM LIGURIA AS THEY TASTE LESS HARD AND 'GRASSY'.

INGREDIENTS FOR 100 CHOCOLATES		ZUTATEN FÜR 100 PRALINEN	
150 g	black olives	150 g	schwarze Oliven
200 g	water	200 g	Wasser
200 g	sugar	200 g	Zucker
200 g	cream, 32 % fat	200 g	Sahne, 32 % Fett
500 g	white couverture	500 g	weiße Kuvertüre
100 g	olive oil	100 g	Olivenöl

COATING	**ÜBERZUG**
bitter couverture	Bitterkuvertüre

Relieffolie zurechtschneiden

Cut a shape out of the pattern sheet

1

Relieffolie auf die frisch mit Bitterkuvertüre überzogenen Pralinen auflegen

Place the pattern shape onto the bitter couverture coating

2

Folie leicht andrücken

Press the pattern down slightly

3

Pralinen aushärten lassen, dann Folie vorsichtig abziehen

Allow the chocolates to set and then carefully remove the pattern

4

MAKING THE PARTS

Remove the stones from the olives and chop them finely. Bring the water and sugar to the boil, add the chopped olives and simmer for a few minutes to allow the salt from the olives to dissolve. Pour the liquid through a sieve and allow the olives to cool down somewhat.

In the meantime, bring the cream to the boil, pour over the finely chopped couverture and blend to form a smooth ganache. Fold in the oil gradually and finally add the olives.

Fill the bitter chocolate half shells with the mixture, leave overnight to form a skin and cover with tempered bitter couverture. Decorate with a pattern sheet.

HERSTELLUNG

Oliven entkernen und fein hacken. Wasser mit dem Zucker aufkochen, die Olivenstückchen zugeben und ein paar Minuten leicht köcheln lassen, sodass sich das Salz aus den Oliven löst. Den Sud durch ein Sieb gießen und dann die Oliven etwas abkühlen lassen.

In der Zwischenzeit die Sahne aufkochen, über die fein gehackte Kuvertüre geben und zu einer glatten Ganache mischen. Nach und nach das Öl und zum Schluss die Oliven unterziehen.

Die Masse in Bitterhalbschalen abfüllen, über Nacht verhauten lassen und mit temperierter Bitterkuvertüre überziehen. Mit einer Relieffolie dekorieren.

SALZKARAMELL

SALT CARAMEL

DIES IST EIN REZEPT VON ROBERT WIDMANN, DEN ICH GERNE ALS MEINEN ZWEITEN VATER BEZEICHNE. ER IST EIN WICHTIGER BEGLEITER IN MEINEM BERUFLICHEN UND LÄNGST AUCH IN MEINEM PRIVATEN LEBEN. ER LIEBT DIESEN KARAMELL. DAS SALZ MACHT SEINEN GESCHMACK SO AUSSERGEWÖHNLICH. ABER FRAGEN SIE MICH NICHT, WIE LANGE ICH GESUCHT HABE, BIS ICH DAS GEEIGNETE FAND.

THIS IS A RECIPE BY ROBERT WIDMANN WHO I LIKE TO CALL MY SECOND FATHER. HE IS AN IMPORTANT MENTOR IN MY PROFESSIONAL LIFE AS WELL AS, FOR SOME TIME NOW, IN MY PRIVATE LIFE. HE LOVES THIS CARAMEL. IT IS THE SALT THAT MAKES ITS TASTE SO UNUSUAL. BUT DON'T ASK ME HOW LONG I HAD TO SEARCH TO FIND THE RIGHT ONE.

ZUTATEN FÜR 160 PRALINEN		INGREDIENTS FOR 160 CHOCOLATES	
	Bitterhalbschalen		*bitter chocolate halfshells*
	SALZKARAMELL		**SALT CARAMEL**
360 g	*Zucker*	360 g	*sugar*
600 g	*Sahne, 32 % Fett*	600 g	*cream, 32 % fat*
240 g	*Glukose*	240 g	*glucose*
1	*Vanilleschote (Mark)*	1	*vanilla pod (pith)*
3 g	*Murray River – Australian Pink Flake Salt*	3 g	*Murray River – Australian Pink Flake Salt*
150 g	*Butter*	150 g	*unsalted butter*
	ÜBERZUG		**COATING**
	Bitterkuvertüre		*bitter couverture*
	DEKORATION		**DECORATION**
	Murray River – Australian Pink Flake Salt		*Murray River – Australian Pink Flake Salt*

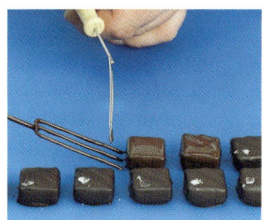

Pralinen mit temperierter Kuvertüre überziehen, überflüssige Kuvertüre abstreifen und Pralinen absetzen

Coat the chocolates with tempered couverture, wipe off any excess and leave to set

1

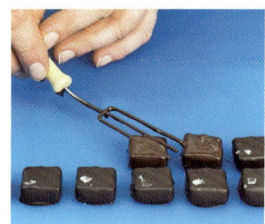

Mit der Überziehgabel ein Dekor auf der Oberfläche anbringen

Use a dipping fork to apply a pattern to the surface

2

Einen Salzkristall an einer Ecke auflegen

Place a salt crystal in one corner

3

MAKING THE PARTS

Melt the sugar into a light caramel. Bring the cream to the boil with the glucose, the vanilla pith and the salt and then pour it over the caramel. Boil the mixture to 104 °C, allow to cool down and then mix in the butter at 35 °C.

Let the mixture cool down completely and fill into the bitter chocolate half shells, leave overnight to form a skin and then coat with tempered couverture. Make a pattern with a dipping fork and add a salt crystal.

HERSTELLUNG

Den Zucker zu einem hellen Karamell schmelzen. Die Sahne mit der Glukose, dem Vanillemark und dem Salz aufkochen und den Karamell damit ablöschen. Die Masse auf 104 °C kochen, abkühlen lassen und bei 35 °C die Butter untermixen.

Die vollständig abgekühlte Masse in Bitterhalbschalen abfüllen, über Nacht verhauten lassen, dann mit temperierter Kuvertüre überziehen. Mit einem Gabeldekor und einem Salzkristall dekorieren.

BALSAMICO CARAMEL

BALSAMICO IST EINE SEHR LECKERE ANGELEGENHEIT. IN MODENA HABE ICH DEN UNTERSCHIED ZWISCHEN DISCOUNT-BALSAMICO UND DEN HOCHWERTIGEN, GEREIFTEN VARIANTEN KENNENGELERNT. BEI DIESEM REZEPT KANN MAN AUCH MIT GÜNSTIGEREM BALSAMICO EINEN KÖSTLICHEN KARAMELL HERSTELLEN.

BALSAMIC VINEGAR IS QUITE A DELICIOUS THING. I HAVE OFTEN TRAVELLED TO MODENA IN ITALY, THE CITY KNOWN FOR ITS BALSAMIC VINEGAR. IT IS WHERE I LEARNED THE DIFFERENCE BETWEEN A CHEAP BALSAMIC VINEGAR AND THE SUPERIOR QUALITY VERSIONS THAT HAVE MATURED FOR MANY MONTHS. WITH THIS RECIPE YOU CAN ALSO USE A CHEAPER BRAND OF BALSAMIC VINEGAR.

INGREDIENTS FOR 90 CHOCOLATES		ZUTATEN FÜR 90 PRALINEN	
	bitter couverture		*Bitterkuvertüre*
	WILD STRAWBERRY GANACHE		**WALDERDBEERGANACHE**
50 g	*fructose*	50 g	*Fruchtzucker*
100 g	*whipping cream*	100 g	*Sahne*
5 g	*long pepper*	5 g	*langer Pfeffer*
15 g	*grated zest of an untreated orange*	15 g	*unbehandelter Orangenschalenabrieb*
2 g	*salt*	2 g	*Salz*
300 g	*white couverture*	300 g	*weiße Kuvertüre*
200 g	*wild strawberry puree*	200 g	*Walderdbeerpüree*
50 g	*unsalted butter*	50 g	*Butter*
	BALSAMICO CARAMEL		**BALSAMICOKARAMELL**
160 g	*sugar*	160 g	*Zucker*
80 g	*balsamic vinegar*	80 g	*Balsamico*
	DECORATION		**DEKORATION**
	dried strawberries		*getrocknete Erdbeeren*
	gold leaf		*Blattgold*

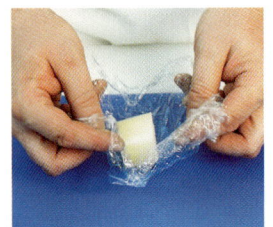

Schaumstoffwürfel vollständig in Frischhaltefolie einpacken

Wrap the rubber foam cubes in plastic wrap so that they are completely covered

1

Damit die Folie sehr straff sitzt, oben zum „Bonbon" drehen

Tighten the plastic wrap by twisting the ends into a knob

2

Schaumstoffbonbon teilweise in temperierte Kuvertüre tauchen, überflüssige Kuvertüre etwas abstreifen

Partially dip each foam cube into tempered couverture and wipe off any excess couverture

3

4

5

6

HERSTELLUNG

Schaumstoffwürfel vollständig in Frischhaltefolie einpacken, bis fast zur Hälfte in temperierte Bitterkuvertüre eintauchen. Abstreifen, absetzen und aushärten lassen, dann die eingepackten Schaumstoffwürfel aus den Formen lösen und Folie abziehen.

Fruchtzucker karamellisieren lassen. Mit der erwärmten Sahne ablöschen, Pfeffer fein mörsern und dann mit dem Orangenschalenabrieb sowie dem Salz zugeben. Karamell aufkochen und über die fein gehackte Kuvertüre gießen. Zu einer glatten Masse rühren, eventuell durch ein Sieb passieren, dann das Walderdbeerpüree zugeben. Butter untermixen und abkühlen lassen.

MAKING THE PARTS

Take some rubber foam cubes, wrap them completely in plastic wrap and dip up to the middle in the tempered bitter couverture. Wipe off any excess, place down and leave to set; then remove the foam cubes from the chocolate shapes and gently take off the plastic wrap.

Caramelise the fructose. Heat up the cream and pour over the fructose, finely grind the peppercorns with a pestle and mortar and add, together with the orange zest and salt. Bring the caramel to the boil and pour over the finely chopped couverture. Stir into a smooth mixture (pass through a sieve if necessary) and then add the wild strawberry puree. Blend in the butter and leave to cool.

Zum Aushärten absetzen
Leave to set

Schaumstoffwürfel aus der Form lösen
Remove the foam cubes from the chocolate shapes

Folie vorsichtig abziehen
Carefully remove the plastic wrap

Melt the sugar into a caramel, warm up the balsamic vinegar a little and pour it over the caramel – do not reheat as this would make it bitter. Allow the caramel to cool.

Fill the bitter couverture cups just ²/₃ with the ganache, wait until it forms a skin and then fill to the top with the caramel. Decorate the chocolates with a slice of dried strawberry and a dab of gold leaf.

Den Zucker zu Karamell schmelzen, den Balsamico etwas anwärmen, dann den Karamell damit ablöschen – nicht mehr aufkochen, sonst wird er bitter. Den Balsamicokaramell abkühlen lassen.

Bitterkuvertüreförmchen zu ²/₃ mit der Ganache füllen, verhauten lassen, dann mit dem Balsamicokaramell verschließen. Pralinen mit einer getrockneten Erdbeerscheibe und einem Goldtupfen garnieren.

WEISSE HASELNUSSTRÜFFEL
WHITE HAZELNUT TRUFFLES

ALS ICH ZUM ERSTEN MAL RICHTIG GUTEN HASELNUSSBRAND KOSTEN DURFTE, WUSSTE ICH SOFORT, DARAUS KANN MAN ETWAS GANZ BESONDERES KREIEREN. BEI ERSTKLASSIGER QUALITÄT DES DESTILLATES SOWIE DER VERWENDETEN KUVERTÜRE KANN MAN VOLLSTÄNDIG AUF DIE VERWENDUNG VON NUSSPASTEN ODER NOUGAT VERZICHTEN.

WHEN I HAD THE CHANCE TO TASTE REALLY GOOD HAZELNUT BRANDY FOR THE FIRST TIME I KNEW INSTANTLY THAT THIS COULD BE USED TO CREATE SOMETHING VERY SPECIAL. WHEN USING FIRST-CLASS BRANDY AND COUVERTURE IT IS POSSIBLE TO GO COMPLETELY WITHOUT NUT PASTES OR NOUGAT.

INGREDIENTS FOR 140 CHOCOLATES		ZUTATEN FÜR 140 PRALINEN	
HAZELNUT MOULDS		**HASELNUSS-HOHLFORMEN**	
	white couverture		weiße Kuvertüre
HAZELNUT GANACHE		**HASELNUSSGANACHE**	
250 g	cream, 32 % fat	250 g	Sahne, 32 % Fett
80 g	glucose	80 g	Glukose
660 g	white couverture	660 g	weiße Kuvertüre
50 g	unsalted butter	50 g	Butter
80 g	hazelnut brandy, 40 % vol.	80 g	Haselnussbrand, 40 %-vol.
	peeled and lightly roasted hazelnuts		geschälte und leicht geröstete Haselnüsse
DECORATION		**DEKORATION**	
	green cocoa butter		grüne Kakaobutter

Leicht angefrostete Praline mit grüner Kakaobutter besprühen. Die selbst hergestellte Schablone hilft, dass die Farbe zielgenau aufgebracht wird

Spray the semi-frozen chocolate with green cocoa butter. Make up your own template to help you to apply the colour spray accurately.

1

HERSTELLUNG

Für die Pralinenformen weiße Kuvertüre temperieren, Schablonen ausgießen und gut aushärten lassen, dann ausformen.

Für die Ganache Sahne und Glukose aufkochen, über die gehackte weiße Kuvertüre gießen und zu einer homogenen Masse verarbeiten. Die Butter bei etwa 30 °C unterziehen und zuletzt den Haselnussbrand unterrühren.

In jede Pralinenform eine geröstete Haselnuss geben und mit der Ganache auffüllen. Über Nacht verhauten lassen und mit temperierter Kuvertüre verschließen. Nach dem Ausformen die Pralinen leicht anfrieren und den Blattansatz leicht mit grüner Kakaobutter ansprühen.

Einige Stunden ruhen lassen, damit die Farbe beim Anfassen nicht schmiert.

MAKING THE PARTS

To make the shapes for the chocolates, temper the white couverture, pour it into the moulds and allow to set well; remove from the moulds.

For the ganache, bring the cream and glucose to the boil, pour over the chopped white couverture and work into an even mixture. Fold in the butter at about 30 °C and finally stir in the hazelnut brandy.

Put one roasted hazelnut into each chocolate shape and fill with the ganache. Leave overnight to form a skin and then cover with tempered couverture. Put the chocolates into the freezer for a short while and then spray the leaf base with a little green cocoa butter.

Allow to rest for a few hours to that the colour does not smudge when touching.

TOMATENGANACHE MIT SPECKKROKANT

TOMATO GANACHE WITH SPECK BRITTLE

Wir haben einige aussergewöhnliche Pralinen in unserem Angebot — seien es die bekannten Käsepralinen, die Hessenpraline, gefüllt mit grüner Sosse, oder meine Parfümkollektion. Diese neuen Geschmackskompositionen können den Kunden überfordern. Deshalb ist immer darauf zu achten, wem und wie solche Neuheiten präsentiert werden.

We have some exceptional types of chocolates in our range — there are the well-known cheese chocolates, the "Hessenpraline" filled with green sauce and my perfume collection. It is quite possible that these new combinations of flavours present a bit of a challenge to customers. For this reason it is always important to be discerning about how to present such novelties, and to whom.

Zutaten für 130 Pralinen

SPECKKROKANT

500 g	Isomalt
100 g	durchwachsener Speck oder Bacon

TOMATENGANACHE

15 g	Tomatenpulver
60 g	Tomatenmark
30 g	Invertzucker
½	Tahitivanilleschote (Mark)
375 g	Sahne
560 g	Vollmilchkuvertüre
45 g	Wacholderbrand oder Gin
35 g	Butter

DEKORATION

getrocknete Babytomatenchips

Ingredients for 130 chocolates

SPECK BRITTLE

500 g	isomalt
100 g	streaky speck or bacon

TOMATO GANACHE

15 g	tomato powder
60 g	tomato puree
30 g	invert sugar
½	Tahiti vanilla pod (pith)
375 g	whipping cream
560 g	milk couverture
45 g	juniper brandy or gin
35 g	unsalted butter

DECORATION

dried cherry tomato chips

Speckkrokant über einen Metallstab rollen.
Das Ende unregelmäßig abreißen

Roll the speck brittle using a metal rod –
tear off each end to leave a jagged edge

1

Fertiges Speckröllchen

Completed speck brittle rolls

2

HERSTELLUNG

Isomalt auflösen, auf eine Silikon-Back-matte ausgießen und auskühlen lassen. In der Zwischenzeit den Speck auf kleiner Flamme auslassen, bis er komplett knusprig ist – das ist sehr wichtig. Den Isomalt in kleine Stücke brechen und zusammen mit dem trockenen Speck in einem Kutter fein zerkleinern. Das Pulver gleichmäßig auf einer Silikon-Backmatte verteilen und im Ofen zum Schmelzen bringen. Dann mit einer zweiten Backmatte bedecken und einem Rollholz dünn ausrollen. In 3 cm breite Streifen schneiden und über einen kleinen Metallstab, Durchmesser 1 cm, kleine Röllchen abmodellieren. Das Ende unregelmäßig abreißen, dadurch bekommt man die wilde Optik. Die vorbereiteten „Speckröllchen" lassen sich trocken in einem luftdicht verschließbaren Behälter einige Tage aufbewahren.

Tomatenpulver (kann man auch durch einfaches Trocknen und Pulverisieren von Tomatenchips selbst herstellen), Tomatenmark, Invertzucker, Vanillemark und die Sahne aufkochen. Die Masse auf 32 °C abkühlen lassen, die temperierte Kuvertüre untermixen, dann den Wacholderbrand und zum Schluss die Butter untermischen. Sobald die Ganache stabil ist, kann man sie leicht aufmontieren und mit einem Spritzbeutel mit einer 6er-Lochtülle in die Speckröllchen eindressieren. Mit getrockneten Babytomatenchips ausgarnieren.

MAKING THE PARTS

Dissolve the isomalt, pour onto a silicone baking mat and leave to cool down. In the meantime, render the speck or bacon on low heat until it is completely crispy – this is very important. Break the isomalt into small pieces and, together with the dry speck, mince to a fine powdery consistency in a mincer. Spread the powder evenly onto a silicone baking mat and place into the oven to melt. Then cover with a second baking mat and use a rolling pin to roll it out thinly. Cut into 3 cm wide strips and, using a small metal rod about 1 cm in diameter, form small rolls. Tear off the ends to leave a rough edge and achieve a rustic look. Once you have prepared these "speck brittle rolls" you can store them for a few days in an air-tight container.

Bring the tomato powder, tomato puree, invert sugar, vanilla pith and cream to the boil. (Note: you can make tomato powder yourself by drying and pulverising tomato chips.) Allow the mixture to cool down to 32 °C, blend in the tempered couverture, then add the juniper brandy or gin and mix in the butter. As soon as the ganache has become firm, it can be worked easily. Fill the speck brittle rolls with the ganache using a piping bag with round hole nozzle no. 6. Garnish with dried cherry tomato chips.

MORCHELTRÜFFEL MIT APRIKOSEN

MOREL TRUFFLES WITH APRICOTS

DIESE KREATION IST EINE TYPISCHE „RESTAURANTPRALINE", DENN DERARTIG AUSSERGEWÖHNLICHE KREATIONEN LASSEN SICH HÄUFIG BESSER IM RESTAURANT EINSETZEN, ALS IN DER KLASSISCHEN KONDITOREI. TROTZDEM SOLLTE MAN IMMER ÜBER DEN TELLERRAND SCHAUEN UND OFFEN FÜR NEUES BLEIBEN.

THIS CREATION IS A TYPICAL CHOCOLATE FOR A RESTAURANT MENU BECAUSE SUCH UNUSUAL CREATIONS ARE OFTEN EASIER TO USE IN A RESTAURANT THAN IN A CLASSIC CONFECTIONER'S SHOP. NEVERTHELESS, WE SHOULD ALWAYS LOOK BEYOND OUR USUAL HORIZONS AND BE OPEN TO NEW THINGS.

INGREDIENTS FOR 80 CHOCOLATES

BITTER COUVERTURE WAFERS

500 g	bitter couverture
5 g	Ceylon cinnamon powder
50 g	Cru Miel (honey powder)

APRICOT MOREL GANACHE

25 g	dried morel mushrooms
100 g	cream, 32 % fat
20 g	invert sugar
150 g	apricot puree
100 g	bitter couverture
250 g	milk couverture
30 g	unsalted butter
30 g	apricot brandy, 40 % vol.

DECORATION
dried apricots

ZUTATEN FÜR 80 PRALINEN

BITTERKUVERTÜRE-PLÄTTCHEN:

500 g	Bitterkuvertüre
5 g	Ceylonzimtpulver
50 g	Cru Miel (Honigpulver)

APRIKOSEN-MORCHEL-GANACHE

25 g	getrocknete Morcheln
100 g	Sahne, 32 % Fett
20 g	Invertzucker
150 g	Aprikosenpüree
100 g	Bitterkuvertüre
250 g	Vollmilchkuvertüre
30 g	Butter
30 g	Aprikosenbrand, 40 %-vol.

DEKORATION
getrocknete Aprikosen

HERSTELLUNG

Bitterkuvertüre temperieren, mit dem Zimt und dem Cru Miel mischen und zwischen zwei festen Folien sehr dünn ausrollen. Sobald sich die Folie ablösen lässt, mit einem erwärmten, löffelbiskuitförmigen Ausstecher Plättchen ausstechen – für jede Praline 3 Plättchen.

Morcheln in kaltem Wasser waschen, abtropfen, in der Sahne einweichen und sobald sie weich sind, mit dem Invertzucker aufkochen. Masse pürieren und durch ein feines Sieb passieren. Das Aprikosenpüree zugeben und alles auf 32 °C erwärmen. Die Kuvertüren temperieren, zugeben und zu einer homogenen Masse verarbeiten. Zuletzt die Butter und den Aprikosenbrand zugeben und leicht aufmontieren. Die Ganache auf ein Schokoplättchen aufdressieren, ein Schokoplättchen aufsetzen, nochmals Ganache, dann wieder ein Schokoplättchen aufsetzen und mit Ganache abschließen.

Praline mit einem Stück Trockenaprikose dekorieren.

1

Temperierte Kuvertüre auf stabile Folie geben, mit einer zweiten Folie abdecken

Place the tempered couverture onto some firm foil and cover with a second foil

2

Kuvertüre mit einem Rollholz sehr dünn ausrollen

Use a rolling pin to roll out the couverture very thinly

3

So bald sich die Folie ablösen lässt, diese abziehen

As soon as possible remove the foil

4

Löffelbiskuitförmigen Ausstecher erwärmen und Schokoladenplättchen ausstechen

Warm up the ladies' finger cutter and cut out the chocolate wafers

5

Untere Folie abziehen

Remove the lower foil

MAKING THE PARTS

Temper the bitter couverture, mix with the cinnamon and the Cru Miel and roll out very thinly between two firm foils. As soon as it is possible to take off the foil, use a warmed up cutter in the shape of a ladies' finger to cut out the wafers – 3 for each chocolate.

Wash the morel mushrooms in cold water, allow excess water to drip off and soak in the cream. As soon as the mushrooms have softened, boil up with the invert sugar. Puree the mixture and then pass through a fine sieve. Add the apricot puree and boil everything to 32 °C. Temper the couvertures, add to the mixture and stir until well blended. Finally add the butter and the apricot brandy and fold in. Pipe the ganache onto a chocolate wafer, place another wafer on top followed by a second layer of ganache, the third wafer and the final layer of ganache.

Decorate the chocolate with a piece of dried apricot.

STERNSCHNUPPEN

FALLING STARS

Was wäre Weihnachten ohne Sterne? Man sieht sie in jeder Bäckerei und Konditorei. Allerdings kann man sich durch besondere Formen oder durch ein ausgefallenes Gewürz von seinen Mitbewerbern absetzen. Denn Lebkuchengewürz ist nicht gleich Lebkuchengewürz. Es gibt so zahlreiche Varianten – lassen Sie sich davon inspirieren.

What would Christmas be without stars? During the Christmas season they can be seen in all bakeries and patisseries. However, with special shapes or unusual spices one can stand out from the competition. Not every gingerbread spice is the same. There are many variations of the theme – let yourself be inspired by the example below.

Zutaten für 150 Pralinen		Ingredients for 150 chocolates	
Bitterkuvertüre-plättchen		**Bitter couverture wafers**	
500 g	Bitterkuvertüre	500 g	bitter couverture
Weihnachts-Ganache		**Christmas ganache**	
600 g	Vollmilchkuvertüre	600 g	milk couverture
100 g	Bitterkuvertüre	100 g	bitter couverture
400 g	Sahne	400 g	whipping cream
30 g	Lebkuchengewürz	30 g	gingerbread spice
200 g	Butter	200 g	unsalted butter
50 g	Jagertee-Konzentrat	50 g	Jagertee concentrate
Überzug		**Coating**	
	Vollmilchkuvertüre		milk couverture
	Bitterkuvertüre		bitter couverture

Weihnachtsganache mit einer Sterntülle in kleinen Tupfen auf die Kuvertüreplättchen dressieren

Use a star-shaped nozzle to pipe the Christmas ganache in small dabs onto the couverture wafers

1

Rechts und links der Pralinen Stangen anlegen

Place bars to the right and left of the chocolates

2

Stabile Folie auflegen

Cover with a firm foil

3

Tupfen durch gleichmäßig vorsichtiges Andrücken einer Arcylglasplatte zu Sternen pressen

Place a Perspex sheet on top of the foil and gently press down so that the dabs are pushed down into a star shape

4

MAKING THE PARTS

Temper the bitter couverture and roll out very thinly between two firm foils. As soon as it is possible to take off the foil, use a warmed up circular cutter to cut out the wafers – 1 for each chocolate.

Temper the couvertures. Bring the cream to the boil together with the gingerbread spice, pass through a fine sieve, allow to cool down to 32 °C and stir into the two couvertures. Add the softened butter and the Jagertee concentrate. Work these into the mixture so that it thickens up and then use a piping bag with a star-shaped nozzle to apply small stars onto the couverture wafers. Place a bar to the right and left of the chocolates, cover with a firm foil and then use a sheet of Perspex to carefully squash the chocolates until the Perspex sheet comes to rest on the bars. Allow the chocolates to set fully and then coat with tempered milk couverture.

Decorate by applying a criss-cross pattern with tempered bitter couverture.

HERSTELLUNG

Bitterkuvertüre temperieren, zwischen zwei festen Folien sehr dünn ausrollen. Sobald sich die Folie ablösen lässt, mit einem erwärmten, kreisförmigen Ausstecher Plättchen ausstechen – für jede Praline 1 Plättchen.

Kuvertüren temperieren. Sahne mit dem Lebkuchengewürz aufkochen, durch ein feines Sieb passieren, auf 32 °C abkühlen lassen und unter die beiden Kuvertüren rühren. Die weiche Butter und das Jagertee-Konzentrat zugeben. Die Masse leicht aufmontieren, so dass sie dressierfähig wird, dann mit dem Spritzbeutel und der Sterntülle kleine Tupfen auf die Kuvertüreplättchen dressieren. Rechts und links der Pralinen Stangen anlegen, eine feste Folie auflegen und Pralinen mit einer Acrylglasplatte vorsichtig flach drücken, bis die Acrylglasplatte auf den Stangen aufliegt. Pralinen komplett auskristallisieren lassen und mit temperierter Vollmilchkuvertüre überziehen.

Zur Ausgarnierung temperierte Bitterkuvertüre über Kreuz spinnen.

HIMBEER-SCHOKOLADEN-FRUCHTGELEE
RASPBERRY CHOCOLATE FRUIT JELLY

Fruchtgelee wurde in Deutschland ursprünglich immer mit Agar-Agar hergestellt. Erst mit dem Einzug der französischen Konditorei kam Pektin zum Einsatz und hat Agar-Agar fast vollständig verdrängt. Die umfassende Renaissance verdankt Agar-Agar den spanischen Molekularköchen. Ich habe mein Fruchtgelee schon immer mit Agar-Agar hergestellt und habe stets sehr gute Ergebnisse damit erzielt.

Originally in Germany fruit jelly was always made with agar agar. It was not until French patisserie methods came to Germany that pectin became popular and almost completely replaced agar agar. Agar agar owes its comprehensive come-back to the Spanish chefs of the school of molecular gastronomy. I for my part have always made my fruit jellies with agar agar and have always had very good results.

INGREDIENTS FOR 80 CHOCOLATES		ZUTATEN FÜR 80 PRALINEN	
RASPBERRY CHOCOLATE FRUIT JELLY		**HIMBEER-SCHOKOLADEN-FRUCHTGELEE**	
500 g	raspberries	500 g	Himbeeren
250 g	sugar	250 g	Zucker
5 g	agar agar	5 g	Agar-Agar
100 g	cocoa paste (Criollo type)	100 g	Kakaomasse (Criollosorte)
	crude cane sugar		Rohr-Rohzucker
COATING		**ÜBERZUG**	
	bitter couverture		Bitterkuvertüre

Gelee in spezielle Silikonformen einfüllen

Fill the special silicone moulds with jelly

1 ——————————————————————————————

Nach dem Ausgelieren mit Rohr-Rohzucker bestreuen

Once set, apply a sprinkling of crude cane sugar

2 ——————————————————————————————

Überflüssigen Zucker abklopfen

Tap to dislodge any excess sugar

3 ——————————————————————————————

Fruchtgelee einzeln ausformen

Remove the fruit jelly from the moulds

4 ——————————————————————————————

HERSTELLUNG

Die Himbeeren und den Zucker mischen und 2 Minuten bei maximaler Hitze erwärmen. Den Saft abpassieren, 500 g davon abmessen. Das Agar-Agar zugeben, mischen und aufkochen. Die Kakaomasse zugeben und untermixen, sofort mit einem Fülltrichter in die Spezialsilikonform füllen und etwa 30 Minuten bei Raumtemperatur gelieren lassen. Anschließend im Kühlschrank durchgelieren lassen, mit Rohr-Rohzucker bestreuen, ausformen und auf einem Gitter trocknen lassen. Fruchtgelee in temperierter Bitterkuvertüre absetzen.

MAKING THE PARTS

Mix the raspberries and sugar and heat up for 2 minutes on maximum heat. Drain off the juice and put 500 g into a separate container. Add the agar agar, mix and bring to the boil. Add the cocoa paste and blend in; immediately fill the special silicone moulds with the mixture, using a filling funnel and leave at room temperature for about 30 minutes. Put into a refrigerator to allow the gelling process to complete, sprinkle some crude cane sugar over it, take out of the moulds and leave to dry on a grid. Decorate the fruit jelly with tempered bitter couverture.

SALBEI-CURRY-TRÜFFEL

SAGE AND CURRY TRUFFLES

AUCH WENN ICH FÜR DIE INDISCHE KÜCHE EIN RICHTIGES FAIBLE HABE, IST INDIEN DENNOCH EIN LAND, DAS AUF MEINER „KULINARISCHEN" LANDKARTE NOCH FEHLT. INDISCHE GEWÜRZE SIND DAS A UND O FÜR DIE TOLLEN CURRYS. SIE KÖNNEN DIE MISCHUNGEN GANZ EINFACH SELBST HERSTELLEN UND SO SICHERSTELLEN, DASS AUCH WIRKLICH NUR DIE ZUTATEN ENTHALTEN SIND, DIE IHNEN SCHMECKEN.

ALTHOUGH I HAVE A REAL WEAKNESS FOR INDIAN CUISINE, INDIA IS NEVERTHELESS A COUNTRY THAT IS STILL MISSING ON MY CULINARY MAP. INDIAN SPICES ARE THE BEGINNING AND END OF REALLY EXCITING CURRIES. IT IS VERY EASY TO MAKE UP THE MIXTURES YOURSELF AND THUS MAKE SURE THAT THEY ONLY CONTAIN THOSE INGREDIENTS YOU REALLY LIKE.

ZUTATEN FÜR 80 PRALINEN

SALBEI-CURRY-GANACHE

160 g	Butter
20 g	Salbeiblätter, frisch gehackt
5 g	Currypulver (je nach Intensität die Menge variieren)
350 g	weiße Kuvertüre
190 g	Kokosnusscreme

DEKORATION

Ananaschips-Tüten

weiße Kuvertüre

Currypulver

INGREDIENTS FOR 80 CHOCOLATES

SAGE CURRY GANACHE

160 g	unsalted butter
20 g	sage leaves, freshly chopped
5 g	curry powder (adjust the quantity to suit the intensity of the powder's flavour)
350 g	white couverture
190 g	coconut cream

DECORATION

pineapple chip cones

white couverture

curry powder

Dünne Ananascheiben in einem Trockengerät trocknen lassen

Cut thin slices of pineapple and allow to dry in a drying unit

1

Ananasscheiben noch warm dritteln und sofort zu Tütchen drehen und in Lochtüllen einlegen

While the pineapple slices are still warm, cut into three segments and form into cones immediately; place into piping nozzles

2

MAKING THE PARTS

Boil up the butter with the sage leaves, leave to steep for a while, then put through a sieve to separate the sage leaves. Leave the butter to cool and then work in the curry powder. Temper the white couverture and add to the mixture. Finally work in the coconut cream. Use a piping bag with a round-hole nozzle to pipe the sage curry ganache into the pineapple cones and leave to set.

Dip the ends into tempered white couverture and leave to set again. Use a small piping bag to draw a line with couverture and dip that into the curry powder. The powder will stick to the line on the chocolate.

HERSTELLUNG

Butter mit den Salbeiblättern aufkochen, nach kurzer Ziehzeit die Salbeiblätter absieben, die Butter erkalten lassen und mit dem Currypulver aufmontieren. Die weiße Kuvertüre temperieren und einlaufen lassen. Zuletzt die Kokosnusscreme unterarbeiten. Die Salbei-Curry-Ganache mit einer Lochtülle in die Ananastütchen eindressieren und erstarren lassen.

Die Enden in temperierte weiße Kuvertüre eintauchen, erneut erstarren lassen mit einem Garniertütchen eine Kuvertürelinie ziehen und diese in das Currypulver tauchen. So bleibt das Pulver als Linie auf der Praline.

BASILIKUM-LIMETTEN-SANDWICH

BASIL-LIME SANDWICH

AUF EINER MEINER REISEN DURCH ASIEN HABE ICH THAI-BASILIKUM UND BASILIKUMSAAT KENNEN GELERNT. EIGENTLICH WIRD AUS DEN SAMEN TEE HERGESTELLT, BEI DIESER KREATION ALLERDINGS KAM ER BEI DER HERSTELLUNG VON KNUSPERPLÄTTCHEN ZUM EINSATZ. LEIDER IST DER THAI-BASILIKUM IN DER VERWENDUNG ETWAS SCHWIERIG, DA SEIN AROMA SEHR FLÜCHTIG IST, DESHALB EIGNET ER SICH BESONDERS GUT FÜR RESTAURANTPRALINEN, DIE SOFORT VERZEHRT WERDEN.

ON ONE OF MY TRAVELS THROUGH ASIA I CHANCED UPON THAI BASIL AND BASIL SEED. TRADITIONALLY, THE SEEDS ARE USED TO MAKE AN INFUSION BUT IN THIS CREATION I HAVE USED IT TO MAKE CRISPY WAVERS. UNFORTUNATELY, THAI BASIL IS SOMEWHAT DIFFICULT TO USE AS ITS AROMA IS VERY VOLATILE; FOR THIS REASON IT IS PARTICULARLY SUITABLE FOR RESTAURANT CHOCOLATES, WHICH ARE MADE FOR IMMEDIATE CONSUMPTION.

INGREDIENTS FOR 120 CHOCOLATES

SUGAR WAFERS
250 g	isomalt
20 g	basil seed

BASIL OIL
450 g	fresh basil
500 g	sunflower seed oil

GANACHE
300 g	whipping cream
	Grated zest from 2 limes
100 g	lime juice
500 g	bitter couverture
100 g	basil oil

ZUTATEN FÜR 120 PRALINEN

ZUCKERPLÄTTCHEN
250 g	Isomalt
20 g	Basilikumsaat

BASILIKUMÖL
450 g	frisches Thai-Basilikum
500 g	Sonnenblumenöl

GANACHE
300 g	Sahne
	Abrieb von 2 Limetten
100 g	Limettensaft
500 g	Bitterkuvertüre
100 g	Basilikumöl

HERSTELLUNG

Isomalt auflösen, auf eine Silikon-Back-matte ausgießen und erkalten lassen, dann mit einem Kutter fein zerkleinern und mit einem Sieb und einer Schablone 2 x 2 cm große Isomalt-Quadrate auf eine Backmat-te sieben. Mit der Basilikumsaat bestreuen, Isomalt bei 180 °C im Ofen verflüssigen, bis er wieder klar ist. Auskühlen lassen und trocken lagern.

Das frische Basilikum mit dem Sonnen-blumenöl in einen Pacojet-Becher füllen, frosten und bei Bedarf pacossieren.

Die Sahne mit dem Limettenabrieb auf-kochen, gut durchmixen, den Limettensaft zugeben und auf 32 °C temperieren. Die temperierte Bitterkuvertüre zugeben und zu einer homogenen Masse verarbeiten. Zum Schluss das Basilikumöl zugeben und zu einer glatten Ganache mixen. In einen vorbereiteten Rahmen ausgießen und dann erkalten lassen. In 1 x 1 cm große Würfel schneiden, die Ganache wie ein Sandwich zwischen zwei Isomalt-Plättchen geben.

1

Isomalt grob brechen und in den Kutter geben

Break up the isomalt and put into the cutter

2

Isomalt im Kutter fein zerkleinern

Crush the isomalt in the cutter to a fine consistency

3

Teflon-Backmatte mit einer Schablone belegen und den Isomaltstaub aufsieben

Place a stencil onto a Teflon baking mat before passing the isomalt through a sieve

4

Schablone vorsichtig abnehmen

Carefully remove the stencil

5

Basilikumsaat aufstreuen

Apply a sprinkling of basil seed

MAKING THE PARTS

Dissolve the isomalt and pour onto a sili-cone baking mat, leave to cool, put into a cutter to crush to a fine consistency; place a 2 x 2 cm stencil on a baking sheet and pass the isomalt through a sieve to make small isomalt squares. Apply a sprinkling of basil seed, put the isomalt into the oven at 180 °C until it becomes liquid and clear again. Leave to cool and store in a dry place.

Put the basil with the sunflower seed oil into a Pacojet container, freeze and paco-tise if required.

Bring the cream and the lime zest to the boil, mix well, add the lime juice and temper to 32 °C. Add the tempered bitter couverture and work into a homogenous mixture. Finally add the basil oil and mix

into a smooth ganache. Pour into a pre-pared frame and leave to set. Cut into 1 x 1 cm cubes, place the ganache between two isomalt wafers to make a little "sand-wich".

HONIGWELTEN-TRÜFFEL

WORLDS-OF-HONEY TRUFFLES

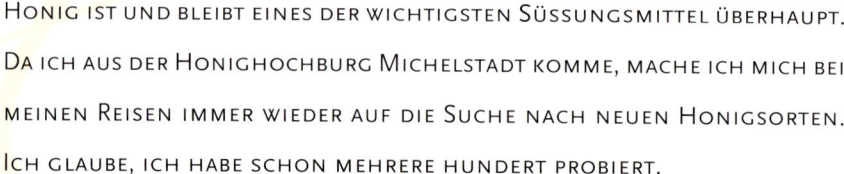

HONIG IST UND BLEIBT EINES DER WICHTIGSTEN SÜSSUNGSMITTEL ÜBERHAUPT.
DA ICH AUS DER HONIGHOCHBURG MICHELSTADT KOMME, MACHE ICH MICH BEI
MEINEN REISEN IMMER WIEDER AUF DIE SUCHE NACH NEUEN HONIGSORTEN.
ICH GLAUBE, ICH HABE SCHON MEHRERE HUNDERT PROBIERT.

HONEY IS, AND ALWAYS HAS BEEN, ONE OF THE MOST IMPORTANT SWEETENERS.
AS I COME FROM MICHELSTADT, WHICH IS FAMOUS FOR ITS HONEY, I TAKE A
SPECIAL INTEREST IN HONEY AND KEEP LOOKING FOR NEW TYPES DURING MY
TRAVELS. I THINK I HAVE PROBABLY TASTED SEVERAL HUNDRED DIFFERENT KINDS.

ZUTATEN FÜR 150 PRALINEN		INGREDIENTS FOR 150 CHOCOLATES	
SCHNITTGANACHE		**GANACHE FOR CUTTING**	
180 g	Sahne	180 g	whipping cream
140 g	Litschi-Honig	140 g	lychee honey
480 g	Milchkuvertüre	480 g	milk couverture
50 g	weiche Butter	50 g	softened butter
	etwas temperierte Kuvertüre		a little tempered couverture
	zum Bestreichen		for spreading
GANACHE ZUM DRESSIEREN		**GANACHE FOR DECORATING**	
140 g	Tannenhonig	140 g	spruce honey
40 g	Wasser	40 g	water
140 g	Sahne	140 g	whipping cream
150 g	Bitterkuvertüre	150 g	bitter couverture
300 g	Milchkuvertüre	300 g	milk couverture
20 g	Butter	20 g	unsalted butter
50 g	Met	50 g	mead
DEKORATION		**DECORATION**	
	leicht verdünnte Milchkuvertüre		slightly diluted milk couverture
	Honigpollen		Honey pollen

1 cm breite Schnittganachestreifen auf ein Blech setzen, zweite Ganache mit einer 3er-Lochtülle schneckenförmig auf die Schnittganachestreifen aufdressieren

Place the 1 cm wide ganache strips on a baking sheet. Use a size 3 hole nozzle to pipe spiral shapes onto the ganache strips.

1

Durch das gleichmäßige Aufdressieren entsteht ein schönes Wellenmuster

With a steady hand pretty wave patterns can be created.

2

MAKING THE PARTS

Bring the cream to the boil, add the honey and dissolve; allow the mixture to cool down to 32 °C. Add the tempered couverture and stir into a smooth ganache. Work in the butter and then fill the mixture into a 0.5 cm high frame you have prepared for this purpose. Leave the ganache to set overnight. Spread the tempered couverture thinly over the top and cut into 1 cm wide strips using a cutting guitar. Place the strips onto a baking sheet, leaving small gaps between them. Leave to set.

Caramelise the honey, reduce slightly, then add water and bring to the boil with the cream. Pour the liquid over the finely chopped couvertures and blend to form a smooth ganache. Add the softened butter and work in the mead. Cover the mixture with plastic wrap and leave to set overnight. Stir the set ganache to loosen, then decorate the ganache strips using a size 3 hole nozzle to pipe on spiral shapes. Leave again to set; use a cutter to cut the strips into 2 cm long pieces. Coat the chocolates with the slightly diluted milk couverture and decorate with honey pollen.

HERSTELLUNG

Die Sahne aufkochen, den Honig zugeben, auflösen, dann Masse auf 32 °C abkühlen lassen. Die temperierte Kuvertüre zugeben und zu einer glatten Ganache verrühren. Die weiche Butter unterarbeiten und einen vorbereiteten Rahmen 0,5 cm hoch füllen. Die Ganache über Nacht auskristallisieren lassen. Am nächsten Tag mit temperierter Kuvertüre dünn von einer Seite bestreichen und mit der Schneidegeige in 1 cm breite Streifen schneiden. Leicht auseinandergesetzt auf ein Blech setzen.

Den Honig karamellisieren, leicht reduzieren, dann mit Wasser ablöschen und mit der Sahne aufkochen. Die Flüssigkeit über die fein gehackten Kuvertüren geben und zu einer glatten Ganache verarbeiten. Die weiche Butter zugeben und den Met unterarbeiten. Die Masse mit Klarsichtfolie abdecken, über Nacht kristallisieren lassen und am nächsten Tag leicht aufmontieren. Die Ganache mit einer 3er-Lochtülle schneckenförmig auf die Schnittganachestreifen aufdressieren. Nochmals kristallisieren lassen und dann mit der Schneidegeige auf 2 cm Länge schneiden. Die Pralinen mit leicht verdünnter Vollmilchkuvertüre überziehen und mit den Honigpollen dekorieren.

PANDAN-KOKOS-GANACHE

PANDAN COCONUT GANACHE

DIE AUSSERGEWÖHNLICHEN AROMEN VON PANDANBLÄTTERN UND YLANG-YLANG VERZAUBERN JEDEN, DER SIE EINMAL PROBIERT HAT. NATÜRLICH KÖNNTE MAN FÜR DIESES REZEPT AUCH EINE EINFACHE KOKOSGANACHE VERWENDEN, ALLERDINGS WÜRDE MAN EINEN UNVERGLEICHLICHEN GAUMENSCHMAUS VERPASSEN. DENN ASIEN MIT SEINER GANZEN EXOTIK LÄSST GRÜSSEN.

THE EXTRAORDINARY AROMAS OF PANDAN LEAVES AND YLANG-YLANG HAVE A SPELL-BINDING MAGIC TO MOST PEOPLE. OF COURSE, ONE COULD JUST USE A SIMPLE COCONUT GANACHE FOR THIS RECIPE, BUT THAT WOULD MEAN FOREGOING AN INCOMPARABLE DELICACY. THIS IS A PIECE OF ASIA WITH ALL ITS EXOTIC LURE.

INGREDIENTS FOR 120 CHOCOLATES

PANDAN COCONUT GANACHE

160 g	whipping cream
160 g	coconut puree
80 g	chopped Pandan leaves
80 g	freeze-dried coconut powder
560 g	white couverture
8	drops ylang-ylang essential oil (culinary grade)

DECORATION

bitter couverture wavers
bitter couverture wavers with a spreading of green and white cocoa butter

ZUTATEN FÜR 120 PRALINEN

PANDAN-KOKOS-GANACHE

160 g	Sahne
160 g	Kokospüree
80 g	gehackte Pandanblätter
80 g	gefriergetrocknetes Kokosnusspulver
560 g	weiße Kuvertüre
8	Tropfen Ylang-Ylang-Duftöl

DEKORATION

Bitterkuvertüreplättchen
Bitterkuvertüreplättchen mit aufgestrichener grüner und weißer Kakaobutter

Folie auf eine Acrylglasplatte auflegen

Place the foil onto a sheet of Perspex

HERSTELLUNG

1

Die Sahne und das Kokospüree mit den gehackten Pandanblättern aufkochen und etwa 5 Minuten ziehen lassen, dann durch ein Passiertuch absieben, das Kokospulver zugeben und gut durchmixen. Die temperierte Kuvertüre zugeben und mit dem Duftöl zu einer glatten Masse aufmontieren. Die Pandan-Kokos-Ganache mit einer Lochtülle in kleinen Tupfen auf ein Bitterkuvertüreplättchen dressieren, ein zweites Bitterkuvertüreplättchen auflegen, nochmals etwas Ganache aufdressieren und mit einem dekorierten Kuvertüreplättchen abschließen.

Grün gefärbte Kakaobutter aufgießen, mit einem breiten Pinsel verstreichen und anziehen lassen

Pour on the green-coloured cocoa butter and spread with a wide brush; leave to set

2

Weiß gefärbte Kakaobutter aufgießen, ebenfalls verstreichen und anziehen lassen

Pour on the white-coloured cocoa butter; spread and leave to set

3

Temperierte Bitterkuvertüre aufgießen

Pour on the tempered bitter couverture

4

MAKING THE PARTS

Kuvertüre mit der Winkelpalette gleichmäßig dünn ausstreichen

Spread the couverture thinly and evenly with an angled spatula

Bring the cream, coconut puree and Pandan leaves to the boil and leave to steep for 5 minutes; strain through a cloth, add the coconut powder and mix well. Add the tempered couverture and stir into a smooth mixture, adding the essential oil. Use a round piping nozzle to pipe the Pandan coconut ganache in small dabs onto a bitter couverture waver, place a second bitter couverture waver on top, pipe on another bit of ganache and then finish off with a decorated couverture waver.

5

Sobald die Kuvertüre anzieht, mit einem leicht erwärmten, tropfenförmigen Ausstecher Plättchen ausstechen

As soon as the couverture begins to set use a slightly warmed up cutter in the shape of a drop to cut out the wavers

6

MODERN WAY-KARAMELL

MODERN WAY CARAMEL

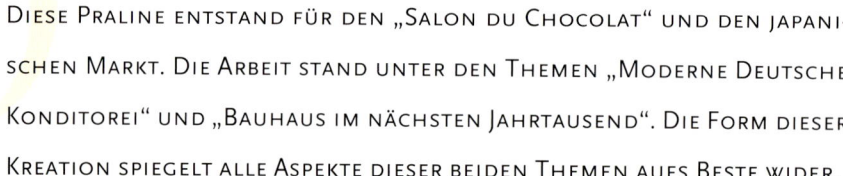

Diese Praline entstand für den „Salon du Chocolat" und den japanischen Markt. Die Arbeit stand unter den Themen „Moderne Deutsche Konditorei" und „Bauhaus im nächsten Jahrtausend". Die Form dieser Kreation spiegelt alle Aspekte dieser beiden Themen aufs Beste wider.

This chocolate was created for the "Salon du Chocolat" and the Japanese market under the headings "Modern German Patisserie" and "Bauhaus in the Next Millenium".

Zutaten für 120 Pralinen		Ingredients for 120 chocolates	
	Quadratische Pralinenformen		**Square chocolate moulds**
	dunkle Sprühkuvertüre		dark spray couverture
	gelbe Kakaobutter		yellow cocoa butter
	weiße Kuvertüre		white couverture
	Lebkuchengewürz		**Gingerbread spices**
30 g	Zimtblüte	30 g	cinnamon flowers
40 g	Ingwer	40 g	ginger
10 g	Muskatblüte	10 g	mace
5 g	Nelken	5 g	cloves
1	Vanilleschote	1	vanilla pod
	Karamellganache		**Caramel ganache**
100 g	Fruchtzucker	100 g	fructose
50 g	Malzsirup	50 g	malt syrup
50 g	Orangensaft, frisch	50 g	fresh orange juice
200 g	Sahne	200 g	whipping cream
5 g	Lebkuchengewürzmischung	5 g	gingerbread spice mixture
100 g	gekochtes Muskatkürbispüree	100 g	boiled mace pumpkin puree
500 g	Milchkuvertüre	500 g	milk couverture
40 g	Whisky	40 g	whisky
10 g	Rosenwasser	10 g	rose water

*Spezialform mit verdünnter, dunkler Sprüh-
kuvertüre aussprühen*

*Spray the special mould with diluted dark
spray couverture*

1

*Das innere Quadrat mit dem Finger wieder
sauber wischen*

Wipe out the inner square neatly

2

*Gelbe Kakaobutter auf das innere Quadrat
auftragen*

Line the inside with yellow cocoa butter

3

MAKING THE PARTS

First spray the mould with diluted dark couverture, wipe out the inner square neatly with your finger and then place yellow cocoa butter onto the inner square. As soon as it has set, line the moulds with the tempered white couverture and prepare for filling.

Grind all the ingredients for the gingerbread spice mixture finely, blend them together and store in an air-tight container.

Caramelise the fructose, add the malt syrup and pour the orange juice and cream over it. Add 5 g of the gingerbread spice mixture and the pumpkin puree, bring to the boil for a moment and pour over the finely chopped milk couverture. Work into a smooth consistency, allow to cool slightly, then add the whisky and rose water.

Fill the prepared moulds with the mixture, leave to set overnight and then close off with tempered white couverture. Take the chocolates out of the moulds once set.

HERSTELLUNG

Zuerst die Form mit verdünnter, dunkler Kuvertüre aussprühen, mit dem Finger das innere Quadrat sauber wischen und gelbe Kakaobutter auf das innere Quadrat auftragen. Sobald sie angezogen hat, die Formen mit der temperierten weißen Kuvertüre ausgießen und zum Füllen vorbereiten.

Alle Zutaten der Lebkuchengewürzmischung fein mahlen, mischen und luftdicht verpackt aufbewahren.

Fruchtzucker karamellisieren, den Malzsirup zugeben und mit dem Orangensaft und der Sahne ablöschen. 5 Gramm des Lebkuchengewürzes und das Kürbispüree zugeben, einmal kurz aufkochen und über die fein gehackte Milchkuvertüre gießen. Zu einer glatten Masse verarbeiten, leicht abkühlen lassen, dann den Whisky und das Rosenwasser zugeben.

Die Masse in die vorbereiteten Formen füllen, über Nacht auskristallisieren lassen, dann mit temperierter weißer Kuvertüre verschließen. Pralinen ausformen.

SHARKY CREMINOS

Die Form dieser Praline, die eigentlich für Eiswürfel vorgesehen ist, stammt aus einer berühmten Serie – aus dem Odenwald. Das Rezept für die Cremino-Füllung kommt von Stefano, meinem Freund aus Italien. Diese Füllung ist in Italien, in zahlreichen Varianten, eine der klassischen Pralinenfüllungen.

The shape of this chocolate, which was really intended for ice cubes, stems from a famous series – from the Odenwald region. The recipe for the Cremino filling is from Stefano, my friend from Italy. There, this filling, in its many permutations, is one of the classic fillings for chocolates.

INGREDIENTS FOR 100 CHOCOLATES		ZUTATEN FÜR 100 PRALINEN	
	SHARKY MOULDS		**SHARKYFORMEN**
	blue pearl dust		perlmuttblaue Metallicfarbe
	bitter couverture		Bitterkuvertüre
	CREMINO FILLING		**CREMINO-FÜLLUNG**
500 g	white couverture	500 g	weiße Kuvertüre
100 g	cocoa butter	100 g	Kakaobutter
250 g	pistachio paste, 100 %	250 g	Pistazienpaste, 100 %
50 g	concentrated butter	50 g	Butterreinfett
	INSIDE LAYER		**EINLAGE**
	roasted pistachios		geröstete Pistazien

HERSTELLUNG

Sharkyformen mit der perlmuttblauen Metallicfarbe auspudern, dann mit temperierter Bitterkuvertüre dünn ausgießen.

Für die Füllung die weiße Kuvertüre auflösen, mit der aufgelösten Kakaobutter mischen und zusammen temperieren, dann die Pistazienpaste untermixen und zum Schluss das weiche Butterreinfett untermischen.

In jede Pralinenform eine Pistazie einlegen, mit der Cremino-Füllung auffüllen, anziehen lassen und mit temperierter Bitterkuvertüre verschließen. Praline in der Kühlung kurz anziehen lassen, dann vorsichtig ausformen.

MAKING THE PARTS

Apply a dusting of pearl dust to the Sharky moulds, then coat thinly with tempered bitter couverture.

Melt the white couverture and mix with the melted cocoa butter; temper the two together and mix in the pistachio paste. Finally mix in the concentrated butter.

Place one pistachio into each chocolate mould, fill with the Cremino filling, allow to set and then top with tempered bitter couverture. Put the chocolates into a fridge to set, then remove carefully from the moulds.

KAFFIR-MINT-NOIR

KAFFIR MINT NOIR

Eigentlich ist Singapur viel zu warm für Schokolade. Doch auf einem der vielen Märkte bekam ich durch Zufall ein Stückchen Schokolade zu probieren und stellte fest, dass es wunderbar mit den Kaffirlimettenblättern harmonierte, die ich zuvor gekostet hatte. Das Ganze wird durch die Nana-Minze erfrischend abgerundet.

You would think that Singapore is too hot for chocolate. Nevertheless, on one of the many markets by chance I was given a small piece of chocolate to taste and found that it harmonised wonderfully with the Kaffir lime leaves I had tried just before. The whole thing is rounded off with the refreshing Nana mint.

Zutaten für 150 Pralinen		Ingredients for 150 chocolates	
Pralinenformen		**Chocolate moulds**	
	rot-metallic-farbene Kakaobutter		cocoa butter with red metallic colouring
	Bitterkuvertüre		bitter couverture
Füllung		**Filling**	
100 g	Kaffirlimettensaft	100 g	Kaffir lime juice
20	Kaffirlimettenblätter	20	Kaffir lime leaves
25 g	Nana-Minze	25 g	Nana mint
300 g	natürliches Kokosnussfett	300 g	natural coconut fat
1000 g	Bitterkuvertüre	1000 g	bitter couverture

Pralinenformen mit rot-metallic-farbener Kakao-butter mit dem Thermoairbrush aussprühen

Use a thermal airbrush to spray the insides of the chocolate moulds with metallic cocoa butter

1

Fertige Pralinen ausformen

Remove the chocolates from the moulds

2

MAKING THE PARTS

Spray the inside of the moulds with the metallic-red cocoa butter, leave to dry, then pour in some tempered bitter couverture.

To make the filling, bring the Kaffir lime juice to the boil, pour it over the Kaffir lime leaves and the Nana mint and leave to steep for 15 minutes, then pass through a sieve. Pour the juice and the liquid coconut fat into the tempered couverture, put the mixture onto a marble slab and table it until it is tempered. Now pour it into the prepared moulds, leave to set overnight and finish off with tempered bitter couverture. Carefully remove the chocolates from the moulds.

HERSTELLUNG

Pralinenformen mit rot-metallic-farbener Kakaobutter aussprühen, etwas trocknen lassen, dann mit temperierter Bitterkuvertüre ausgießen.

Für die Füllung den Kaffirlimettensaft aufkochen, über die Kaffirlimettenblätter und die Nana-Minze gießen und 15 Minuten ziehen lassen, dann absieben. Den Saft und das flüssige Kokosfett in die temperierte Kuvertüre gießen, das Ganze auf der Marmorplatte so lange tablieren, bis es temperiert ist. Dann in die vorbereiteten Formen füllen, über Nacht kristallisieren lassen und mit temperierter Bitterkuvertüre verschließen. Die Pralinen vorsichtig ausformen.

BITTER INKA GOLD

INSPIRIERT ZU DIESER PRALINE WURDE ICH DURCH MEINEN AUFENTHALT IN ARGENTINIEN. ALS ICH ZUM ERSTEN MAL MATETEE PROBIERTE, MUSSTE ICH MICH SCHÜTTELN – ER WAR SO BITTER. ABER NACHDEM MAN MIR IMMER WIEDER NEU NACHSCHENKTE UND ICH DANN EINE ORANGENVARIANTE PROBIEREN DURFTE, WAR ICH SO BEGEISTERT, DASS ICH SOFORT LUST BEKAM, DAMIT EIN NEUES REZEPT ZU KREIEREN.

THE INSPIRATION FOR THIS CHOCOLATE CAME DURING MY STAY IN ARGENTINA. WHEN I TASTED MATE TEA FOR THE FIRST TIME I SHOOK INVOLUNTARILY – SUCH WAS THE INTENSITY OF ITS BITTERNESS. BUT AFTER MY CUP WAS FILLED AGAIN AND AGAIN AND I HAD THE PRIVILEGE OF TRYING AN ORANGE VERSION I REALLY GOT INTO THE SPIRIT OF IT AND RESOLVED THERE AND THEN TO CREATE A NEW RECIPE WITH MATE AS AN INGREDIENT.

INGREDIENTS FOR 100 CHOCOLATES

CHOCOLATE MOULDS
gold lustre dust

bitter couverture

DULCE DE LECHE
1 large can of sweetened condensed milk

FILLING
200 g whole milk

30 g orange mate tea

about 150 g whipping cream

700 g milk couverture, min. 40 % cocoa content

100 g unsalted butter

ZUTATEN FÜR 100 PRALINEN

PRALINENFORMEN
Metallic-Goldpuder

Bitterkuvertüre

DULCE DE LECHE
1 große Dose gesüßte Kondensmilch

FÜLLUNG
200 g Vollmilch

30 g Orangen-Matetee

etwa 150 g Sahne

700 g Vollmilchkuvertüre, mind. 40 % Kakaoanteil

100 g Butter

1

2

3

HERSTELLUNG

Pralinenformen mit Metallic-Goldpuder auspinseln, etwas ausklopfen, damit nicht zu viel in der Form hängen bleibt und mit temperierter Bitterkuvertüre ausgießen.

Für die Dulce de Leche eine große ungeöffnete Dose gesüßte Kondensmilch im Wasserbad etwa 4 Stunden simmern lassen, öffnen und auskühlen lassen. Etwa 3 g Dulce de Leche in jede Pralinenform füllen.

Vollmilch aufkochen und über den Tee gießen. Maximal 5 Minuten ziehen lassen. Dann durch ein Passiertuch pressen und mit der Sahne auf 300 ml Fond auffüllen.

Den Fond nochmals auf 32 °C erwärmen und die temperierte Kuvertüre eingießen. Daraus eine glatte Ganache rühren, die weiche Butter einarbeiten, dann in die vorbereitete Form füllen. Über Nacht kristallisieren lassen, mit temperierter Bitterkuvertüre verschließen und ausformen.

MAKING THE PARTS

Use a brush to apply the gold lustre dust to the inside of the moulds, tap lightly to remove excess dust, then coat with tempered bitter couverture.

To make the dulce de leche, simmer the unopened can of sweetened condensed milk in a pan of hot water for 4 hours, open the can and leave to cool fully. Fill each chocolate mould with about 3 g of dulce de leche.

Bring the milk to the boil and pour over the tea. Let it steep for a maximum of 5 minutes. Press the liquid through a straining cloth and add enough cream to make up to 300 ml.

Heat the mixture again until it reaches 32 °C and add the tempered couverture. Stir to make a smooth ganache, work in the softened butter and fill the prepared moulds. Leave to set overnight, then close with tempered bitter couverture and remove from the moulds.

*Pralinenformen mit Metallic-Goldpuder
auspinseln*

*Apply the gold lustre dust with a brush
to the inside of the moulds*

*Form etwas ausklopfen, damit nicht zu viel
Goldpuder hängen bleibt*

*Tap the moulds lightly to remove any excess
powder*

4

*Durch leichtes Klopfen an der Form bewegen sich
möglicherweise entstandene Blasen nach oben*

*Tap the moulds lightly so that any air bubbles
rise to the surface*

*Die Formen mit temperierter Bitterkuvertüre
auffüllen*

Coat the moulds with tempered bitter couverture

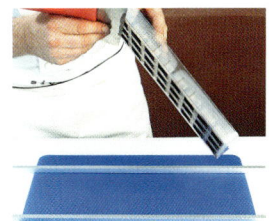

5

*Die Form umdrehen und auf zwei Stangen ablegen,
damit die Kuvertüre abfließen kann. Überschüs-
sige Kuvertüre von oben nach unten abschaben*

*Turn the moulds upside down, resting them on two
bars so that the couverture can run out. Scrape off
any excess couverture, moving from top to bottom*

SPARGELTRÜFFEL

ASPARAGUS TRUFFLES

Spargel ist wunderbar süsslich und eignet sich deshalb hervorragend zur Herstellung toller Desserts. Und was für Desserts gilt, gilt auch für Pralinen. Allerdings steht und fällt der Geschmack dieser Praline mit der Qualität des Spargels. Wer Spargel ausserhalb der Saison verarbeitet, muss damit rechnen, dass er bitter ist.

Asparagus has a delightful sweet nuance in its flavour and is therefore an outstanding ingredient for making great deserts. And what applies to deserts is also true for chocolates. Having said that, the taste of the chocolate depends entirely on the quality of the asparagus. Asparagus that is not in season is likely to be bitter.

INGREDIENTS FOR 90 CHOCOLATES		ZUTATEN FÜR 90 PRALINEN	
CHOCOLATE MOULDS		**PRALINENFORMEN**	
	red cocoa butter		rote Kakaobutter
	white couverture		weiße Kuvertüre
ASPARAGUS PUREE		**SPARGELPÜREE**	
250 g	asparagus	250 g	Spargel
FILLING		**FÜLLUNG**	
50 g	glucose syrup	50 g	Glukosesirup
100 g	whipping cream	100 g	Sahne
200 g	asparagus puree	200 g	Spargelpüree
250 g	white couverture	250 g	weiße Kuvertüre
50 g	cocoa butter	50 g	Kakaobutter
50 g	softened unsalted butter	50 g	weiche Butter
50 g	asparagus schnaps	50 g	Spargelschnaps

3

*Metalleinlage für die Spezialform leicht
mit Speiseöl einölen, passgenau geschnittene
Folie auflegen*

Brush the metal inserts of the special moulds
with cooking oil, place a piece of foil on top that
fits the shape exactly

1

4

Folie sorgfältig glatt aufbringen

Carefully rub the foil until smooth

2

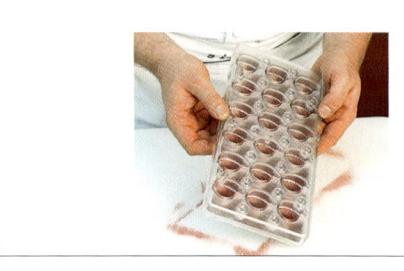

5

Folie mit rot gefärbter Kakaobutter einstreichen

Cover with red-coloured cocoa butter

Metalleinlage mit der eingefärbten Folie in die Spezialform einlegen

Place the metal insert with the coloured foil into the special mould

Fertig vorbereitete Pralinenformen

Fully prepared chocolate moulds

MAKING THE PARTS

To make the chocolate moulds, brush the metal inserts of the special moulds with cooking oil, place a piece of foil on top that has been cut to fit the shape exactly, rub until smooth and then cover with red-coloured cocoa butter. Place the metal inserts into the special moulds and pour in tempered white couverture.

To make the asparagus puree, cook the asparagus in a steamer until soft, take out and let the water drop off, make into a very fine puree and pass through a fine sieve.

To make the filling, bring the glucose syrup to the boil with the cream, add 200 g of the asparagus puree and leave to cool down to 32 °C. Add the tempered white couverture, the tempered cocoa butter the softened butter and schnaps and stir into a smooth and consistent mixture; fill the moulds with the mixture. Leave to set overnight and then top off with tempered white couverture. Take the chocolates out of their moulds and decorate with tempered white couverture.

HERSTELLUNG

Für die Pralinenformen die Metalleinlage der Spezialform leicht mit Speiseöl einölen, passgenau geschnittene Folie auflegen, glatt streichen und mit rot gefärbter Kakaobutter einstreichen. Metalleinlage in die Spezialform einlegen und mit temperierter weißer Kuvertüre ausgießen.

Für das Spargelpüree den Spargel im Dampfgarer weich kochen, dann abtropfen lassen, sehr fein pürieren und durch ein feines Sieb passieren.

Für die Füllung den Glukosesirup mit der Sahne aufkochen, 200 g des Spargelpürees zugeben und auf 32 °C abkühlen lassen. Die temperierte weiße Kuvertüre sowie die temperierte Kakaobutter zugeben, mit der Butter und dem Schnaps zu einer homogenen Masse mixen und in die vorbereiteten Formen füllen. Über Nacht auskristallisieren lassen, dann mit temperierter weißer Kuvertüre verschließen. Ausformen und mit temperierter weißer Kuvertüre garnieren.

KÖNIGSBERGER HERZEN

KÖNIGSBERG HEARTS

MARZIPAN IST EINE DER ÄLTESTEN SÜSSSPEISEN. IM ALTEN VENEDIG TRIEB MAN DEN MARZIPANKULT AUF DIE SPITZE: MAN VERGOLDETE GANZE, AUS MARZIPAN MODELLIERTE HOFSTÄDTE, SOLANGE BIS KEIN GOLD MEHR ZUM VERGOLDEN DER KIRCHEN VORHANDEN WAR. ERST DANN WURDE ES VERBOTEN.

MARZIPAN IS ONE OF THE OLDEST SWEETS THERE IS. IN VENICE THE MARZIPAN FASHION TOOK ON EXTREME FORMS: MARZIPAN WAS USED TO MODEL WHOLE TOWNS WHICH WERE DECORATED WITH GOLD TO THE EXTENT THAT THE GOLD RAN OUT FOR DECORATING THE CHURCHES. THEN FINALLY IT WAS OUTLAWED.

INGREDIENTS FOR 100 CHOCOLATES		**ZUTATEN FÜR 100 PRALINEN**	
	MARZIPAN		**MARZIPAN**
700 g	marzipan raw mixture	700 g	Marzipanrohmasse
35 g	rose water	35 g	Rosenwasser
	BLACKBERRY/ROSE GANACHE		**BROMBEER-ROSEN-GANACHE**
60 g	whipping cream	60 g	Sahne
25 g	glucose syrup	25 g	Glukosesirup
75 g	blackberry puree	75 g	Brombeerpüree
30 g	rose jelly	30 g	Rosengelee
150 g	bitter couverture, 66 % cocoa content	150 g	Bitterkuvertüre, 66 % Kakaoanteil
3	drops of rose oil (adjust quantity according to the quality of the oil)	3	Tropfen Rosenöl (je nach Qualität etwas weniger oder mehr)
15 g	rose schnaps, 40 % vol.	15 g	Rosenschnaps, 40 %-vol.
15 g	unsalted butter	15 g	Butter
	TO COVER		**VERSCHLIESSEN**
140 g	fondant	140 g	Fondant
35 g	glucose syrup	35 g	Glukosesirup
35 g	rose water	35 g	Rosenwasser
15 g	beetroot juice concentrate	15 g	Rote-Bete-Saft-Konzentrat

1

2

3

HERSTELLUNG

Marzipanrohmasse mit dem Rosenwasser
verkneten (bitte achten Sie darauf, dass
beim Rosenwasser der Wassergehalt nicht
zu hoch ist, sonst kann es sein, dass der
Marzipan zu feucht ist und es Probleme
beim Ausstechen gibt). Gleichmäßig zwischen Schienen ausrollen.

Das Marzipan mit Spezialausstechern
ausstechen, Marzipankörper über Nacht
trocken lassen und am nächsten Tag mit
einem Gasbrenner oder einem Salamander abflämmen. Danach mit aufgelöstem
Gummi Arabicum abglänzen.

Für die Ganache Sahne mit Glukosesirup
und dem Brombeerpüree aufkochen, das
Rosengelee untermixen und auf 32 °C
abkühlen lassen, die temperierte Bitterkuvertüre zugeben und dann die Masse
homogenisieren. Die restlichen Zutaten
unterarbeiten und in die vorbereiteten Mar-
zipanförmchen füllen. Verhauten lassen.

MAKING THE PARTS

Add the rose water to the marzipan raw
mixture and knead it into a smooth consistency (please make sure that the water
content of the rose water is not too high,
otherwise the marzipan may get to moist
and give problems when cutting shapes
out of it). Roll out evenly between two rails.

Use special cutters to cut out shapes from
the marzipan, leave to dry out overnight
and on the next day flame off with a gas
torch or in a Salamander infrared process
heater. Brush on some dissolved gum arabic to produce a shiny finish.

To make the ganache, bring the cream,
the glucose syrup and the blackberry jelly
to the boil, mix in the rose jelly and allow
to cool down to 32 °C; add the tempered
bitter couverture and homogenise the mixture. Work in the remaining ingredients
and fill the ganache into the prepared
marzipan shapes. Leave to form a skin.

Marzipan mit einem Silikonrollholz auf einer Silikonmarzipanmatte mit Hilfe von Schienen gleichmäßig ausrollen

Using a silicone rolling pin, roll out the marzipan on a silicone marzipan mat with guide rails on either side to achieve an even thickness

Drei verschiedene Königsberger Spezialausstecher

Three different shape cutters for the Königsberg hearts

Herzen ausformen

Take the hearts out of the forms

4

Herzen mit dem Königsberger Spezialausstecher ausstechen

Use the cutters to cut out the marzipan shapes

Fertig abgeflämmte Königsberger Marzipanherzen

The completed Königsberg hearts with flame finish

5

Heat up the fondant with the glucose syrup to about 40 °C, dilute with the rose water and the beetroot juice concentrate, temper and spread on the ganache with a small piping bag. Again leave to set overnight.

For a better shelf life it is also possible to use a food-grade lacquer for the glossy finish on this type of chocolate.

Fondant mit Glukosesirup auf etwa 40 °C erwärmen, mit dem Rosenwasser und dem Rote-Bete-Saft-Konzentrat verdünnen und temperiert mit einem Garniertütchen auf die Ganache verteilen. Erneut über Nacht anziehen lassen.

Diese Art von Praline kann man, zwecks der Haltbarkeit, auch mit Lebensmittellack abglänzen.

SCENTED GERANIUM

Die beste Ideenquelle ist für mich das Reisen. Zu dieser Praline wurde ich bei Harrods in London inspiriert, als ich in der riesigen Gemüse-abteilung die essbaren Blüten sah. Es war sofort um mich geschehen. Leider gibt es in Deutschland noch keine grosse „Fan-Gemeinde" für essbare Blüten, aber was nicht ist, kann ja noch werden. Übrigens: Unser Landrat liebt diese Praline.

I get my best ideas when I am travelling. The inspiration for these chocolates came to me when I was browsing through the huge green-grocer section at Harrods in London and saw these edible flowers. I was smitten instantly. Unfortunately, Germany does not, as yet, have a large fan base for edible flowers, but perhaps that will change in the future. By the way, our District Councillor loves this chocolate.

Ingredients for 140 chocolates		**Zutaten für 140 Pralinen**	
Chocolate moulds		**Pralinenformen**	
	red cocoa butter		rote Kakaobutter
	milk couverture		Vollmilchkuvertüre
Scented geranium ganache		**Duftgeranien-ganache**	
400 g	whole milk	400 g	Vollmilch
50 g	scented geranium leaves	50 g	Duftgeranienblätter
100 g	glucose syrup	100 g	Glukosesirup
200 g	whipping cream	200 g	Sahne
600 g	milk couverture	600 g	Vollmilchkuvertüre
100 g	unsalted butter	100 g	Butter

4

Kochende Milch über
die Duftgeranienblätter gießen

Pour boiling milk over the scented
geranium leaves

1

5

Etwa 5 Minuten ziehen lassen

Allow to steep for about 5 minutes

2

6

Durch ein Passiertuch gießen und gut auspressen

Pass through a straining cloth and squeeze
the liquid from the leaves

3

7

140 g der Duftgeranienmilch mit Glukosesirup und Sahne erneut aufkochen und über die fein gehackte Vollmilchkuvertüre gießen

Reheat 140 g of the scented milk with the glucose syrup and cream and pour over the finely chopped milk couverture

---

Langsam zu einer glatten Ganache rühren

Slowly stir into a smooth ganache

Die glatte Ganache

The smooth ganache

Bei maximal 35 °C weiche Butter unterarbeiten

Work in the softened butter at a maximum of 35 °C

MAKING THE PARTS

Wipe the inside of the chocolate moulds with the red cocoa butter. As soon as the cocoa butter has set, coat with the milk couverture.

To make the filling, bring the milk to the boil and pour it over the geranium leaves. Cover and leave to steep for about 5 minutes, press through a straining cloth, then pour 140 g of the liquid into a separate container. Add the glucose syrup and the cream and bring back to the boil. Pour over the finely chopped milk couverture and slowly stir into a smooth ganache. When it reaches a maximum of 35 °C work in the softened butter. Fill the prepared forms with the ganache and leave it to set overnight. Finish off with the tempered couverture and remove from the moulds once set.

HERSTELLUNG

Die Pralinenformen mit der roten Kakaobutter auswischen. Sobald die Kakaobutter angezogen hat, mit Vollmilchkuvertüre ausgießen.

Für die Füllung die Milch aufkochen, über die Duftgeranienblätter gießen, zugedeckt etwa 5 Minuten ziehen lassen, dann durch ein Passiertuch pressen und 140 g der Flüssigkeit weiterverarbeiten. Die Sahne und den Glukosesirup zugeben und erneut aufkochen. Über die feingehackte Vollmilchkuvertüre gießen und langsam zu einer glatten Ganache rühren. Bei maximal 35 °C die weiche Butter unterarbeiten. Die Ganache in die vorbereiteten Formen füllen und über Nacht auskristallisieren lassen. Mit temperierter Vollmilchkuvertüre verschließen und ausformen.

CASSIS ELDER ROYAL

FÜR MICH IST DIES EINE DER ELEGANTESTEN PRALINEN, DIE ICH KENNE. MIT DER FROSTERSTEMPELTECHNIK KANN MAN ZAHLLOSE VARIANTEN HERSTELLEN. ZUM EINEN MIT GEKAUFTEN STEMPELN, ZUM ANDEREN SIND DER FANTASIE BEI DER KREATION EIGENER ENTWÜRFE KEINE GRENZEN GESETZT.

FOR ME THIS IS ONE OF THE MOST ELEGANT CHOCOLATES I KNOW. USING THE COLD-STAMPING TECHNOLOGY IT IS POSSIBLE TO PRODUCE MANY VARIATIONS. YOU CAN BUY THESE STAMPS BUT ALSO USE YOUR IMAGINATION TO PRODUCE YOUR OWN CREATIONS — THERE ARE NO LIMITS TO WHAT YOU CAN DO.

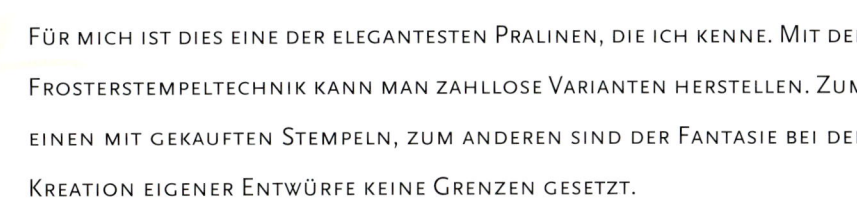

INGREDIENTS FOR 150 CHOCOLATES		ZUTATEN FÜR 150 PRALINEN	
CHOCOLATE MOULDS		**PRALINENFORMEN**	
	blue pearl dust		perlmutblauer Metallic-Puder
	bitter couverture		Bitterkuvertüre
	gold lustre dust		Goldpuder
CASSIS GANACHE		**CASSISGANACHE**	
250 g	cassis puree	250 g	Cassispüree
100 g	whipping cream	100 g	Sahne
50 g	invert sugar	50 g	Invertzucker
550 g	white couverture	550 g	weiße Kuvertüre
50 g	unsalted butter	50 g	Butter
100 g	Champagne	100 g	Champagner
50 g	Marc de Champagne	50 g	Marc de Champagne
ELDER FLOWER CARAMEL		**HOLUNDERBLÜTEN-KARAMELL**	
150 g	sugar	150 g	Zucker
75 g	unsalted butter	75 g	Butter
150 g	elder flower syrup	150 g	Holunderblütensirup

Fertig ausgeformte Pralinen

The completed chocolates with the moulds removed

1

Oberfläche mit einem Schwämmchen und Goldstaub abreiben

Use a small sponge to apply gold dust to the surface

2

HERSTELLUNG

Pralinenformen mit dem perlmuttblauen Metallicpulver ausstauben, dann mit temperierter Bitterkuvertüre ausgießen.

Für die Cassisganache das Cassispüree mit der Sahne und dem Invertzucker aufkochen, über die fein gehackte Kuvertüre geben und zu einer glatten Masse verarbeiten. Die Butter, dann den Champagner und das Marc de Champagne luftfrei untermixen. Ganache auf etwa 30 °C abkühlen lassen, dann die vorbereiteten Formen zu ²/₃ damit füllen. Verhauten lassen.

Für den Holunderblütenkaramell den Zucker karamellisieren, mit der Butter verrühren und dem Holunderblütensirup ablöschen. Den Holunderblütenkaramell abkühlen lassen, dann die vorgefüllte Form bis 1 mm unter den Rand auffüllen. Der Rand muss absolut frei von Karamell sein, da die Praline sonst tropft.

Für das Verschließen der Pralinen eine Folie in der Größe und Form der Pralinen zurechtschneiden, dünn mit temperierter Kuvertüre bestreichen und vorsichtig an der einen Kante der Form auflegen. Behutsam auf die ganze Form abrollen. Mit einem Rollholz vorsichtig darüber rollen. Sobald die Kuvertüre fest ist, kann man die flüssig gefüllten Pralinen ausformen.

Mit temperierter Bitterkuvertüre je einen kleinen Tupfen auf die Praline geben, mit einem gefrosteten Stempel abstempeln und sobald sich die Kuvertüre wieder stabilisiert hat, die Oberfläche mit Goldstaub abreiben.

MAKING THE PARTS

Apply a dusting of blue pearl dust to the chocolate moulds and then coat thinly with the tempered bitter couverture.

To make the cassis ganache, bring the cassis puree, cream and invert sugar to the boil, pour over the finely chopped couverture and blend to form a smooth ganache. Mix in the butter, Champagne and Marc de Champagne taking care to exclude air. Let the ganache cool down to about 30 °C and fill the prepared moulds just over ²/₃ with the ganache. Leave to form a skin.

To make the elder flower caramel, caramelise the sugar, stir in the butter and pour on the elder flower syrup. Leave the caramel to cool, then pour into the moulds to within 1 mm from the top. It is imperative that the edge is free from caramel to stop the chocolate from seeping out.

For closing the chocolates, cut a piece of foil to the size and shape of the chocolates, cover thinly with tempered couverture and carefully place on the edge of the mould, starting from one side. Gently roll it out over the whole mould. Use a rolling pin to carefully level it flat. As soon as the couverture has set, the caramels can be removed from the moulds.

Add a small dab of tempered couverture onto each chocolate, make an imprint with the deep-frozen stamp and as soon as the couverture has become firm again, dust with a little gold dust.

ÜBERRASCHUNGS-MANDELSPLITTER

ALMOND SLIVER SURPRISE

MANDELSPLITTER UND NOCHMALS MANDELSPLITTER! FÜR KINDER, EGAL OB GROSS ODER KLEIN, IST UND BLEIBT DIE VOLLMILCHVARIANTE DAS BESTE WAS ES GIBT. BESONDERS AN OSTERN AUF EINEM GROSSEN OSTEREI IST DAS DER HIT.

ALMOND SLIVERS IN MANY FORMS! FOR CHILDREN, SMALL OR NOT SO SMALL, THE MILK-CHOCOLATE VARIATION IS THE BEST THERE IS. THIS IS A FAVOURITE — ESPECIALLY AT EASTER TIME ON A LARGE CHOCOLATE EASTER EGG.

ZUTATEN FÜR 70 MANDEL-SPLITTER		INGREDIENTS FOR 70 ALMOND SLIVERS	
75 g	Läuterzucker 1:1	75 g	sugar syrup 1:1
500 g	Mandelstifte	500 g	almond slivers
150 g	Puderzucker	150 g	icing sugar
10 g	gefriergetrocknetes Zitronenpulver	10 g	freeze-dried lemon powder
20 g	Peta Zeta von SOSA alternativ: Fizzy von Adrià	20 g	Peta Zeta by SOSA alternatively: Fizzy by Adrià
50 g	Cornflakes	50 g	cornflakes
600 g	temperierte Vollmilchkuvertüre	600 g	tempered milk couverture
100 g	Puderzucker zum Bestauben	100 g	icing sugar for dusting

MAKING THE PARTS

Mix the sugar syrup and almond slivers, add a dusting of 50 g of icing sugar and mix again. Put the almond sliver mixture onto a baking sheet and roast in the oven at 190 °C. Keep turning it.

Allow to cool, mix with the freeze-dried lemon powder, Peta Zetas, the ground cornflakes and the tempered couverture and spoon small heaps onto special paper or a silicone sheet. Apply a dusting of icing sugar while the couverture is setting.

HERSTELLUNG

Den Läuterzucker und die Mandelsplitter mischen, 50 g Puderzucker darüber stäuben und nochmals mischen. Die Mandelsplittermasse auf ein Backblech geben und im Ofen bei 190 °C rösten. Dabei immer wieder wenden.

Auskühlen lassen, mit dem gefriergetrockneten Zitronenpulver, Peta Zetas, den im Mörser zerriebenen Cornflakes und der temperierten Kuvertüre mischen und kleine Häufchen auf Spezialpapier oder eine Silikonmatte setzen. Während die Kuvertüre anzieht mit Puderzucker bestauben.

TIP

Use an almond sliver stencil.

TIPP

Benutzen Sie eine Mandelsplitterschablone.

JASMIN-KIRSCHBLÜTEN-KRUSTENLIKÖR-PRALINEN

JASMINE, CHERRY FLOWERS AND CRUSTED LIQUEUR CHOCOLATES

KRUSTENLIKÖR-PRALINEN SIND EINFACH EIN GENUSS! DIESE MIT KIRSCHWASSER, KIRSCHBLÜTENÖL UND JASMINBLÜTEN-GRÜNTEE IST BESONDERS LECKER, DENN DIE GESCHMACKSNOTEN ERGÄNZEN SICH AUF DAS BESTE. EIN HAUCH VON ASIEN UND ETWAS ODENWALDER-FLAIR – WENN DAS NICHT MULTI-KULTI IST.

CRUSTED LIQUEUR CHOCOLATES ARE DELIGHTFUL! THIS ONE, WITH KIRSCH, CHERRY FLOWER OIL AND JASMINE-FLAVOURED GREEN TEA IS PARTICULARLY TASTY BECAUSE THESE DIFFERENT FLAVOURS COMPLEMENT EACH OTHER PERFECTLY.

INGREDIENTS FOR 100 CHOCOLATES		ZUTATEN FÜR 100 PRALINEN	
	plaster stamps		Gipsstempel
	POWDER MIXTURE		**PUDERGEMISCH**
	wheat powder		Weizenpuder
	corn starch		Maisstärke
	SYRUP		**SIRUP**
200 g	water	200 g	Wasser
30 g	green tea with jasmine flowers	30 g	Grüntee mit Jasminblüten
500 g	sugar	500 g	Zucker
180 g	kirsch, 40 % vol.	180 g	Kirschwasser, 40 %-vol.
35 g	alcohol, 96 % vol.	35 g	Weingeist, 96 %-vol.
5	drops cherry flower oil	5	Tropfen Kirschblütenöl
	DECORATION		**DEKORATION**
	milk couverture		Vollmilchkuvertüre
	white couverture		weiße Kuvertüre
	dried jasmine flowers		getrocknete Jasminblüten

Herstellung

Ein Pudergemisch aus zwei Teilen Weizenpuder und einem Teil Maisstärke herstellen. Das gut trockene Pudergemisch zwei Mal sieben, in Puderkästen verdichten, dann mit Gipsstempeln die Likörpralinenformen eindrücken. Etwas Pudergemisch für das Absieben der Pralinen beiseite lassen.

Wasser auf 80 °C erwärmen, über den Tee gießen, 1 Minute ziehen lassen und durch ein Passiertuch abpressen. 150 g Tee mit dem Zucker mischen und schnell auf 120 °C kochen. Dann vom Herd nehmen, sofort die Alkohole und das Kirschblütenöl zugeben, zudecken und den Alkohol leicht unterschwenken. Den noch heißen Sirup in einen Fülltrichter geben und in die vorbereiteten Pralinenformen füllen. Pralinen mit einem Sieb und dem vorbereiteten Pudergemisch abpudern und über Nacht stehen lassen. Den Likörkörper vorsichtig wenden und nochmals über Nacht stehen lassen, so dass sich rundum eine feine Zuckerkruste bildet.

Die Likörkörper mit einem feinen Pinsel abpudern, mit temperierter Milchkuvertüre überziehen und dann, wenn diese angezogen hat, mit temperierter weißer Kuvertüre in der Mitte überspinnen. Jede Praline mit einer getrockneten Jasminblüte dekorieren.

Making the parts

Mix two parts of wheat powder together with one part of corn starch to make a powder blend. Keep the powder as dry as possible, pass it twice through a sieve and compact into powder boxes. Use the plaster stamps to press the desired shape of the liqueur chocolates into the powder. Keep a little of the powder blend aside for dusting later.

Heat the water to 80 °C, pour over the tea, allow to steep for 1 minute and then pass through a straining cloth. Put the sugar into 150 g of the tea and boil up quickly to 120 °C. Remove the syrup from the heat, add the alcohols and cherry flower oil immediately, cover the pan and gently sway it so that the alcohol blends with the syrup. Pour the hot syrup into a filling funnel and fill the prepared chocolate forms with syrup. Use the powder blend you have set aside and pass it through a sieve to dust the chocolates; leave them to stand overnight. Carefully turn over the liqueur shapes and again leave to stand overnight so that a fine sugar crust forms all over.

Use a fine brush to dust the liqueur shapes before covering them with tempered milk couverture; when this has set use tempered white couverture to make a pattern in the middle. Decorate each chocolate with a dried jasmine flower.

Puderkasten (es geht auch der Deckel eines
Tortenkartons) mit getrocknetem Pudergemisch
füllen und glatt streichen

*Fill the powder box with the dried powder blend
and level off smooth. If you have no powder box
you can simply use the lid of a cake carton*

Mit Gipsstempeln, die gleichmäßig auf
einen Holzstab geklebt sind, Vertiefungen
in das verdichtete Puder eindrücken

*Glue the plaster stamps evenly onto a wooden
batten and use this to press the shapes into the
compacted powder*

Nach einem Tag wenden

Turn over after a day

5

Mit einem Fülltrichter den heißen Sirup gleichmäßig in die trockenen Puderformen einfüllen

*Use a filling funnel to evenly fill the hot syrup
into the dry powder forms*

Vorsichtig mit einem Pinsel oder, falls vorhanden,
mit einer Auspudermaschine auspudern

*Apply a dusting with a brush or, if available,
a dusting machine*

6

Sofort mit trockenem Pudergemisch überpudern

*Apply a dusting immediately, using the dry
powder blend*

Die fertige Kruste ist gleichmäßig und dünn

The finished crust is even and thin

7

EIS

ICE CREAM

AFRICAN CIRCUS

EINER MEINER KLASSIKER IM NEUEN GEWAND. DIE ANANAS HABE ICH SCHON AUF VERSCHIEDENSTE ARTEN VARIIERT, ABER DIES IST UND BLEIBT MEINE LIEBLINGSVERSION.

THIS IS ONE OF MY CLASSICS IN A NEW CLOAK. I HAVE USED PINEAPPLE IN MANY VARIATIONS BUT THIS ONE IS STILL MY FAVOURITE VERSION.

INGREDIENTS FOR 12 PERSONS

RED SUGAR LOLLIES

150 g	*sugar*
45 g	*glucose syrup*
15 g	*water*

Mix all ingredients together and bring to the boil, remove the froth and boil to 160 °C, continually "cleaning" the mixture. Pour the mixture onto a silicone baking mat and leave to cool, use a Thermomix or cutter to crush into a powder.

Mix some freeze-dried red fruit powder into the powder, quantity to your taste but usually between 4 and 10 g, depending on the type of fruit powder.

Place some round stencils onto a Teflon baking mat and pass the mixture through a sieve to cover the stencils. Carefully remove the stencils, place in the oven at 180 °C for 4 minutes until the powder begins to melt. Allow to cool, place on a silicone baking mat and decorate with a boiled sugar thread; wrap up air-tight immediately.

ZUTATEN FÜR 12 PERSONEN

ROTE ZUCKERLOLLYS

150 g	*Zucker*
45 g	*Glukosesirup*
45 g	*Wasser*

Alle Zutaten miteinander aufkochen, abschäumen und unter ständigem Reinwaschen auf 160 °C kochen. Masse auf eine Silikon-Backmatte gießen und auskühlen lassen, dann mit dem Thermomix oder einem Kutter pulverisieren.

Pulver nach Geschmack mit gefriergetrocknetem, roten Fruchtpulver mischen. Die Menge kann je nach Sorte zwischen 4 und 10 g variieren.

Teflon-Backmatte mit runden Schablonen belegen, dann Mischung darüber sieben. Schablonen vorsichtig entfernen und bei 180 °C für etwa 4 Minuten im Ofen anschmelzen. Nach dem Erkalten auf eine Silikon-Backmatte legen und mit einem gekochten Zuckerfaden als Stab überspinnen und sofort luftdicht verpacken.

KOKOSNUSSFINANZIERS

27 g	Kokosraspeln, leicht geröstet
12 g	Puderzucker
12 g	Mehl
25 g	flüssige Butter
40 g	Eiweiß
17 g	Zucker
5 g	alter Rum

Alle Zutaten miteinander verrühren und in eine Silikon-Backform füllen. Teig bei 175 °C etwa 15 Minuten saftig backen und für die Spieße in kleine Würfel schneiden.

COCONUT FINANCIERS

27 g	grated coconut, lightly roasted
12 g	icing sugar
12 g	flour
25 g	liquid butter (unsalted)
40 g	egg white
17 g	sugar
5 g	aged rum

Stir all ingredients together and fill into a silicone baking mould. Put in the oven and bake at 175 °C for 15 minutes, take out and cut into small cubes for the skewers.

GEGRILLTE ANANAS

1	Ananas
4	Vanilleschoten
200 g	Zucker
300 g	Weißwein
50 g	Ingwer, frisch gerieben
1	Banane, geschält und gewürfelt
5	Pimentkörner
50 g	alter Rum

Ananas schälen, die Vanilleschoten in 3 cm lange Stücke schneiden, dann die Ananas damit spicken.

Zucker in einer kleinen Pfanne leicht karamellisieren lassen, mit Wein ablöschen, dann die restlichen Zutaten zugeben. Gespickte Ananas im Ofen bei 160 °C für etwa 30 Minuten garen, dabei in regelmäßigen Abständen mit dem Gewürzsud übergießen.

Die Ananas für die Spieße in passende Würfel schneiden und abwechselnd mit den Kokosnussfinanziers aufspießen. Als Unterlage für das Savarin einige Ananas klein schneiden.

GRILLED PINEAPPLE

1	pineapple
4	vanilla pods
200 g	sugar
300 g	white wine
50 g	ginger, freshly ground
1	banana, peeled and diced
5	grains of allspice
50 g	aged rum

Peel the pineapple, cut the vanilla pods into 3 cm long pieces and use them to spike the pineapple.

Put the sugar into a small frying pan and heat until it begins to caramelise, add the wine and then the remaining ingredients. Put the pineapple into the oven for 30 minutes at 160 °C, basting it with the spice mixture at regular intervals.

Cut the pineapple into suitably sized cubes and spike them onto the skewers, alternating with the coconut financiers. Chop up some of the pineapple as a base for the savarins.

SAVARINS

7 g	yeast
13 g	sugar
50 g	milk
75 g	whole egg
30 g	egg yolk
1 g	salt
2 g	lemon zest (from 1 lemon)
125 g	flour
40 g	unsalted butter

Dissolve the yeast with the sugar in the lukewarm milk, add the egg, egg yolk, spices and flour and work everything into a smooth pastry. Cover the pastry and leave to rise, then work in the butter, leave to rise again, fold together and put into a piping bag with a round nozzle to pipe into the silicone moulds until these are about $^2/_3$ full. Leave to rise again and then bake at 180 °C for about 15 minutes (the time can vary for different moulds). The savarins keep well in a deep freezer.

SAVARINS

7 g	Hefe
13 g	Zucker
50 g	Milch
75 g	Vollei
30 g	Eigelb
1 g	Salz
2 g	Abrieb von 1 Zitrone
125 g	Mehl
40 g	Butter

Hefe mit dem Zucker in der lauwarmen Milch auflösen, dann Ei, Eigelb, Gewürze und Mehl zugeben und alles zu einem glatten Teig verarbeiten. Diesen zugedeckt gehen lassen, dann die Butter unterarbeiten, erneut gehen lassen, zusammenschlagen und mit einer Lochtülle und einem Spritzbeutel zu $^2/_3$ Höhe in Silikonformen eindressieren. Anschließend erneut gehen lassen und bei 180 °C für etwa 15 Minuten backen (je nach Form kann die Backzeit variieren). Die Savarins können tiefgekühlt sehr gut gelagert werden.

SOAKING

200 g	sugar
250 g	water
	Zest from 1 lemon
	Zest from 1 orange
1	vanilla pod
1	twig of mint
50 g	aged rum

Bring the sugar and spices to the boil in the water, drain the water and add the rum. Use this sauce to soak to savarins, if required.

TRÄNKE

200 g	Zucker
250 g	Wasser
	Abrieb von 1 Zitrone
	Abrieb von 1 Orange
1	Vanilleschote
1	Minzzweig
50 g	alter Rum

Den Zucker mit Wasser und Gewürzen aufkochen, dann absieben und den Rum zugeben. Bei Bedarf die Savarins damit tränken.

Rosa-Pfefferbeeren-Eis mit Vanille (warme Herstellung) (ergibt 1000 g)

7 g	rosa Pfefferbeeren
333 g	Vollmilch
1	Bourbon-Vanilleschote
133 g	Eigelb
166 g	Zucker
33 g	Trockenglukose
333 g	Sahne

Die Pfefferbeeren leicht mörsern und mit Milch, Vanilleschote und -mark aufkochen. Danach Vanilleschote entnehmen. Eigelb mit Zucker und Trockenglukose schaumig schlagen, dann mit der heißen Milch auf 85 °C pasteurisieren, schließlich auf 65 °C abkühlen lassen. Die Sahne zugeben. Die Masse auf 4 °C abkühlen und reifen lassen, anschließend absieben und in einer Eismaschine abfrieren.

Red pepper berry ice cream with vanilla (hot production method) (makes 1000 g)

7 g	red pepper berries
333 g	whole milk
1	Bourbon vanilla pod
133 g	egg yolk
166 g	sugar
33 g	dry glucose
333 g	whipping cream

Lightly crush the pepper berries in a mortar and bring to the boil with the milk, vanilla pod and vanilla pith. Take out the vanilla pod. Beat the egg yolk with the sugar and dry glucose until frothy, pasteurise with the hot milk to 85 °C and finally allow to cool down to 65 °C. Add the cream. Cool the mixture down to 4 °C and leave to mature, drain off and freeze in an ice-cream maker.

Wassergelee aus karamellisiertem Honig

300 g	Leatherwood-Honig
	Wasser
500 g	Honigwasser
10 g	Gellan

Honig karamellisieren und bis zu einem Gesamtgewicht von 500 g mit Wasser ablöschen.
Honigwasser bei Raumtemperatur mit Gellan mischen, aufkochen, abschäumen und auf ein erwärmtes Blech ausgießen. Nach dem Erkalten in die gewünschten Formen schneiden (Tagliatelle und Umhüllungen für Fruchtspieße). Das Wassergelee lässt sich auf maximal 130 °C erneut erhitzen.

Water jelly made from caramelised honey

300 g	leatherwood honey
	water
500 g	honey water
10 g	gellan

Caramelise the honey and add water until the whole mixture weight 500 g.
Mix the honey water with the gellan at room temperature, bring to the boil, take the froth off the surface and pour onto a warmed-up baking sheet. Once it has cooled down, cut out the required shapes (Tagliatelle and shrouds for the fruit skewers). The water jelly can be reheated to a maximum of 130 °C.

PEANUT / SESAME CRUMBS

125 g	*peanut oil*
50 g	*roasted sesame oil*
47	*peanuts, roasted and chopped*
67 g	*Maltodextrin*
1	*vanilla pod (pith)*
1 g	*salt*

Mix all ingredients together.

ERDNUSS-SESAMSTREUSEL

125 g	*Erdnussöl*
50 g	*geröstetes Sesamöl*
47	*Erdnüsse, geröstet und gehackt*
67 g	*Maltodextrin*
1	*Vanilleschote (Mark)*
1 g	*Salz*

Alle Zutaten miteinander vermischen.

DECORATION

peel of lime

red currants

DEKORATION

Limettenschale

rote Johannisbeeren

KINDHEITSTRÄUME

CHILDHOOD DREAMS

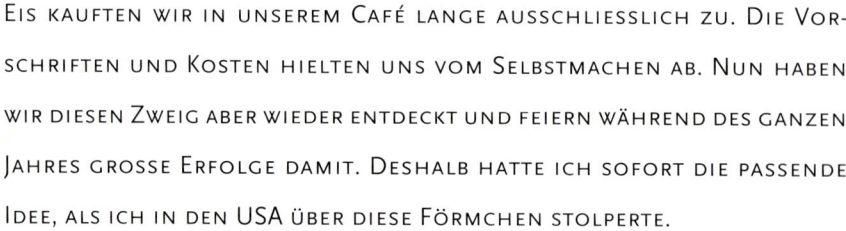

Eis kauften wir in unserem Café lange ausschliesslich zu. Die Vorschriften und Kosten hielten uns vom Selbstmachen ab. Nun haben wir diesen Zweig aber wieder entdeckt und feiern während des ganzen Jahres grosse Erfolge damit. Deshalb hatte ich sofort die passende Idee, als ich in den USA über diese Förmchen stolperte.

In our café we used to buy in the ice-cream. Regulations and costs prevented us from making it ourselves. However, now we have rediscovered this branch of our profession and go from success to success throughout the year. That's why these little moulds that I came across in the USA immediately prompted me to an idea for a recipe.

ZUTATEN FÜR 12 PERSONEN

HIMBEERSOSSE

50 g	Zucker
50 g	Portwein
2 g	Xanthan
200 g	Himbeerpüree, leicht angefroren

Den Zucker hell karamellisieren und mit Portwein ablöschen. Dann mit Xanthan und Himbeerpüree stabil aufmixen, durch ein feines Sieb passieren und gut gekühlt lagern.

INGREDIENTS FOR 12 PERSONS

RASPBERRY SAUCE

50 g	sugar
50 g	port
2 g	xanthan gum
200 g	raspberry puree, very slightly frozen

Caramelise the sugar to a light colour and pour the port over it. Add in the xanthan gum and raspberry puree and blend until stiff, pass through a fine sieve and store in a cool place.

HIMBEER-MANGO-PARFAIT
IN WEISSER SCHOKOLADE

140 g	Eiweiß
210 g	Zucker
75 g	Himbeerpüree
75 g	Mangopüree
	Abrieb und Saft von 1 Bio-Zitrone
475 g	halb geschlagene Sahne
	etwas weiße Kuvertüre

Eiweiß zu Schnee schlagen, in der Zwischenzeit den Zucker mit etwas Wasser auf 119 °C kochen und in dünnem Strahl in den Schnee einlaufen lassen. Kalt schlagen, dann die Masse halbieren, zur einen Hälfte das Himbeerpüree und zur anderen Hälfte das Mangopüree geben. Zitronensaft und -abrieb unterheben, dann jeweils die Hälfte der Sahne. Je eine Sorte in einen Spritzbeutel geben und glatt und gleichmäßig aufeinander legen. Dann aufschneiden, die beiden Beutel in einen dritten Beutel mit Spezialtülle geben und Stieleisförmchen befüllen. Anschließend einfrieren, gefroren ausformen, dann eine Folie mit temperierter, weißer Kuvertüre dekorieren und das Parfait darin einrollen. Bis zur Verwendung tiefgekühlt lagern.

RASPBERRY MANGO PARFAIT
IN WHITE CHOCALATE

140 g	egg white
210 g	sugar
75 g	raspberry puree
75 g	mango puree
	zest and juice from 1 organic lemon
475 g	half-whipped cream
	some white couverture

Beat the egg white until stiff, meanwhile boil the sugar with a little water at 119 °C and add to the beaten egg white in a thin stream. Beat until cold, divide the mixture into half portions, add the raspberry puree to one half and the mango puree to the other half. Fold in the lemon juice and zest followed by half of the cream for each part. Put the mixtures into a piping bag each and lay smoothly and evenly on top of each other. Then cut open, put the content of the two bags into a third bag with a special nozzle and fill the mixture into moulds for ice-cream lollies. Put into the freezer, remove from the moulds when frozen, decorate a foil with tempered white couverture and use this to wrap around the parfait. Store in the freezer until used.

1

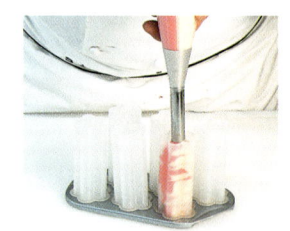

2

3

PISTAZIENFINANZIERS

25 g	Puderzucker
55 g	Pistazien, fein gerieben, leicht geröstet
25 g	Mehl
50 g	geschmolzene Butter
80 g	Eiweiß
35 g	Zucker

Alle Zutaten miteinander verrühren und in eine Silikon-Backform einfüllen. Dann bei 175 °C etwa 15 Minuten backen. Ausgekühlte Finanziers mit je einer frischen Himbeere und einem Tupfen Kaltgelee dekorieren.

PISTACHIO FINANCIERS

25 g	icing sugar
55 g	pistachios, finely ground, lightly roasted
25 g	flour
50 g	melted butter (unsalted)
80 g	egg white
35 g	sugar

Stir all ingredients together and fill into a silicone baking form. Bake at 175 °C for about 15 minutes. Once the financiers have cooled down completely, decorate with a fresh raspberry and a dab of cold jelly each.

Zwei verschiedenfarbige Parfaitmassen in getrennte Spritzbeutel füllen, dann glatt und gleichmäßig aufeinander legen

Fill two separate piping bags with the two differently coloured parfait mixtures, then lay smoothly and evenly on top of each other

---

Spritzbeutel aufschneiden, in einen dritten Spritzbeutel mit Tülle geben und in Spezial-förmchen füllen

Cut the piping bag open, fill the content into a third piping bag with a nozzle and pipe the mixture into the special little moulds

---

Stiele eindrücken, abfrieren und später ausformen

Push in the sticks, freeze and remove from the moulds later

PUFF PASTRY BED

	butter block:
375 g	butter fat
150 g	flour, type 550

	pastry:
15 g	sea salt
150 g	water
3 g	vinegar
135 g	flour, type 405
112 g	butter fat

To make the butter block, kneed the butter fat and flour, shape into a rectangular block and cool thoroughly.

To make the pastry, dissolve the salt in water, add vinegar and flour and kneed into a smooth pastry. Then kneed in the butter fat, cover and put in a cold place; when cold shape the pastry into a ball, cut this crosswise and pull the sections outwards. Insert the butter block, close the four ends back together and apply 2 double workings at 2-hour intervals; roll out to a thickness of 3 mm and place on a baking sheet that you have sprayed with water. Apply a dusting of icing sugar, bake at 220 °C for about 20 minutes and cut to the required size. Store in a dry place.

BLÄTTERTEIGBETT

	Butterstück:
375 g	Butterfett
150 g	Mehl, Typ 550

	Teig:
15 g	Meersalz
150 g	Wasser
3 g	Essig
135 g	Mehl, Typ 405
112 g	Butterfett

Für das Butterstück Butterfett und Mehl verkneten, zu einem quadratischen Ziegel formen und durchkühlen.

Für den Teig Salz in Wasser auflösen, dann Essig und Mehl zugeben und zu einem glatten Teig verkneten. Anschließend Butterfett unterkneten, zugedeckt kaltstellen und zu einer Kugel formen, diese über Kreuz einschneiden, dann die Ecken auseinander ziehen. Das Butterstück auflegen, die vier Enden wieder verschließen und im Abstand von 2 Stunden je 2 doppelte Touren geben, auf 3 mm Stärke ausrollen und auf ein mit Wasser besprühtes Backblech absetzen. Mit Puderzucker absieben, bei 220 °C etwa 20 Minuten backen und auf gewünschte Größe zuschneiden. Trocken lagern.

DECORATION

chocolate décor
seal
chopped pistachios

DEKORATION

Schokoladendekor
Siegel
gehackte Pistazien

WEDDING CONES

MAN KÖNNTE DENKEN, ZUR HOCHZEIT BRAUCHT MAN UNBEDINGT AUCH HOCH-
ZEITSGLOCKEN. ABER DIE LASSEN SICH NUN MAL LEIDER SCHLECHT BEFÜLLEN.
ABER ICH FINDE, DIESE DURCHSICHTIGEN TÜTCHEN EIGNEN SICH HERVORRAGEND
FÜR EIN KLEINES, ABER FEINES EISDESSERT ZUM STEHEMPFANG.

ONE MIGHT THINK THAT WEDDING BELLS ARE A MUST FOR A WEDDING. BUT
UNFORTUNATELY, THEY ARE NOT EASY TO FILL. BUT I FIND THAT THESE TRANS-
PARENT CONES ARE PERFECTLY SUITABLE FOR A SELECT ICE-CREAM DESSERT AT A
STAND-UP RECEPTION.

INGREDIENTS FOR **20** PERSONS		ZUTATEN FÜR **20** PERSONEN	
ARLETTES PUFF PASTRY (ABOUT **100** PCS.)		**ARLETTES BLÄTTERTEIGGEBÄCK** (ETWA **100** STÜCK)	
	Butter block:		*Butterstück:*
375 g	*butter fat*	375 g	*Butterfett*
150 g	*flour, type 550*	150 g	*Mehl, Typ 550*
	Pastry:		*Teig:*
15 g	*sea salt*	15 g	*Meersalz*
150 g	*water*	150 g	*Wasser*
2 g	*vinegar*	2 g	*Essig*
135 g	*flour, type 405*	135 g	*Mehl, Typ 405*
110 g	*butter fat*	110 g	*Butterfett*
	some vanilla icing sugar		*etwas Vanillepuderzucker*

Making the parts see next page.

Zubereitung siehe nächste Seite.

ARLETTES BLÄTTERTEIGGEBÄCK

Für das Butterstück Butterfett und Mehl
verkneten, dann zu einem quadratischen
Ziegel formen und durchkühlen.
Für den Teig Meersalz in Wasser auflösen,
dann Essig und Mehl zugeben und zu
einem glatten Teig verkneten. Butterfett
unterkneten und zugedeckt kaltstellen.
Teig anschließend zu einer Kugel formen,
diese über Kreuz einschneiden und auseinander ziehen. Butterstück auflegen,
Enden wieder verschließen und im Abstand von 2 Stunden je 2 doppelte Touren
geben. Teig mit Vanillepuderzucker bestäuben und auf 2 mm Stärke sowie 30 cm
Breite ausrollen, dann leicht mit Wasser
befeuchten und zu einer Rolle formen.
Rolle tiefkühlen und mit der Aufschnitt-
maschine in dünne Scheiben schneiden.
Erneut mit Vanillepuderzucker bestäuben,
wieder dünn ausrollen und auf einem gefetteten Backblech absetzen. Abschließend
mit Puderzucker absieben und bei 200 °C
etwa 10 Minuten backen. Trocken lagern.

ARLETTES PUFF PASTRY

To make the butter block, knead the butter
fat and flour, shape into a rectangular block
and cool thoroughly.
To make the pastry, dissolve the sea salt in
water, add vinegar and flour and knead into a smooth pastry. Work in the butterfat,
cover and refrigerate. Then shape the pastry into a ball, cut this crosswise and pull
the sections outwards. Insert the butter
block, close the ends back together and apply 2 double workings at 2-hour intervals.
Apply a dusting of vanilla icing sugar and
roll out to a thickness of 2 mm and a width
of 30 cm, wet with a little water and form a
roll. Deep-freeze the roll and then cut into
thin slices using a slicing machine. Apply
another dusting of vanilla icing sugar, again
roll out thinly and place on a greased baking sheet. Apply a final dusting with icing
sugar and bake at 200 °C for about 10 minutes. Store in a dry place.

1

2

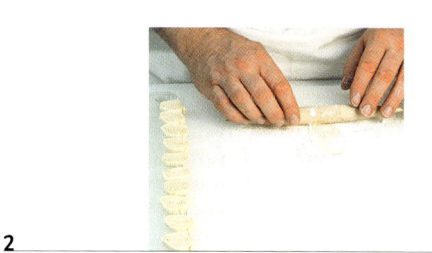

GELIERTER ROSENSEKT

1,1 g	Agar-Agar
500 g	Riesling Sekt
50 g	Rosensirup

Alle Zutaten mischen und kurz aufkochen.
Dann leicht abgekühlt in die Flöten füllen
und gelieren lassen.

JELLIED ROSE CHAMPAGNE

1.1 g	agar agar
500 g	Riesling Champagne
50 g	rose syrup

Mix all ingredients and boil up briefly.
Once the liquid has cooled down a little,
pour into the cones where it will set.

Tiefgekühlte, in Scheiben geschnittene Blätter-teigrolle in Puderzucker wälzen

Roll the slices of deep-frozen puff pastry roll in icing sugar

Blätterteigrolle erneut dünn auswalzen, auf einem gefetteten Backblech absetzen und mit Puderzucker absieben

Again, roll out the puff pastry roll thinly, place on a greased baking sheet and apply a dusting of icing sugar

ROSE RASPBERRY CREAM

250 g	whipping cream
25 g	rose syrup
25 g	raspberry puree

Mix all ingredients together, fill into an Espuma foaming beaker and insert 2 gas cartridges.

ROSEN-HIMBEERSAHNE

250 g	Sahne
25 g	Rosensirup
25 g	Himbeerpüree

Alle Zutaten mischen, in den Espuma-Siphon füllen und dann 2 Gaspatronen aufschrauben.

PASSION FRUIT JELLY

1.25 g	agar agar
250 g	passion fruit juice
1/2	vanilla pod (pith)
50 g	sugar

Mix all ingredients and boil up briefly. Once the liquid has cooled down a little, pour into a silicone mould and, after it has set, cut into cubes. Mix with fresh raspberries and the pulp of passion fruit.

MARACUJAGELEE

1,25 g	Agar-Agar
250 g	Maracujasaft
1/2	Vanilleschote (Mark)
50 g	Zucker

Alle Zutaten mischen und kurz aufkochen. Leicht abgekühlt in eine Silikonform füllen und gelieren lassen, dann in Würfel schneiden. Mit frischen Himbeeren und Maracujafruchtfleisch mischen.

RASPBERRY ROSE SORBET
(COLD PRODUCTION METHOD)
(MAKES 1000 G)

42 g	dry glucose
97 g	sugar
170 g	invert sugar
466 g	raspberry puree
203 g	water
17 g	rose syrup
3	drops of rose oil (modify quantity depending on strength)
4 g	fruit acid

Mix the dry ingredients together followed by the remaining ingredients. Use a refractometer to adjust the mixture to 32 °Brix. Place into the ice-cream maker to freeze.

HIMBEER-ROSENSORBET
(KALTE HERSTELLUNG)
(ERGIBT 1000 G)

42 g	Trockenglukose
97 g	Zucker
170 g	Invertzucker
466 g	Himbeerpüree
203 g	Wasser
17 g	Rosensirup
3	Tropfen Rosenöl (je nach Qualität variieren)
4 g	Fruchtsäure

Trockene Zutaten mischen und mit den restlichen Zutaten aufmixen. Mit dem Refraktometer anschließend auf 32 °Brix einstellen. In der Eismaschine gefrieren.

KÖNIG-LUDWIG-EISBOMBE

KING LUDWIG ICE-CREAM BOMB

MEIN FREUND MARKUS KÜHNE WAR IN FÜSSEN AM KÖNIG-LUDWIG-MUSICAL ENGAGIERT UND EIN BESUCH DORT WECKTE MEIN INTERESSE AN DEN GESCHMACK-LICHEN VORLIEBEN SEINER HOHEIT. NUN, SOWEIT MEINE RECHERCHEN STIMMEN, MÜSSTE DIESE WAHRHAFT KÖNIGLICHE EISBOMBE IHM WOHL GEMUNDET HABEN. AUCH WENN SIE NICHT GANZ IN BLAU UND WEISS DAHERKOMMT.

MY FRIEND MARKUS KÜHNE WAS INVOLVED AT THE KÖNIG-LUDWIG-MUSICAL IN FÜSSEN AND WHEN I VISITED HIM THERE I BECAME INTERESTED IN THE CULI-NARY PREFERENCES OF HIS HIGHNESS. WELL, IF MY RESEARCH IS CORRECT, THIS TRULY ROYAL ICE-CREAM BOMB SHOULD HAVE PLEASED HIM THOROUGHLY. EVEN THOUGH IT IS NOT EXACTLY DRESSED IN THE ROYAL COLOURS, BLUE AND WHITE.

4 EISBOMBEN Ø 18 CM

LAVENDEL-BAISERBODEN

150 g	Eiweiß
400 g	Zucker
1 g	Salz
100 g	Puderzucker
5 g	Lavendelblüten

4 ICE-CREAM BOMBS Ø 18 CM

LAVENDER MERINGUE BASE

150 g	egg white
400 g	sugar
1 g	salt
100 g	icing sugar
5 g	lavender flowers

Eiweiß mit etwas Zucker und dem Salz zu einem steifen Schnee schlagen. Den rest-lichen Zucker nach und nach einlaufen lassen. Puderzucker und Lavendelblüten fein mörsern. Unterheben und mit dem Spritzbeutel und einer 6er-Lochtülle eine Scheibe, die etwas kleiner als die Form ist, auf eine Backmatte garnieren. Diese bei 120 °C für etwa 4 Stunden „trocknen".

Add some sugar and the salt to the egg white and beat until stiff. Let the remain-ing sugar run into the egg in small doses. Crush the icing sugar with the lavender flowers into a fine dust. Fold into the mix-ture, then use a piping bag with a round nozzle size 6 to pipe a disk that is a little smaller than the mould onto a baking mat. "Dry" the mixture in the oven at 120 °C for about 4 hours.

WEISSE GLASUR (ÜBERZUG)

6 g	Gelatine
12 g	Wasser
120 g	Milch
72 g	Glukose
30 g	Sahne
390 g	weiße Kuvertüre

Gelatine in Wasser einweichen. Die Milch mit Glukose und Sahne aufkochen. Weiße Kuvertüre zugeben, dann alles miteinander mischen und homogenisieren.

TIPP

Alle Glasuren nur im fast kalten Zustand verwenden.

WHITE ICING (COATING)

6 g	gelatine
12 g	water
120 g	milk
72 g	glucose
30 g	whipping cream
390 g	white couverture

Soak the gelatine in water. Boil the milk with the cream and glucose. Add the white couverture, mix everything together and homogenise.

TIP

Do not use icing until it is almost cold.

WEISSE-JOHANNISBEEREN-MILCHEIS (WARME HERSTELLUNG) (KERN INNEN)

70 g	Zucker
34 g	Magermilchpulver
13 g	Trockenglukose
1 g	Vanillemark
178 g	Vollmilch
46 g	Invertzucker
141 g	Püree aus weißen Johannisbeeren
41 g	Sahne

Trockene Zutaten mischen. Die Milch und den Invertzucker zugeben, dann bei 85 °C pasteurisieren und auf 65 °C abkühlen. Fruchtpüree und Sahne zugeben, bei 4 °C reifen lassen und abfrieren.

WHITE CURRANT DAIRY ICE-CREAM (HOT PRODUCTION METHOD) (INNER CENTRE)

70 g	sugar
34 g	skimmed milk powder
13 g	dry glucose
1 g	vanilla pith
178 g	whole milk
46 g	invert sugar
141 g	white currant puree
41 g	whipping cream

Mix the dry ingredients. Add the milk and invert sugar, then pasteurise at 85 °C and cool down to 65 °C. Add the fruit puree and cream, allow to mature at 4 °C and then put into the freezer.

MANDARIN CHAMPAGNE SORBET (OUTER CENTRE)

288 g	dry glucose
144 g	sugar
7 g	neutral (cold) ice-cream binding agent (vary in accordance with manufacturer's instructions)
100 g	water
79 g	mandarin juice
	Zest from 3 organic mandarins
180 g	Champagne

Mix the dry ingredients, then add the water, mandarin juice and zest and mix well. Slightly freeze in the ice-cream maker, then add the Champagne and freeze fully.

MANDARINEN-CHAMPAGNER-SORBET (KERN AUSSEN)

288 g	Trockenglukose
144 g	Zucker
7 g	neutrales (kaltes) Eisbindemittel (je nach Hersteller variieren)
100 g	Wasser
79 g	Mandarinensaft
	Abrieb von 3 Bio-Mandarinen
180 g	Champagner

Trockene Zutaten mischen, dann Wasser, Mandarinensaft und -schale zugeben und gut aufmixen. In der Eismaschine anfrieren, dann den Champagner zugeben und vollständig abfrieren.

ORANGE PARFAIT (COVER)

193 g	whole egg
270 g	sugar
128 g	orange juice concentrate
	Zest from 3 organic oranges
610 g	half-whipped cream

Beat the whole egg until frothy In the meantime, boil the sugar with a little water at 119 °C and add to the beaten egg in a thin stream. Beat until cold and then fold in the juice concentrate and the orange zest followed by the cream.

ORANGENPARFAIT (MANTEL)

193 g	Vollei
270 g	Zucker
128 g	Orangensaftkonzentrat
	Abrieb von 3 Bio-Orangen
610 g	halb geschlagene Sahne

Vollei schaumig schlagen. In der Zwischenzeit Zucker mit etwas Wasser auf 119 °C kochen und in dünnem Strahl in den Eischaum einlaufen lassen. Kalt schlagen, zunächst das Saftkonzentrat und die Orangenschale, dann die Sahne unterheben.

DECORATION

bubbles and sugar décor made from Isomalt
chocolate décor
fresh white currants
candied lavender
orange slices

DEKORATION

Blasen-und Zuckerdekor aus Isomalt
Schokoladendekor
frische weiße Johannisbeeren
kandierter Lavendel
Orangenchips

RED FRUIT JELLY

In Norddeutschland kommt man nicht umhin Rote Grütze zu essen. Ich mag sie wirklich sehr gerne, auch wenn sie nichts Aussergewöhnliches ist. Aber genau das reizt mich: Klassiker in neuem Licht erscheinen zu lassen.

As a child I often went to the north of Germany you don't come back from there without having tasted red fruit jelly. I really like it very much even though it is not something extra-special. But for me that is the challenge: to present classic dishes with a new twist.

WRAPPED-UP ICE-CREAM

FIORI DI PANNA
(HOT PRODUCTION METHOD)
(MAKES 1000 G)

183 g	sugar
24 g	dextrose
30 g	milk powder
30 g	stabiliser for ice-cream made with cream
610 g	milk, 3.5 %
122 g	cream, 35 %

Mix the dry ingredients, bring the milk to the boil, add the dry ingredients and pasteurise at 85 °C. Cool the mixture down to 60 °C, add the cream and then cool down to 4 °C. Allow to mature and then place into the ice-cream maker to freeze.

EINGEPACKTES EIS

FIORI DI PANNA
(WARME HERSTELLUNG)
(ERGIBT 1000 G)

183 g	Zucker
24 g	Dextrose
30 g	Milchpulver
30 g	Stabilisator für Sahnemilcheis
610 g	Milch, 3,5 %
122 g	Sahne, 35 %

Trockene Zutaten mischen, Milch aufkochen, dann trockene Zutaten zugeben und bei 85 °C pasteurisieren. Eismasse herunterkühlen und bei 60 °C Sahne zugeben, anschließend auf 4 °C abkühlen. Reifen lassen und in der Eismaschine abfrieren.

1

2

ROTE-GRÜTZE-MILCHEIS
(WARME HERSTELLUNG)
(ERGIBT 1000 G)

124 g	Zucker
60 g	Magermilchpulver
4 g	neutrales Eisbindemittel
22 g	Trockenglukose
1 g	Ceylonzimt
¹/₂	Vanilleschote (Mark)
	Abrieb ¹/₄ Bio-Zitrone
30 g	Invertzucker
311 g	Vollmilch
374 g	Fruchtpüree (Waldbeer oder Mischung nach Wahl)
4 g	Fruchtsäure
71 g	Sahne

Trockene Zutaten mischen, Milch aufkochen, trockene Zutaten zugeben und bei 85 °C pasteurisieren. Das Fruchtpüree und die Fruchtsäure zugeben, Mix herunterkühlen und dann bei 60 °C Sahne zugeben. Eismasse auf 4 °C abkühlen, reifen lassen und in der Eismaschine abfrieren.

Zum Einpacken das Eis mit einem Nockenportionierer vorportionieren und erneut anfrieren. Danach die aufgelöste Bitterkuvertüre in Form eines Netzes auf ein gefrorenes Rohr spritzen, das Netz dann sofort abnehmen und die Eisnocke darin einwickeln.

RED FRUIT JELLY ICE-CREAM
(HOT PRODUCTION METHOD)
(MAKES 1000 G)

124 g	sugar
60 g	skimmed milk powder
4 g	neutral ice-cream binding agent
22 g	dry glucose
1 g	Ceylon cinnamon
¹/₂	vanilla pod (pith)
	Zest from ¹/₄ organic lemon
30 g	invert sugar
311 g	whole milk
374 g	fruit puree (forest berries or any of your choice)
4 g	fruit acid
71 g	whipping cream

Mix the dry ingredients, bring the milk to the boil, add the dry ingredients and pasteurise at 85 °C. Add the fruit puree and fruit acid, cool the mixture down to 60 °C and then add the cream. Cool the mixture down to 4 °C, allow to mature and place into the ice-cream maker to freeze.

Use an egg-shaped scoop to scoop out ice-cream portions and freeze these again slightly. Dissolve the bitter couverture and spray it onto a frozen tube in the shape of a net, take off the net immediately and use it to wrap up the ice-cream portions.

Waffelmasse in ein vorgeheiztes Waffeleisen eindressieren

Ladle the batter into a preheated waffle iron

Getrocknete Kiwischeibe auflegen, dann Waffeleisen erneut schließen, so dass die Kiwischeibe anbacken kann

Add the dried kiwi fruit slice, close the waffle iron again so that the slice can merge with the waffle

3

Fast vollständig ausgebackene Waffel

The waffle before it is fully baked

Fertig ausgebackene Kiwiwaffel

Finished kiwi waffle

4

## RED FRUIT JELLY (ABOUT 20 SERVINGS)		## ROTE GRÜTZE (ETWA 20 PORTIONEN)

	RED FRUIT JELLY			ROTE GRÜTZE
500 g	white wine		500 g	Weißwein
250 g	puree of forest berries		250 g	Waldbeerpüree
300 g	sugar		300 g	Zucker
100 g	sago pearls		100 g	Sagoperlen
1	vanilla pod		1	Vanilleschote
2	cinnamon sticks		2	Zimtstangen
	Zest from 1 organic orange			Abrieb von 1 Bio-Orange
500 g	red currants		500 g	rote Johannisbeeren
200 g	cherries		200 g	Kirschen
250 g	blackberries		250	Brombeeren
400 g	raspberries		400 g	Himbeeren
100 g	bilberries		100 g	Waldheidelbeeren
20 g	aged rum		20 g	alten Rum

Soak the forest berry puree, sugar, sago pearls and spices in the wine, then bring to the boil, take out the spices and add the fruit. Bring the mixture to the boil and cool off by adding the rum. Store in a cool place.

Wein mit Waldbeerpüree, Zucker, Sago-perlen und Gewürzen quellen lassen, dann aufkochen, Gewürze entfernen und Früchte zugeben. Mischung kurz aufko-chen und mit Rum abschrecken. Gekühlt lagern.

TIP:
Instead of the sago one can also use arrow root starch, which results in a clear jelly.

TIPP:
Anstelle des Sago kann man auch Pfeil-wurzstärke verwenden, dadurch bleibt die Grütze klar.

KIWIWAFFEL
(ETWA 120 STÜCK)

100 g	Puderzucker
185 g	Mehl, Typ 405
2 g	Meersalz
1 g	Backpulver
¹/₂	Vanilleschote (Mark)
3 g	Ceylon Zimt
150 g	Wasser
175 g	Vollmilch
10 g	Vollei
50 g	flüssige Butter
1	Kiwischeibe pro Waffel

Alle trockenen Zutaten mischen, flüssige Zutaten nach und nach unterrühren. Dabei darauf achten, dass die Butter nur flüssig, nicht heiß ist, sonst reagiert das Backpulver zu früh. Teig vor der Verarbeitung für kurze Zeit stehen lassen.
Das Waffeleisen auf 220 °C vorheizen und mit Trennspray einfetten. Den Teig in das Waffeleisen geben, die Backzeit sollte etwa 1,5 Minuten betragen. Kurz vor dem Ende der Backzeit das Waffeleisen öffnen und eine getrocknete Kiwischeibe auflegen. Das Waffeleisen kurz schließen, damit sich die Waffel mit der Kiwischeibe verbinden kann. Trocken lagern.

KIWI WAFFLE
(ABOUT 120 PCS.)

100 g	icing sugar
185 g	flour, type 405
2 g	sea salt
1 g	baking powder
¹/₂	vanilla pud (pith)
3 g	Ceylon cinnamon
150 g	water
175 g	whole milk
10 g	whole egg
50 g	liquid butter (unsalted)
1	dried slice of kiwi fruit per waffle

Mix all dry ingredients, then add the liquid ingredients in small doses and stir well. Make sure that the butter is liquid but not hot, otherwise the baking powder will react too soon. Let the batter stand for a short while before making the waffles.
Preheat the waffle iron to 220 °C and apply a spray of separating fat. Add a portion of batter into the waffle iron and bake for about 1¹/₂ minutes. Shortly before the end of the baking time, open the waffle iron and place a dried slice of kiwi fruit onto the waffle. Close the waffle iron again so that the kiwi fruit slice can become part of the waffle. Store in a dry place.

DEKORATION

halb geschlagene Sahne
(bei Bedarf mit Aromasirup
versetzen)

DECORATION

half-whipped cream
(laced with an aroma syrup
if desired)

AUSTRALIAN CHRISTMAS-WAVE

AUSTRALIAN CHRISTMAS WAVE

WER WEIHNACHTEN MAL BEI TROPISCHEN TEMPERATUREN ERLEBT HAT, KOMMT UNWEIGERLICH ZUM SCHLUSS, DASS GEWÜRZE NICHT NUR ZUR KLASSISCHEN DEUTSCHEN WEIHNACHT PASSEN. MAN KANN DAMIT WÄHREND DES GANZEN JAHRES HERRLICHE DESSERTS ZAUBERN. ES IST, WIE IMMER, EINE FRAGE DER OFFENHEIT GEGENÜBER NEUEM UND UNGEWOHNTEM.

ANYBODY WHO HAS EXPERIENCED CHRISTMAS AT TROPICAL TEMPERATURES WILL COME TO THE CONCLUSION THAT ONE CAN USE OUR TRADITIONAL CHRISTMAS SPICES ALSO ON OTHER OCCASIONS. THEY CAN BE USED TO CREATE WONDERFUL DESSERTS THROUGHOUT THE YEAR. AS ALWAYS, IT IS A QUESTION OF HOW OPEN WE ARE TO SOMETHING NEW AND UNUSUAL.

4 EISTORTEN Ø 18 CM

KOKOSDAQUOISE

225 g	Eiweiß
5 g	Trockeneiweiß
75 g	Zucker
190 g	Kokosraspeln
185 g	Zucker, extrafein
25 g	Mehl

Eiweiß mit Trockeneiweiß und 75 g Zucker zu einem festen Schnee schlagen. Die restlichen Zutaten anschließend mischen und unter den Schnee heben. Masse mit einem Spritzbeutel und einer 8er-Lochtülle in Form der Eisbombe auf eine Backmatte aufdressieren und bei 200 °C anbacken. Bei 170 °C etwa 30 Minuten ausbacken.

4 ICE-CREAM CAKES Ø 18 CM

COCONUT DACQUOISE

225 g	egg white
5 g	dried egg white
75 g	sugar
190 g	grated coconut
185 g	sugar, extra fine
25 g	flour

Beat the egg white with the dried egg white and 75 g sugar until firm. Mix the other ingredients together and fold into the beaten egg. Use a piping bag with round nozzle size 8 to pipe the mixture onto a baking mat in the shape of the ice-cream bomb and start baking at 200 °C. Continue to bake at 170 °C for about 30 minutes.

SPICY PINEAPPLE SORBET
(COLD PRODUCTION METHOD)
(INSIDE LAYER)

17 g	dry glucose
36 g	sugar
91 g	water
2 g	red pepper berries, crushed
1 g	chilli strings
68 g	invert sugar
186 g	pineapple puree

Mix the dry ingredients and stir in invert sugar and pineapple puree. Use a refractometer to adjust the mixture to 31 °Brix. Place into the ice-cream maker to freeze.

SPICY ANANASSORBET
(KALTE HERSTELLUNG)
(EINLAGE)

17 g	Trockenglukose
36 g	Zucker
91 g	Wasser
2 g	rosa Pfefferbeeren, gemörsert
1 g	Chilifäden
68 g	Invertzucker
186 g	Ananaspüree

Die trockenen Zutaten mischen, Invertzucker und Ananaspüree untermixen. Die Masse mit dem Refraktometer auf 31 °Brix einstellen. In der Eismaschine abfrieren.

COCONUT-RUM-RAISIN ICE-CREAM
(HOT PRODUCTION METHOD)
(INSIDE LAYER)

15 g	skimmed milk powder
38 g	dry glucose
53 g	sugar
3 g	neutral ice-cream binding agent (in accordance with manufacturer's instructions)
190 g	coconut milk
69 g	whipping cream
10 g	aged rum
15 g	rum raisins

Mix the dry ingredients with the coconut milk and pasteurise at 85 °C, cool down to 65 °C and add the cream. Allow to mature at 4 °C and freeze in the ice-cream maker. As soon as the freezing process is nearly complete, mix the rum with the raisins and add to the ice-cream.

KOKOS-RUM-ROSINEN-EIS
(WARME HERSTELLUNG)
(EINLAGE)

15 g	Magermilchpulver
38 g	Trockenglukose
53 g	Zucker
3 g	neutrales Eisbindemittel (nach Herstellerangaben)
190 g	Kokosmilch
69 g	Sahne
10 g	alter Rum
15 g	Rumrosinen

Trockene Zutaten mit der Kokosmilch mischen und bei 85 °C pasteurisieren, dann auf 65 °C herunterkühlen und die Sahne zugeben. Bei 4 °C reifen lassen und in der Eismaschine gefrieren. Sobald der Gefriervorgang fast abgeschlossen ist, Rum mit den Rosinen mischen und zugeben.

MARACUJAEIS-PARFAIT (MANTEL)

140 g	Eiweiß
210 g	Zucker
150 g	Maracujapüree
475 g	halb geschlagene Sahne

Das Eiweiß zu Schnee schlagen, in der Zwischenzeit den Zucker mit etwas Wasser auf 119 °C kochen und im dünnen Strahl in den Schnee einlaufen lassen. Kalt schlagen, zuerst das Püree unterheben, später die Sahne. Die Masse in die, mit einem Silikonstempel ausgelegte, vorgefrorene Form füllen, die beiden Einlagen abwechselnd in Schichten aufdressieren und mit dem Kokosboden abdeckeln. Dann durchfrieren. Anschließend vorsichtig ausformen.

PASSION FRUIT ICE-CREAM PARFAIT (COVER)

140 g	egg white
210 g	sugar
150 g	passion fruit puree
475 g	half-whipped cream

Beat the egg white until stiff, meanwhile boil the sugar with a little water at 119 °C and add to the beaten egg white in a thin stream. Beat cold, then fold in the puree followed later by the cream. Put the mixture into the pre-frozen form into which you have placed a silicone stamp, pipe the two ice-cream sorts in layers one on top of the other and cover with the coconut base. Freeze thoroughly. Carefully remove from the form.

1

2

3

DEKORATION

Sprühkuvertüre in gelb, orange und braun
Schokoladendekor
karamellisierte Ananaschips
Kokoschips
rosa Pfefferbeeren
frische Maracuja

DECORATION

spray couverture in yellow, orange and brown
chocolate decor
caramelised pineapple crisps
coconut crisps
red pepper berries
fresh passion fruit

Relieffolie mit weißer Kakaobutter beträufeln

Pour a little white cocoa butter onto the relief foil

4

Mit einer kleinen Winkelpalette verteilen, bis das Muster der Folie wieder sichtbar wird

Spread everything with a small angled spatula until the pattern in the foil is visible again

---

Gelbe Kakaobutter darüber sprenkeln

Spread a little yellow cocoa butter over it

5

Relieffolie mit gewünschtem Muster

Relief foil with the pattern of your choice

Rote Pigmentfarbe aufstreuen

Follow on with a sprinkling of some red food colouring

6

Temperierte Bitterkuvertüre aufbringen und mit einer Winkelpalette gleichmäßig verteilen

Apply the tempered bitter couverture and spread evenly with an angled spatula

---

7

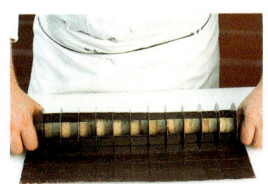

Mit der Schneidewalze in gleichmäßige Quadrate schneiden

Use a cutting wheel to cut into even squares

8

Fertige Schokoladenplättchen abformen

Take the completed chocolate wafers out

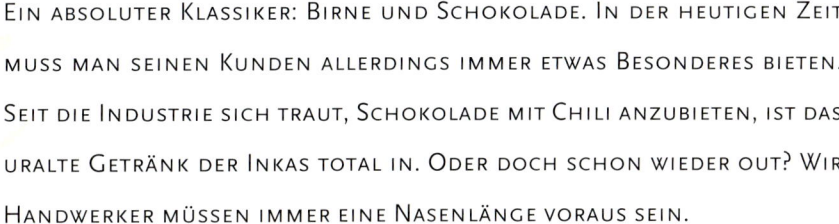

BEAUTIFUL HELENA

EIN ABSOLUTER KLASSIKER: BIRNE UND SCHOKOLADE. IN DER HEUTIGEN ZEIT MUSS MAN SEINEN KUNDEN ALLERDINGS IMMER ETWAS BESONDERES BIETEN. SEIT DIE INDUSTRIE SICH TRAUT, SCHOKOLADE MIT CHILI ANZUBIETEN, IST DAS URALTE GETRÄNK DER INKAS TOTAL IN. ODER DOCH SCHON WIEDER OUT? WIR HANDWERKER MÜSSEN IMMER EINE NASENLÄNGE VORAUS SEIN.

AN ABSOLUTE CLASSIC: PEAR AND CHOCOLATE. BUT THESE DAYS YOU ALWAYS HAVE TO OFFER YOUR CUSTOMERS SOMETHING SPECIAL. SINCE INDUSTRIAL PRODUCERS HAVE DARED TO OFFER CHOCOLATE WITH CHILLI, THIS ANCIENT DRINK OF THE INCAS HAS BECOME VERY POPULAR. OR IS IT ALREADY ON ITS WAY OUT? WE TRADESMEN ALWAYS HAVE TO BE AHEAD OF THE GAME.

INGREDIENTS FOR 12 PERSONS	ZUTATEN FÜR 12 PERSONEN
PEAR SESAME OIL SORBET (COLD PRODUCTION METHOD) (MAKES 1000 G)	**BIRNEN-SESAMÖL-SORBET (KALTE HERSTELLUNG) (ERGIBT 1000 G)**

50 g	dry glucose	50 g	Trockenglukose
115 g	sugar	115 g	Zucker
210 g	water	210 g	Wasser
20 g	invert sugar	20 g	Invertzucker
600 g	pear puree	600 g	Birnenpüree
5 g	lime juice	5 g	Limettensaft
10 g	roasted sesame oil	10 g	geröstetes Sesamöl
5 g	pear brandy	5 g	Birnenbrand

Mix the dry ingredients. Add the other ingredients, use a refractometer to adjust to 32 °Brix and then freeze in the ice-cream maker.

Trockene Zutaten mischen. Die restlichen Zutaten zugeben und mit dem Refraktometer auf 32 °Brix einstellen und in der Eismaschine abfrieren.

SCHOKOLADEN-CHILI-EIS (WARME HERSTELLUNG) (ERGIBT 1000 G)

137 g	Zucker
18 g	Dextrose
13 g	Milchpulver
2 g	neutrales Eisbindemittel
½	Vanilleschote (Mark und Schote)
14	Tropfen Tabasco
11 g	Invertzucker
55 g	Eigelb
457 g	Milch
183 g	Kuvertüre, 70 %
110 g	Sahne

Trockene Zutaten mischen, dann die Gewürze, Invertzucker und Eigelb zugeben. Die Milch zum Kochen bringen, die hergestellte Mischung zugeben, Vanilleschote entnehmen und bei 85 °C pasteurisieren. Kuvertüre untermixen, auf 60 °C herunterkühlen und Sahne zugeben. Eismasse auf 4 °C herunterkühlen und reifen lassen, anschließend in der Eismaschine abfrieren.

CHOCOLATE CHILLI ICE-CREAM (HOT PRODUCTION METHOD) (MAKES 1000 G)

137 g	sugar
18 g	dextrose
13 g	milk powder
2 g	neutral ice-cream binding agent
½	vanilla pod (pith and pod)
14	drops Tabasco
11 g	invert sugar
55 g	egg yolk
457 g	milk
183 g	couverture, 70 %
110 g	whipping cream

Mix the dry ingredients, add the spices, egg yolk and invert sugar. Bring the milk to the boil, add the above mixture, take out the vanilla pod and pasteurise at 85 °C. Mix in the couverture, cool down to 60 °C and add the cream. Cool the mixture down to 4 °C and leave to mature, then freeze in the ice-cream maker.

1

2

3

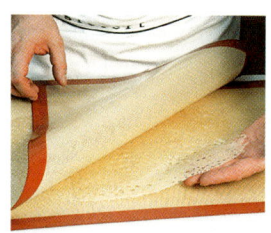

4

BIRNEN

50 g	Zucker
100 g	Weißwein
10 g	Zitronensaft
2 g	Zimtblüten, fein gemahlen
500 g	Birnen, geschält, entkernt und gewürfelt

Den Zucker hell karamellisieren und mit Weißwein ablöschen. Zitronensaft und Zimtblüten zugeben, Birnen kurz unterschwenken und gekühlt lagern.

PEARS

50 g	sugar
100 g	white wine
10 g	lemon juice
2 g	cinnamon flowers, finely ground
500 g	peeled, cored and diced pears

Caramelise the sugar to a light colour and pour the white wine over it. Add the lemon juice and cinnamon flowers followed by the pears, turn over briefly and store in a cool place.

5

6

Florentinermasse im Kutter pulverisieren

Pulverise the Florentine mixture in a cutter

CHOCOLATE CHILLI VERMICELLI

50 g	sugar
50 g	unsalted butter
70 g	flour
20 g	cocoa powder
10 g	cocoa nibs
1 g	Pimentón de Espelette
	some lemon zest

SCHOKOLADEN-CHILI-STREUSEL

50 g	Zucker
50 g	Butter
70 g	Mehl
20 g	Kakaopulver
10 g	Kakaonibs
1 g	Pimentón de Espelette
	etwas Zitronenschalenabrieb

Gleichmäßig auf einer Silikon-Backmatte verteilen

Spread the mixture evenly on a silicone baking mat

Mix all ingredients at room temperature and bake at 160 °C in a preheated oven until the vermicelli are nice and crunchy.

Zutaten bei Zimmertemperatur mischen und bei 160 °C im vorgeheizten Backofen zu knusprigen Streuseln vorbacken.

Mit einer zweiten Backmatte belegen

Place a second baking sheet on top

FLORENTINE BUBBLE SUGAR

200 g	sugar
100 g	water
20 g	glucose syrup
20 g	unsalted butter

FLORENTINER BLASENZUCKER

200 g	Zucker
100 g	Wasser
20 g	Glukosesirup
20 g	Butter

Backmatte direkt nach dem Backen abziehen, um die Blasen in die Masse zu bringen

Immediately after baking, pull the top baking sheet off so that bubbles form in the mixture

Boil the sugar and glucose syrup in the water up to 155 °C, add the butter and turn gently, then pour the mixture onto a silicone baking mat. Leave to cool before grinding the sugar mixture to a fine powder in a cutter; store in a dry place. When you want to make the decoration, spread the powder on a baking mat evenly and thinly and place a second baking mat on top. Put into the oven at 180 °C until the sugar has melted, pull off the second baking mat and make the shapes from the sugar while it is still warm. Store in a dry place.

Zucker, Wasser und Glukosesirup auf 155 °C kochen, Butter unterschwenken und auf eine Silikon-Backmatte gießen. Nach Erkalten im Kutter zu einem feinen Pulver mahlen und trocken lagern. Bei Bedarf das Pulver auf eine Backmatte geben, dünn ausstreichen mit einer zweiten Backmatte belegen. Im Ofen bei 180 °C verschmelzen, zweite Backmatte direkt abziehen und noch warm in Form bringen. Trocken lagern.

Zuckermasse zurechtschneiden

Cut the sugar mixture into the desired shape

Zum Dekor formen

Make the shape wanted for the decor

DECORATION

chilli strings

DEKORATION

Chilifäden

SCHWARZWALDMÄDCHEN

BLACK FOREST GIRL

Was wäre Deutschland ohne seine Klassiker? Aber auch Klassiker brauchen ab und zu mal einen neuen Anstrich. Oder in den Worten meines Freundes Kolja Kleeberg: „Ohne Evolution keine Revolution".

What would Germany be without its classics? But even classics can do with a facelift from time to time. Or in the words of my friend Kolja Kleeberg: "without evolution no revolution".

ZUTATEN FÜR 12 PERSONEN

KIRSCHGELEE

2,5 g	Agar-Agar
400 g	Kirschsaft
100 g	Orangensaft
1	Vanilleschote (Mark)
100 g	Zucker

Alle Zutaten mischen und kurz aufkochen. Leicht abgekühlt in Gläser füllen.

INGREDIENTS FOR 12 PERSONS

CHERRY JELLY

2.5 g	agar agar
400 g	cherry juice
100 g	orange juice
1	vanilla pod (pith)
100 g	sugar

Mix all ingredients and boil up briefly. Fill into glasses once the mixture has cooled a little.

SCHOKOLADENSAHNE

140 g	*Bitterkuvertüre, 70 %*
125 g	*Sahne*
40 g	*Vollmilch*
50 g	*Vollei, pasteurisiert*

Kuvertüre zuerst auflösen, dann die restlichen Zutaten zugeben und erwärmen. Masse mit dem Mixstab homogenisieren und in einen Espuma-Schäumer geben, dann 2 Gaspatronen aufschrauben. Bis zur Verwendung mit der Spitze nach unten kaltstellen und bei Bedarf verwenden.

CHOCOLATE CREAM

140 g	*bitter couverture, 70 %*
125 g	*whipping cream*
40 g	*whole milk*
50 g	*whole egg, pasteurised*

First dissolve the couverture, then add the other ingredients and warm up. Use a hand-held blender to homogenise the mixture, put into an Espuma siphon and fit 2 gas cartridges. Store in the refrigerator with the point downwards, use when required.

SAUERKIRSCHKOMPOTT

6	*Blatt Gelatine*
700 g	*Sauerkirschen, tiefgekühlt und aufgetaut*
100 g	*Honig*
30 g	*Amaretto*

Gelatine in kaltem Wasser einweichen und auspressen. Kirschsaft absieben, mit Honig und Amaretto mischen und über Nacht ziehen lassen. Kirschsaft erwärmen, Gelatine darin auflösen, anschließend Kirschen zugeben. Kompott erkalten lassen.

MORELLO CHERRY SAUCE

6	*sheets of gelatine*
700 g	*frozen morello cherries, defrosted*
100 g	*honey*
30 g	*Amaretto*

Soak the gelatine in cold water and squeeze out. Separate the cherries from the juice, mix the honey and Amaretto with the juice and leave to steep overnight. Heat up the cherry juice, dissolve the gelatine in it and then add the cherries. Leave the sauce to cool down.

KIRSCHWASSERSAHNE

500 g	*Sahne*
3 g	*Xanthan*
100 g	*Läuterzucker*
50 g	*Kirschwasser*

Zutaten durchmixen und in eine Espuma-Flasche geben. 2 Gaspatronen aufschrauben und gekühlt verwenden.

KIRSCH CREAM

500 g	*whipping cream*
3 g	*xanthan gum*
100 g	*sugar syrup*
50 g	*kirsch*

Blend all ingredients together and put into an Espuma bottle. Fit 2 gas cartridges and use chilled.

KIRSCH GRANITÉ

100 g	sugar
350 g	water
50 g	kirsch

Bring the sugar and water to the boil, leave to cool and stir in the kirsch. Pour the liquid into small silicone moulds, freeze and then grate into a granité when needed.

KIRSCHWASSERGRANITÉ

100 g	Zucker
350 g	Wasser
50 g	Kirschwasser

Zucker und Wasser aufkochen, abkühlen lassen und Kirschwasser unterrühren. Sud in kleine Silikonförmchen füllen, gefrieren und bei Bedarf mit einer Reibe zu Granité reiben.

MARBLED CHOCOLATE VANILLA ICE-CREAM

CLASSIC VANILLA ICE-CREAM (HOT PRODUCTION METHOD) (MAKES 1000 G)

188 g	sugar
25 g	dextrose
19 g	milk powder
2.5 g	neutral ice-cream binding agent
1	vanilla pod
72 g	egg yolk
627 g	milk
63 g	whipping cream

Mix the dry ingredients and add the egg yolk. Bring the milk to the boil, add the mixed ingredients, take out the vanilla pod and pasteurise at 85 °C. Cool the mixture down to 60 °C and add the cream. Cool down further to 4 °C and leave to mature before freezing in the ice-cream maker.

MARMORIERTES SCHOKOLADEN-VANILLEEIS

KLASSISCHES VANILLEEIS (WARME HERSTELLUNG) (ERGIBT 1000 G)

188 g	Zucker
25 g	Dextrose
19 g	Milchpulver
2,5 g	neutrales Eisbindemittel
1	Vanilleschoten
72 g	Eigelb
627 g	Milch
63 g	Sahne

Trockene Zutaten mischen, dann Eigelb zugeben. Milch zum Kochen bringen, den Zutatenmix zugeben, die Schote heraus-nehmen und bei 85 °C pasteurisieren. Eis-masse auf 60 °C herunterkühlen, dann Sahne zugeben. Bis auf 4 °C weiter abküh-len und reifen lassen, schließlich in der Eismaschine abfrieren.

SCHOKOLADENEIS (WARME HERSTELLUNG) (ERGIBT 1000 G)

139 g	Zucker
19 g	Dextrose
14 g	Milchpulver
1,9 g	neutrales Eisbindemittel
1	Vanilleschote
12 g	Invertzucker
56 g	Eigelb
463 g	Milch
185 g	Kuvertüre, 70 %
111 g	Sahne

Trockene Zutaten mischen, dann Eigelb und Invertzucker zugeben. Die Milch zum Kochen bringen, anschließend Zutaten-mix zugeben, Schote entfernen und bei 85 °C pasteurisieren. Kuvertüre untermixen, auf 60 °C herunterkühlen und Sahne zugeben. Bis auf 4 °C weiter abkühlen und reifen lassen, schließlich in der Eismaschine abfrieren.

Beide Eismassen abwechselnd im Portionierer marmorieren.

CHOCOLATE ICE-CREAM (HOT PRODUCTION METHOD) (MAKES 1000 G)

139 g	sugar
19 g	dextrose
14 g	milk powder
1.9 g	neutral ice-cream binding agent
1	vanilla pod
12 g	invert sugar
56 g	egg yolk
463 g	milk
185 g	couverture, 70 %
111 g	whipping cream

Mix the dry ingredients, add egg yolk and invert sugar. Bring the milk to the boil, add the mixed ingredients, take out the vanilla pod and pasteurise at 85 °C. Mix in the couverture, cool down to 60 °C and add the cream. Cool down further to 4 °C and leave to mature before freezing in the ice-cream maker.

Marble the two ice-cream mixtures in a scoop.

1

2

3

SCHOKOLADENSTREUSEL

50 g	Zucker
50 g	Butter
70 g	Mehl
20 g	Kakaopulver
10 g	Kakaonibs
3 g	Zitronenabrieb

Zutaten bei Zimmertemperatur mischen und bei 160 °C im vorgeheizten Backofen zu knusprigen Streuseln vorbacken.

CHOCOLATE VERMICELLI

50 g	sugar
50 g	unsalted butter
70 g	flour
20 g	cocoa powder
10 g	cocoa nibs
3 g	lemon zest

Mix all ingredients at room temperature and bake at 160 °C in a preheated oven until the vermicelli are nice and crunchy.

Kakaomasse in die Baisermasse einlaufen lassen

Let the cocoa paste run into the meringue mixture

4

Karamellisierte Kakaonibs aufstreuen

Apply a sprinkling of caramelised cocoa nibs

Beide Massen miteinander vermischen

Blend the two mixtures

5

Fertig getrocknete Dekorationen

Finished dried decoration

Schokoladenbaisermasse bogenförmig mit Hilfe eines Spritzbeutels und einer Lochtülle auf eine Teflon-Backmatte dressieren

Use a piping bag with a round nozzle to pipe the chocolate meringue mixture onto a Teflon baking mat in the shape of bows

CHOCOLATE MERINGUE DECORATION WITH COCOA NIBS

150 g	egg white
300 g	sugar
1 g	salt
25 g	cocoa paste
50 g	caramelised cocoa nibs

Beat the egg white with 100 g sugar and salt gradually until firm. In the meantime, boil 200 g sugar with a little water at 119 °C and add to the beaten egg in a thin stream. Keep going slowly with the mixture until it has cooled down to 20 °C, then fold in the cocoa paste. Use a piping bag with a round nozzle size 4 to pipe the meringue mixture onto Teflon baking mats in the shape of bows; add a sprinkling of cocoa nibs. Pre-bake in the oven at 110 °C for about 15 minutes, then dry at 50 °C in the drying cabinet for at least 12 hours.

SCHOKOLADENBAISER-DEKORATION MIT KAKAONIBS

150 g	Eiweiß
300 g	Zucker
1 g	Salz
25 g	Kakaomasse
50 g	karamellisierte Kakaonibs

Eiweiß mit 100 g Zucker und Salz nach und nach zu einem stabilen Schnee schlagen. In der Zwischenzeit 200 g Zucker mit etwas Wasser auf 119 °C kochen und in einem feinen Strahl in den Eischnee laufen lassen. Masse langsam weiterlaufen lassen, bis sie 20 °C erreicht hat, dann die Kakaomasse flüssig unterziehen. Baisermasse mit Hilfe des Spritzbeutels und einer 4er-Lochtülle in Bögen auf Teflon-Backmatten dressieren und dann mit den Kakaonibs bestreuen. Im Ofen bei 110 °C etwa 15 Minuten anbacken, dann bei 50 °C im Trockenschrank mindestens 12 Stunden austrocknen.

CHICAGO CLASSIC

MEINE FREUNDE IN DER CHICAGO MOLDSCHOOL HABEN EINFACH DIE TOLLSTEN SILIKONFORMEN. ICH WUSSTE SOFORT, ALS ICH DAS ALTE TAPETENMUSTER UND DIE DIAMANTENFORM SAH, DASS MAN ETWAS WUNDERBARES DARAUS MACHEN KANN.

MY FRIENDS IN THE CHICAGO MOLDSCHOOL HAVE THE MOST FANTASTIC SILICONE MOULDS. WHEN I SAW THE OLD WALLPAPER PATTERN AND THE DIAMOND SHAPE, I KNEW IMMEDIATELY THAT I COULD DO SOMETHING FABULOUS WITH THAT.

4 ICE-CREAM CAKES Ø 20 CM	4 EISTORTEN Ø 20 CM
VIOLET SPONGE (BASE)	**VEILCHENBISKUIT (BODEN)**

120 g	egg yolk	120 g	Eigelb
135 g	sugar	135 g	Zucker
230 g	egg white	230 g	Eiweiß
90 g	flour	90 g	Mehl
90 g	unsalted butter	90 g	Butter
6	drops of violet oil (modify quantity depending on strength)	6	Tropfen Veilchenöl (je nach Qualität variieren)
70 g	candied violets	70 g	kandierte Veilchen

Beat the egg yolk with 60 g sugar and separately the egg white with 75 g sugar until firm, fold the egg yolk mixture and the flour in alternating steps into the egg white, melt the butter, add a little mixture to the butter and then fold the butter and the violet oil into the mixture. Use a piping bag with a round nozzle size 8 to pipe the mixture onto baking paper in the required shape and sprinkle with the chopped up candied violets. Bake at 200 °C for about 12 minutes.

Eigelb mit 60 g Zucker und Eiweiß mit 75 g Zucker getrennt stabil aufschlagen, dann Eigelbmasse abwechselnd mit dem Mehl unter das Eiweiß ziehen, zerlassene Butter etwas angleichen und mit dem Veilchenöl unterziehen. Mit Hilfe eines Dressierbeutels und einer 8er-Lochtülle in der gewünschten Form auf Backpapier aufdressieren, dann gehackte, kandierte Veilchen aufstreuen. Bei 200 °C etwa 12 Minuten backen.

ROTWEIN-CASSIS-EIS
(KALTE HERSTELLUNG)
(EINLAGE)

200 g	Zucker
40 g	Trockenglukose
20 g	Magermilchpulver
1 g	Vanillemark
36 g	neutrales Eisbindemittel
360 g	Cassispüree
460 g	Rotwein
352 g	Milch
120 g	Sahne

Trockene Zutaten mischen, Cassispüree und die Hälfte des Rotweins zugeben, dann Milch und Sahne untermixen. Masse in der Eismaschine anfrieren, sobald die Masse zu gefrieren beginnt, den Rest des Rotweins zugeben. Vollständig gefroren in rechteckige Formen einfüllen, erneut frieren und ausformen.

RED WINE CASSIS ICE-CREAM
(COLD PRODUCTION METHOD)
(INSIDE LAYER)

200 g	sugar
40 g	dry glucose
20 g	skimmed milk powder
1 g	vanilla pith
36 g	neutral ice-cream binding agent
360 g	cassis puree
460 g	red wine
352 g	milk
120 g	whipping cream

Mix the dry ingredients, add the cassis puree and half of the red wine, then mix in the milk and cream. Slightly freeze the mixture in the ice-cream maker; when it starts to freeze, add the remaining red wine. When fully frozen, put the mixture into rectangular moulds, freeze again and then take out of the mould.

TRANSPARENTE ROTWEINGLASUR
(ÜBERZUG)

12 g	Pektin
450 g	Zucker
300 g	Rotwein
200 g	Trockenglukose

Pektin mit 50 g Zucker mischen, beides mit Rotwein aufkochen, 400 g Zucker zugeben und dann erneut aufkochen. Anschließend Trockenglukose zugeben und wieder aufkochen. Absetzen lassen und abschäumen. Die Überzugstemperatur sollte bei 25 °C liegen.

TRANSPARENT RED WINE GLAZE
(COATING)

12 g	pectin
450 g	sugar
300 g	red wine
200 g	dry glucose

Mix the pectin with 50 g sugar and bring to the boil with the red wine, add 400 g sugar and bring back to the boil. Add the dry glucose and again bring to the boil. Allow to settle and remove the froth. Use the glaze when its temperature is about 25 °C.

Wild berry parfait (cover)

360 g	whole egg
504 g	sugar
480 g	puree of wild berries
	Zest from 2 organic lemons
1140 g	half-whipped cream

Beat the whole egg until frothy. In the meantime, boil the sugar with a little water at 119 °C and add to the beaten egg in a thin stream. Beat cold and then fold in the puree with the lemon zest followed by the cream. Place a rectangular frame onto a silicone decor mat, fill with the parfait, add the ice-cream and cover with the sponge base. Allow to freeze thoroughly and then remove the silicone decor mat with a sharp tug. Carefully remove the frame.

Waldbeer-Parfait (Mantel)

360 g	Vollei
504 g	Zucker
480 g	Waldbeerpüree
	Abrieb von 2 Bio-Zitronen
1140 g	halb geschlagene Sahne

Das Vollei schaumig schlagen. In der Zwischenzeit den Zucker mit etwas Wasser auf 119 °C kochen und in dünnem Strahl in den Eischaum einlaufen lassen. Kalt schlagen, zunächst Püree und Zitronenschale, dann Sahne unterheben. Einen rechteckigen Rahmen auf eine Silikon-Dekormatte legen, das Parfait einfüllen, dann das Eis einlegen und mit Biskuit abdeckeln. Durchfrieren lassen und die Silikon-Dekormatte mit einem Ruck abziehen. Den Rahmen vorsichtig ausformen.

Decoration

fan-shaped chocolate decoration
chocolate arc and diamonds
in metallic paint
fresh grapes
candied violets

Dekoration

fächerförmiges Schokoladendekor
metallicfarbene Schokoladen-
bogen und -diamanten
frische Trauben
kandierte Veilchen

CHINESE DELIGHT

CHINESE DELIGHT

DIE IDEE ZU DIESEM AUSSERGEWÖHNLICHEN DESSERT ENTSTAND EIGENTLICH NUR DURCH DIESEN WUNDERSCHÖNEN TELLER. VON JEDER MEINER REISEN BRINGE ICH AUSGEFALLENES GESCHIRR ODER ANDERE UTENSILIEN MIT. MITTLERWEILE HABEN DER FOTOGRAF MATTHIAS HOFFMANN UND ICH FAST SCHON EINEN WETTBEWERB UNTEREINANDER, WER WOHL DIE SCHÖNSTEN SACHEN ENTDECKT.

THE IDEA FOR THIS UNUSUAL DESSERT WAS PROMPTED REALLY BY THIS BEAUTIFUL PLATE. FROM EACH OF MY JOURNEYS I BRING BACK SOME UNUSUAL CROCKERY OR OTHER UTENSILS. BY NOW THE PHOTOGRAPHER, MATTHIAS HOFFMANN, AND I HAVE A FRIENDLY COMPETITION BETWEEN US WHO DISCOVERS THE MOST BEAUTIFUL ITEMS.

ZUTATEN FÜR 10 PERSONEN	INGREDIENTS FOR 10 PERSONS
AGAR-AGAR-SPAGHETTI	**AGAR AGAR SPAGHETTI**

2,5 g	Agar-Agar	2.5 g	agar agar
500 g	Wasser	500 g	water
50 g	Zucker	50 g	sugar
1	Vanilleschote (Mark)	1	vanilla pod (pith)

Agar-Agar mit dem Wasser mischen, kurz aufkochen, dann die restlichen Zutaten zugeben und nochmals kurz aufkochen. Die Masse durch ein feines Sieb gießen, in einem passenden Gefäß dünn gelieren lassen, anschließend feine Spaghetti zuschneiden und gekühlt lagern.

Mix the agar agar with the water, bring to the boil, add the other ingredients and boil again briefly. Pour the mixture through a fine sieve into a suitable container, allow to gel thinly, then cut fine spaghetti and store in a cool place.

ERDBEER-PAPRIKASOSSE

50 g	Zucker
200 g	Erdbeerpüree
150 g	gelbe Paprika, geschält und gewürfelt

Zucker zu einem hellen Karamell schmelzen und mit dem Püree ablöschen. Paprika zugeben, kurz aufkochen und nach dem Abkühlen über die Spaghetti gießen.

STRAWBERRY PEPPER SAUCE

50 g	sugar
200 g	strawberry puree
150 g	yellow pepper, peeled and diced

Melt sugar into a light caramel and pour the puree over it. Add the pepper, bring to the boil and pour over the spaghetti once it has cooled down.

1

2

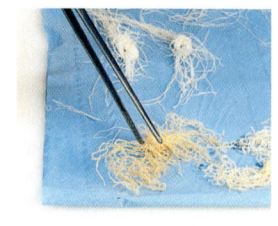

3

ERDBEER-RHABARBERSORBET (KALTE HERSTELLUNG) (ERGIBT 1000 G)

353 g	Rhabarber, geschält und in Stücke geschnitten
41 g	Trockenglukose
165 g	Zucker
3 g	Eisbindemittel (Menge kann je nach Hersteller variieren)
	Abrieb von ¹/₂ Orange
210 g	Wasser
235 g	Erdbeerpüree

Rhabarber mit Zucker, Trockenglukose, Bindemittel, Orangenschale und Wasser mischen, aufkochen und pürieren. Masse rasch herunterkühlen, das Erdbeerpüree zugeben, aufmixen und im Refraktometer auf 26 °Brix einstellen.

STRAWBERRY RHUBARB SORBET (COLD PRODUCTION METHOD) (MAKES 1000 G)

353 g	rhubarb, peeled and diced
41 g	dry glucose
165 g	sugar
3 g	ice-cream binding agent (quantity can vary for different manufacturers)
	Zest from ¹/₂ orange
210 g	water
235 g	strawberry puree

Mix the rhubarb with the sugar, dry glucose, binding agent, orange zest and water, bring to the boil and make into a puree. Cool the mixture rapidly, add and mix in the strawberry puree, adjust to 26 °Brix in a refractometer.

Kleine Knoten aus türkischem Spaghetti-Teig herstellen

Make small knots from the Turkish spaghetti pastry

Teigknoten in heißem Frittieröl frittieren und mit einem Sieb herausnehmen

Deep-fry the pastry knots in hot oil and remove with a sieve

Auf einem Küchenpapier abtropfen lassen

Allow to drain off on a paper towel

TURKISH SPAGHETTI

200 g	Turkish spaghetti pastry (finished product)
500 g	deep-frying oil
50 g	vanilla icing sugar

Use the spaghetti pastry to form small knots, deep-fry in the oil at 160 °C, allow to drain off on a paper towel and apply a light dusting of vanilla icing sugar.

TÜRKISCHE SPAGHETTI

200 g	türkischer Spaghetti-Teig (Fertigprodukt)
500 g	Frittieröl
50 g	Vanillepuderzucker

Aus dem fertigen Spaghetti-Teig kleine Knoten herstellen, im 160 °C heißen Frittieröl frittieren und auf einem Küchenpapier abtropfen lassen, dann mit Vanillepuderzucker leicht abpudern.

MACADAMIA VERMICELLI

15 g	macadamia nuts, ground and roasted
30 g	sugar
40 g	unsalted butter
75 g	flour
1 g	sea salt
2 g	lemon zest

Add the macadamia nuts to the other ingredients and knead into a crumby pastry; spread onto a silicone baking mat. Bake dry at 150 °C for about 15 minutes.

MACADAMIASTREUSEL

15 g	Macadamianüsse, gerieben und geröstet
30 g	Zucker
40 g	Butter
75 g	Mehl
1 g	Meersalz
2 g	Zitronenschalenabrieb

Die Macadamianüsse mit den restlichen Zutaten zu einem bröseligen Teig verkneten und auf eine Silikon-Backmatte streuen. Bei 150 °C etwa 15 Minuten trocken ausbacken.

DAS GOLDENE DREIECK

THE GOLDEN TRIANGLE

ASIEN UND DIE DORTIGE ESSKULTUR WERDEN BEI UNS IN EUROPA IMMER BELIEBTER. WIR HABEN VIELE WUNDERBARE ZUTATEN KENNENGELERNT. BEI DIESER KREATION ERGÄNZEN SICH ASIENS LEMONGRAS UND LITSCHI AUF DAS BESTE MIT JOGHURT UND ERDBEEREN AUS EUROPA.

ASIA AND THE ASIAN CUISINE ARE BECOMING MORE AND MORE POPULAR IN EUROPE. WE HAVE LEARNED ABOUT MANY WONDERFUL INGREDIENTS. IN THIS CREATION, ASIA'S LEMON GRASS AND LYCHEE ARE A PERFECT COMPLEMENT TO EUROPE'S YOGHURT AND STRAWBERRIES.

4 ICE-CREAM CAKES Ø 18 CM	4 EISTORTEN Ø 18 CM
STRAWBERRY MACAROON (BASE AND DECORATION)	**ERDBEERMACARON (BODEN UND DEKORATION)**
150 g egg white	150 g Eiweiß
310 g icing sugar	310 g Puderzucker
40 g cornflour	40 g Speisestärke
125 g grated almonds, extra fine	125 g Mandelgrieß, extrafein
30 g strawberry powder	30 g Erdbeerpulver

Making the parts see next page.

Zubereitung siehe nächste Seite.

ERDBEERMACARON

Eiweiß mit 180 g Puderzucker und Speise-stärke zu einem festen Schnee schlagen. Anschließend Mandelgries, restlichen Puderzucker und Erdbeerpulver mischen, vorsichtig unterheben und bei Bedarf mit Lebensmittelfarbe färben. Dann für die Dekoration auf ein mit Backpapier belegtes Backblech mit Hilfe eines Dressierbeutels mit 8er-Lochtülle kleine Tupfen dressieren. Außerdem für die äußere Form der Eisbombe Dreiecke, die etwas kleiner sind als die verwendete Ringgröße aufdressieren. Kurze Zeit abstehen lassen und im vorgeheizten Ofen bei 160 °C 15 – 20 Minuten backen.

STRAWBERRY MACAROON

Beat the egg white with 180 g icing sugar and the cornflour until firm. Mix the grated almonds, the remaining icing sugar and the strawberry powder, fold into the egg mixture and add in some food colouring if required. To make the decorations, use a piping bag with a round nozzle size 8 to pipe small dabs on baking paper on a baking sheet. Also pipe on triangles for the outer form of the ice-cream bomb – these should be a bit smaller than the ring you will use. Allow to stand for a short while and then bake in a preheated oven at 160 °C for 15 to 20 minutes.

ERDBEER-JOGHURT-LEMONGRAS-EIS (EINLAGE)

120 g	Vollmilch
100 g	Lemongras
195 g	Zucker
36 g	Dextrose
30 g	Magermilchpulver
1 g	Salz
600 g	Joghurt
15 g	Zitronensaft
120 g	Erdbeerpüree
90 g	Sahne

Milch mit geklopftem Lemongras aufkochen, ziehen lassen und absieben, dann die trockenen Zutaten mischen, mit dem Milchsud vermengen und bei 85 °C pasteurisieren. Joghurt, Zitronensaft und Erdbeerpüree untermixen, bei 65 °C die Sahne untermixen, dann reifen lassen und gefrieren. Eis in vorbereitete Form einfüllen.

STRAWBERRY YOGHURT LEMONGRASS ICE-CREAM (INSIDE LAYER)

120 g	whole milk
100 g	lemongrass
195 g	sugar
36 g	dextrose
30 g	skimmed milk powder
1 g	salt
600 g	yoghurt
15 g	lemon juice
120 g	strawberry puree
90 g	whipping cream

Boil the milk with the lemongrass after beating it, allow to steep and drain the milk into a container, mix the dry ingredients together, add to the milk and pasteurise at 85 °C. Mix in the yoghurt, lemon juice and strawberry puree, mix in the cream at 65 °C, allow to mature and then put into the freezer. Fill the ice-cream into the prepared mould.

LYCHEE SORBET
(COVER)

75 g	dry glucose
150 g	sugar
25 g	invert sugar
550 g	lychee puree
444 g	water
6.25 g	fruit acid

Mix the dry glucose and sugar, add the other ingredients and adjust to 29 °Brix in a refractometer.

DECORATION

white and red spray
cocoa butter
chocolate decor made from red
and copper-coloured cocoa butter
fresh lychee and dried
strawberry chip
macaroons
silver leaf
cold jelly coloured with
red metallic food colouring

LITSCHISORBET
(MANTEL)

75 g	Trockenglukose
150 g	Zucker
25 g	Invertzucker
550 g	Litschipüree
444 g	Wasser
6,25 g	Fruchtsäure

Trockenglukose und Zucker mischen, die restlichen Zutaten untermixen und mit dem Refraktometer auf 29 °Brix einstellen.

DEKORATION

weiße und rote Sprüh-
kakaobutter
Schokoladendekor aus roter und
kupferfarbener Kakaobutter
frischer Litschi- und
getrockneter Erdbeerchip
Macarons
Blattsilber
Kaltgelee, gefärbt mit roter
Metallicfarbe

EISSANDWICH TOBBI

ICE-CREAM SANDWICH TOBBI

Als Kind gab es nichts Tolleres für mich, als eine Kugel Vanilleeis mit der Zunge zwischen zwei Waffeln herauszuschlecken. Mein Freund Antonio aus Italien hat mich wieder an diese alte Spezialität erinnert, das Werkzeug dazu habe ich mal wieder aus den USA mitgebracht. Haben Sie nicht auch solche herrlichen Kindheitserinnerungen?

When I was a child there was nothing more exciting for me than to lick a ball of vanilla ice-cream between two waffles. My friend Antonio from Italy has reminded me of this old speciality and again I have brought back the tools for it from the USA. Do you not also have such wonderful childhood memories?

Zutaten für 12 Personen	Ingredients for 12 persons
Schokoladen-Sablé Breton (etwa 12 Sandwiches)	**Chocolate Sablé Breton (about 12 sandwiches)**

	Schokoladen-Sablé Breton			Chocolate Sablé Breton
100 g	Kakaomasse		100 g	cocoa paste
50 g	Wasser		50 g	water
465 g	Butter		465 g	unsalted butter
150 g	Puderzucker		150 g	icing sugar
2 g	Meersalz		2 g	sea salt
20 g	Eigelb, gestockt und passiert		20 g	egg yolk, coagulated and strained
425 g	Mehl		425 g	flour
85 g	Maisstärke		85 g	corn starch
50 g	Nougat de Montélimar-Streusel		50 g	Nougat de Montélimar vermicelli

Zubereitung siehe nächste Seite.

Making the parts see next page.

SCHOKOLADEN-SABLÉ BRETON

Kakaomasse und Wasser zu einer Paste anrühren und mit den restlichen Zutaten zu einem Teig verkneten. Gut durchkühlen lassen und in einer Form 4 Millimeter stark ausrollen, mit gehacktem Nougat bestreuen und bei 165 °C etwa 25 Minuten backen. Erst nach dem Backen ausstechen, um zu vermeiden, dass der Teig breit läuft.

CHOCOLATE SABLÉ BRETON

Stir the cocoa paste into the water to make a paste, add the other ingredients and kneed into a pastry. Allow to cool thoroughly, roll out in a form to a thickness of 4 mm, sprinkle the chopped-up nougat over it and bake at 165 °C for about 25 minutes. Do not cut the shapes until after baking to avoid the pastry spreading.

VOLLMILCH-SCHOKOLADENEIS (WARME HERSTELLUNG) (ERGIBT 1000 G)

15 g	Magermilchpulver
50 g	Zucker
5 g	neutrales Eisbindemittel
600 g	Milch
40 g	Eigelb
100 g	Invertzucker
185 g	Milchkuvertüre, 40 %
50 g	Sahne

Trockene Zutaten mischen, Milch, Eigelb und Invertzucker zugeben und bei 85 °C pasteurisieren. Die Milchkuvertüre untermixen, Masse herunterkühlen, bei 60 °C Sahne zugeben und dann alles bis auf 4 °C abkühlen. Reifen lassen und in der Eismaschine abfrieren.

WHOLE MILK CHOCOLATE ICE-CREAM (HOT PRODUCTION METHOD) (MAKES 1000 G)

15 g	skimmed milk powder
50 g	sugar
5 g	neutral ice-cream binding agent
600 g	milk
40 g	egg yolk
100 g	invert sugar
185 g	milk couverture, 40 %
50 g	whipping cream

Mix the dry ingredients, add the milk, egg yolk and invert sugar and pasteurise at 85 °C. Mix in the milk couverture, cool down the mixture, at 60 °C add the cream and then cool everything down to 4 °C. Allow to mature and then place into the ice-cream maker to freeze.

Passend ausgestochenen Schokoladenmürbteig in eine Spezialform einlegen

Cut the chocolate shortcrust in the shape of the form and place into the special form

Beide Eissorten mischen und mit einem Portionierer 2 Kugeln in die Form einfüllen

Mix both types of ice-cream and fill the forms with the mixture

Mit einem Stempel abpressen

Use a stamp to make an impression

4

Fertiges Eissandwich, dieses vor dem Servieren mit verdünnter Kakaobutter absetzen

The ice-cream sandwich is complete – apply thinned cocoa butter to set it off before serving

Mit einem zweiten Mürbteigkeks abdeckeln

Put a second shortcrust layer on top

5

WHITE NOUGAT ICE-CREAM (HOT PRODUCTION METHOD) (MAKES 1000 G)

154 g	sugar
21 g	dextrose
26 g	milk powder
26 g	stabiliser for ice-cream made with cream
513 g	milk, 3.5 %
51 g	light cream nougat
102 g	cream, 35 %
5 g	aroma oil Fiori di Sicilia
102 g	Nougat de Montélimar, chopped

Mix the dry ingredients, add the milk and pasteurise. Add the cream nougat at 85 °C, allow the mixture to cool, add the cream and oil at 60 °C and then cool everything down to 4 °C. Once it has matured, put the mixture into the ice-cream maker to freeze and add the Nougat de Montélimar just before the end of the freezing process.

WEISSES NOUGATEIS (WARME HERSTELLUNG) (ERGIBT 1000 G)

154 g	Zucker
21 g	Dextrose
26 g	Milchpulver
26 g	Stabilisator für Sahnemilcheis
513 g	Milch, 3,5 %
51 g	hellen Sahnenougat
102 g	Sahne, 35 %
5 g	Aromaöl Fiori di Sicilia
102 g	Nougat de Montélimar, gehackt

Trockene Zutaten mischen, Milch zugeben und pasteurisieren. Bei 85 °C Sahnenougat untermixen, Mischung herunterkühlen, dann bei 60 °C Sahne und Öl zugeben und alles auf 4 °C abkühlen. Nach dem Reifen in der Eismaschine abfrieren und kurz vor Ende des Gefriervorgangs den Nougat de Montélimar zufügen.

EISSCHOKOLADE SULMONA
ICE-CREAM CHOCOLATE SULMONA

MEIN FREUND FABRIZIO LEBT IN DEN ABRUZZEN. ICH HABE IHM EINMAL DIE EISKARTE FÜR SEINE DEUTSCHEN GÄSTE ÜBERSETZT, DABEI STOLPERTE ICH ÜBER DIESE SPEZIALITÄT. DA ICH SIE NICHT KANNTE WAR ICH NEUGIERIG UND HABE SIE SOFORT AUSPROBIERT. DIE ERFRISCHENDE KOMBINATION AUS SCHOKOLADE UND MINZE EIGNET SICH HERVORRAGEND ALS SOMMERSPEZIALITÄT.

MY FRIEND FABRIZIO LIVES IN THE ABRUZZO REGION. I ONCE TRANSLATED A MENU FOR HIS GERMAN GUESTS AND CAME ACROSS THIS SPECIALITY. AS I DIDN'T KNOW IT I WAS CURIOUS AND TRIED IT OUT IMMEDIATELY. THE REFRESHING COMBINATION OF CHOCOLATE WITH MINT MAKES AN IDEAL SUMMER SPECIALITY.

CLASSIC ITALIAN VANILLA ICE-CREAM (HOT PRODUCTION METHOD) (MAKES 1000 G)		KLASSISCHES ITALIENISCHES VANILLEEIS (WARME HERSTELLUNG) (ERGIBT 1000 G)	
188 g	sugar	188 g	Zucker
25 g	dextrose	25 g	Dextrose
19 g	milk powder	19 g	Milchpulver
2.5 g	neutral ice-cream binding agent	2,5 g	neutrales Eisbindemittel
1	vanilla pod	1	Vanilleschote
	Zest from $^1/_2$ lemon		Abrieb von $^1/_2$ Zitrone
12 g	coffee beans, lightly roasted in a frying pan	12 g	Kaffeebohnen, leicht in der Pfanne angeröstet
75 g	egg yolk	75 g	Eigelb
627 g	milk	627 g	Milch
63 g	whipping cream	63 g	Sahne

Making the parts see next page.

Zubereitung siehe nächste Seite.

Klassisches italienisches Vanilleeis (warme Herstellung)

Trockene Zutaten mischen und Eigelb einrühren. Milch zum Kochen bringen, anschließend Zutatenmix zugeben, Vanilleschote entnehmen und bei 85 °C pasteurisieren. Die Masse herunterkühlen und bei 60 °C die Sahne zugeben. Herunterkühlen auf 4 °C, reifen lassen und vor dem Gefrieren durch ein feines Sieb passieren. Dann in der Eismaschine abfrieren.

Classic Italian vanilla ice-cream (hot production method)

1

Mix the dry ingredients and stir in the egg yolk. Bring the milk to the boil, add the mixed ingredients, take out the vanilla pod and pasteurise at 85 °C. Cool the mixture down to 60 °C and add the cream. Cool down to 4 °C, allow to mature and pass through a fine sieve before freezing it. Place into the ice-cream maker to freeze.

2

3

Minzsosse

6 g	Pektin
225 g	Zucker
150 g	Wasser
100 g	Trockenglukose
3	Tropfen Pefferminzöl (je nach Intensität variieren) grüner Lebensmittelfarbstoff oder natürliche Farbextrakte

Mint sauce

6 g	pectin
225 g	sugar
150 g	water
100 g	dry glucose
3	drops of peppermint oil (can be more or less, depending on the intensity of the oil) green food colouring or natural colour extracts

4

Das Pektin und 50 g Zucker mischen, mit Wasser aufkochen, dann 175 g Zucker zugeben und erneut aufkochen. Nach Zugabe der Trockenglukose, Soße nochmals aufkochen, absetzten lassen und abschäumen. Nach dem Erkalten mit Minzöl und Farbstoff abschmecken.

Mix the pectin with 50 g sugar and bring to the boil with the water, add 175 g sugar and bring back to the boil. After adding the dry glucose, boil the sauce again, leave to settle and remove the froth. Once it has cooled down, add colouring and mint oil to taste.

Schokoladentuillemasse tupfenförmig in ausreichend großem Abstand auf Teflon-Backmatten dressieren

Pipe dabs of the chocolate tuille mixture with sufficient spacing between them onto Teflon baking mats

Fertig gebackene Schokoladentuille

Finished chocolate tuille after baking

Tuille noch warm auf einen Metallstab aufrollen

Roll the tuille onto a metal bar while still warm

Fertig aufgerollte Schokoladentuille

Finished chocolate tuille rolled up

DRINKING CHOCOLATE
(MAKES 1000 G)

667 g	whole milk
133 g	whipping cream
67 g	glucose syrup
1	stick of Ceylon cinnamon
133 g	bitter couverture, 70 %

Bring the milk, cream and glucose to the boil with the cinnamon stick. Take out the cinnamon, chop up the couverture and mix it in. Before serving the drinking chocolate, add some of the mint sauce to taste.

TRINKSCHOKOLADE
(ERGIBT 1000 G)

667 g	Vollmilch
133 g	Sahne
67 g	Glukosesirup
1	Stange Ceylonzimt
133 g	Bitterkuvertüre, 70 %

Milch, Sahne und Glukose mit der Zimtstange aufkochen. Diese entfernen, dann Kuvertüre fein hacken und untermixen. Vor dem Anrichten die Trinkschokolade mit der Minzsoße abschmecken.

CHOCOLATE TUILLE ROLL
(ABOUT 40 PCS.)

150 g	sugar
2.5 g	pectin
100 g	unsalted butter
50 g	glucose syrup
50 g	orange juice
20 g	ground cocoa bean pieces
20 g	cocoa powder

Mix the sugar with the pectin and boil together with the butter, glucose syrup and orange juice. Stir in the ground cocoa beans and cocoa powder and then put in a refrigerator. Use a piping bag to pipe small dabs onto a Teflon baking mat, leaving larger spaces between them, bake at 180 °C for about 15 minutes and leave to cool a little. While still warm, roll onto a metal bar; store in a dry place.

SCHOKOLADENTUILLEROLLE
(ETWA 40 STÜCK)

150 g	Zucker
2,5 g	Pektin
100 g	Butter
50 g	Glukosesirup
50 g	Orangensaft
20 g	gemahlener Kakaobohnenbruch
20 g	Kakaopulver

Zucker und Pektin mischen, mit Butter, Glukosesirup und Orangensaft aufkochen. Dann Kakaobohnenbruch und Kakaopulver unterrühren, anschließend kaltstellen. Mit dem Spritzbeutel kleine Tupfen in größeren Abständen auf eine Teflon-Backmatte spritzen, bei 180 °C etwa 15 Minuten backen und leicht abkühlen lassen. In noch warmem Zustand auf einen Metallstab aufrollen. Trocken lagern.

DECORATION

1	cream swirl per glass

DEKORATION

1	Sahnerosette je Glas

EXOTIC DREAMS

EXOTIC DREAMS

In einem Eiscafé sind tolle Becher das A und O. Der Gast wählt zum grossen Teil auch nach der Optik aus. Zum Glück – denn wenn in unserem Café ein Riesencoupe bestellt wird und die anderen Gäste darauf aufmerksam werden, dann kommen sicher einige davon auf die gleiche Idee.

In an ice-cream parlour the most important items on the menu are sumptuous Coppas. Guests will often make their choice based on looks. That's a good thing – because if somebody in our Café orders a giant Coppa and the other guests notice it, some of them will surely get tempted to try the same thing.

EXOTISCHE GRÜTZE (ERGIBT 1000 G)

1,3 g	Agar-Agar
365 g	Blutorangensaft
245 g	Maracujasaft
60 g	Zucker
30 g	Sagoperlen
120 g	gewürfelte Mango
120 g	gewürfelte Papaya
60 g	Zuchtheidelbeeren

Alle Zutaten, bis auf die Früchte, mischen und dann quellen lassen. Anschließend aufkochen, die Früchte zugeben und gekühlt lagern.

EXOTIC FRUIT JELLY (MAKES 1000 G)

1,3 g	agar agar
365 g	blood orange juice
245 g	passion fruit juice
60 g	sugar
30 g	sago pearls
120 g	diced mango
120 g	diced papaya
60 g	cultivated bilberries

Mix all ingredients, except for the fruit, and leave to soak. Bring the mixture to the boil, add the fruit and store in a cool place.

KANDIERTE ZUCKERPLATTE

1250 g	Zucker
500 g	Wasser

Beide Zutaten auf 74 °Brix kochen. Mit einem Fülltrichter in Silikonformen füllen, mit Kristallzucker abstreuen und für etwa zwei Tage ohne Vibrationen kristallisieren lassen. Vorsichtig die Zuckeroberfläche abnehmen und auf einem Gitter abtropfen lassen. Trocken lagern.

KOKOSBAISER
(ETWA 65 STÜCK)

75 g	Eiweiß
150 g	Zucker
1 g	Salz
50 g	Puderzucker
50 g	Kokosraspeln, leicht geröstet

Eiweiß mit etwas Zucker und dem Salz zu einem steifen Schnee schlagen, restlichen Zucker nach und nach einlaufen lassen. Puderzucker und Kokosflocken gemischt unterheben und mit Hilfe eines Spritzbeutels mit einer 8er-Lochtülle kleine Tupfen auf eine Backmatte garnieren. Masse bei 120 °C für etwa 4 Stunden „trocknen".

CANDIED SUGAR DISK

1250 g	sugar
500 g	water

Boil the two ingredients to 74 °Brix. Use a funnel to pour the liquid into silicone moulds, sprinkle some granulated sugar over it and allow to crystallise for two days without vibrations. Carefully remove the sugar surface and place on a grille to drain. Store in a dry place.

COCONUT MERINGUE
(ABOUT 65 PCS.)

75 g	egg white
150 g	sugar
1 g	salt
50 g	icing sugar
50 g	grated coconut, lightly roasted

Add a little sugar and the salt to the egg white and beat until stiff, then slowly add the remaining sugar in small doses. Mix the icing sugar with the coconut and fold into the mixture, use a piping bag with a round nozzle size 8 to pipe small dabs onto a baking mat. "Dry" the mixture in the oven at 120 °C for about 4 hours.

PINEAPPLE FENNEL SORBET
(HOT PRODUCTION METHOD)
(MAKES 1000 G)

43 g	dry glucose
89 g	sugar
170 g	invert sugar
230 g	water
2	sachets fennel tea
468 g	pineapple puree

Mix the sugar together with the dry glucose. Add the invert sugar and water, bring to the boil, use this to infuse the tea and leave to steep. Take out the tea sachets after 5 minutes, add the puree and use a refractometer to adjust to 31°Brix. Place into the ice-cream maker to freeze.

ANANAS-FENCHEL-SORBET
(WARME HERSTELLUNG)
(ERGIBT 1000 G)

43 g	Trockenglukose
89 g	Zucker
170 g	Invertzucker
230 g	Wasser
2	Beutel Fencheltee
468 g	Ananaspüree

Die Trockenglukose und den Zucker mischen. Den Invertzucker und Wasser zugeben, aufkochen, dann den Tee damit überbrühen und ziehen lassen. Teebeutel nach 5 Minuten entfernen, Püree zugeben und mit dem Refraktometer auf 31°Brix einstellen. In der Eismaschine abfrieren.

KIWIFRUIT SORBET
(COLD PRODUCTION METHOD)
(MAKES 1000 G)

35 g	dry glucose
183 g	sugar
140 g	invert sugar
288 g	water
349 g	kiwifruit puree
4 g	fruit acid

Mix the dry glucose together with the sugar. Add invert sugar and water followed by the puree and fruit acid. Use a refractometer to adjust the mixture to 32°Brix. Place into the ice-cream maker to freeze.

KIWISORBET
(KALTE HERSTELLUNG)
(ERGIBT 1000 G)

35 g	Trockenglukose
183 g	Zucker
140 g	Invertzucker
288 g	Wasser
349 g	Kiwipüree
4 g	Fruchtsäure

Die Trockenglukose und den Zucker mischen. Den Invertzucker und Wasser zugeben, dann Püree und Fruchtsäure. Mit dem Refraktometer auf 32°Brix einstellen. In der Eismaschine abfrieren.

DECORATION

cream dabs

DEKORATION

Sahnetupfen

FIELDS OF CHANGE

DIE ANANAS GEHÖRT ZU DEN FRÜCHTEN, DIE MIT HILFE VON ENZYMEN EIWEISS LÖSEN KÖNNEN. UM DIESE FRUCHT MIT EIWEISSHALTIGEN PRODUKTEN ZU MISCHEN, SOLLTE MAN SIE IMMER ERHITZEN. DENN SONST KANN ES BITTER, ODER – WENN MAN GELATINE VERWENDET – NICHT FEST WERDEN.

PINEAPPLE IS ONE OF SEVERAL TYPES OF FRUIT THAT CAN DISSOLVE PROTEIN WITH THE HELP OF ENZYMES. IN ORDER TO MIX THIS FRUIT WITH PRODUCTS THAT CONTAIN PROTEIN ONE SHOULD ALWAYS HEAT IT UP. OTHERWISE THE MIXTURE MAY TURN BITTER OR – WHERE GELATINE IS USED – MAY NOT BECOME FIRM.

INGREDIENTS FOR 15 PERSONS	ZUTATEN FÜR 15 PERSONEN
CARAMELISED PINEAPPLE	**KARAMELLISIERTE ANANAS**

250 g	*baby pineapple*	250 g	*Babyananas*
50 g	*maple syrup*	50 g	*Ahornsirup*
1	*vanilla pod*	1	*Vanilleschote*
	(with the pith scraped out, dried and cut into 2 cm long pieces)		*(ausgeschabt, getrocknet, in 2 cm lange Stücke geschnitten)*

Peel the pineapple and spike with the vanilla pod. Lightly caramelise the maple syrup in a frying pan, place the pineapple into the pan and lightly fry on all sides, making sure it doesn't change colour. Leave the fruit in the pan, place into the preheated oven at 180 °C until it is cooked but still firm to the bite; this may take 15 minutes or more, depending on the size of the pineapple. Baste the fruit with the maple syrup from time to time. Once cooked, take out the vanilla pod, leave to cool, cut to the required size and store in a cool place.

Ananas schälen und mit der Vanilleschote spicken. Ahornsirup in einer Pfanne leicht karamellisieren und die gespickte Ananas darin von allen Seiten anbraten, ohne das sie Farbe annimmt. Anschließend in der Pfanne belassen und im vorgeheizten Ofen bei 180 °C, je nach Größe der Ananas, für mindestens 15 Minuten bissfest garen. Dabei ab und zu mit dem Ahornsirup übergießen. Nach dem Garen die Vanilleschote entfernen, auskühlen lassen, in die gewünschte Größe schneiden und gekühlt lagern.

HASELNUSSFINANZIERS

55 g	Haselnüsse, fein gerieben und leicht geröstet
25 g	Puderzucker
25 g	Mehl
50 g	Nussbutter, leicht abgekühlt
80 g	Eiweiß
35 g	Zucker

Alle Zutaten miteinander verrühren und in eine Silikon-Backform füllen. Bei 175 °C etwa 15 Minuten backen.

HAZELNUT FINANCIERS

55 g	hazelnuts, finely ground and lightly roasted
25 g	icing sugar
25 g	flour
50 g	nut butter, chilled
80 g	egg white
35 g	sugar

Stir all ingredients together and fill into a silicone baking mould. Bake at 175 °C for about 15 minutes.

1

2

SALBEIZUCKERBLÄTTER

	Zutaten für den neutralen Zucker:
300 g	Zucker
90 g	Glukosesirup
90 g	Wasser

Alle Zutaten miteinander aufkochen, abschäumen und unter ständigem Reinwaschen auf 160 °C kochen, dann auf eine Silikon-Backmatte gießen und auskühlen lassen. Mit einem Kutter oder dem Thermomix pulverisieren. Nach Geschmack mit gefriergetrocknetem Fruchtpulver, Gewürzen oder Kräutern mischen. Je nach Sorte kann die Menge von 4 g bis 10 g variieren.
Eine Teflon-Backmatte mit einer Blätterschablone belegen, die Zuckermischung darübersieben. Schablone vorsichtig entfernen und bei 180 °C für etwa 4 Minuten erneut im Ofen anschmelzen. Erkalten lassen, mit einem gekochten Zuckerfaden als Stab überspinnen und sofort luftdicht verpacken.

SAGE SUGAR LEAVES

	Ingredients for the neutral sugar:
300 g	sugar
90 g	glucose syrup
90 g	water

Bring all ingredients to the boil, remove the froth and boil at 160 °C, continually "cleaning" the mixture, pour onto a silicone mat and leave to cool. Use a cutter or Thermomix to grind the sugar into a powder. Add freeze-dried fruit powder, herbs or spices to taste. Depending on the type, the quantity can vary between 4 g and 10 g. Cover a Teflon baking mat with a leaf stencil and sift the sugar mixture over the stencil. Carefully remove the stencils, place in the oven at 180 °C for about 4 minutes until the sugar begins to melt. Leave to cool, decorate with a boiled sugar thread; wrap up air-tight immediately.

Eine Teflon-Backmatte mit einer Blätterschablone belegen und die Salbeizucker-Mischung durch ein Sieb darauf geben

Place leaf stencil on a Teflon baking mat and spread the sage sugar mixture over it passing it through a sieve

Schablone vorsichtig entfernen und im Ofen anschmelzen, so dass sich die Zuckerkristalle verbinden

Carefully remove the stencil and put into the oven until the sugar begins to melt and the crystals merge

ARGAN-OIL APRICOT PUMPKIN JELLY

5	sheets of gelatine
25 g	glucose syrup
80 g	icing sugar
50 g	apricot puree
50 g	pumpkin puree
100 g	Isomalt
1	vanilla pod
2 g	cinnamon flowers
100 g	almond oil
100 g	Argan oil

Soak the gelatine in cold water. Add the glucose syrup, icing sugar, apricot and pumpkin puree, Isomalt, vanilla pod and cinnamon flowers together into a Thermomix and then run at 90 °C for 15 minutes. Squeeze the gelatine and add it to the mixture, pour through a sieve and then back into the Thermomix to cool it down to 45 °C. Add the two oils in small doses. As soon as the oil has been worked in, pour the mixture into a suitable frame, leave to cool and chill with a cover on the frame. Cut to the required size.

ARGANÖL-APRIKOSEN-KÜRBIS-GELEE

5	Blatt Gelatine
25 g	Glukosesirup
80 g	Puderzucker
50 g	Aprikosenpüree
50 g	Kürbispüree
100 g	Isomalt
1	Vanilleschote
2 g	Zimtblüten
100 g	Mandelöl
100 g	Arganöl

Gelatine in kaltem Wasser einweichen. Glukosesirup, Puderzucker, Aprikosen- und Kürbispüree, Isomalt, Vanilleschote und Zimtblüten im Thermomix auf 90 °C 15 Minuten lang laufen lassen. Dann die Gelatine ausgepresst zugeben, Masse durch ein Sieb gießen und dann weiterlaufend im Thermomix auf 45 °C abkühlen. Nach und nach die beiden Öle zugeben. Sobald das Öl untergearbeitet ist, Masse in einen passenden Rahmen gießen, erkalten lassen und abgedeckt kühlen. Auf die passende Größe zuschneiden.

JOGHURT-APRIKOSEN-KARAMELL-EIS
(WARME HERSTELLUNG)
(ERGIBT 1000 G)

73 g	Zucker
105 g	Vollmilch
1/2	Bourbon-Vanilleschote (Mark)
85 g	Zucker
29 g	Dextrose
24 g	Magermilchpulver
5 g	neutraler Stabilisator
1 g	Salz
73 g	Sahne
487 g	Joghurt
97 g	Aprikosenpüree
19 g	Zitronensaft

73 g Zucker zu einem aromatischen Karamell schmelzen, Milch mit dem Mark der Vanilleschote aufkochen und den Karamell damit ablöschen. Restliche trockene Zutaten mischen und mit der Karamellmilch verrühren. Bei 85 °C pasteurisieren und während des Abkühlungsprozesses bei 65 °C mit den restlichen Zutaten mischen. Die Mischung rasch auf 4 °C abkühlen und in der Eismaschine abgefrieren.

YOGHURT APRICOT CARAMEL
ICE-CREAM
(HOT PRODUCTION METHOD)
(MAKES 1000 G)

73 g	sugar
105 g	whole milk
1/2	Bourbon vanilla pod (pith)
85 g	sugar
29 g	dextrose
24 g	skimmed milk powder
5 g	neutral stabiliser
1 g	salt
73 g	whipping cream
487 g	yoghurt
97 g	apricot puree
19 g	lemon juice

Melt the 73 g sugar until it caramelises, boil the milk with the pith of the vanilla pod and then pour it over the caramel. Mix the remaining dry ingredients together and stir into the caramel milk. Pasteurise at 85 °C and while the mixture is cooling down, mix in the other ingredients at 65 °C. Cool the mixture quickly to 4 °C and put into the ice-cream maker to freeze.

DEKORATION

geröstete Kürbiskerne
Kürbiskernöl

DECORATION

roasted pumpkin seeds
pumpkin seed oil

FIORI DI SICILIA-EISTORTE

CASSATA FIORI DI SICILIA

LEIDER HABE ICH VON DER INSEL SIZILIEN NUR DEN WEG VOM HAFEN BIS ZUM FLUGHAFEN KENNENGELERNT. ABER DIE EINDRÜCKE, DIE ICH AUS ERZÄHLUNGEN MEINER DORTIGEN KOLLEGEN BEKOMME, BRINGEN MICH IMMER WIEDER ZUM TRÄUMEN. ICH GLAUBE SOGAR, DASS DIE WIEGE DER KONDITOREI DORT GESTANDEN HABEN MUSS.

WHEN I WAS IN SICILY I DIDN'T SEE MUCH OF THE ISLAND BUT THE IMPRESSIONS I HAVE GAINED FROM THE STORIES OF MY COLLEAGUES THERE CONVEY A DREAM-LIKE QUALITY THAT I TREASURE. I AM CONVINCED THAT THE CRADLE OF PATISSERIE MUST HAVE STOOD ON THAT ISLAND.

4 EISTORTEN Ø 18 CM

PISTAZIENDAQUOISE (BODEN)

225 g	Eiweiß
5 g	Trockeneiweiß
75 g	Zucker
90 g	Pistazien, feingerieben
100 g	Mandelgrieß
185 g	Zucker, extrafein
25 g	Mehl

Eiweiß und Trockeneiweiß mit 75 g Zucker zu einem festen Schnee schlagen, dann die restlichen Zutaten mischen und unter den Schnee heben. Masse mit einem Spritzbeutel und einer 8er-Lochtülle in Form der Eisbombe auf eine Backmatte aufdressieren, bei 200 °C anbacken und bei 170 °C etwa 30 Minuten ausbacken.

4 ICE-CREAM CAKES Ø 18 CM

PISTACHIOS DACQUOISE (BASE)

225 g	egg white
5 g	dried egg white
75 g	sugar
90 g	finely grated pistachios
100 g	grated almonds
185 g	sugar, extra fine
25 g	flour

Mix the egg white with the dried egg white and 75 g sugar and beat until firm, mix the remaining ingredients and fold them into the egg mixture. Use a piping bag with round nozzle size 8 to pipe the mixture onto a baking mat in the shape of the ice-cream bomb, start baking at 200 °C and continue to bake at 170 °C for about 30 minutes.

RICOTTA LEMON SORBET
(HOT PRODUCTION METHOD)
(INSIDE LAYER)

185 g	sugar
50 g	dextrose
25 g	skimmed milk powder
3 g	neutral ice-cream binding agent
	Zest from 2 lemons
300 g	water
100 g	ricotta
160 g	lemon juice
3	drops aroma oil Fiori di Sicilia

Mix the dry ingredients with the lemon zest and bring to the boil in water. Pour through a sieve and mix with the ricotta, lemon juice and aroma oil; put into the ice-cream maker to freeze. Use a piping bag with a large round nozzle to pipe rings onto the pistachio base and freeze.

RICOTTA-ZITRONEN-SORBET
(WARME HERSTELLUNG)
(EINLAGE)

185 g	Zucker
50 g	Dextrose
25 g	Magermilchpulver
3 g	neutrales Eisbindemittel
	Abrieb von 2 Zitronen
300 g	Wasser
100 g	Ricotta
160 g	Zitronensaft
3	Tropfen Aromaöl Fiori di Sicilia

Trockene Zutaten mit Zitronenabrieb mischen und mit Wasser aufkochen. Absieben und mit Ricotta, Zitronensaft und Aromaöl aufmixen, dann in der Eismaschine abfrieren. Ringförmig mit einem Spritzbeutel und großer Lochtülle auf den Pistazienboden dressieren, dann einfrieren.

CHOCOLATE NOUGAT ICE-CREAM
(HOT PRODUCTION METHOD)
(INSIDE LAYER)

107 g	sugar
14 g	dextrose
11 g	milk powder
2 g	neutral ice-cream binding agent
43 g	egg yolk
14 g	invert sugar
360 g	milk
72 g	couverture, 70 %
72 g	almond bitter nougat
104 g	whipping cream

Mix the dry ingredients, add egg yolk and invert sugar. Mix in the milk and pasteurise at 85 °C. Add the couverture and nougat, cool down to 65 °C and then add the cream. Cool the mixture down to 4 °C and place into the ice-cream maker to freeze. Use a piping bag with a round nozzle to fill in the gaps between the lemon-ricotta-ice-cream rings, freeze and fill up with the cassata parfait.

SCHOKOLADEN-NOUGAT-EIS
(WARME HERSTELLUNG)
(EINLAGE)

107 g	Zucker
14 g	Dextrose
11 g	Milchpulver
2 g	neutrales Eisbindemittel
43 g	Eigelb
14 g	Invertzucker
360 g	Milch
72 g	Kuvertüre, 70 %
72 g	Mandelbitternougat
104 g	Sahne

Trockene Zutaten mischen, Eigelb und Invertzucker zugeben. Milch untermixen und bei 85 °C pasteurisieren. Kuvertüre und Nougat zugeben, herunterkühlen und bei 65 °C Sahne zugeben. Eismasse auf 4 °C abkühlen, in der Eismaschine abfrieren. Mit einem Dressierbeutel und einer Lochtülle die Freiräume zwischen dem Zitronen-Ricotta-Eis-Ringen ausspritzen, festfrieren und mit dem Cassata-Parfait auffüllen.

Isomalt auflösen und mit Zitronenöl aromatisieren

Dissolve Isomalt and add some of the lemon oil for flavour

1

Schmetterling-Silikonform durch Isomalt-mischung ziehen

Pull the butterfly silicone mould through the Isomalt mixture

2

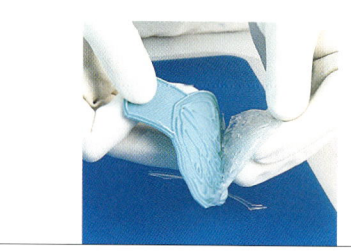

3

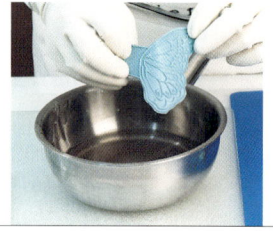

4

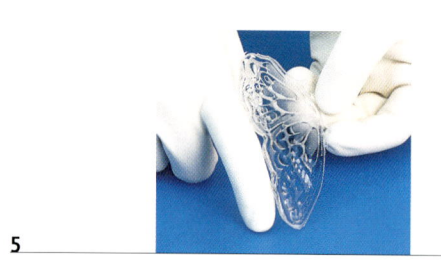

5

CASSATA-PARFAIT (MANTEL)

75 g	gehackte Pistazien
37 g	Orangeat
37 g	Zitronat
112 g	Belegkirschen
37 g	Kirschwasser
90 g	Eigelb
75 g	Vollei
187 g	Zucker
750 g	halb geschlagene Sahne
75 g	gehackte Bitterkuvertüre

Die Pistazien und die kandierten Früchte über Nacht in Kirschwasser einweichen. Eigelb, Vollei und Zucker bei 85 °C pasteurisieren, dann kalt schlagen. Sahne, kandierte Früchte und Kuvertüre unterheben, in den vorgefrorenen Ring einfüllen und somit das bereits gefrorene Zitronen-Ricotta-Sorbet und das Schokoladen-Nougat-Eis „auffüllen". Anschließend mit der Pistaziendaquoise abdeckeln und durchfrieren. Danach ausformen.

CASSATA PARFAIT (COVER)

75 g	chopped pistachios
37 g	candied orange peel
37 g	candied lemon peel
112 g	decorating cherries
37 g	kirsch
90 g	egg yolk
75 g	whole egg
187 g	sugar
750 g	half-whipped cream
75 g	chopped bitter couverture

Soak the pistachios and candied fruit in kirsch overnight. Pasteurise the egg yolk, whole egg and sugar at 85 °C and then beat cold. Fold in the cream, candied fruit and couverture, put into the pre-frozen ring and fill up the ring with the lemon-ricotta sorbet and the chocolate-nougat ice-cream. Cover with the pistachio dacquoise and freeze thoroughly. Take out of the ring.

Silikonform abtropfen lassen

*Allow excess liquid to drain from
the silicone mould*

*Nach dem Erkalten Schmetterlingsflügel
abformen*

*Once cold, take the butterfly wings out
of the mould*

Fertiger Flügel

A finished wing

FLAMED LEMON MERINGUE (COATING)

400 g	sugar
	Zest from 1 lemon
200 g	egg white

Boil 350 g sugar and lemon zest with a little water to 119 °C. In the meantime, beat the egg white with 50 g sugar until firm, then let a thin stream of the boiling sugar run into the egg, beat cold and use this to spread over the cassata. Finish off by flaming the surface with a gas torch.

GEFLÄMMTER ZITRONENBAISER (ÜBERZUG)

400 g	Zucker
	Abrieb von 1 Zitrone
200 g	Eiweiß

350 g Zucker und die Zitronenschale mit etwas Wasser auf 119 °C kochen. In der Zwischenzeit das Eiweiß und 50 g Zucker zu einem festen Schnee schlagen, dann den kochenden Zucker in einem feinen Strahl in das Eiweiß laufen lassen, kalt schlagen und die Eistorte damit einstreichen. Abschließend mit einem Gasbrenner abflämmen.

DECORATION

sugar butterfly
dried slice of lemon
caramelised hazelnuts
chopped pistachios

DEKORATION

Zuckerschmetterling
getrocknete Zitronenscheibe
karamellisierte Haselnüsse
gehackte Pistazien

FOREST GARDEN

EIN SOUFFLÉ IST BEI ALLEN GÄSTEN IMMER GERNE WILLKOMMEN – UND WENN ES DANN NOCH EIN GEFRORENES IST, KANN EIGENTLICH NICHTS MEHR SCHIEF GEHEN.

SOUFFLÉS ARE ALWAYS POPULAR WITH OUR GUESTS – SO WHEN IT IS A FROZEN ONE THERE'S NOTHING MUCH THAT CAN GO WRONG.

INGREDIENTS FOR 10 PERSONS

FROZEN FOREST BERRY SOUFFLÉ

140 g	egg white
210 g	sugar
2 g	finely chopped cinnamon flowers
150 g	puree of forest berries
	Zest from 1 organic orange
475 g	half-whipped cream

Beat the egg white until stiff, meanwhile boil the sugar with a little water and the cinnamon flowers at 119 °C and add to the beaten egg white in a thin stream. Cold-beat the mixture and fold in the puree and orange zest followed by the cream. Line the pre-frozen moulds with baking paper, fill with the soufflé mixture and freeze thoroughly. Then carefully remove the paper.

ZUTATEN FÜR 10 PERSONEN

GEFRORENES WALDBEERSOUFFLÉ

140 g	Eiweiß
210 g	Zucker
2 g	fein gemahlene Zimtblüten
150 g	Waldbeerpüree
	Abrieb von 1 Bio-Orange
475 g	halb geschlagene Sahne

Eiweiß steif schlagen, in der Zwischenzeit Zucker mit etwas Wasser und den Zimt-blüten auf 119 °C kochen und in dünnem Strahl in den Schnee einlaufen lassen. Die Masse kalt schlagen und zunächst Püree und Orangenschale unterheben, dann die Sahne. Vorgefrorene Formen mit Back-papier auslegen, die Soufflé-Masse einfül-len und vollständig durchfrieren. Danach vorsichtig das Papier entfernen.

ORANGENBAISER ZUM ABFLÄMMEN UND BAISERNEST FÜR DAS EIS

300 g	*Eiweiß*
600 g	*Zucker*
1 g	*Salz*
5 g	*natürliches Orangenöl*

Eiweiß mit 200 g Zucker und Salz nach und nach zu einem stabilen Schnee schlagen. In der Zwischenzeit 400 g Zucker mit etwas Wasser auf 119 °C kochen und in einem feinen Strahl in den Eischnee laufen lassen. Die Masse langsam weiterlaufen lassen bis sie auf 20 °C abgekühlt ist, dann das Öl zugeben. Mit einem Spritzbeutel und Spezial-Tüllen auf Backmatten zunächst kleine Nester dressieren, diese bei 110 °C etwa 15 Minuten im Ofen anbacken, dann bei 50 °C im Trockenschrank mindestens 12 Stunden austrocknen.
Außerdem mit Hilfe einer Spezialtülle das Waldbeereis-Soufflé mit dem Baiser dekorieren und abflämmen. Anschließend sofort wieder einfrieren.

ORANGE MERINGUE FOR FLAMING AND MERINGUE NEST FOR THE ICE-CREAM

300 g	*egg white*
600 g	*sugar*
1 g	*salt*
5 g	*natural orange oil*

Beat the egg white with 200 g sugar and salt gradually until firm. In the meantime, boil 400 g sugar with a little water at 119 °C and add to the beaten egg in a thin stream. Keep going slowly with the mixture until it has cooled down to 20 °C, then add the oil. Use a piping bag and special nozzles to pipe small nests onto baking mats, bake these slightly in the oven at 110 °C for about 15 minutes, then place into the drying cabinet at 50 °C for at least 12 hours. Use a special nozzle to decorate the forest berry ice-cream soufflé with the meringue and flame lightly. Then put back in the deep freeze immediately.

1

2

CASSIS WALNUT OIL SAUCE

1	sheet of gelatine
12 g	glucose syrup
40 g	icing sugar
40 g	cassis puree
25 g	pear puree
50	Isomalt
¹/₂	vanilla pod
50 g	almond oil
50 g	walnut oil

Soak the gelatine in cold water. Add the glucose syrup, icing sugar, fruit puree, Isomalt and vanilla pod into the Thermomix and run at 90 °C for 15 minutes. Squeeze the gelatine and add it to the mixture, pour through a sieve and then back into the Thermomix to cool it down to 45 °C. Then add the oils in small doses; as soon as all of the oil has been worked in, pour the mixture into a bowl, leave to cool, cover and put into the chiller. Stir the sauce and apply with a silicone brush.

CASSIS-WALNUSSÖLSOSSE

1	Blatt Gelatine
12 g	Glukosesirup
40 g	Puderzucker
40 g	Cassispüree
25 g	Birnenpüree
50 g	Isomalt
¹/₂	Vanilleschote
50 g	Mandelöl
50 g	Walnussöl

Die Gelatine in kaltem Wasser einweichen. Glukosesirup, Puderzucker, Fruchtpüree, Isomalt und Vanilleschote im Thermomix auf 90 °C Einstellung 15 Minuten lang laufen lassen. Anschließend die Gelatine ausgepresst zugeben, Masse durch ein Sieb gießen und weiterlaufend im Thermomix auf 45 °C abkühlen. Anschließend die Öle nach und nach zugeben, sobald das ganze Öl untergearbeitet ist, die Masse in eine Schüssel gießen, erkalten lassen und abgedeckt kühlen. Soße durchrühren und mit einem Silikonpinsel anrichten.

Fruchtpüree mit Hilfe einer Soßenflasche auf eine, mit einer Puzzleschablone belegte Teflon-Backmatte auftragen

Use a sauce bottle to spread the fruit puree onto a puzzle stencil that has been placed onto a Teflon baking mat

Fertig im Ofen getrocknete Puzzleteile

Finished puzzle pieces after drying in the oven

DRIED FOREST BERRY PUZZLE PIECES

0.75 g	xanthan gum
50 g	sugar
250 g	puree of forest berries

Mix the xanthan gum and sugar followed by the forest berry puree. Apply the resulting puree evenly onto a puzzle stencil that has been placed onto a Teflon baking mat. Remove the stencil and dry in the oven at max. 60 °C until it is firm. Store the puzzle pieces together with a desiccant in an airtight container.

GETROCKNETE WALDBEER-PUZZLETEILE

0,75 g	Xanthan
50 g	Zucker
250 g	Waldbeerpüree

Xanthan und Zucker mischen, dann mit dem Waldbeerpüree mixen. Dieses Püree gleichmäßig durch eine Puzzleschablone auf eine Teflon-Backmatte auftragen. Schablone entfernen und im Ofen bei maximal 60 °C solange trocknen, bis es fest ist. Die Puzzleteile zusammen mit einem Trockenmittel luftdicht lagern.

SCHOKOLADENDEKORATION

100 g	Bitterküvertüre

Die temperierte Bitterkuvertüre dünn zwischen zwei festen Folien ausrollen, sobald sich die Folien lösen lassen, in passende Stücke schneiden und brechen.

CHOCOLATE DECORATION

100 g	bitter couverture

Roll out the tempered couverture thinly between two firm foils; as soon as the foils can be parted, cut into suitable pieces and break.

HOLUNDERBLÜTEN-JOGHURT-EIS (WARME HERSTELLUNG) (ERGIBT 1000 G)

118 g	Zucker
31 g	Dextrose
26 g	Magermilchpulver
1 g	Salz
105 g	Vollmilch
523 g	Joghurt
13 g	Zitronensaft
105 g	Holunderblütensirup
78 g	Sahne

Die trockenen Zutaten mit Milch mischen und bei 85 °C pasteurisieren. Anschließend Joghurt, Zitronensaft und Holunderblütensirup untermixen, bei 65 °C Sahne untermixen und reifen lassen. Danach gefrieren.

ELDERFLOWER YOGHURT ICE-CREAM (HOT PRODUCTION METHOD) (MAKES 1000 G)

118 g	sugar
31 g	dextrose
26 g	skimmed milk powder
1 g	salt
105 g	whole milk
523 g	yoghurt
13 g	lemon juice
105 g	elder flower syrup
78 g	whipping cream

Mix the dry ingredients with the milk and pasteurise at 85 °C. Mix in the yoghurt, lemon juice and elderflower syrup, when the mixture has reached 65 °C mix in the cream and leave to mature. Then place into the deep freeze.

DEKORATION

	frische Beeren

DECORATION

	fresh berries

MEIN KLEINES AQUARIUM

MY SMALL AQUARIUM

EINE MEINER LUSTIGSTEN ERFAHRUNGEN IN SACHEN AGAR-AGAR: IN EINER STARK VERDÜNNTEN LÖSUNG KANN MAN DINGE SCHWEBEN LASSEN – EGAL, OB ES EIN MINZBLATT ODER EINE TOTE FLIEGE IST. EINER MEINER KURSTEILNEHMER WAR SO FREI DIES AUSZUTESTEN. ICH BESCHRÄNKE MICH DANN DOCH LIEBER AUF LECKERE ZUTATEN.

ONE OF MY FUNNIEST EXPERIENCES WAS IN CONNECTION WITH AGAR AGAR: IN A HEAVILY DILUTED SOLUTION THINGS WILL FLOAT – AND THAT COULD BE A LEAF OF MINT, A DEAD FLY OR ANYTHING. ONE OF MY COURSE PARTICIPANTS TRIED THIS EXPERIMENT RATHER LITERALLY. I MYSELF PREFER TO FOCUS MY ATTENTION MORE ON TASTY INGREDIENTS.

ZUTATEN FÜR 20 PERSONEN

GELIERTE MINZCONSOMMÉ (ETWA 20 PORTIONEN)

500 g	Wasser
1,1 g	Agar-Agar
25 g	Minzsirup (je nach Qualität variieren)

Wasser mit Agar-Agar-Pulver mischen und aufkochen. Dann mit dem Minzsirup mixen und in Gläsern erkalten lassen.

INGREDIENTS FOR 20 PERSONS

JELLIED MINT CONSOMMÉ (ABOUT 20 SERVINGS)

500 g	water
1.1 g	agar agar
25 g	mint syrup (modify quantity depending on strength)

Add the agar agar to the water, mix and bring to the boil. Then mix in the mint syrup and leave to cool in glasses.

APRICOT CAVIAR
(ABOUT 20 SERVINGS)

250 g	*mineral water*
1.3 g	*Citras*
1.8 g	*algin*
250 g	*apricot puree*

Mix the mineral water with Citras, add the algin and mix again. Bring to the boil, leave to cool down to room temperature and mix in the apricot puree.

CALCIC MIXTURE FOR SPHERIFICATION (CAVIAR-SIZED GLOBULES)

6.5 g	*calcic*
1000 g	*still mineral water*

Use a whisk to stir the calcic into the mineral water until it has dissolved. Prepare a bowl with a litre of water to wash the spheres, and some paper towel.
Attention: water that has been mixed with calcic for spherification will block the drainage system when poured into the sink! To make the spheres pull the apricot mix into a syringe and add put drops into the calcic water. Once it has turned to jelly, take out with a sieve, wash in the neutral water and put the sieve with spheres onto the paper towel to drain off. Put the spheres, some mint leaves and gold leaf into the mint consommé. As an option one can lace the apricot mixture with mint liqueur or add some green food colouring.

APRIKOSENKAVIAR
(ETWA 20 PORTIONEN)

250 g	*Mineralwasser*
1,3 g	*Citras*
1,8 g	*Algin*
250 g	*Aprikosenpüree*

Mineralwasser mit Citras mischen, dann Algin zugeben und erneut mischen. Anschließend aufkochen, auf Raumtemperatur abkühlen lassen und Aprikosenpüree untermixen.

CALCIC-MISCHUNG FÜR SPHERAS IN KAVIARGRÖSSE

6,5 g	*Calcic*
1000 g	*stilles Mineralwasser*

Calcic und das Mineralwasser mit einem Schneebesen mischen, bis es aufgelöst ist. Eine Schüssel mit einem Liter Wasser zum Waschen der Spheras sowie Küchenpapier bereitstellen.
Achtung: Wasser, Calcic-Mischung sowie Spheras-Mischung direkt gemischt blockieren den Abfluss!
Zur Herstellung der Spheras, den Aprikosen-Mix in eine Spritze ziehen und tröpfchenweise in das Calcic-Wasser geben. Gelieren lassen, mit einem Sieb herausnehmen, im neutralen Wasser waschen und das Sieb auf Küchenpapier abtropfen lassen. Spheras zusammen mit einigen Minzblättern und Blattgold in die Minzconsommé geben. Als Variation einen Schuss Minzlikör zur Aprikosenmischung geben, wahlweise auch etwas grüne Lebensmittelfarbe.

APRIKOSEN-MILCHEIS
(WARME HERSTELLUNG)
(ERGIBT 1000 G)

352 g	Vollmilch
49 g	Invertzucker
141 g	Zucker
67 g	Magermilchpulver
3,5 g	neutraler Eisstabilisator
25 g	Trockenglukose
1/2	Vanilleschote (Mark)
81 g	Sahne
282 g	Aprikosenpüree

Milch und Invertzucker erwärmen, dann alle trockenen Zutaten und das Mark der Vanilleschote mischen und unter die Milch mixen. Masse auf 85 °C pasteurisieren und auf 65 °C herunterkühlen, dann Sahne und Aprikosenpüree untermixen, schnell auf 4 °C herunterkühlen und mit der Eismaschine gefrieren.

TIPP
Bei Verwendung eines Pacojets kann man vollkommen auf den Zucker verzichten.

APRICOT DAIRY ICE-CREAM
(HOT PRODUCTION METHOD)
(MAKES 1000 G)

352 g	whole milk
49 g	invert sugar
141 g	sugar
67 g	skimmed milk powder
3.5 g	neutral ice-cream stabiliser
25 g	dry glucose
1/2	vanilla pod (pith)
81 g	whipping cream
282 g	apricot puree

Warm up the milk and invert sugar, mix all dry ingredients and the vanilla pith together and then stir into the milk. Pasteurise the mixture at 85 °C, cool down to 65 °C to mix in the cream and apricot puree, then chill down quickly to 4 °C and put into the ice-cream maker to freeze.

TIP
When using a Pacojet it is possible to omit the sugar completely.

SCHOKOLADENBISKUIT

70 g	Butter
25 g	Muscovadozucker (Rohrohrzucker)
50 g	Vollei
55 g	Eigelb
125 g	flüssige Bitterkuvertüre, 74 %
167 g	Eiweiß
62 g	Zucker, extrafein
1 g	Salz

Butter und Muscovadozucker schaumig schlagen, nach und nach Vollei und Eigelb zugeben, dann Kuvertüre unterlaufen lassen. Aus Eiweiß, Zucker und Salz einen stabilen Schnee schlagen und unterheben. Masse gleichmäßig auf eine Silikon-Backmatte verteilen und bei 160 °C im Umluftofen etwa 12 Minuten backen.

CHOCOLATE SPONGE

70 g	unsalted butter
25 g	muscovado sugar (unrefined cane sugar)
50 g	whole egg
55 g	egg yolk
125 g	liquid bitter couverture, 74%
167 g	egg white
62 g	sugar, extra fine
1 g	salt

Beat the butter with the muscovado sugar until frothy, add the whole egg and egg white in small doses and finally let the couverture run into it. Beat the egg white, sugar and salt until firm and fold into the mixture. Spread the mixture evenly onto a silicone baking mat and bake at 160 °C in a fan-assisted oven for about 12 minutes.

Pear jelly

250 g	pear puree
1/2	vanilla pod (pith)
255 g	sugar
6 g	pectin
55 g	dry glucose
3 g	citric acid solution (1:1)
3 g	pear brandy

Heat the pear puree with the pith of the vanilla pod up to 50 °C, mix 55 g sugar with the pectin and add to the puree. Bring the mixture to the boil, mix 200 g sugar with the glucose powder, divide this into two or three portions and stir into the mixture. Heat up to 107 °C and start the gelling process by adding the citric acid solution. Then add the pear brandy and pour onto a prepared silicone baking mat with an upstand. Spread out evenly and leave to gel. Once it has cooled down, place a layer of sponge over the jelly and cut into even strips.

Birnengelee

250 g	Birnenpüree
1/2	Vanilleschote (Mark)
255 g	Zucker
6 g	Pektin
55 g	Trockenglukose
3 g	Zitronensäurelösung (1:1)
3 g	Birnenbrand

Birnenpüree mit dem Mark der Vanilleschote auf 50 °C erwärmen, dann 55 g Zucker mit Pektin mischen und dem Püree zugeben. Mischung aufkochen, 200 g Zucker mit dem Glukosepulver mischen und in zwei bis drei Portionen unterrühren. Hergestellte Masse auf 107 °C erhitzen und unter Zugabe der Zitronensäurelösung den Gelierungsprozess einleiten. Mit dem Birnenbrand ablöschen und auf eine vorbereitete Silikon-Backmatte mit Rand ausgießen. Gleichmäßig verstreichen und gelieren lassen. Direkt nach Erkalten mit dem Biskuit aufschichten und in gleichmäßige Streifen schneiden.

Decoration

mint leaves
gold leaf
hazelnut slices
chocolate spaghetti
(see page 308)
fresh blackberries

Dekoration

Minzblätter
Blattgold
Haselnussscheiben
Schokoladenspaghetti
(siehe Seite 308)
frische Brombeeren

HERZHAFTE SORBETS:
STEINPILZ, SHRIMPS, ROQUEFORT

SAVOURY SORBETS:
CEP, SHRIMPS, ROQUEFORT

Herzhaftes Eis ist in. Egal wo, mittlerweile werden solche Kreationen im kompletten Menü eingesetzt. Von meinen zahlreichen Besuchen der Eismesse in Rimini kenne ich diese schon sehr lange, aber bei meinem Freund Alexander Dressel habe ich zum ersten Mal bewusst ein herzhaftes Eis zu einem Fischgang genossen. Damals waren wir noch jung und wild. Heute gilt so etwas schon als normal. Schön, wenn man etwas bewegt.

Savoury ice-creams are in fashion. These creations are now popular in full menus in many places. I have known these for a long time from my frequent visits to the ice-cream fair in Rimini, but the first time I have enjoyed a savoury ice-cream with a fish dish was with my friend Alexander Dressel. In those days we were still young and wild. Nowadays this sort of thing is considered normal. It is nice when one can move something.

Filling quantity for one Pacojet pot

Füllung für 1 Pacojet-Dose

GORGONZOLA-EIS
(WARME HERSTELLUNG)

20 g	Milchpulver
50 g	Dextrose
4 g	Salz
1 g	Kräuter der Provence-Mischung
730 g	Vollmilch
25 g	Sahne
80 g	Roquefort

Trockene Zutaten mischen, Milch unterrühren und bei 85 °C pasteurisieren. Auf 65 °C abkühlen lassen, die Sahne und den Käse untermixen, dann die Masse in einen Pacojet-Behälter geben, für 24 Stunden tiefkühlen und bei Bedarf pacossieren.

GORGONZOLA ICE-CREAM
(HOT PRODUCTION METHOD)

20 g	milk powder
50 g	dextrose
4 g	salt
1 g	Herbes de Provence
730 g	whole milk
25 g	whipping cream
80 g	Roquefort cheese

Mix the dry ingredients, stir in the milk and pasteurise at 85 °C. Allow to cool down to 65 °C, mix in the cream and cheese, put the mixture into a Pacojet container, deep-freeze for 24 hours and pacotise if required.

SHRIMPS-EIS
(WARME HERSTELLUNG)

50 g	Milchpulver
90 g	Dextrose
6 g	Salz
1 g	Paprikapulver, edelsüß
500 g	Vollmilch
200 g	Shrimps, in der Schale gebraten, geschält, feingewürfelt
20 g	Hummerbutter

Trockene Zutaten mischen, Milch unterrühren und bei 85 °C pasteurisieren. Die Shrimps und die Hummerbutter untermixen, dann die Masse in einen Pacojet-Behälter geben und für 24 Stunden tiefkühlen. Bei Bedarf pacossieren.

SHRIMPS ICE-CREAM
(HOT PRODUCTION METHOD)

50 g	milk powder
90 g	dextrose
6 g	salt
1 g	paprika powder, sweet
500 g	whole milk
200 g	shrimps, fried in their shells, peeled and finely diced
20 g	lobster butter

Mix the dry ingredients, stir in the milk and pasteurise at 85 °C. Mix in the shrimps and lobster butter, put the mixture into a Pacojet container and deep-freeze for 24 hours. Pacotise if required.

Gefrorene Eisgrundmischung mit eingeweichten Steinpilzen belegen

Place the soaked ceps onto the frozen basic ice-cream mixture

Fertig pacossiertes Eis

Finished pacotised ice-cream

CEP YOGHURT ICE-CREAM (HOT PRODUCTION METHOD)

540 g	whole milk
40 g	milk powder
90 g	dextrose
6 g	salt
80 g	whipping cream
80 g	yoghurt
50 g	dried ceps

Mix the dry ingredients with the milk and pasteurise at 85 °C. Let the mixture cool down to 65 °C, add the cream and yoghurt, mix well and deep-freeze for 24 hours. Soak the ceps in a little water, place onto the frozen basic ice-cream mixture and pacotise if required.

IMPORTANT

Do not put portions into ice-cream cones.

STEINPILZ-JOGHURT-EIS (WARME HERSTELLUNG)

540 g	Vollmilch
40 g	Milchpulver
90 g	Dextrose
6 g	Salz
80 g	Sahne
80 g	Joghurt
50 g	getrocknete Steinpilze

Trockene Zutaten mit der Milch mischen und bei 85 °C pasteurisieren. Masse auf 65 °C abkühlen lassen, Sahne und Joghurt zugeben, aufmixen und 24 Stunden tiefkühlen. Steinpilze in etwas Wasser einweichen, auf die gefrorene Grundeismischung geben und bei Bedarf pacossieren.

WICHTIG

Bitte nicht in eine Eistüte portionieren.

INDIAN SUMMERDRINK

INDIAN SUMMER DRINK

INDIEN MIT SEINER GEWÜRZHOCHBURG KERALA IM SÜDEN IST EIN WAHRES EL DORADO FÜR GEWÜRZFANS WIE MICH. FAST ALLE GEWÜRZE DER WELT FINDET MAN AUF DIESEM FLECKCHEN ERDE. SCHON BEI EINEM EINFACHEN SPAZIERGANG FALLEN EINEM DIE ZUTATEN SOZUSAGEN IN DEN SCHOSS.

INDIA, AND ESPECIALLY KERALA IN THE SOUTH WITH ALL ITS SPICES, IS A TRUE EL DORADO FOR SPICE FANS LIKE MYSELF. IN THIS CORNER OF THE GLOBE YOU CAN FIND ALMOST ALL SPICES THAT EXIST IN THE WORLD. JUST GO FOR A SHORT WALK AND THE INGREDIENTS WILL ALMOST FALL INTO YOUR LAP.

ZUTATEN FÜR 12 PERSONEN

EISTEE-PUNSCH

2000 g	starker, gebrühter schwarzer Assam-Tee
10 g	Zimtblüten
120 g	Honig
100 g	Rum
40 g	Tamarindenpaste

Alle Zutaten mischen und auf 80 °C erwärmen, durch ein feines Sieb passieren, danach gekühlt lagern.

INGREDIENTS FOR 12 PERSONS

ICE TEA PUNCH

2000 g	strong infused Assam tea
10 g	cinnamon flowers
120 g	honey
100 g	rum
40 g	tamarind paste

Mix all ingredients together and heat up to 80 °C, pass through a fine sieve and store in a cool place.

GEWÜRZTES MILCHEIS
(WARME HERSTELLUNG)
(ERGIBT 1000 G)

183 g	Zucker
24 g	Dextrose
30 g	Milchpulver
30 g	Stabilisator für Sahne-Milcheis
610 g	Milch, 3,5 %
2	Stangen Ceylonzimt
2	Gewürznelken
10	Kardamomkapseln
1	Vanilleschote
122 g	Sahne, 35 %

Trockene Zutaten mischen, Milch mit den Gewürzen aufkochen, die Gewürze entnehmen und trockene Zutaten zugeben. Masse bei 85 °C pasteurisieren. Eismix herunterkühlen, bei 60 °C Sahne zugeben und auf 4 °C abkühlen. Reifen lassen, dann durch ein feines Sieb passieren und in der Eismaschine abfrieren.

SPICY ICE-CREAM
(HOT PRODUCTION METHOD)
(MAKES 1000 G)

183 g	sugar
24 g	dextrose
30 g	milk powder
30 g	stabiliser for ice-cream made with cream
610 g	milk, 3.5 %
2	sticks of Ceylon cinnamon
2	whole cloves
10	cardamom pods
1	vanilla pod
122 g	cream, 35 %

Mix all ingredients, bring the milk and spices to the boil, take out the spices and add the dry ingredients. Pasteurise the mixture at 85 °C. Cool the mixture down to 60 °C, add the cream and cool down to 4 °C. Leave to mature, pass through a fine sieve and put into the ice-cream maker to freeze.

MANGOSAHNE

500 g	Sahne
200 g	Mangopüree
50 g	Puderzucker

Alle Zutaten im Espuma-Siphon mischen und 2 Gaspatronen aufschrauben.

MANGO CREAM

500 g	whipping cream
200 g	mango puree
50 g	icing sugar

Mix all ingredients in an Espuma foaming beaker and insert 2 gas cartridges.

ALMOND TUILLE SCROLL

75 g	*sugar*
1.2 g	*pectin*
50 g	*unsalted butter*
25 g	*glucose syrup*
25 g	*orange juice*
10 g	*grated almonds*

Mix the sugar with the pectin and boil together with the butter, glucose syrup and orange juice. Stir in the grated almonds and put into a cold place.

Use a piping bag to pipe fine lines onto a Teflon baking mat, bake at 180 °C for about 15 minutes. Allow the pastry to cool down a little, while still warm roll onto a metal rod to form a scroll. Store in a dry place.

MANDELTUILLELOCKE

75 g	*Zucker*
1,2 g	*Pektin*
50 g	*Butter*
25 g	*Glukosesirup*
25 g	*Orangensaft*
10 g	*Mandelgrieß*

Zucker und Pektin mischen, mit Butter, Glukosesirup und Orangensaft aufkochen. Mandelgrieß unterrühren, kaltstellen. Mit dem Spritzbeutel kleine Linien auf eine Teflon-Backmatte spritzen, bei 180 °C etwa 15 Minuten backen. Den Teig leicht abkühlen lassen, aber in noch warmem Zustand lockenförmig auf einen Metallstab aufrollen. Trocken lagern.

INKA ICE-CREAM CAKE

ARGENTINIEN UND MEINE FREUNDE VON DER MAUSI-SEBESS-SCHULE HABEN MICH ZU DIESER KREATION MIT DULCE DE LECHE INSPIRIERT. ICH HABE SIE ZUERST ETWAS SPARSAMER EINGESETZT ALS ICH SIE IN DEN ARGENTINISCHEN RESTAURANTS SERVIERT BEKOMMEN HABE, DA ICH DACHTE, FÜR UNSEREN EUROPÄISCHEN GESCHMACK WÄRE SIE MÖGLICHERWEISE ZU SÜSS. ABER MITTLERWEILE LIEBE ICH SIE SOGAR, GANZ NACH SÜDAMERIKANISCHER TRADITION, AUF MEINEM FRÜHSTÜCKSBRÖTCHEN.

ARGENTINA AND MY FRIENDS AT THE MAUSI-SEBESS SCHOOL HAVE PROVIDED THE INSPIRATION FOR THIS CREATION WITH DULCE DE LECHE. AT FIRST I USED IT SOMEWHAT MORE SPARINGLY COMPARED TO HOW IT WAS SERVED TO ME IN THE ARGENTINIAN RESTAURANTS BECAUSE I THOUGHT THAT IT WOULD BE A BIT TOO SWEET FOR OUR EUROPEAN TASTE. BUT NOW I LIKE IT SO MUCH THAT I EVEN SPREAD IT ON MY BREAKFAST ROLL, JUST LIKE THEY DO IT IN SOUTH AMERICA.

4 ICE-CREAM CAKES Ø 18 CM

ALMOND CRUST WITH COCOA BEAN PIECES

300 g	marzipan raw mixture
180 g	whole egg
40 g	egg yolk
70 g	flour, type 550
80 g	caramelised cocoa bean pieces
2 g	baking powder
90 g	unsalted butter

Making the parts see next page.

4 EISTORTEN Ø 18 CM

MANDELBODEN MIT KAKAOBOHNENBRUCH

300 g	Marzipanrohmasse
180 g	Vollei
40 g	Eigelb
70 g	Mehl, Typ 550
80 g	karamellisierter Kakaobohnenbruch
2 g	Backpulver
90 g	Butter

Zubereitung siehe nächste Seite.

MANDELBODEN MIT KAKAOBOHNENBRUCH

Marzipanrohmasse in der Mikrowelle erwärmen und mit Vollei und Eigelb zuerst glatt, dann schaumig schlagen.
Mehl und Kakaobohnenbruch mit Backpulver vermischen, unter die Masse melieren, zum Schluss Butter unterziehen. In eine passende Form füllen und bei 180 °C für etwa 20 Minuten backen.

KAFFEE-KARAMEL-AMARETTO-TRÄNKE

500 g	Zucker
500 g	Kaffee
100 g	Amarettolikör

Zucker karamellisieren lassen, mit dem Kaffee ablöschen und sobald die Mischung erkaltet ist, den Amaretto unterrühren.

KARAMELLFÜLLUNG (DULCE DE LECHE) (FÜLLUNG)

80 g	Zucker
65 g	Glukosesirup
110 g	Sahne
1 g	Meersalz
½	Vanilleschote
15 g	Honig
	Abrieb und Saft von 1 Orange
30 g	Butter

Zucker mit Glukosesirup karamellisieren und mit der erwärmten Sahne ablöschen. Anschließend mit den anderen Zutaten auf 104 °C kochen, dann abkühlen lassen, die Vanilleschote entnehmen und bei 35 °C die Butter untermixen.

ALMOND CRUST WITH COCOA BEAN PIECES

Heat the marzipan raw mixture in the microwave, beat together with the whole egg and egg yolk until smooth and then more until it is frothy.
Mix the flour and cocoa bean pieces with baking powder, stir gently into the mixture and finally fold in the butter. Fill a suitable tin with the mixture and then bake at 180 °C for about 20 minutes.

COFFEE CARAMEL AMARETTO SOAKING

500 g	sugar
500 g	coffee
100 g	amaretto

Caramelise the sugar, pour the coffee over the sugar and stir in the amaretto when the mixture has cooled down.

CARAMEL FILLING (DULCE DE LECHE) (FILLING)

80 g	sugar
65 g	glucose syrup
110 g	whipping cream
1 g	sea salt
½	vanilla pod
15 g	honey
	Zest and juice of 1 orange
30 g	unsalted butter

Caramelise the sugar with the glucose syrup and add the cream after heating it up moderately. Add the other ingredients and boil up to 104 °C, allow to cool, take out the vanilla pod and mix in the butter at 35 °C.

ORANGE CHOCOLATE ICE-CREAM (HOT PRODUCTION METHOD) (INSIDE LAYER)

107 g	sugar
14 g	dextrose
11 g	skimmed milk powder
1 g	neutral stabiliser
43 g	egg yolk
357 g	milk
143	bitter couverture, 70 %
	Zest from 2 oranges
7	drops of orange oil (modify quantity de pending on strength)
104 g	whipping cream
11 g	invert sugar

Mix the dry ingredients together, mix in the milk and egg yolk and pasteurise at 85 °C. Make a ganache from the couverture, cream and invert sugar and mix in with the base mixture after it has cooled to 65 °C. Cool down quickly to 4 °C, allow to mature and freeze in the ice-cream maker. Decant into a suitable mould, freeze thoroughly, remove from the mould and keep ready for the next step.

ORANGEN-SCHOKOLADENEIS (WARME HERSTELLUNG) (EINLAGE)

107 g	Zucker
14 g	Dextrose
11 g	Magermilchpulver
1 g	neutraler Stabilisator
43 g	Eigelb
357 g	Milch
143 g	Bitterkuvertüre, 70 %
	Abrieb von 2 Orangen
7	Tropfen Orangenöl (je nach Qualität variieren)
104 g	Sahne
11 g	Invertzucker

Die trockenen Zutaten vermengen, mit Eigelb und Milch mischen und auf 85 °C pasteurisieren. Aus Kuvertüre, Sahne und Invertzucker eine Ganache herstellen und unter die auf 65 °C abgekühlte Basismasse mixen. Rasch auf 4 °C herunterkühlen, reifen lassen und in der Eismaschine gefrieren. In eine passende Form einfüllen, durchgefrieren, ausformen und zum Weiterverarbeiten bereitstellen.

Kaffee-Karamell-Parfait (Mantel)

302 g	Zucker
391 g	Milch
227 g	Eigelb
18 g	löslicher Kaffee
661 g	geschlagene Sahne

Zucker karamellisieren, mit der erwärmten Milch ablöschen und unter das Eigelb rühren. Auf 85 °C pasteurisieren und kalt schlagen, dann die geschlagene Sahne unterheben. In eine Form geben, eine dünne Karamell-Schicht einfüllen und mit dem ausgeformten Schokoladeneis auffüllen. Den Schokoladenbiskuit auflegen und gut durchfrieren, dann ausformen und mit der gelben Sprühkuvertüre absprühen. Von einer Seite mit Bittersprühkuvertüre besprühen, eine Schablone auflegen und mit gelber Sprühkuvertüre das Muster aufsprühen.

Coffee caramel parfait (cover)

302 g	sugar
391 g	milk
227 g	egg yolk
18 g	instant coffee
661 g	whipped cream

Caramelise the sugar, pour the warm milk over it and stir into the egg yolk. Pasteurise at 85 °C, then beat until cold and fold in the whipped cream. Put the mixture into a mould, add a thin layer of caramel and fill up with the chocalate ice-cream. Place the chocolate biscuit on top and freeze thoroughly, take out of the mould and spray with the yellow spray couverture. Spray on one side with bitter spray couverture, then spray on the pattern with a stencil and the yellow spray couverture.

Dekoration

Dekor aus Isomalt
ganze Kakaobohnen

Decoration

Isomalt decor
whole cocoa beans

NACHBARS GARTENSONNE

NEIGHBOUR'S GARDEN SUN

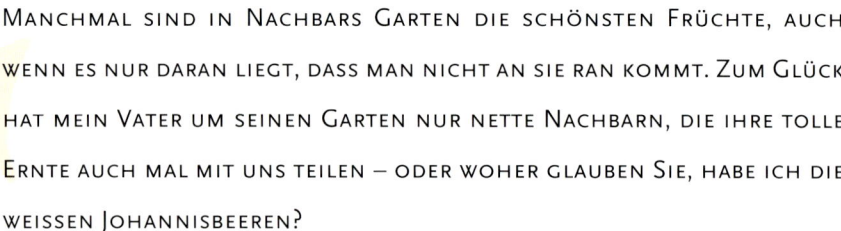

MANCHMAL SIND IN NACHBARS GARTEN DIE SCHÖNSTEN FRÜCHTE, AUCH
WENN ES NUR DARAN LIEGT, DASS MAN NICHT AN SIE RAN KOMMT. ZUM GLÜCK
HAT MEIN VATER UM SEINEN GARTEN NUR NETTE NACHBARN, DIE IHRE TOLLE
ERNTE AUCH MAL MIT UNS TEILEN – ODER WOHER GLAUBEN SIE, HABE ICH DIE
WEISSEN JOHANNISBEEREN?

SOMETIMES THE NICEST FRUIT SEEMS TO BE IN THE NEIGHBOUR'S GARDEN EVEN
JUST FOR THE SOLE REASON THAT WE CAN'T HAVE IT. I AM LUCKY IN THAT THE
NEIGHBOURS AROUND MY FATHER'S GARDEN ARE ALL FRIENDLY AND OFTEN
SHARE THEIR GORGEOUS HARVEST WITH US – WHERE ELSE DO YOU THINK I
COULD FIND THESE WHITE CURRANTS?

ZUTATEN FÜR 12 PERSONEN	INGREDIENTS FOR 12 PERSONS
WEISSE JOHANNISBEEREN IN PROSECCOGELEE	**WHITE CURRANTS IN PROSECCO JELLY**

	WEISSE JOHANNISBEEREN IN PROSECCOGELEE		WHITE CURRANTS IN PROSECCO JELLY
8	*Blatt Gelatine*	8	*sheets of gelatine*
500 g	*Prosecco*	500 g	*Prosecco*
50 g	*Zucker*	50 g	*sugar*
	weiße Johannisbeeren		*White currants*

Die Gelatine in kaltem Wasser einweichen.
Zucker zum Prosecco geben. Die Gelatine,
ausgepresst und aufgelöst, nach und nach
mit dem Prosecco mischen, so dass die
Kohlensäure weitgehend erhalten bleibt.
Langsam in passende, schräg gestellte Gläser füllen, mit einigen weißen Johannisbeeren füllen und gelieren lassen.

Soak the gelatine in cold water. Add the
sugar to the Prosecco. Squeeze and dissolve
the gelatine and mix step by step with the
Prosecco so that most of the carbonic acid
remains. Slowly decant the mixture into
suitable glasses that are leaning against
something so that they are at an angle, fill
with some white currants and then leave
to gel.

CASSIS SORBET
(HOT PRODUCTION METHOD)

50 g	dry glucose
5 g	neutral ice-cream binding agent
170 g	sugar
1	bay leaf
2 g	vanilla pith
390 g	water
385 g	cassis puree

Mix all dry ingredients, boil with the water and remove the bay leaf. Add the cassis puree and then use a refractometer to adjust to 32 °Brix. Allow the mixture to mature at 4 °C and freeze in the ice-cream maker.

CASSISSORBET
(WARME HERSTELLUNG)

50 g	Trockenglukose
5 g	neutrales Eisbindemittel
170 g	Zucker
1	Lorbeerblatt
2 g	Vanillemark
390 g	Wasser
385 g	Cassispüree

Alle trockenen Zutaten mischen, mit Wasser aufkochen und das Lorbeerblatt entfernen. Das Cassispüree zugeben und mit dem Refraktometer auf 32 °Brix einstellen. Masse bei 4 °C reifen lassen und in der Eismaschine abfrieren.

PISTACHIO ICE-CREAM
(HOT PRODUCTION METHOD)

40 g	milk powder
120 g	sugar
5 g	neutral ice-cream binding agent
40 g	invert sugar
30 g	egg yolk
625 g	whole milk
35 g	pistachio paste, 100 %
35 g	pistachios, finely ground
70 g	unsalted butter
5 g	kirsch

Mix the dry ingredients, add the invert sugar, egg yolk and milk and pasteurise at 85 °C. When the mixture has cooled down to 65 °C, mix in the pistachio paste, ground pistachios, butter and kirsch. Place into the ice-cream maker to freeze.

PISTAZIENEIS
(WARME HERSTELLUNG)

40 g	Milchpulver
120 g	Zucker
5 g	neutrales Eisbindemittel
40 g	Invertzucker
30 g	Eigelb
625 g	Vollmilch
35 g	Pistazienpaste, 100 %
35 g	fein geriebene Pistazien
70 g	Butter
5 g	Kirschwasser

Trockene Zutaten mischen, dann Invertzucker, Eigelb und Milch zugeben und bei 85 °C pasteurisieren. Pistazienpaste, geriebene Pistazien, Butter und Kirschwasser bei 65 °C untermixen. In der Eismaschine abfrieren.

MANGOSALAT

75 g	*Zucker*
75 g	*Glukosesirup*
150 g	*Maracujasaft*
450 g	*Mango, geschält, entkernt und gewürfelt*

Zucker und Glukosesirup hell karamellisieren, dann mit Maracujasaft ablöschen, abschließend Mangowürfel unterschwenken. Gekühlt lagern.

MANGO SALAD

75 g	*sugar*
75 g	*glucose syrup*
150 g	*passion fruit juice*
450 g	*peeled, cored and diced mangos*

Caramelise the sugar and glucose syrup to a light colour, pour in the passion fruit juice and finally add the diced mango. Store in a cool place.

CASSIS-BANANEN-SOSSE

50 g	*Zucker*
100 g	*Glukosesirup*
100 g	*Cassispüree*
140 g	*Bananenpüree*

Zucker hell karamellisieren, Glukose zugeben. Cassis- und Bananenpüree nach und nach zugeben, die Mischung einmal aufkochen.

CASSIS BANANA SAUCE

50 g	*sugar*
100 g	*glucose syrup*
100 g	*cassis puree*
140 g	*banana puree*

Caramelise the sugar to a light colour and add the glucose. Add the cassis and banana puree in small doses and bring the mixture to the boil.

Teig so auf eine genoppte Silikon-Backmatte streichen, dass ein Lochmuster zu sehen ist

Spread the pastry onto a studded silicone baking mat so that the hole pattern becomes visible

Nach dem Backen vorsichtig aus der Silikon-Backmatte ausformen

After baking, remove carefully from the silicone baking mat

Die noch heiße Eiswaffel mit einem runden Ausstecher in Form bringen

Use a round cutter to cut the shapes from the ice waffle while it is still hot

PERFORATED ICE-CREAM WAFFLE

100 g	*unsalted butter*
100 g	*icing sugar*
2 g	*vanilla pith*
1 g	*cinnamon*
1 g	*salt*
100 g	*egg white*
100 g	*flour*

Mix the butter with the spices and the icing sugar after passing it through a sieve, then work in the egg white and flour in turns; make sure that the mixture does not become frothy. Spread the pastry onto a studded silicone mat so that the hole pattern becomes visible. After baking, remove carefully and then use a round cutting shape to cut the waffle while it is still hot.

GELOCHTE EISWAFFEL

100 g	*Butter*
100 g	*Puderzucker*
2 g	*Vanillemark*
1 g	*Zimt*
1 g	*Salz*
100 g	*Eiweiß*
100 g	*Mehl*

Butter mit durchgesiebtem Puderzucker und den Gewürzen mischen, dann abwechselnd Eiweiß und Mehl unterarbeiten, dabei darauf achten, dass die Masse nicht schaumig wird. Den Teig so auf eine genoppte Silikon-Backmatte streichen, dass ein Lochmuster zu sehen ist. Nach dem Backen vorsichtig ausformen und die noch heiße Waffel mit einem runden Ausstecher in Form bringen.

DECORATION

sprig of white currants

DEKORATION

Johannisbeerrispe

JAPANESE GARDEN

Natürlich ist diese Eisbombe meine Sicht der Dinge und nicht wirklich traditionell japanisch. Aber für mich gibt es nichts Schöneres als einen japanischen Garten. Ich hoffe, ich werde diesem gerecht.

Of course, this ice-cream bomb is not really a traditional Japanese dish but just reflects my view of things. For me, there is nothing more beautiful than a Japanese garden. I hope this recipe does justice to the idea.

---

4 ICE-CREAM BOMBS Ø 18 CM

GREEN TEA ALMOND CRUST (DACQUOISE)

225 g	egg white
5 g	dried egg white
75 g	sugar
190 g	grated almonds
185 g	sugar, extra fine
25 g	flour
5 g	Matcha green tea powder

Mix the egg white with the dried egg white and 150 g sugar and beat until firm, mix the remaining ingredients and fold them into the egg mixture. Use a piping bag with round nozzle size 8 to pipe the mixture onto a baking mat in the diameter of the ice-cream bomb, start baking at 200 °C and continue to bake at 170 °C for about 30 minutes.

---

4 EISBOMBEN Ø 18 CM

GRÜNTEEMANDELBODEN (DAQUOISE)

225 g	Eiweiß
5 g	Trockeneiweiß
75 g	Zucker
190 g	Mandelgrieß
185 g	Zucker, extrafein
25 g	Mehl
5 g	Matcha-Grünteepulver

Eiweiß, Trockeneiweiß und 150 g Zucker zu einem festen Schnee schlagen, dann die restlichen Zutaten mischen und unter den Schnee heben. Die Masse mit einem Spritzbeutel und einer 8er-Lochtülle im Durchmesser der Eisbombe auf eine Backmatte aufdressieren, bei 200 °C anbacken und bei 170 °C etwa 30 Minuten ausbacken.

Kirsch-Tränke für den Boden

125 g	Zucker
125 g	Wasser
25 g	Kirschwasser, 40 %

Zucker mit Wasser aufkochen, sobald die Mischung erkaltet ist, Kirschwasser unterrühren und den Boden damit tränken.

Grüntee-Kirschblüteneis (warme Herstellung) (Mantel)

385 g	Zucker
55 g	Trockenglukose
82 g	Milchpulver
14 g	Matcha-Grünteepulver
193 g	Eigelb
1761 g	Vollmilch
110 g	Butter
7	Tropfen Kirschblütenessenz (je nach Qualität variieren)

Die trockenen Zutaten mischen, dann mit Eigelb und Milch aufmixen, bei 85 °C pasteurisieren und auf 65 °C herunterkühlen. Dann die Butter untermixen und sobald erkaltet, Essenz zugeben, reifen lassen und abfrieren. Die vorgefrorene Eisform damit auschemisieren.

Kirsch soaking for the crust

125 g	sugar
125 g	water
25 g	kirsch, 40 %

Boil the sugar with the water, when the mixture is cold again, stir in the kirsch and pour over the crust.

Green tea cherry blossom ice-cream (hot production method) (cover)

385 g	sugar
55 g	dry glucose
82 g	milk powder
14 g	Matcha green tea powder
193 g	egg yolk
1761 g	whole milk
110 g	unsalted butter
7	drops of cherry blossom essence (modify quantity depending on strength)

Mix the dry ingredients, add in and mix the egg yolk and the milk, pasteurise this mixture at 85 °C and cool down to 65 °C. Then stir in the butter and when the mixture is cold add the essence, leave to mature and freeze. Line a pre-frozen ice-cream mould with this mixture.

CHERRY BANANA SORBET (COLD PRODUCTION METHOD) (CENTRE)

70 g	dry glucose
189 g	sugar
386 g	morello cherry puree
281 g	banana puree
4 g	fruit acid
14 g	invert sugar
456 g	water

Mix the dry glucose together with the sugar. Mix in the fruit purees and the other ingredients and adjust to 32 °Brix in a refractometer. Put in a deep-freeze, fill the ice-cream bomb with the sorbet, put on the crust and freeze thoroughly. Take out of the mould, spray with white spray couverture and green tea spray couverture. Use a piping bag to apply the green tea icing.

KIRSCH-BANANEN-SORBET (KALTE HERSTELLUNG) (KERN)

70 g	Trockenglukose
189 g	Zucker
386 g	Sauerkirschpüree
281 g	Bananenpüree
4 g	Fruchtsäure
14 g	Invertzucker
456 g	Wasser

Trockenglukose und Zucker mischen. Fruchtpürees und die restlichen Zutaten untermixen und mit dem Refraktometer auf 32 °Brix einstellen. Abfrieren, die Eisbombe damit füllen, dann Boden auflegen und durchfrieren. Anschließend ausformen, mit weißer Sprühkuvertüre und Grünteesprühkuvertüre absprühen. Mit Hilfe einer Garniertüte Grüntee-Glasur aufdekorieren.

DECORATION

white spray couverture
green tea spray couverture
green tea icing (white icing and Matcha green tea powder)
fresh cherries
silver leaf
candied cherry blossoms
sugar decoration

DEKORATION

weiße Sprühkuvertüre
Grüntee-Sprühkuvertüre
Grüntee-Glasur (weiße Glasur und Matcha-Grünteepulver)
frische Kirschen
Blattsilber
kandierte Kirschblüten
Zuckerdekoration

KING LOUIE, DIE ZWEITE

KING LOUIS THE SECOND

Was ist des Deutschen liebstes Kind? Natürlich Pommes rot-weiss, äh blau-weiss! Diese Kreation ist immer ein Hingucker in unserem Café und so etwas braucht man, um im Gespräch zu bleiben. Bei uns im Odenwald gibt es eine Kartoffel-Spezialitätenwoche für die ich schon manche Spezialität kreiert habe.

What is German children's favourite food? It must be "chips red/white" (with ketchup and mayonnaise) — or is it blue/white? This creation always gets the looks in our café and you need something like that to keep you in people's minds and conversations.

ZUTATEN FÜR 12 PERSONEN		INGREDIENTS FOR 12 PERSONS	
LILA KARTOFFELPARFAIT		**PURPLE POTATO PARFAIT**	
150 g	Vollei	150 g	whole egg
5 g	Stollen-Gewürzmischung	5 g	Stollen spice mixture
210 g	Zucker	210 g	sugar
200 g	Kartoffelpüree aus lila Kartoffeln	200 g	potato puree from purple potatoes
	Abrieb von 1 Bio-Zitrone		Zest from 1 organic lemon
475 g	halb geschlagene Sahne	475 g	half-whipped cream

Vollei mit der Gewürzmischung schaumig schlagen. In der Zwischenzeit Zucker und etwas Wasser auf 119 °C kochen und in dünnem Strahl in den Eischaum einlaufen lassen. Masse kalt schlagen und zuerst Püree und Zitronenschale unterheben, dann Sahne. Mischung in eine Silikonform füllen, einfrieren und gefroren zu Pommes frites schneiden.

Beat the whole egg with the spice mixture until frothy. In the meantime, boil the sugar with a little water at 119 °C and add to the beaten egg in a thin stream. Beat the mixture until cold and then fold in the puree and lemon zest followed by the cream. Fill the mixture into a silicone mould, freeze and once frozen, cut into chip shapes.

KOKOSMAYONNAISE

200 g	*Kokospüree*
50 g	*Puderzucker*
	etwa 6 g Xanthan
30 g	*Kokoslikör*

Alle Zutaten mischen und mit einem Mixstab stabil aufmixen. Mit einer Dosierflasche aufbringen.

COCONUT MAYONNAISE

200 g	*coconut puree*
50 g	*icing sugar*
	about 6 g xanthan gum
30 g	*coconut liqueur*

Blend all ingredients together and user a mixer to mix until firm. Apply with the help of a dosing bottle.

SÜSSES ROTE-BOHNEN-KETCHUP

100 g	*Rote Bohnen (Azuki)*
100 g	*weißer Rohrzucker*
100 g	*Portwein*
20 g	*Kirschwasser*

Die Rote Bohnen in kaltem Wasser einweichen, Wasser abgießen und mit dem Rohrzucker im Portwein weich kochen. Anschließend Kirschwasser untermixen und gekühlt in Einmachgläsern lagern.

SWEET RED BEAN KETCHUP

100 g	*red beans (azuki or aduki)*
100 g	*white cane sugar*
100 g	*port*
20 g	*kirsch*

Soak the beans in cold water, drain the water and boil in the port with the cane sugar until soft. Then mix in the kirsch and store in preserve glasses in a refrigerator.

EISWAFFELBLATT

50 g	*Butter*
50 g	*Puderzucker*
1 g	*Vanillemark*
1 g	*Zimt*
1 g	*Salz*
50 g	*Eiweiß*
50 g	*Mehl*

Butter mit durchgesiebtem Puderzucker und den Gewürzen mischen, abwechselnd Eiweiß und Mehl unterarbeiten. Darauf achten, dass die Masse nicht schaumig wird. Anschließend durch eine Schablone auf eine Backmatte streichen und bei 170 °C etwa 15 Minuten backen. Dann jedes Blatt, noch heiß, zwischen zwei Zuckerstempeln abstempeln, damit sich das Blattmuster abzeichnet. Trocken lagern.

ICE WAFFLE LEAF

50 g	*unsalted butter*
50 g	*icing sugar*
1 g	*vanilla*
1 g	*cinnamon*
1 g	*salt*
50 g	*egg white*
50 g	*flour*

Mix the butter with the spices and the icing sugar after passing it through a sieve, then work in the egg white and flour in turns, making sure that the mixture does not become frothy. Spread over a stencil that has been placed on a baking mat and bake at 170 °C for about 15 minutes. While still hot, press each leaf between two sugar stamps to imprint the leaf pattern. Store in a dry place.

PINEAPPLE SESAME JELLY

3	*sheets of gelatine*
12 g	*glucose syrup*
40 g	*icing sugar*
50 g	*pineapple puree*
50 g	*Isomalt*
1/2	*vanilla pod*
50 g	*almond oil*
50 g	*roasted sesame oil*

Soak the gelatine in cold water. Then add the glucose syrup, icing sugar, pineapple puree, Isomalt and vanilla pod into the Thermomix and run at 90 °C for 15 minutes. Squeeze the gelatine and add it to the mixture, pour through a sieve and then back into the Thermomix to cool it down to 45 °C. Then add the oils in small doses; as soon as all of the oil has been worked in, pour the mixture into a suitable frame and leave to cool. Cover and chill. Use cutting rings to cut the circles and sprinkle some sugar over them.

ANANAS-SESAMÖL-GELEE

3	*Blatt Gelatine*
12 g	*Glukosesirup*
40 g	*Puderzucker*
50 g	*Ananaspüree*
50 g	*Isomalt*
1/2	*Vanilleschote*
50 g	*Mandelöl*
50 g	*geröstetes Sesamöl*

Gelatine in kaltem Wasser einweichen. Glukosesirup, Puderzucker, Ananaspüree, Isomalt und Vanilleschote im Thermomix auf 90 °C Einstellung 15 Minuten lang laufen lassen. Anschließend die Gelatine ausgepresst zugeben, Masse durch ein Sieb gießen und weiterlaufend im Thermomix auf 45 °C abkühlen. Die Öle nach und nach zugeben und sobald das ganze Öl untergearbeitet ist, die Masse in einen passenden Rahmen gießen und erkalten lassen. Abgedeckt kühlen. Abschließend in passender Größe ausstechen und zuckern.

DECORATION

red currants
chocolate decor
(see page 294)

DEKORATION

rote Johannisbeeren
Schokoladendekor
(siehe Seite 294)

MY LITTLE POWERBOAT

AUCH DIESE FORM HABE ICH AUS DEN USA MITGEBRACHT. UND DA ICH SCHON ALS KLEINES KIND EIS AM STIEL SELBST GEMACHT HABE, HABE ICH MICH GEFRAGT, WARUM ES HEUTE MIT SOLCH TOLLEN FORMEN NICHT AUCH GEHEN SOLLTE. ES HAT GEKLAPPT – EIS AM STIEL MAL ANDERS.

THIS IS ANOTHER MOULD I HAVE BROUGHT BACK FROM THE USA. AND SINCE I HAVE BEEN MAKING MY OWN ICE LOLLIES SINCE I WAS A SMALL CHILD, I WONDERED WHETHER IT WOULD ALSO WORK WITH THESE EXCITING NEW MOULDS. IT DID – AN ICE LOLLY WITH A DIFFERENCE.

INGREDIENTS FOR 12 PERSONS

SHORTCRUST FOR THE BOAT SHAPE

230 g	unsalted butter
75 g	icing sugar
1 g	sea salt
10 g	egg yolk, coagulated and strained
215 g	flour
43 g	corn starch
	some bitter couverture

Mix all ingredients together and kneed into a pastry, chill thoroughly and then roll out to a thickness of about 3 mm. Line the small boat moulds with the pastry and bake blind at 165 °C for about 25 minutes. Apply some tempered bitter couverture to the boat shapes after they have cooled down.

ZUTATEN FÜR 12 PERSONEN

EISSCHIFFCHEN MÜRBTEIG

230 g	Butter
75 g	Puderzucker
1 g	Meersalz
10 g	Eigelb, gestockt und passiert
215 g	Mehl
43 g	Maisstärke
	etwas Bitterkuvertüre

Alle Zutaten zu einem Teig verkneten, gut kühlen und etwa 3 Millimeter stark ausrollen. Kleine Schiffsförmchen mit dem Teig auslegen und bei 165 °C etwa 25 Minuten blind backen. Die Schiffchen ausgekühlt in temperierter Bitterkuvertüre absetzen.

RED-BULL-WASSEREIS
(ERGIBT 1000 G)

300 g	Red-Bull-Konzentratflüssigkeit
300 g	Wasser
22,5 g	Xanthan
1	Vanilleschote (Mark)
150 g	Mangopüree
150 g	Himbeerpüree
15 g	Rote-Bete-Saftkonzentrat
	etwas geschlagene Sahne

Alle Zutaten aufmixen und dann die Mischung halbieren. Zur einen Hälfte das Mangopüree zugeben, zur anderen das Himbeerpüree und 15 g Rote-Bete-Saftkonzentrat.

Zuerst eine dreieckige Stieleis-Form zu zwei Dritteln mit der gelben Flüssigkeit füllen, gefrieren, den Rest mit der roten auffüllen und dann erneut gefrieren. Vor dem Servieren ausformen und mit etwas geschlagener Sahne im Boot befestigen.

RED BULL WATER ICE
(MAKES 1000 G)

300 g	Red Bull concentrate
300 g	water
22.5 g	xanthan gum
1	vanilla pod (pith)
150 g	mango puree
150 g	raspberry puree
15 g	beetroot juice concentrate
	some whipped cream

Mix all ingredients together and then divide into two equal portions. Add 150 g mango puree to one portion and 150 g raspberry puree and 15 g beetroot juice concentrate to the other portion.

Fill a triangular ice lolly mould up to two thirds with the yellow liquid, freeze, fill up the rest with the red liquid and then freeze again. Take out of the mould and fix with a little whipped cream in the boat before serving.

ZUCKERWELLEN

200 g	Isomalt

Isomalt auflösen und auf eine Backmatte gießen, erkalten lassen und im Kutter grob hacken. Das entstandene Pulver mit einer Schablone auf eine Backmatte aufbringen und im Ofen bei 160 °C verschmelzen. Trocken lagern.

SUGAR WAVES

200 g	Isomalt

Dissolve the Isomalt, pour onto a baking mat, leave to cool and chop up in a cutter. Use a stencil to sprinkle the Isomalt onto a baking sheet, place into the oven at 160 °C so that the powder melts together. Store in a dry place.

Grob zerkleinerte Isomaltkristalle auf eine, mit einer Schablone belegte Teflon-Backmatte streuen.

Crush the Isomalt into course crystals and sprinkle onto a Teflon baking mat, using a stencil to make the shapes

1

Isomaltkristalle gleichmäßig auf der Backmatte verteilen

Spread the Isomalt crystals evenly on the baking mat

2

Schablone vorsichtig abnehmen

Carefully remove the stencil

3

Fertige Zuckerkristallwellen

Finished sugar crystal waves

4

ORANGE APRICOT SAUCE

125 g	sugar
225 g	apricot puree
100 g	orange juice concentrate
1.5 g	xanthan gum
25 g	Grand Marnier

Caramelise 25 g sugar to a light colour, add the fruit puree and juice concentrate. Mix the xanthan gum and the remaining 100 g of the sugar, add and boil briefly. Add the Grand Marnier and mix everything thoroughly. Store in a cool place.

ORANGEN-APRIKOSENSOSSE

125 g	Zucker
225 g	Aprikosenpüree
100 g	Orangensaftkonzentrat
1,5 g	Xanthan
25 g	Grand Marnier

25 g Zucker hell karamellisieren, Fruchtpüree und Saftkonzentrat zugeben. Xanthan und 100 g Zucker mischen, zugeben und kurz aufkochen. Dann den Grand Marnier zugeben und alles gut durchmixen. Gekühlt lagern.

MELBA 3000

MELBA 3000

EINEN DER BEKANNTESTEN EISBECHER HABEN WIR DEM BERÜHMTEN KOCH AUGUSTE ESCOFFIER UND EINER SÄNGERIN NAMENS NELLY MELBA ZU VERDANKEN. ESCOFFIER HAT DIESE EISSPEZIALITÄT DAMALS IN EINEM GESCHNITZTEN EISSCHWAN SERVIERT. LEIDER HAT DAZU HEUTE KEINER MEHR DIE ZEIT, ABER WENN MAN EINE SILIKONFORM BENUTZT, KANN MAN ES EINFACHER UND GENAUSO EFFEKTVOLL MACHEN.

FOR ONE OF THE BEST-KNOWN ICE-CREAM RECIPES WE HAVE TO THANK THE FAMOUS CHEF, AUGUSTE ESCOFFIER, AND A SINGER CALLED NELLY MELBA. AT THE TIME, ESCOFFIER SERVED THIS ICE-CREAM SPECIALITY IN A SWAN CARVED FROM ICE. UNFORTUNATELY, NOBODY HAS THE TIME TO DO THAT THESE DAYS, BUT WITH THE HELP OF A SILICONE MOULD ONE CAN ACHIEVE THE SAME EFFECT IN AN EASIER WAY.

ZUTATEN FÜR 12 PERSONEN	INGREDIENTS FOR 12 PERSONS
OLIVENÖL-JOGHURTEIS	**OLIVE OIL WITH YOGHURT ICE-CREAM**

	Olivenöl-Joghurteis			Olive oil with yoghurt ice-cream
180 g	Olivenöl		180 g	olive oil
1 g	Orangenblütenwasser		1 g	orange blossom water
350 g	Magerjoghurt		350 g	low-fat yoghurt
180 g	Orangenblütenhonig		180 g	orange blossom honey
180 g	Wasser		180 g	water
10 g	Cointreau-Likör, 40 %		10 g	Cointreau liqueur, 40 %
10 g	Zitronensaft		10 g	lemon juice

Alle Zutaten mixen und dann in einen Pacojet-Behälter einfüllen. Für 24 Stunden tiefkühlen und bei Bedarf pacossieren.

Mix all ingredients and pour into a Pacojet container. Deep-freeze for 24 hours and pacotise if required.

EISSCHALE

Mineralwasser in eine Silikonform füllen und gefrieren. Bei Bedarf ausformen.

BLUTORANGENSCHAUM

250 g	Blutorangensaft
25 g	Puderzucker
1 g	Orangenblütenwasser
2 g	Lecite

Alle Zutaten mit einem Mixstab sehr luftig aufmixen. Vor dem Anrichten kurz abstehen lassen, so dass sich der überflüssige Saft absetzen kann.

HIMBEER-PAPRIKA-SORBET (ERGIBT 1000 G)

137 g	Zucker
29 g	Portwein
1	Vanilleschote
34 g	Trockenglukose
229 g	gelbe Paprika, geschält, entkernt und fein gewürfelt
343 g	Himbeerpüree
229 g	Wasser

Zucker in einer Pfanne leicht karamellisieren, mit Portwein ablöschen und die Vanilleschote mit dem ausgekratzten Mark, der Trockenglukose und der Paprika zugeben. Kurz aufkochen bis die Paprika weich ist, dann Vanilleschote entfernen, Himbeerpüree zugeben und gut pürieren. Zuletzt mit dem Wasser auf 29 °Brix einstellen.

ICE BOWL

Fill a silicone mould with mineral water and freeze. Take out of the mould when needed.

BLOOD ORANGE FOAM

250 g	blood orange juice
25 g	icing sugar
1 g	orange blossom water
2 g	Lecite

Use a hand-held blender to mix all ingredients – keep the mixture as "airy" as possible. Let the mixture stand for a while so that the excess juice can settle.

RASPBERRY CAPSICUM SORBET (MAKES 1000 G)

137 g	sugar
29 g	port
1	vanilla pod
34 g	dry glucose
229 g	yellow capsicum (pepper), peeled, cored and chopped into small dice
343 g	raspberry puree
229 g	water

Lightly caramelise the sugar in a frying pan, add the port followed by the vanilla pod with the scraped-out pith, the dry glucose and the capsicum. Boil for a short while until the capsicum is soft, remove the vanilla pod, add the raspberry puree and puree everything well. Finally add the water to adjust the mixture to 29 °Brix.

WHITE PEACH WITH OLIVES, CUMQUAT AND ANGELICA DICE

100 g	sugar
100 g	water
50 g	black olives, stoned and diced
50 g	white port
50 g	candied angelica, diced
100 g	cumquats, in slices
400 g	white peach, stoned and cut into thin wedges

Bring the water and sugar to the boil. Add the olives and allow to steep on low heat for about 5 minutes. Add the port, angelica and cumquat slices, boil again lightly for about 5 minutes and then strain through a sieve. Warm up the liquid, add the white peaches and reheat to a moderate temperature. Add the strained ingredients, leave to cool and steep.

CHOCOLATE DECORATION

Spread the tempered bitter couverture thinly onto a pattern foil. As soon as the couverture begins to set, use a knife to pull bent half moons to the outside, starting from the centre. Roll the foil diagonally and leave to cool. As soon as the foil comes off, take the chocolates out.

DECORATION

chocolate spaghetti
(see page 308)

WEISSER PFIRSICH MIT OLIVEN, KUMQUAT UND ANGELIKAWÜRFELN

100 g	Zucker
100 g	Wasser
50 g	schwarze Oliven, kernlos und gewürfelt
50 g	weißer Portwein
50 g	kandierte Angelika, gewürfelt
100 g	Kumquat, in Scheiben
400 g	weißer Pfirsich, entkernt und in dünnen Spalten

Zucker und Wasser aufkochen. Die Oliven zugeben und dann unter leichtem Köcheln etwa 5 Minuten ziehen lassen. Portwein, Angelika und Kumquatscheiben zugeben, erneut für etwa 5 Minuten leicht köchelnd ziehen lassen und absieben. Flüssigkeit erwärmen, weiße Pfirsiche zugeben und leicht erwärmen. Abgesiebte Zutaten zugeben, erkalten und ziehen lassen.

SCHOKOLADENDEKORATION

Temperierte Bitterkuvertüre dünn auf eine Folie streichen. Sobald die Kuverture anzieht, von der Mitte aus mit einem Messer gebogene Halbmonde nach außen ziehen. Folie diagonal aufrollen und erkalten lassen. Sobald sich die Folie löst, abformen.

DEKORATION

Schokoladenspaghetti
(siehe Seite 308)

MONSUN

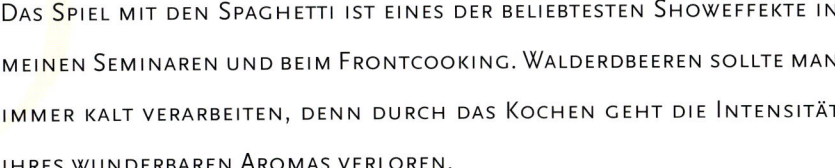

DAS SPIEL MIT DEN SPAGHETTI IST EINES DER BELIEBTESTEN SHOWEFFEKTE IN MEINEN SEMINAREN UND BEIM FRONTCOOKING. WALDERDBEEREN SOLLTE MAN IMMER KALT VERARBEITEN, DENN DURCH DAS KOCHEN GEHT DIE INTENSITÄT IHRES WUNDERBAREN AROMAS VERLOREN.

THE GAME WITH THE SPAGHETTI IS ONE OF THE MOST FAVOURITE SHOW EFFECTS IN MY SEMINARS AND DISPLAY-COOKING SESSIONS. WOODLAND STRAWBERRIES SHOULD ALWAYS BE PROCESSED COLD BECAUSE IN COOKING THEY LOSE THE INTENSITY OF THEIR AROMA.

CHOCOLATE CHILLI SPAGHETTI (ABOUT 20 SERVINGS)

2.5 g	agar agar
250 g	milk
50 g	cocoa paste
50 g	sugar
10	drops Tabasco

Bring the agar agar to the boil in the milk. Dissolve the cocoa paste and the sugar in the milk, add the Tabasco, bring back to the boil and then use a sauce bottle to fill the mixture into thin plastic hoses. Place into ice water and leave to gel. Remove from the ice water, dry and store in a cool place. To remove the spaghetti from the hoses you can use an Espuma siphon with a special nozzle.

SCHOKOLADEN-CHILI-SPAGHETTI (ETWA 20 PORTIONEN)

2,5 g	Agar-Agar
250 g	Milch
50 g	Kakaomasse
50 g	Zucker
10	Tropfen Tabasco

Agar-Agar in der Milch aufkochen. Kakaomasse und Zucker darin auflösen, Tabasco zugeben, nochmals aufkochen und mit einer Soßenflasche in dünne Kunststoffschläuche füllen. Anschließend in Eiswasser geben und gelieren lassen. Aus dem Eiswasser nehmen, abtrocknen und gekühlt lagern. Bei Bedarf mit Hilfe eines Espuma-Schäumers mit Spezialdüse ausformen.

1

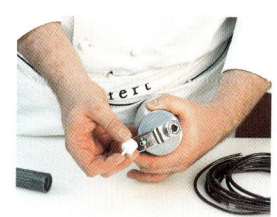

2

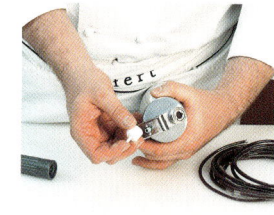

3

Cassisbaiser
(etwa 100 Stück)

150 g	Eiweiß
300 g	Zucker
15 g	gefriergetrocknetes Cassispulver
60 g	Wasser

Eiweiß, 150 g Zucker und Cassispulver zu einem stabilen Schnee schlagen. In der Zwischenzeit den restlichen Zucker mit dem Wasser auf 119 °C kochen und in die Eiweißmasse laufen lassen. Die Mischung bis zu einer Temperatur von 20 °C kalt schlagen, dann mit einer 10er-Lochtülle tupfenförmig auf eine Teflon-Backmatte dressieren. Die Tupfen mit Cassispulver absieben und mit einem befeuchteten Daumen zu einer Seite auswischen. Mit geöffnetem Zug bei 100 °C für mindestens 4 Stunden trocknen.

Cassis meringue
(about 100 pcs.)

150 g	egg white
300 g	sugar
15 g	freeze-dried cassis powder
60 g	water

Add 150 g of the sugar and the cassis powder to the egg white and beat until stiff. In the meantime, boil the remaining sugar with the water to 119 °C and pour slowly into the egg white mixture. Beat the mixture until it cools down to 20 °C, then use a piping bag with a round nozzle, size 10, to pipe it in small dabs onto a Teflon baking mat. Sprinkle the cassis powder over the dabs through a sieve and then use your moistened thumb to drag the mixture from the centre outwards. Dry at 100 °C for at least 4 hours with the door open.

Walderdbeersorbet
(ergibt 1000 g)

164 g	Zucker
41 g	Trockenglukosepulver
318 g	Wasser
455 g	Walderdbeerpüree
23 g	Orangensaft

Den Zucker und das Trockenglukosepulver mischen, dann mit den restlichen Zutaten für 2 Minuten aufmixen. Mit dem Refraktometer auf 28 °Brix einstellen und in der Eismaschine abfrieren.

Woodland strawberry sorbet
(makes 1000 g)

164 g	sugar
41 g	dry glucose powder
318 g	water
455 g	wild strawberry puree
23 g	orange juice

Mix the sugar and dry glucose powder, add the other ingredients and keep mixing for about 2 minutes. Use a refractometer to adjust to 28 °Brix and then freeze in the ice-cream maker.

Warme Schokoladen-Agar-Agar-Masse mit einer Soßenflasche in Mini-Schläuche einfüllen und zum Gelieren direkt in Eiswasser geben

Use a sauce bottle to fill the warm chocolate agar agar mixture into the mini hoses and place them into ice water for gelling

Spezialaufsatz auf ISI Espuma-Schäumer aufschrauben

Screw the special nozzle onto an ISI Espuma siphon

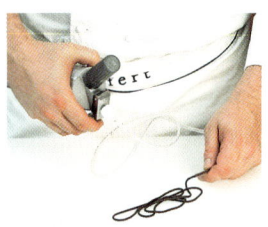

4

Mit dem Druck der Gaspatrone die Spaghetti aus den Minischläuchen pressen

Use the pressure from the gas to press the spaghetti from the mini hoses

Espuma-Schäumer mit einer Gaspatrone befüllen

Fit a gas bottle to the Espuma siphon

5

Fertige Schokoladenspaghetti

Finished chocolate spaghetti

POMEGRANATE GRANITÉ (ABOUT 20 SERVINGS)

200 g	fresh pomegranate juice
100 g	water
90 g	sugar
1	Tahiti vanilla pod
	Zest from 1 orange
175 g	Dornfelder red wine

Mix the pomegranate juice with the water and sugar, add the vanilla pod and pith as well as the orange zest and bring to the boil. Take the pod out, add the red wine and pour the mixture into a small rectangular silicone mould. Put into the freezer and once frozen use a fine grater to produce the ice flakes. Store in the freezer.

DECORATION

chilli strings
strawberries

GRANATAPFELGRANITÉ (ETWA 20 PORTIONEN)

200 g	frischer Granatapfelsaft
100 g	Wasser
90 g	Zucker
1	Tahiti-Vanilleschote
	Abrieb von 1 Orange
175 g	Dornfelder Rotwein

Granatapfelsaft mit Wasser, Zucker, Vanilleschote und Mark sowie Orangenschale mischen und aufkochen. Danach Schote entnehmen, Rotwein zugeben und in eine kleine rechteckige Silikonform gießen. Gefrieren lassen und mit einer feinen Reibe zu Flocken hobeln. Gefroren lagern.

DEKORATION

Chilifäden
Erdbeeren

RITMO DE LA NOCHE

RITMO DE LA NOCHE

RITMO DE LA NOCHE

DER NUSSBECHER – EIGENTLICH EIN TYPISCHER KLASSIKER. ÜBERDENKEN SIE JEDOCH ALLES, WAS SIE JE BEIGEBRACHT BEKOMMEN HABEN UND WAGEN SIE SICH AN NEUE VARIATIONEN.

A NUT SUNDAE – IN A SENSE A TYPICAL CLASSIC. BUT YOU SHOULD REVISE EVERYTHING YOU HAVE BEEN TOLD BEFORE AND DARE TO TRY NEW COMPOSITIONS.

MANGOPAPIER

1,5 g	Xanthan
100 g	Zucker
500 g	Mangopüree

Xanthan und Zucker mischen, mit dem Mangopüree mixen. Die Mischung gleichmäßig, etwa 1 Millimeter dick, auf eine Silikon-Backmatte streichen und dann im Ofen bei maximal 60 °C solange trocknen, bis es fest ist. In noch warmem Zustand schalenartig ausformen und zusammen mit einem Trockenmittel luftdicht lagern.

MANGO PAPER

1.5 g	xanthan gum
100 g	sugar
500 g	mango puree

Mix the xanthan gum with the sugar followed by the mango puree. Spread this mixture evenly onto a silicone baking mat, about 1 mm thick, and dry in the oven at max. 60 °C until it is firm. While still warm, take off the sheet in the form of shells and store in an air-tight container, together with desiccant.

DULCE-DE-LECHE-SOSSE MIT AHORNSIRUP

500 g	ungesüßte Kondensmilch
500 g	Ahornsirup

Beide Zutaten mischen und im Thermomix bis zur Soßenkonsistenz reduzieren lassen. Dies kann je nach Wassergehalt mehrere Stunden dauern.

DULCE DE LECHE SAUCE WITH MAPLE SYRUP

500 g	unsweetened condensed milk
500 g	maple syrup

Mix both ingredients together and reduce in a Thermomix until it reaches the consistency of sauce. Depending on the water content, this may take several hours.

HASELNUSSEIS (WARME HERSTELLUNG) (ERGIBT 1000 G)

128 g	Zucker
32 g	Dextrose
16 g	Magermilchpulver
5 g	neutrales Eisbindemittel
1 g	Salz
51 g	Eigelb
641 g	Vollmilch
38 g	Haselnussmark, 100%
80 g	Sahne
6 g	Haselnusslikör

Trockene Zutaten mischen, dann Eigelb und Milch zugeben und bei 85°C pasteurisieren. Haselnussmark untermixen und auf 65°C herunterkühlen. Abschließend Sahne und Likör untermixen und in der Eismaschine abfrieren.
Achtung! Nusseis kann durch das Nussöl überfrieren und in der Eismaschine schnell sandig werden.

HAZELNUT ICE-CREAM (HOT PRODUCTION METHOD) (MAKES 1000 G)

128 g	sugar
32 g	dextrose
16 g	skimmed milk powder
5 g	neutral ice-cream binding agent
1 g	salt
51 g	egg yolk
641 g	whole milk
38 g	hazelnut paste, 100 %
80 g	whipping cream
6 g	hazelnut liqueur

Mix the dry ingredients, add the egg yolk and milk and pasteurise at 85°C. Mix in the hazelnut paste and cool down to 65°C. Finally add the cream and liqueur and put into the ice-cream maker to freeze.
Important! Owing to the nut oil content it is possible that this ice-cream over-freezes and becomes flaky in the ice-cream maker.

Yuzu salt caramel ice-cream

(Yuzu is a special Japanese citrus fruit available in well-stocked Asian delicatessen shops. As an alternative you can use orange zest mixed 1:1 with sea salt.)

Caramel

185 g	sugar
135 g	whipping cream
5 g	Yuzu salt

Caramelise the sugar to a light colour, add the warmed-up cream and salt and boil until you can draw strings. (A total of about 250 g caramel mixture)

Ice-cream
(hot production method)
(makes 1000 g)

118 g	sugar
34 g	dextrose
34 g	skimmed milk powder
5 g	neutral ice-cream binding agent
675 g	whole milk
250 g	Yuzu salt caramel paste
102 g	whipping cream

Mix the dry ingredients, add the milk and pasteurise at 85 °C; mix in 34 g caramel paste and cool down to 65 °C. Then fold in the cream and place into the ice-cream maker to freeze. Use the remaining 216 g of caramel paste to create a marbling pattern in an ice tray.

Yuzu-Salz-Karamelleis

Yuzu ist eine spezielle japanische Zitrusfrucht, die man in gut sortierten, asiatischen Feinkostgeschäften bekommt. Ersatzweise kann man Orangenschale 1:1 mit Meersalz gemischt verwenden.

Karamell

185 g	Zucker
135 g	Sahne
5 g	Yuzu-Salz

Den Zucker hell karamellisieren lassen, dann mit der erwärmten Sahne ablöschen, Salz zugeben und bis zur Fadenprobe einkochen. (Insgesamt etwa 250 g Karamellmasse)

Eis
(warme Herstellung)
(ergibt 1000 g)

118 g	Zucker
34 g	Dextrose
34 g	Magermilchpulver
5 g	neutrales Eisbindemittel
675 g	Vollmilch
250 g	Yuzu-Salz-Karamellpaste
102 g	Sahne

Trockene Zutaten mischen, dann Milch zugeben und bei 85 °C pasteurisieren, 34 g Karamellpaste untermixen und auf 65 °C herunterkühlen. Danach Sahne untermixen und in der Eismaschine abfrieren. Eis mit den restlichen 216 g Karamellpaste in der Eiswanne marmorieren.

1

2

3

4

5

FRITTIERTER EISKRISTALL

70 g	Mehl
1 g	Salz
30 g	Zucker
8 g	Vanillezucker
50 g	Vollei
80 g	Vollmilch

Alle trockenen Zutaten mischen und dann mit Ei und Milch zu einer glatten Masse anrühren. Kurz quellen lassen und mit einem, in Frittierfett vorgeheizten Rosenküchle-Eisen, nacheinander Eiskristalle ausfrittieren. Diese auf Küchenpapier absetzen und vor dem Servieren leicht mit Puderzucker absieben.

ICE CRYSTAL WAFFLE

70 g	flour
1 g	salt
30 g	sugar
8 g	vanilla sugar
50 g	whole egg
80 g	whole milk

Mix all dry ingredients together and blend with the egg and milk to make a smooth batter without lumps. Allow to stand for a short while and then use a waffle iron that has been preheated in deep-frying fat to make the waffles in the shape of ice crystals. Place the waffles on a paper towel and apply a light dusting of icing sugar before serving.

KROKANTSTREUSEL

15 g	Glukosesirup
125 g	Zucker
50 g	gehobelte Mandeln

Den Glukosesirup schmelzen, nach und nach den Zucker zugeben und ebenfalls schmelzen lassen. Dann gehobelte Mandeln unterrühren und auf eine Backmatte geben. Eine zweite Backmatte auflegen und dünn ausrollen, alles fein hacken, anschließend trocken lagern.

BRITTLE VERMICELLI

15 g	glucose syrup
125 g	sugar
50 g	sliced almonds

Melt the glucose syrup, add the sugar in small doses and wait until this has melted too. Then stir in the almond slices and put the mixture onto a baking mat. Place a second baking mat on top and roll out thinly; chop into fine pieces and store in a dry place.

Rosenküchle-Eisen im Frittierfett vorheizen

Preheat the waffle iron in the deep-frying fat

*Vorgeheiztes Eisen nur bis zur Oberkante
in den Teig tauchen*

*Dip the preheated iron into the batter,
but only up to the top edge of the iron*

SMALL MERINGUE STICK IN TWO COLOURS AND CHOCOLATE MERINGUE TWIRL

150 g	egg white
300 g	sugar
1 g	salt
3 g	natural vanilla essence

ZWEIFARBIG DRESSIERTES BAISERSTÄNGELCHEN UND SCHOKOLADENBAISERSCHNECKE

150 g	Eiweiß
300 g	Zucker
1 g	Salz
3 g	natürliche Vanilleessenz

Teig in heißem Frittierfett ausbacken

Dip the iron with the batter into the deep-frying fat

Beat the egg white with 100 g sugar, salt and vanilla gradually until firm. In the meantime, boil 200 g sugar with a little water at 119 °C and add to the beaten egg in a thin stream. Continue blending the mixture slowly until it reaches 20 °C, then add a choice of aromas to your taste, such as freeze-dried fruit powder, cocoa powder or others. Use a piping bag and nozzle to pipe the mixture onto baking mat, soaked woodblocks or silicone baking moulds and part-bake in the oven at 110 °C for about 15 minutes. Then dry at 50 °C in a drying cabinet for at least 12 hours.

Eiweiß mit 100 g Zucker, Salz und Vanille nach und nach zu einem stabilen Schnee schlagen. In der Zwischenzeit 200 g Zucker mit etwas Wasser auf 119 °C kochen und in einem feinen Strahl in den Schnee laufen lassen. Masse langsam weiterlaufen lassen bis sie 20 °C erreicht hat, dann nach Belieben mit gefriergetrocknetem Fruchtpulver, Kakaopulver oder anderen Aromen aromatisieren. Mit Spritzbeutel und Tüllen auf Backmatten, vorgewässerte Holzklötzchen oder Silikon-Backformen dressieren und bei 110 °C etwa 15 Minuten im Ofen anbacken. Bei 50 °C im Trockenschrank mindestens 12 Stunden austrocknen.

Teig mit einer Nadel vom Eisen lösen

Use a needle to detach the waffle from the iron

Fertige Schneekristalle

Finished snow crystals

DECORATION

cream dabs
almonds
pistachios

DEKORATION

Sahnetupfen
Mandeln
Pistazien

SWISS NEW CLASSIC

SWISS NEW CLASSIC

EINER DER ABSOLUTEN SCHWEIZER KLASSIKER IN SACHEN KUCHEN IST MIT SICHERHEIT DIE RÜBLITORTE. EINFACH LECKER – ABER WAS PASSIERT WENN MAN SIE MAL EIN WENIG AUFPEPPT? PROBIEREN SIE ES AUS!

WITHOUT ANY DOUBT, ONE OF THE TRUE SWISS CLASSICS IN TERMS OF CAKE IS "RÜBLITORTE". IT IS SIMPLY SCRUMPTIOUS – BUT WHAT HAPPENS WHEN YOU GIVE A BIT OF EXTRA PIZZAZZ? TRY IT OUT!

INGREDIENTS FOR 12 PERSONS

CARROT QUARK ICE-CREAM (HOT PRODUCTION METHOD) (MAKES 1000 G)

303 g	sugar
56 g	dextrose
1 g	salt
7 g	neutral ice-cream binding agent
334 g	carrot juice
178 g	peeled carrots
33 g	lemon juice
89 g	low-fat quark

Mix the dry ingredients together and add the carrot juice. Put the carrots in the juice extractor, pasteurise the extracted juice and the remains of the carrots at 85 °C. Puree the mixture, add the lemon juice and quark, stir well and freeze in the ice-cream maker.

ZUTATEN FÜR 12 PERSONEN

KAROTTEN-QUARK-EIS (WARME HERSTELLUNG) (ERGIBT 1000 G)

303 g	Zucker
56 g	Dextrose
1 g	Salz
7 g	neutrales Eisbindemittel
334 g	Karottensaft
178 g	geschälte Karotten
33 g	Zitronensaft
89 g	Magerquark

Alle trockenen Zutaten mischen, Karottensaft zugeben. Karotten entsaften, dann ausgepressten Saft und Reste der Karotten bei 85 °C pasteurisieren. Anschließend die Mischung pürieren, Zitronensaft und den Quark zugeben, untermixen und in der Eismaschine abfrieren.

2

Acrylglasplatte mit einer Folie belegen, temperierte Bitterkuvertüre mit einem Kamm auftragen

Place a foil onto a sheet of Perspex, spread the tempered bitter couverture with a comb onto the foil

1

3

HASELNUSS-STREUSEL

50 g	Zucker
50 g	Butter
90 g	Mehl
10 g	Haselnüsse, geröstet und gerieben
2 g	Zitronenabrieb

Zutaten bei Zimmertemperatur mischen und bei 160 °C im vorgeheizten Backofen zu knusprigen Streuseln vorbacken.

HAZELNUT VERMICELLI

50 g	sugar
50 g	unsalted butter
90 g	flour
10 g	hazelnuts, roasted and grated
2 g	lemon zest

Mix all ingredients at room temperature and bake at 160 °C in a preheated oven until the vermicelli are nice and crunchy.

KAROTTENSCHAUM

125 g	Karottensaft
5 g	Akazienhonig
2 g	Zitronensaft
1 g	Lecite

Alle Zutaten mit einem Mixstab luftig aufschlagen und den Schaum setzen lassen.

CARROT FOAM

125 g	carrot juice
5 g	acacia honey
2 g	lemon juice
1 g	Lecite

Use a hand-held blender to beat all ingredients into an airy mixture and let the foam settle.

Aufgetragene Bitterkuvertüre mit Silberperlen bestreuen

Sprinkle some silver pearls onto the bitter couverture

Schokoladenstreifen mit einem Messer separieren

Use a knife to separate the chocolate strips

ORANGE ICE-CREAM	**ORANGEN-EIS**	
(HOT PRODUCTION METHOD)	**(WARME HERSTELLUNG)**	
(MAKES 1000 G)	**(ERGIBT 1000 G)**	

112 g	sugar	112 g	Zucker
54 g	skimmed milk powder	54 g	Magermilchpulver
2,5 g	neutral ice-cream binding agent	2,5 g	neutrales Eisbindemittel
20 g	dry glucose	20 g	Trockenglukose
28 g	invert sugar	28 g	Invertzucker
279 g	whole milk	279 g	Vollmilch
430 g	orange juice	430 g	Orangensaft
64 g	whipping cream	64 g	Sahne
11 g	Grand Marnier	11 g	Grand Marnier

Mix the dry ingredients, add the invert sugar, whole milk and orange juice and pasteurise at 85 °C. Allow the mixture to cool down to 65 °C, then add the cream and leave to mature at 4 °C. Put into the ice-cream maker to freeze and shortly before the end of the freezing process add the Grand Marnier.

Trockene Zutaten mischen, dann Invertzucker, Vollmilch und Orangensaft dazugeben und bei 85 °C pasteurisieren. Die Mischung auf 65 °C herunterkühlen, dann Sahne zugeben und bei 4 °C reifen lassen. In der Eismaschine gefrieren und kurz vor Ende des Gefriervorgangs den Grand Marnier zugeben.

PRALINÉ ESPUMA

PRALINÉ-ESPUMA

420 g	almond bitter nougat	420 g	Mandelbitternougat
375 g	whipping cream	375 g	Sahne
120 g	whole milk	120 g	Vollmilch
150 g	whole egg, pasteurised	150 g	Vollei, pasteurisiert

Dissolve the nougat, then add the other ingredients and warm up. Use a hand-held blender to homogenise the mixture, put into an Espuma siphon and fit 2 gas cartridges. Put into the refrigerator with the point downwards until you want to use the mixture.

Nougat auflösen, dann die restlichen Zutaten zugeben und erwärmen. Masse mit dem Mixstab homogenisieren, in einen Espuma-Schäumer geben und 2 Gaspatronen aufschrauben. Bis zur Verwendung mit der Spitze nach unten kaltstellen.

NUSSBISKUIT

85 g	Zucker
100 g	Eigelb
150 g	Eiweiß
150 g	Zucker
60 g	Mehl
60 g	Weizenpuder
40 g	Haselnüsse, fein gerieben und geröstet

Eigelb mit 85 g Zucker und Eiweiß mit 150 g Zucker getrennt stabil aufschlagen, dann Eigelbmasse abwechselnd mit einer Mischung aus Mehl, Weizenpuder und Haselnüssen unter das Eiweiß ziehen. In etwa 1 Zentimeter Höhe auf eine Backmatte streichen und bei 180 °C etwa 15 Minuten backen. In Größe der verwendeten Gläser ausstechen.

NUT SPONGE

85 g	sugar
100 g	egg yolk
150 g	egg white
150 g	sugar
60 g	flour
60 g	wheat powder
40 g	hazelnuts, finely ground and roasted

Beat the egg yolk with 85 g sugar and separately the egg white with 150 g sugar until firm, fold the egg yolk mixture and a mixture of flour, wheat powder and hazelnuts in alternating steps into the egg white. Spread onto a baking mat, finishing with a thickness of about 1 cm, and bake at 180 °C for about 15 minutes. Cut out round shapes to suit the glasses used for serving.

KONFIERTE KAROTTEN-SPAGHETTI

100 g	Läuterzucker
10 g	Zitronensaft
100 g	junge Karotten, in feine Streifen geschnitten

Läuterzucker mit Zitronensaft aufkochen und die Karotten darin bissfest kochen.

CANDIED CARROT SPAGHETTI

100 g	sugar syrup
10 g	lemon juice
100 g	young carrots, cut into thin strips

Boil the sugar syrup with the lemon juice, add the carrots and boil until they are cooked but still firm.

DEKORATION

frische Brombeeren
Schokoladen-Silberperlen-Sticks

DECORATION

fresh blackberries
chocolate silver pearl sticks

Japan lässt grüssen. Dieses Land mit seiner aussergewöhnlichen Kultur ist für mich einer der faszinierendsten Orte, die ich jemals bereist habe. Ich hoffe, ich kann seiner Anziehungskraft mit meiner kleinen Hommage gerecht werden.

A homage to Japan. This country with its extraordinary culture is one of the most fascinating places for me that I have ever visited. I hope my small offering does justice to this country with its charismatic appeal.

Zutaten für 12 Personen

Ananas-Grüntee-Gelee

5 g	Matcha-Grünteepulver
50 g	Zucker
1,5 g	Agar-Agar
250 g	Ananassaft

Trockene Zutaten mischen und mit dem Saft aufkochen. Abschäumen und in eine Silikonform gießen. 30 Minuten bei Raumtemperatur gelieren lassen, dann im Kühlschrank vollständig durchgelieren lassen.

Ingredients for 12 persons

Pineapple / green tea jelly

5 g	Matcha green tea powder
50 g	sugar
1,5 g	agar agar
250 g	pineapple juice

Mix the dry ingredients together and boil with the juice. Remove the froth and pour the liquid into a silicone mould. Leave to gel at room temperature for 30 minutes, then put into the refrigerator until fully gelled.

MILK MERINGUE

500 g	whole milk
50 g	dry glucose
1.5 g	Lecite

Heat the milk to 50 °C, add the dry glucose and Lecite and beat very airily. Let the mixture settle down, put into a silicone mould and dry in the oven at 50 °C; cut into suitably sized pieces and store in a dry place until needed.

MILCHBAISER

500 g	Vollmilch
50 g	Trockenglukose
1,5 g	Lecite

Milch auf 50 °C erwärmen, dann Trockenglukose und Lecite zugeben und sehr luftig aufschlagen. Schaum absetzen lassen, diesen in einer Silikonform bei 50 °C im Ofen trocknen lassen, dann in passende Stücke schneiden und bis zur Verwendung trocken lagern.

SWEET CHERRY SORBET

2 g	lemon peel
1 g	vanilla pith
1 g	ground cinnamon flowers
156 g	sugar
39 g	dry glucose
247 g	water
556 g	sweet cherry puree

Mix the dry ingredients, add the water and bring to the boil. Leave the mixture to steep before passing through a sieve. Add the cherry puree and then use a refractometer to adjust to 30 °Brix. Place into the ice-cream maker to freeze.

SÜSSKIRSCHSORBET

2 g	Zitronenschale
1 g	Vanillemark
1 g	gemahlene Zimtblüte
156 g	Zucker
39 g	Trockenglukose
247 g	Wasser
556 g	Süßkirschenpüree

Trockene Zutaten mischen, das Wasser zugeben und aufkochen. Mischung ziehen lassen und absiehen. Kirschpüree zugeben und mit dem Refraktometer auf 30 °Brix einstellen. In der Eismaschine abfrieren.

GERÖSTETER POPCORN-MANDELKUCHEN

125 g	Marzipanrohmasse
75 g	Vollei
17 g	Eigelb
28 g	Mehl, Typ 550
1 g	Backpulver
38 g	flüssige Butter
17 g	geröstetes Popcorn, fein gehackt

Marzipan in der Mikrowelle erwärmen und mit Vollei und Eigelb zunächst glatt, dann schaumig schlagen. Mehl mit Backpulver versieben, dann untermelieren. Zum Schluss flüssige Butter unter die Masse ziehen, das Popcorn unterheben und in Silikonförmchen füllen. Bei 180 °C etwa 20 Minuten backen.

ROASTED POPCORN ALMOND CAKE

125 g	marzipan raw mixture
75 g	whole egg
17 g	egg yolk
28 g	flour, type 550
1 g	baking powder
38 g	liquid butter (unsalted)
17 g	roasted popcorn, finely chopped

Heat the marzipan in the microwave, beat together with the whole egg and egg yolk until smooth and then more until it is frothy. Pass the flour and baking powder through a sieve and stir into the mixture. Finally draw the liquid butter into the mixture, fold in the popcorn and fill into small silicone moulds. Bake at 180 °C for about 20 minutes.

PISTAZIENPARFAIT

1	Blatt Gelatine
100 g	Zucker
80 g	Eigelb
60 g	Pistazienpaste
300 g	halb geschlagene Sahne

Gelatine in kaltem Wasser einweichen. Zucker mit etwas Wasser auf 115 °C kochen. Das Eigelb schaumig schlagen, dann den gekochten Zucker in feinem Strahl in das Eigelb einlaufen lassen und kalt schlagen. Die Gelatine aufgelöst unterziehen, die Pistazienpaste einrühren, zum Schluss die Sahne unterheben. Masse in Silikonformen einfüllen, gefrieren und vorsichtig ausformen. Mit Sprühkuvertüre absprühen, auf den Kuchen setzen und mit einer halben Pistazie dekorieren.

PISTACHIO PARFAIT

1	sheet of gelatine
100 g	sugar
80 g	egg yolk
60 g	pistachio paste
300 g	half-whipped cream

Soak the gelatine in cold water. Boil the sugar with a little water to 115 °C. Beat the egg yolk until frothy, let the boiled sugar run into the egg yolk in a fine stream and then beat until cold. Add the dissolved gelatine, stir in the pistachio paste and finally fold in the cream. Fill the mixture into silicon moulds, freeze and then carefully turn out. Spray with spray couverture, place onto the cake and decorate with half a pistachio.

PINEAPPLE SAGO JELLY

25 g	pearl sago
125 g	white wine
250 g	pineapple juice
25 g	sugar
1	vanilla pod
100 g	pineapple, finely diced

Soak the sago in the wine, add the pineapple juice, sugar and vanilla, boil the mixture until it has a creamy consistency, take out the vanilla pod, stir in the pineapple dice and boil up briefly. Allow to cool down.

ANANAS-SAGO-GRÜTZE

25 g	Perlsago
125 g	Weißwein
250 g	Ananassaft
25 g	Zucker
1	Vanilleschote
100 g	Ananas, fein gewürfelt

Sago in Wein einweichen, Ananassaft, Vanille und Zucker zugeben, die Mischung aufkochen bis sie eine cremige Konsistenz hat, dann die Vanilleschote entnehmen, Ananaswürfel unterrühren und kurz mitkochen. Auskühlen lassen.

CHERRY SUGAR DECOR

150 g	sugar
45 g	glucose syrup
45 g	water

Mix all ingredients together and bring to the boil, remove the froth and boil to 160 °C, continually "cleaning" the mixture. Pour onto a silicone baking mat and leave to cool completely. Use a cutter or thermomix to grind the sugar into a powder. Mix some freeze-dried red cherry fruit powder into the powder, quantity to your taste, but usually between 4 and 10 gram, depending on the type.

Pass this mixture through a sieve onto square stencils that have been placed onto a Teflon baking mat. Carefully remove the stencils, put into the oven at 180 °C for 4 minutes until the powder begins to melt.

KIRSCHZUCKERDEKOR

150 g	Zucker
45 g	Glukosesirup
45 g	Wasser

Alle Zutaten miteinander aufkochen, abschäumen und unter ständigem Reinwaschen auf 160 °C kochen. Dann auf eine Silikon-Backmatte ausgießen und auskühlen lassen. Mit einem Kutter oder mit dem Thermomix pulverisieren.

Je nach Geschmack mit gefriergetrocknetem, roten Kirsch-Fruchtpulver mischen. Die Menge kann, je nach Sorte, zwischen 4 und 10 g variieren.

Die Mischung auf eine, mit quadratischen Schablonen bestückte Teflon-Backmatte sieben. Die Schablonen vorsichtig entfernen und bei 180 °C für etwa 4 Minuten im Ofen anschmelzen.

DECORATION

fresh cherries

DEKORATION

frische Kirschen

TRANSPARENT MOVEMENT

TRANSPARENT MOVEMENT

UND NOCH EIN GLASDESSERT. ODER WIE DER KENNER ZU SAGEN PFLEGT: „AUF DIE VERPACKUNG KOMMT ES AN." SIE IST BEI DIESEM DESSERT BESONDERS SCHÖN, SOLL ABER AUF KEINEN FALL VOM KÖSTLICHEN INHALT ABLENKEN.

HERE IS ANOTHER DESSERT IN A GLASS. AS THEY SAY IN THE TRADE: "IT IS THE PACKAGING THAT MAKES THE DIFFERENCE". THE PACKAGING OF THIS DESSERT IS PARTICULARLY ELEGANT BUT IN NO WAY SHOULD IT DETRACT FROM ITS DELICIOUS CONTENT.

INGREDIENTS FOR 12 PERSONS		ZUTATEN FÜR 12 PERSONEN	
MULLED WINE JELLY		**GLÜHWEINGELEE**	
8	sheets of gelatine	8	Blatt Gelatine
500 g	mulled wine	500 g	Glühwein
2	cinnamon sticks	2	Zimtstangen
	Zest from 1 organic orange		Abrieb von 1 Bio-Orange
20 g	chestnut honey	20 g	Kastanienhonig
2	drops rose oil	2	Tropfen Rosenöl
50 g	sugar	50 g	Zucker

Soak the gelatine in cold water. Heat the other ingredients to 80 °C, allow to steep for a short while and then pour through a sieve. Squeeze the gelatine and add to the mixture. Allow the mixture to cool down, fill slowly into glasses that are placed at an angle and leave to gel.

Die Gelatine in kaltem Wasser einweichen. Die restlichen Zutaten auf 80 °C erwärmen und kurze Zeit ziehen lassen, dann absieben. Gelatine auspressen und untermischen. Mischung abkühlen lassen, langsam in schräg gestellte Gläser füllen und gelieren lassen.

Schokoladen-Lebkuchen-Mousse
(ergibt 1 Liter Bechervolumen)

8	*Blatt Gelatine*
200 g	*Bitterkuvertüre, 70 %*
160 g	*Milch*
180 g	*Sahne*
100 g	*Eiweiß, pasteurisiert*
10 g	*Rum*
5 g	*Lebkuchengewürz*

Die Gelatine in kaltem Wasser einweichen, quellen lassen und auspressen. Kuvertüre schmelzen, Milch und Sahne zugeben, erwärmen, dann Gelatine zugeben und auflösen lassen. Nach dem Erkalten Eiweiß leicht schlagen und dann zusammen mit Rum und Lebkuchengewürz untermischen und in Pacojet-Becher abfüllen. Bei -20 °C 24 Stunden gefrieren. Anschließend zweimal pacossieren, ohne den Luftdruck abzulassen. Mousse 3 bis 4 Stunden ruhen lassen. Dann kleine Nocken abstechen und als Einlage für den Glühweinschaum verwenden. Diese dazu auf das gelierte Glühweingelee geben.

Chocolate gingerbread mousse
(makes 1 litre volume)

8	*sheets of gelatine*
200 g	*bitter couverture, 70 %*
160 g	*milk*
180 g	*whipping cream*
100 g	*egg white, pasteurised*
10 g	*rum*
5 g	*gingerbread spice*

Soak the gelatine in cold water, leave to swell up and then squeeze the liquid from it. Melt the couverture, add the milk and cream, heat up before adding the gelatine, leave to dissolve. After the mixture has cooled down, beat the egg white lightly and mix in together with the rum and gingerbread spice, put into a Pacojet container. Deep-freeze at -20 °C for 24 hours. Pacotise twice without releasing the air pressure. Leave the mousse to stand for 3 to 4 hours. Take out small egg-shaped scoops and use them to add to the mulled wine foam. Spoon this onto the gelled mulled wine jelly.

MULLED WINE MOUSSE

2	sheets of gelatine
250 g	mulled wine
120 g	egg yolk
120 g	sugar
20 g	lemon juice
20 g	orange juice
1 g	Ceylon cinnamon

Soak the gelatine in cold water. Beat the mulled wine with the other ingredients in a bowl in hot water until firm. Beat again to cool down the mixture and draw in the dissolved gelatine. Spoon the mulled wine mousse onto the first layer of mousse but this time with the glass tilted in the opposite direction; leave to gel. Dress the surface with fresh raspberries.

GLÜHWEINSCHAUM

2	Blatt Gelatine
250 g	Glühwein
120 g	Eigelb
120 g	Zucker
20 g	Zitronensaft
20 g	Orangensaft
1 g	Ceylonzimt

Die Gelatine in kaltem Wasser einweichen. Glühwein mit den anderen Zutaten über einem Wasserbad zu stabilem Schaum schlagen. Anschließend noch einmal kalt schlagen und die Gelatine aufgelöst unterziehen. Den Glühweinschaum auf die bereits ins Glas gegebene Mousse-Einlage setzten und erneut schräg gelieren lassen, allerdings in entgegengesetzter Richtung. Die Oberfläche mit frischen Himbeeren belegen.

WOODLAND STRAWBERRY SORBET (MAKES 1000 G)

143 g	sugar
42 g	dry glucose
169 g	invert sugar
371 g	woodland strawberries
270 g	water
	Zest from 1 organic mandarin
4 g	fruit acid

Mix the dry ingredients together followed by the remaining ingredients. Use a refractometer to adjust the mixture to 32 °Brix. Place into the ice-cream maker to freeze.

WALDERDBEERSORBET (ERGIBT 1000 G)

143 g	Zucker
42 g	Trockenglukose
169 g	Invertzucker
371 g	Walderdbeeren
270 g	Wasser
	Abrieb von 1 Bio-Mandarine
4 g	Fruchtsäure

Trockene Zutaten mischen und mit den restlichen Zutaten aufmixen. Mit dem Refraktometer auf 32 °Brix einstellen. In der Eismaschine gefrieren.

DECORATION

chocolate decor

DEKORATION

Schokoladendekor

TUTTI FRUTTI

TUTTI FRUTTI

Der Früchtebecher ist und bleibt das beliebteste Sommereis. Früher konnte man mangels Auswahl oft nur auf Dosenobst zurückgreifen, heute aber kommt man nicht umhin, frische Früchte aus aller Herren Länder zu verwenden. Manchmal finde ich selbst eingemachte Früchte sogar besser als frische, vor allem wenn man die mangelnde Verträglichkeit mancher Früchte mit Eiweissprodukten bedenkt.

This fruit sundae is and remains the most popular summer ice-cream. In former times the choice of fruit was often restricted so that canned fruit had to be used, but nowadays one can select fresh fruit from many foreign countries. At other times I find preserved fruit even better than fresh fruit, particularly some kinds of fruit that are not compatible with egg products.

ERDBEER-GRÜNER-PFEFFER-SORBET (ERGIBT 1000 G)

105 g	Zucker
50 g	Trockenglukose
20 g	Invertzucker
660 g	Erdbeerpüree
160 g	Wasser
5 g	Fruchtsäure
5 g	grüner Pfeffer, fein gemörsert

Trockene Zutaten mischen, alle anderen Zutaten untermixen und mit dem Refraktometer auf 30 °Brix einstellen. Masse in der Eismaschine abfrieren.

STRAWBERRY / GREEN PEPPER SORBET (MAKES 1000 G)

105 g	sugar
50 g	dry glucose
20 g	invert sugar
660 g	strawberry puree
160 g	water
5 g	fruit acid
5 g	green pepper, finely crushed

Mix the dry ingredients together, add all other ingredients and stir, use a refractometer to adjust to 30 °Brix. Place mixture into the ice-cream maker to freeze.

1

2

PINK-DRAGONFRUIT-SORBET
(ERGIBT 1000 G)

190 g	Zucker
40 g	Trockenglukose
16 g	Invertzucker
550 g	Pink-Dragonfruit-Püree
255 g	Wasser
5 g	Fruchtsäure

Trockene Zutaten mischen, alle anderen Zutaten untermixen und mit dem Refraktometer auf 30 °Brix einstellen. Masse in der Eismaschine abfrieren.

PINK DRAGON FRUIT SORBET
(MAKES 1000 G)

190 g	sugar
40 g	dry glucose
16 g	invert sugar
550 g	pink dragon fruit (pitaya) puree
255 g	water
5 g	fruit acid

Mix the dry ingredients together, add all other ingredients and stir, use a refractometer to adjust to 30 °Brix. Place mixture into the ice-cream maker to freeze.

MANGOSORBET
(ERGIBT 1000 G)

165 g	Zucker
50 g	Trockenglukose
275 g	Wasser
500 g	Mangopüree
5 g	Fruchtsäure
10 g	alter Rum

Trockene Zutaten mischen, alle anderen Zutaten bis auf den Rum untermixen und mit dem Refraktometer auf 32 °Brix einstellen. Masse in der Eismaschine abfrieren und sobald das Sorbet stabil gefroren ist, Rum unterlaufen lassen.

MANGO SORBET
(MAKES 1000 G)

165 g	sugar
50 g	dry glucose
275 g	water
500 g	mango puree
5 g	fruit acid
10 g	aged rum

Mix the dry ingredients together, add all other ingredients except the rum and stir, use a refractometer to adjust to 32 °Brix. Freeze the mixture in the ice-cream maker and as soon as the sorbet has frozen to a firm consistency let the rum run into it.

Dunkle Kuvertüre mit Hilfe eines Spritzbeutels
auf eine gefrorene Marmorplatte garnieren

*Use a piping bag to dress the dark couverture
onto a frozen marble slab*

Fertige Spaghetti zusammen nehmen

Gather up a few finished spaghetti …

3

Schokoladenspaghetti auf die richtige Größe
zuschneiden

Cut the chocolate spaghetti to the required size

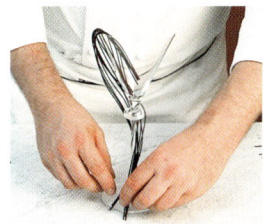

Direkt an ein gekühltes Glas anbringen

and drape them around a chilled glass

4

RED FRUIT SAUCE (MAKES 500 G)

70 g	sugar
3.5 g	xanthan gum
280 g	strawberry puree, slightly frozen
140 g	raspberry puree, slightly frozen
7 g	fruit acid

Mix the sugar with the xanthan gum, add the fruit purees and fruit acid and stir until the sauce becomes stable. Store in a cool place.

ROTE FRUCHTSOSSE (ERGIBT 500 G)

70 g	Zucker
3,5 g	Xanthan
280 g	Erdbeerpüree, leicht angefroren
140 g	Himbeerpüree, leicht angefroren
7 g	Fruchtsäure

Zucker und Xanthan mischen, dann die Fruchtpürees und die Fruchtsäure untermixen, bis die Soße stabil wird. Gekühlt lagern.

DECORATION

mixed fruit of the season
fruit chips
chocolate spaghetti

DEKORATION

gemischte Früchte je nach Saison
Früchtechips
Schokoladenspaghetti

UNA ROSA PER UNA ROSA

Auf einer meiner Reisen durch Italien habe ich mir eines schönen Nachmittags in einer kleinen Gelateria ein Eis gegönnt. Ich war beeindruckt, denn statt der in Deutschland üblichen Bällchen, steckte in meiner Eiswaffel ein kleines Kunstwerk. Dies nachzumachen ist zwar mit etwas Übung verbunden, aber Sie werden sehen, es lohnt sich!

On one of my trips through Italy I went into a gelateria one beautiful afternoon and treated myself to an ice-cream. I was impressed – instead of the scoops we normally get served in Germany, my cone contained a small work of art. To repeat this creation may take a little practice but you will see – it is worth the effort.

ROSENEIS
(WARME HERSTELLUNG)
(ERGIBT 1000 G)

165 g	Zucker
33 g	Dextrose
25 g	Magermilchpulver
1 g	Rosensalz
5 g	neutrales Eisbindemittel
583 g	Vollmilch
5	Bio-Duftrosen
5 g	Zitronensaft
139 g	Sahne
30 g	Rosenwasser
	(je nach Qualität variieren)
13	Rosenblätter, kandiert und gehackt
	Rote-Bete-Saftkonzentrat oder Lebensmittelfarbstoff (bei Bedarf)

Trockene Zutaten mischen. Die Milch lauwarm erhitzen und über die abgezupften Rosenblätter gießen. Abdecken und über Nacht ziehen lassen, dann absieben und mit den trockenen Zutaten bei 85 °C pasteurisieren.

Auf 65 °C abkühlen, dann die Sahne und das Rosenwasser zugeben. Bei 4 °C reifen lassen und in der Eismaschine abfrieren. Kandierte Rosenblätter gegen Ende des Gefriervorganges zugeben.

Die Eismasse als Blütenblätter einer Rose aufspachteln. Beginnend vom Zentrum immer weiter nach außen arbeiten. Die fertige Blüte mit rot gefärbter Kakaobutter mit Hilfe eines Thermo-Airbrushs besprühen. Alternativ kann auf ein Fertigprodukt in der Spraydose zurückgegriffen werden.

ROSE ICE-CREAM
(HOT PRODUCTION METHOD)
(MAKES 1000 G)

165 g	sugar
33 g	dextrose
25 g	skimmed milk powder
1 g	rose salt
5 g	neutral ice-cream binding agent
583 g	whole milk
5	organic scented roses
5 g	lemon juice
139 g	whipping cream
30 g	rose water (modify quantity depen ding on strength)
13	rose petals, candied and chopped
	Beetroot juice concentrate or food colouring (optional)

Mix the dry ingredients. Heat the milk until lukewarm and pour over the rose petals that have been picked off the roses. Cover and leave to steep overnight, strain the milk through a sieve, add the dry ingredients and pasteurise at 85 °C.

Cool down to 65 °C, then add the cream and rose water. Leave the mixture to mature at 4 °C and freeze in the ice-cream maker. Towards the end of the freezing process, add the candied rose petals.

Shape the mixture to resemble the petals of a rose. To do that take a small lump of the mixture and work from the centre to the outside. Spray the finished blossom with red-died cocoa butter using a thermo-airbrush. Alternatively one can also use a proprietary colouring product from a spray can.

1

2

Mit der Eismasse, im Zentrum der späteren Rosenblüte beginnend, Blütenblätter aufspachteln

Make the rose blossom by starting from the centre and adding the petals ...

3

Fertige Eis-Rosenblüte

Finished rose blossom ice-cream

Immer weiter nach außen vorarbeiten

working to the outside

4

Blüte mit rot gefärbter Kakaobutter oder Fertigprodukt aus der Spraydose besprühen

Spray the rose with coloured cocoa butter or a proprietary colouring product from a spray can

WAFFLE CONE (ABOUT 25 PCS.)

200 g	icing sugar
375 g	flour, type 405
4 g	sea salt
2 g	baking powder
1	vanilla pod (pith)
5 g	Ceylon cinnamon
300 g	water
350 g	whole milk
20 g	whole egg
100 g	liquid butter (unsalted)

Mix all dry ingredients, then add the liquid ingredients in small doses and stir well. Make sure that the butter is liquid but not hot, otherwise the baking powder will react too soon. Let the batter rest for a short while before making the waffles.

Preheat the waffle iron to 220 °C and apply a spray of separating fat. Ladle the batter into the waffle iron and bake for about $1^1/_2$ minutes.

WAFFELTÜTE (ETWA 25 STÜCK)

200 g	Puderzucker
375 g	Mehl, Typ 405
4 g	Meersalz
2 g	Backpulver
1	Vanilleschote (Mark)
5 g	Ceylonzimt
300 g	Wasser
350 g	Vollmilch
20 g	Vollei
100 g	flüssige Butter

Alle trockenen Zutaten mischen, flüssige Zutaten nach und nach unterrühren. Darauf achten, dass die Butter nur flüssig, nicht heiß ist, sonst reagiert das Backpulver zu früh. Teig vor der Verarbeitung für kurze Zeit ruhen lassen.

Waffeleisen auf 220 °C vorheizen und mit Trennspray einfetten. Teig einfließen lassen und etwa 1,5 Minuten ausbacken.

WINTERSYMPHONIE

WINTER SYMPHONY

Quadratisch-praktisch-gut! Parfaits nutze ich sehr gerne als schützenden Aussenmantel für meine Eisbomben – denn so haben meine Gäste etwas mehr Zeit die Köstlichkeit anzuschneiden.

It's square, it's practical, it's good. I like to use parfaits as a protective outer coat for my ice-cream bombs – it gives my guests a little more time to make their way to the delicacy inside.

4 Eistorten Ø 18 cm		4 ice-cream cakes Ø 18 cm	
Aprikosenkernboden		**Apricot kernel crust**	
260 g	Persipan	260 g	persipan
160 g	Vollei	160 g	whole egg
35 g	Eigelb	35 g	egg yolk
60 g	Mehl, Typ 550	60 g	flour, type 550
2 g	Backpulver	2 g	baking powder
80 g	flüssige Butter	80 g	liquid butter (unsalted)

Persipan in der Mikrowelle erwärmen und mit Vollei und Eigelb zunächst glatt, dann schaumig schlagen.
Mehl und Backpulver mischen, unter die Masse geben, zum Schluss die Butter unterziehen. In eine Form füllen und bei 180 °C für etwa 20 Minuten backen.

Heat the persipan in the microwave, beat together with the whole egg and egg yolk until smooth and then more until it is frothy.
Mix the flour with the baking powder, add to the mixture and finally draw in the butter. Fill a tin with the mixture and then bake at 180 °C for about 20 minutes.

1

2

3

4

TRÄNKE

125 g	Zucker
125 g	Weißwein
25 g	Aprikosenlikör

Zucker karamellisieren lassen und mit dem Wein ablöschen. Nach dem Erkalten Aprikosenlikör unterrühren.

SOAKING

125 g	sugar
125 g	white wine
25 g	apricot liqueur

Caramelise the sugar and then add the wine. Leave to cool down and then stir in the apricot liqueur.

BROMBEER-LEMON-MYRTLE-SCHOKOLADENEIS (WARME HERSTELLUNG) (KERN)

5 g	Lemon Myrtle
150 g	Zucker
25 g	Dextrose
50 g	Kakaopulver
500 g	Vollmilch
100 g	Brombeerpüree
70 g	Sahne

Trockene Zutaten mischen, mit Milch aufkochen, dann das Püree zugeben und auf 65°C herunterkühlen. Danach die Sahne zugeben, die Masse durch ein Sieb passieren und bei 4°C mindestens 6 Stunden reifen lassen. Anschließend abfrieren und in eine Form füllen, tiefkühlen und ausformen. Eis wird später als Einlage benutzt.

BLACKBERRY LEMON MYRTLE CHOCOLATE ICE-CREAM (HOT PRODUCTION METHOD) (CENTRE)

5 g	lemon myrtle
150 g	sugar
25 g	dextrose
50 g	cocoa powder
500 g	whole milk
100 g	blackberry puree
70 g	whipping cream

Mix the dry ingredients, add to the milk and bring to the boil, add the puree and cool down to 65°C. Then add the cream, pass the mixture through a sieve and leave to mature at 4°C for at least 6 hours. Freeze the mixture, fill into a mould, put into the deep-freezer and then take out of the mould. The ice-cream will later be used to add to the recipe.

Weiße Kuvertüre mit Bitterkuvertüre überspinnen und auf eine gefrorene Marmorplatte auftragen

Use the bitter couverture to apply a net pattern over the white couverture

Schokoladenmasse gleichmäßig mit einer Winkelpalette verteilen

Use an angled spatula to spread the chocolate mixture evenly

Sofort mit einem Messer in gleichmäßige Quadrate schneiden

Use a knife to cut to the mixture into even squares

Quadrate locker zusammennehmen und mittig einschlagen

Gather the squares loosely together and then fold in the middle

YOGHURT APRICOT PARFAIT (COVER)

125 g	apricot puree
200 g	sugar
150 g	egg yolk
1	vanilla pod
125 g	yoghurt
440 g	half-whipped cream

Pasteurise the puree with the sugar, egg yolk and the scraped-out pith and pod of the vanilla at 85 °C. Take out the pod and beat the mixture until cold. Add the yoghurt and stir and then carefully fold in the half-whipped cream. Place the square frames onto a silicone sushi mat and distribute the mixture evenly between them. Insert the chocolate ice-cream and finish off with the apricot kernel crust that has been cut to suit the shape. Freeze the ice bomb, then remove from the mould and spray with yellow and brown spray couverture.

JOGHURT-APRIKOSEN-PARFAIT (MANTEL)

125 g	Aprikosenpüree
200 g	Zucker
150 g	Eigelb
1	Vanilleschote
125 g	Joghurt
440 g	halb geschlagene Sahne

Püree mit Zucker, Eigelb sowie Mark und Schote der ausgeschabten Vanille auf 85 °C pasteurisieren. Schote entfernen und die Masse kalt schlagen. Dann Joghurt unterrühren, danach die halb geschlagene Sahne unterheben. Quadratische Rahmen auf einer Silikon-Sushimatte platzieren und die Masse gleichmäßig darin verteilen. Die Schokoladeneis-Einlage einlegen und mit dem zurechtgeschnittenen Aprikosen kernboden abschließen. Eisbomben einfrieren, dann vorsichtig ausformen und mit gelber sowie brauner Sprühkuvertüre absprühen.

DECORATION

chocolate décor
gold leaf
apricots
blackberries

DEKORATION

Schokoladendekor
Blattgold
Aprikosen
Brombeeren

SPÄTZLE-EIS MIT KAKAOLINSEN UND MANGO-WACHTELEI-SPHERAS

SPÄTZLE ICE-CREAM WITH COCOA LENTILS AND MANGO QUAIL'S EGG SPHERES

Das ich gebürtiger Schwabe bin hört man nicht unbedingt, aber wenn man mir Linsen mit Spätzle vorsetzt, kann ich es nicht mehr verbergen. Zur Eröffnung des neuen Mercedes-Benz-Museums in Stuttgart sollte ich mir etwas ganz Neues einfallen lassen, dabei sollten aber schwäbische Klassiker verwendet werden. Damit war die Idee schon geboren.

For the opening of the new Mercedes Benz Museum in Stuttgart I was asked to come up with something completely new, although the briefing also called for something involving a Swabian classic. That gave me the idea ...

INGREDIENTS FOR 12 PERSONS

COCOA LENTILS

200 g	water
15 g	cocoa powder
60 g	sugar
2.2 g	Kappa
	Orange liqueur syrup
	(Cointreau and sugar syrup)

Bring all the ingredients to the boil, then immediately fill a syringe and place drops onto some baking paper. Once they have gelled, take off immediately and mix with the slightly gelled orange liqueur syrup as a separating agent and store in a cool place.

ZUTATEN FÜR 12 PERSONEN

KAKAOLINSEN

200 g	Wasser
15 g	Kakaopulver
60 g	Zucker
2,2 g	Kappa
	Orangenlikörsirup
	(Cointreau und Läuterzucker)

Alle Zutaten miteinander aufkochen und direkt danach mit einer Spritze aufziehen und auf Backpapier tropfen lassen. Sofort nach dem Gelieren abnehmen und mit angeliertem Orangenlikörsirup als Trennmittel mischen und gekühlt lagern.

Calcic-Mischung für Spheras in Eigelbgrösse

| 3,25 g | Calcic |
| 500 g | stilles Mineralwasser |

Eine Schüssel mit einem Liter Wasser zum Waschen der Spheras sowie Küchenpapier bereitstellen.

Calcic und Mineralwasser in einer weiteren Schüssel mit einem Schneebesen mischen bis es aufgelöst ist. Ein feinmaschiges Sieb einlegen.

Achtung! Wasser, Calcic und die Spheras-Mischung direkt gemischt, blockieren den Abfluss!

Eine Spritze mit der Mangopüree-Mischung aufziehen und vorsichtig kleine Tropfen in das Sieb geben. Nach etwa 1 Minute, die mit einer gelierten Außenhaut versehenen Spheras mit dem Sieb aus der Flüssigkeit nehmen, im klaren Wasser abwaschen und auf einem Küchenpapier abtropfen lassen.

Tipp

Zur Herstellung größerer Spheras kann man sie, wie auf dem Foto abgebildet, statt einer Spritze genauso gut mit einem Portionierlöffel herstellen. Vorgehensweise ist dieselbe wie beschrieben. Jedoch mindestens 3 Minuten gelieren lassen.

Calcic mixture for spherification (egg-yolk-sized spheres)

| 3.25 g | calcic |
| 500 g | still mineral water |

Prepare a bowl with a litre of water to wash the spheres and some paper towel. Use a whisk to mix the calcic with the mineral water in another bowl until it has dissolved. Insert a fine-meshed sieve.

Important! Water that has been mixed with calcic for spherification will block the drainage system when poured into the sink!

Fill a syringe with the mango puree mixture and carefully add small drops into the sieve. After about 1 minute, use the sieve to take the spheres with their gelled outer skin out of the liquid, wash in clear water and leave on some paper towel to dry.

Tip

To make larger spheres you can also use a scoop instead of a syringe, as shown on the photograph. The process is the same as described. Allow to gel for at least 3 minutes.

Mineralwasser und Citras in einem Topf mischen

Mix the Citras with the mineral water in a pan

Ein feinmaschiges Sieb in die Schüssel einlegen, die Mangopüree-Mischung mit einer Spritze aufziehen und vorsichtig kleine Tropfen in das Sieb geben

Place a fine sieve into the bowl, fill a syringe with the mango puree mixture and carefully add small drops into the sieve

5

Algin zugeben und erneut mischen

Add the algin and mix again

Nach etwa 1 Minute, die mit einer gelierten Außenhaut versehenen Spheras mit dem Sieb aus der Flüssigkeit nehmen

After about 1 minute, use the sieve to take the spheres with their gelled outer skin out of the liquid

6

Nach dem Aufkochen und Abkühlen der Mischung Mangopüree untermixen

After boiling and cooling the mixture mix in the mango puree

Fertige, in klarem Wasser abgewaschene Spheras

Finished spheres after washing them in clear water

7

In einer weiteren Schüssel Calcic in das Mineralwasser einrühren bis es aufgelöst ist

Pour mineral water into another bowl and stir in the calcic until it dissolves

MANGO QUAIL'S EGG SPHERES

125 g	mineral water
0.65 g	Citras
0.9 g	algin
125 g	mango puree

Mix the mineral water with Citras, add the algin and mix again. Bring to the boil, leave to cool down to room temperature. Add the mango puree and mix in.

MANGO-WACHTELEI-SPHERAS

125 g	Mineralwasser
0,65 g	Citras
0,9 g	Algin
125 g	Mangopüree

Mineralwasser und Citras mischen, Algin zugeben und erneut mischen. Anschließend aufkochen und auf Raumtemperatur abkühlen lassen. Mangopüree zugeben und untermixen.

Aufgekochte Zutaten mit einer Spritze aufziehen

Pull the boiled ingredients into a syringe ...

1

Zutatenmischung mit der Spritze auf Backpapier aufbringen

... and place drops onto some baking paper

2

Linsen direkt nach dem Gelieren vom Backpapier nehmen

Immediately after they have gelled, take the lentils off the baking paper

3

SPECKKROKANT

12	feine Scheiben Speck oder Bacon, durchwachsen
250 g	Isomalt

Den Speck in einer Pfanne auslassen bis er sehr knusprig ist, dann auf Küchenpapier ablegen. Isomalt auflösen, Speckscheiben darin karamellisieren. Je nach Geschmack kann man auch einen Teil des Specks fein hacken und über die Linsen streuen.

SPECK BRITTLE

12	thin slices of speck or streaky bacon
250 g	Isomalt

Render the speck in a frying pan until it is completely crispy, then place on some paper towel. Dissolve the Isomalt and caramelise the speck slices in it. Alternatively one can also chop the speck into small pieces and sprinkle over the lentils.

Spätzle ice-cream
(hot production method)
(makes 1000 g)

79 g	Spätzle, candied and caramelised
316 g	whole milk
1	Tahiti vanilla pod
111 g	egg yolk
119 g	sugar
475 g	whipping cream

To candy the Spätzle, boil them not in water as usual but in sugar syrup until they are cooked but still firm, then drain the liquid and put the Spätzle on a paper towel to dry. Caramelise the Spätzle with a little sugar in a frying pan.

Boil the milk with the vanilla pith and pod, take out the pod, add the egg yolk and sugar and stir until frothy. Add the milk and then pasteurise the mixture by heating it in a bowl in hot water up to 85 °C. Cool down to 65 °C, add the cream and place into the ice-cream maker to freeze. Towards the end of the freezing process add the Spätzle after chopping them finely.

Spätzle-Eis
(warme Herstellung)
(ergibt 1000 g)

79 g	Spätzle, kandiert und karamellisiert
316 g	Vollmilch
1	Tahiti-Vanilleschote
111 g	Eigelb
119 g	Zucker
475 g	Sahne

Um die Spätzle zu kandieren, nicht wie gewohnt in Wasser, sondern in Läuterzucker bissfest kochen, dann abtropfen lassen und auf Küchenpapier trocknen. Spätzle mit etwas Zucker in einer Pfanne karamellisieren.

Milch mit Vanillemark und -schote aufkochen, dann Schote entnehmen sowie Eigelb und Zucker schaumig rühren. Milch zugießen und Mischung im Wasserbad bei 85 °C pasteurisieren. Auf 65 °C abkühlen und Sahne zugeben, dann in der Eismaschine abfrieren. Gegen Ende des Gefriervorgangs vorbereitete Spätzle fein hacken und zugeben.

Decoration

chocolate decor

Dekoration

Schokoladendekor

SAIL AWAY ODER EHER TAKE AWAY? GLASDESSERTS SIND IN – VOR ALLEM, WENN SIE SO LECKER SIND WIE DIESES HIER. ES IST FÜR MICH COSTA DEL SOL PUR. GLASDESSERTS SIND AUF ALLE FÄLLE EINE ZUSÄTZLICHE MÖGLICHKEIT, UM NEUE UMSÄTZE ZU GENERIEREN.

SAIL AWAY OR SHOULD IT BE "TAKE AWAY"? DESSERTS IN GLASS DISHES ARE VERY POPULAR – ESPECIALLY WHEN THEY TASTE LIKE THIS ONE. FOR ME THEY REPRESENT UNDILUTED COSTA DEL SOL. IN ANY CASE, DESSERTS IN GLASS DISHES ARE AN ADDITIONAL OPTION FOR GENERATING MORE TURNOVER.

ZUTATEN FÜR 12 PERSONEN

FLÜSSIGE ORANGEN-MELONEN-SAGO-GRÜTZE

1,1 g	Agar-Agar
500 g	Orangensaft
50 g	Zucker
25 g	Sagoperlen
200 g	Cantaloupe-Melone, fein gewürfelt

Alle Zutaten, bis auf die Melone mischen und quellen lassen. Aufkochen, Melonenstücke zugeben und gekühlt lagern.

INGREDIENTS FOR 12 PERSONS

LIQUID ORANGE MELON SAGO JELLY

1.1 g	agar agar
500 g	orange juice
50 g	sugar
25 g	sago pearls
200 g	Cantaloupe melon, finely diced

Mix all ingredients, except for the melon, and leave to soak. Then bring to the boil, add the pieces of melon and store in a cool place.

MANDEL-CALISSON-EIS (WARME HERSTELLUNG) (ERGIBT 1000 G)

32 g	Dextrose
64 g	Zucker
16 g	Magermilchpulver
5 g	neutrales Eisbindemittel
1 g	Salz
64 g	Eigelb
645 g	Vollmilch
96 g	Calissons (französische Mandel-spezialität, erhältlich im Feinkostladen)
80 g	Sahne

Trockene Zutaten mischen, Eigelb und Milch zugeben und bei 85 °C pasteurisieren. Calissons untermixen bis die Masse glatt ist, dann bei 65 °C die Sahne untermixen. Bei 4 °C reifen lassen und in der Eismaschine abfrieren.

TIPP

Je nach Geschmack kann man statt der Calissons auch Marzipanrohmasse verwenden.

ALMOND CALLISON ICE-CREAM (HOT PRODUCTION METHOD) (MAKES 1000 G)

32 g	dextrose
64 g	sugar
16 g	skimmed milk powder
5 g	neutral ice-cream binding agent
1 g	salt
64 g	egg yolk
645 g	whole milk
96 g	Calissons (French almond speciality obtainable from delicatessen shops)
80 g	whipping cream

Mix the dry ingredients, add the milk and egg yolk and pasteurise at 85 °C. Mix in the Callisons until the mixture is smooth and then mix in the cream at 65 °C. Leave the mixture to mature at 4 °C and freeze in the ice-cream maker.

TIP

As an option you can also use marzipan raw mixture instead of the Calissons – it results in a slightly different taste.

MANDELBISKUIT

235 g	Zucker
100 g	Eigelb
150 g	Eiweiß
60 g	Mehl
60 g	Weizenpuder
40 g	Mandelgrieß

Eigelb mit 85 g Zucker und Eiweiß mit 150 g Zucker getrennt stabil aufschlagen, dann Eigelbmasse abwechselnd mit einer Mischung aus Mehl, Weizenpuder und Mandelgrieß unter das Eiweiß ziehen. Teig in der Höhe von etwa 1 Zentimeter auf eine Backmatte streichen und bei 180 °C 15 Minuten backen. Anschließend in der Größe der verwendeten Gläser ausstechen.

ALMOND SPONGE

235 g	sugar
100 g	egg yolk
150 g	egg white
60 g	flour
60 g	wheat powder
40 g	grated almonds

Beat the egg yolk with 85 g sugar and separately the egg white with 150 g sugar until firm, fold the egg yolk mixture and a mixture of flour, wheat powder and grated almonds in alternating steps into the egg white. Spread the pastry 1 cm thick onto a baking mat and bake at 180 °C for 15 minutes. Cut out round shapes to suit the glasses used for serving.

FLAMED AMARETTO MERINGUE

2	*sheet of gelatine*
200 g	*egg white, pasteurised*
200 g	*sugar, extra fine*
20 g	*amaretto*

Soak the gelatine in cold water. Warm up the egg white and sugar in a bowl in hot water until the sugar has dissolved completely. Dissolve the gelatine in this mixture and add the amaretto. Put the mixture into an Espuma siphon and fit 2 gas cartridges. Store in a cool place and shake well before use. Pipe the mixture onto a flame-proof base, flame with a gas torch and serve immediately as the meringue will not be stable for long. It is possible, however, to improve the stability by adding Espuma stabilisers such as xanthan gum.

GEFLÄMMTER AMARETTOBAISER

2	*Blatt Gelatine*
200 g	*Eiweiß, pasteurisiert*
200 g	*Zucker, extrafein*
20 g	*Amaretto*

Gelatine in kaltem Wasser einweichen. Eiweiß und Zucker im Wasserbad erwärmen, bis sich der Zucker vollständig gelöst hat. Gelatine in dieser Mischung auflösen und Amaretto zugeben. Masse in einen Espuma-Schäumer geben und 2 Gaspatronen aufschrauben. Gekühlt lagern und vor der Verwendung gut schütteln. Auf eine feuerfeste Unterlage dressieren, dann mit einem Gasbrenner abflämmen und sofort servieren, da das Baiser nicht lange stabil bleibt. Die Stabilität kann jedoch durch die Zugabe von Espumastabilisatoren wie Xanthan verbessert werden.

DECORATION

chocolate decor
sugar decor made from Isomalt
roasted almond

DEKORATION

Schokoladendekor
Zuckerdekor aus Isomalt
geröstete Mandel

SPACEBALLS EISBOMBE

SPACE BALLS ICE-CREAM BOMB

Ich versuche in meinen Kreationen oft Klassiker zu verändern, ohne mich zu weit von den klassischen Formen wegzubewegen. Hier lasse ich die Eisbombe einfach unter einer abnehmbaren Zuckerkuppel verschwinden. Dieser Effekt erinnert mich an weit von der Erde entfernte Planeten im Weltraum.

In my creations I often try to modify classic recipes without moving too far from the classic shape. In this one I simply hide the ice-cream bomb under a removable sugar dome. This effect reminds me of planets that are far away from Earth, deep in space.

4 ICE-CREAM BOMBS Ø 18 CM

STRAWBERRY SORBET (CENTRE)

76 g	dry glucose
8 g	neutral stabiliser
161 g	sugar
247 g	mineral water
30 g	invert sugar
1000 g	strawberry puree
5 g	fruit acid (1:1)

Mix the dry ingredients, add the mineral water and invert sugar and bring to the boil. Stir in the puree and fruit acid and adjust to 30 °Brix. The best results are achieved after at least 4 hours time for maturing. Then mix again and freeze in the ice-cream maker; once frozen fill the ice-cream into silicone moulds in the shape of a semi-sphere.

4 EISBOMBEN Ø 18 CM

ERDBEERSORBET (KERN)

76 g	Trockenglukose
8 g	neutraler Stabilisator
161 g	Zucker
247 g	Mineralwasser
30 g	Invertzucker
1000 g	Erdbeerpüree
5 g	Fruchtsäure (1:1)

Trockene Zutaten mischen, dann Mineralwasser und Invertzucker zugeben und kurz aufkochen. Püree und Fruchtsäure untermischen und auf 30 °Brix einstellen. Das beste Resultat bekommt man nach mindestens 4 Stunden Reifezeit. Danach nochmals mixen und in der Eismaschine gefrieren, schließlich in Silikonhalbkugeln füllen.

1

2

3

4

5

BAISER
(BODEN FÜR SORBET UND PARFAIT)

150 g	Eiweiß
400 g	Zucker
1 g	Salz
100 g	Puderzucker

Das Eiweiß mit etwas Zucker und Salz zu einem steifen Schnee schlagen. Dann den restlichen Zucker nach und nach einlaufen lassen, Puderzucker unterheben und mit Hilfe eines Spritzbeutels mit einer 6er-Lochtülle eine Scheibe auf eine Backmatte garnieren. Ihr Durchmesser sollte etwas kleiner sein als die Form. Restliche Masse aufdressieren und als Boden für das Parfait verwenden. Bei 120 °C für etwa 4 Stunden „trocknen".

MERINGUE BASE
(BASE FOR SORBET AND PARFAIT)

150 g	egg white
400 g	sugar
1 g	salt
100 g	icing sugar

Add some sugar and salt to the egg white and beat until stiff. Then let the remaining sugar run into the egg white in small doses, fold in the icing sugar and use a piping bag with a round nozzle size 6 to pipe a disk onto a baking mat. Its diameter should be a little smaller than the mould. Pipe the remaining mixture and use as base for the parfait. "Dry" the mixture at 120 °C for about 4 hours.

PARFAIT D'AMOUR
(MANTEL)

60 g	Eigelb
150 g	Vollei
262 g	Zucker
1 g	Tonkabohne, frisch gerieben
10 g	Ingwer, frisch gerieben
150 g	Baiser, gehackt
300 g	Erdbeerpüree
150 g	Himbeeren
600 g	Sahne

Eigelb mit Vollei, Zucker, Tonkabohne und Ingwer im Wasserbad auf 85 °C pasteurisieren, anschließend im Eiswasserbad kalt schlagen. Baiser, Erdbeerpüree und grob zerkleinerte Himbeeren mit der Sahne unter die Eiermasse heben. In eine große Silikonform einfüllen, mit dem ausgeformten Erdbeersorbet füllen und mit einer Baiserscheibe abdeckeln. Gut durchfrieren und ausformen.

PARFAIT D'AMOUR
(COVER)

60 g	egg yolks
150 g	whole eggs
262 g	sugar
1 g	tonka bean, freshly ground
10 g	ginger, freshly ground
150 g	meringue, chopped
300 g	strawberry puree
150 g	raspberries
600 g	whipping cream

Pasteurise the egg yolks with the whole eggs, sugar, tonka bean and ginger in a bowl in hot water at 85 °C, then beat in a bowl in ice water until cold. Fold the meringue, strawberry puree and coarsely chopped up raspberries with the cream into the egg mixture. Fill the mixture into a large silicone mould, add the strawberry sorbet and finish off with a meringue "lid". Freeze thoroughly and take out of the mould.

Gefrorene Metallhalbkugel dünn mit Trennspray einfetten, überschüssiges Fett mit einem Tuch abnehmen.

Freeze a metal semi-sphere and spray thinly with separating spray, wipe off any excess fat with a cloth

STRAWBERRY GLAZE (COATING)

12 g	pectin
450 g	sugar
300 g	strawberry juice
200 g	dry glucose

ERDBEERGLASUR (ÜBERZUG)

12 g	Pektin
450 g	Zucker
300 g	Erdbeersaft
200 g	Trockenglukose

Isomalt in Wasser auflösen, leicht abkühlen lassen und netzartig über die Metallhalbkugel spinnen

Dissolve the Isomalt in water, leave to cool a little and then apply to the metal semi-sphere in the shape of a net

Mix the pectin with 50 g sugar and bring to the boil with the strawberry juice – add 400 g sugar. Bring back to the boil, add the dry glucose and boil up again. Allow to settle and remove the froth. Use the glaze when its temperature is 25 °C.

Pektin mit 50 g Zucker mischen, mit Erdbeersaft aufkochen und 400 g Zucker zugeben. Erneut aufkochen, Trockenglukose zugeben und wieder aufkochen. Absetzten lassen und abschäumen. Die Überzugstemperatur sollte 25 °C betragen.

Überhängende Enden mit einer Schere abtrennen

Use scissors to cut off any excess ends

SUGAR DECORATION

300 g	Isomalt
	metal semi-spheres

ZUCKERDEKORATION

300 g	Isomalt
	Metallhalbkugeln

Erkaltetes Isomaltnetz vorsichtig von der Halbkugel lösen

Once the Isomalt net has set, remove it carefully from the semi-sphere

Freeze a metal semi-sphere and spray thinly with separating spray, wipe off any excess fat with a cloth. Dissolve the Isomalt in water, leave to cool and apply to the semi-sphere in the shape of a net. Once it has set, cut off any excess ends with a pair of scissors and take the finished Isomalt net off the semi-sphere.

Eine gefrorene Metallhalbkugel dünn mit Trennspray einfetten, überschüssiges Fett mit einem Tuch abnehmen. Isomalt in Wasser auflösen, abkühlen lassen und mit einem Spatel netzartig auf die Halbkugel aufbringen. Nach dem Erkalten überhängende Enden mit einer Schere abtrennen und das fertige Isomaltnetz vorsichtig von der Halbkugel ablösen.

Fertiger Isomaltdekor

Finished Isomalt décor

MARZIPAN

MARZIPAN

Um die Modellierfähigkeit des Marzipans zu erhöhen, ist es sinnvoll, Puderzucker unterzuarbeiten. Um eine längere Frischhaltung zu gewährleisten, können Frischhaltemittel wie Sorbitol und Glukosesirup zugegeben werden.

Nachträgliches Ansprühen der Figuren mit Kakaobutter oder Lebensmittellack dient dem gleichen Zweck und verhindert ein schnelles Austrocknen der Figuren.

Selbstverständlich kann man das Marzipan nach Wunsch mit verschiedenen Zutaten aromatisieren.

In order to increase the pliability of marzipan it helps to work in some icing sugar. Preservatives such as sorbitol and glucose syrup can be added in order to guarantee a prolonged shelf life.

Spraying the finished figures with cocoa butter or food lacquer serves the same purpose and prevents the figures from drying out too quickly.

Of course it is possible to flavour the marzipan with a number of ingredients to suit your requirements/taste.

Die Arbeitsgeräte für das Modellieren von Marzipan

Tools used for working with marzipan

MODELLING MARZIPAN

1000 g	marzipan raw mixture
35 g	glucose syrup
35 g	sorbitol
600 g	icing sugar

Kneed all ingredients into a smooth mixture and wrap in plastic wrap/cling-film. Store in a cool place.

COLOURING

liquid food colouring

food colouring powders

metallic food colouring powders

cocoa butter for finishing
the figures with a sheen and as
a binder for the dry colouring.

food lacquer

natural colouring such as
freeze-dried fruit or herbs

TOOLS

silicone baking mats

special silicone marzipan mats

relief foils and mats from
various materials

airbrush (normal and thermo)

various brushes

modelling tools

spoons

knives and special marzipan knife

scissors

pattern rolls

decorating bag

spray chocolate (white and dark)

rubber gloves

MODELLIERMARZIPAN

1000 g	Marzipanrohmasse
35 g	Glukosesirup
35 g	Sorbitol
600 g	Puderzucker

Alle Zutaten zu einer glatten Masse kneten und in Frischhaltefolie verpacken. Kühl lagern.

FARBEN

Flüssige Lebensmittelfarben

Pulverförmige Lebensmittelfarben

Pulverförmige Metallic-Lebens-
mittelfarben

Kakaobutter zum Abglänzen
der Figuren und zum Anrühren
der trockenen Farbstoffe

Lebensmittellack

Naturfarben, zum Beispiel
gefriergetrocknete Früchte
oder Kräuter

ARBEITSGERÄTE

Silikon-Backmatten

Spezialsilikonmarzipanmatten

Relieffolien und Matten aus
verschiedenen Materialien

Airbrush (Normal und Thermo)

Verschiedene Pinsel

Modellierstäbe

Löffel

Messer und spez. Marzipanmesser

Scheren

Riefhölzer

Garniertütchen

Spritzschokolade (weiß und dunkel)

Gummihandschuhe

NOAH'S ARK

MEINE MODELLIERTECHNIK WURDE VON EINIGEN MARZIPANKÜNSTLERN GE-
PRÄGT. DER ERSTE WAR CAREL VAN LAERE, DENN MEIN VATER HATTE SEIN BUCH
„NEUE MARZIPANFIGUREN". DANN FASZINIERTE MICH KARL SINDERN, DER DIE
EFFIZIENZ DER KÖRPERTECHNIKEN BEHERRSCHT, ABER AM MEISTEN WAR ES
WOHL FREDY EGGENSCHWILER, DER MEINE TECHNIK BEEINFLUSST HAT.

MY MODELLING TECHNIQUE HAS BEEN INFLUENCED BY A NUMBER OF MARZIPAN
ARTISTS. THE FIRST ONE WAS CAREL VAN LAERE BECAUSE MY FATHER HAD HIS
BOOK "NEUE MARZIPANFIGUREN" (NEW MARZIPAN FIGURES). THEN I WAS FAS-
CINATED BY KARL SINDERN WHO IS A MASTER AT SHAPING BODIES EFFICIENTLY,
BUT MOST OF ALL IT WAS PROBABLY FREDY EGGENSCHWILER WHO INFLUENCED
MY TECHNIQUE.

FLAMED SHIP AND ANCHOR

Model the basic shape of a ship. For the planks of the ship roll out the marzipan not too thin, cut out and use a knife to attach them to the hull. When all planks have been fitted fashion a marzipan strip at the bow of the ship to finish off the boarding. Leave to dry. Use a gas torch to lightly flame the edges. To make the anchor, roll out the black-died marzipan, model the shape of the anchor, fashion the points in the shape of hearts and then use an air brush to apply silver colouring. Attach the anchor to the ship.

GEFLÄMMTES SCHIFF MIT ANKER

Für das Schiff einen Grundkörper model-lieren. Für die Schiffsplanken Marzipan nicht zu dünn ausrollen, ausschneiden und mit dem Messer am Rumpf anbrin-gen. Wenn alle Planken angebracht sind, am Bug einen Marzipanstreifen als Ab-schluss anmodellieren. Trocknen lassen. Kanten mit dem Gasbrenner leicht abfläm-men. Für den Anker schwarz gefärbtes Marzipan ausrollen, Ankerform modellie-ren, die Spitzen herzförmig ansetzen und mit Airbrush silbern schminken. Anker am Schiff befestigen.

FISCH AUF WELLE

Für die Welle blau gefärbtes Marzipan zu einer konischen Rolle formen, abflachen, entgegengesetzt zu einer S-Form aufrollen und dann mit dem Airbrush metallic-blau schminken. Den Fisch aus gelbem Marzipan modellieren. Für den Körper eine Kugel spitz zumodellieren. Die Schwanzflossen auseinander geklappt modellieren, flachdrücken, mit dem Messer masern und mit der Rückenflosse und den Seitenflossen anbringen. Erneut masern und Schuppen eindrücken. Die Augenwülste, die Augenhöhlen und den Mund eindrücken, die Augen mit Garnierschokolade spritzen. Fertigen Fisch mit dem Airbrush orange schminken und auf der Welle befestigen.

AFFE

Für den Körper eine große braune Marzipankugel mit einer kleineren rosa Marzipankugel zusammen modellieren und den birnenförmigen Körper herstellen. Den Bauchnabel einmodellieren. Die Arme aus einer dünnen Rolle modellieren und über dem Grundkörper ansetzen. Für den Kopf eine Kugel, je zur Hälfte aus rosa und braunem Marzipan fertigen, dann birnenförmig modellieren, so dass die dünnere Seite aus rosa Marzipan besteht. Dieses als Gesicht ausarbeiten. Rotes Marzipan als Mund, eine kleine braune Marzipankugel als Nase und große rosa Ohren anmodellieren. Für die Augen naturfarbenes Marzipan verwenden und mit dunkler Garnierschokolade spritzen.

FISH ON A WAVE

To make the wave, form a tapered roll using blue-died marzipan, flatten it, roll it the other way in an S shape and then use an air brush to spray with metallic blue colouring. Model the fish from yellow marzipan. To make the body start with a ball and make it pointed. Model the tail folded apart, press flat, texture it with the knife and then attach the tail together with the back fin and the side fins. Renew the stripy pattern and add the scale patterns. Form the bulges above the eyes, press in the eye sockets and the mouth and spray the eyes with decorating chocolate. Colour the finished fish in orange with an air brush and attach to the wave.

MONKEY

To make the body, join a large brown marzipan ball with a smaller pink one and model into a pear-shaped body. Carve in the shape of the belly button. Make a thin roll and model the arms from it – attach at the top of the basic body. To make the head, roll together a ball using equal portions of pink and brown marzipan, then model into a pear shape with the thinner end consisting of pink marzipan. Work this into a face. Attach red marzipan as a mouth, a small brown marzipan ball as nose and fashion large pink ears. Make the eye sockets using natural-coloured marzipan and spray the eyes with decorating chocolate.

1
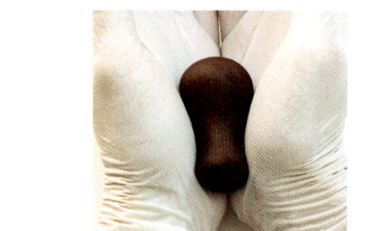

2
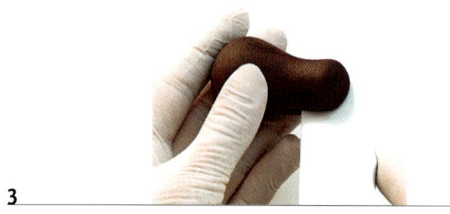

3
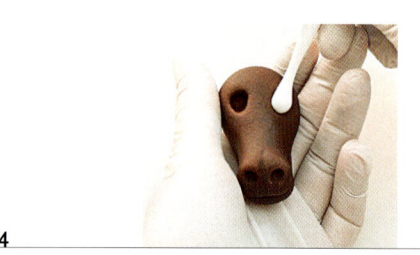

4
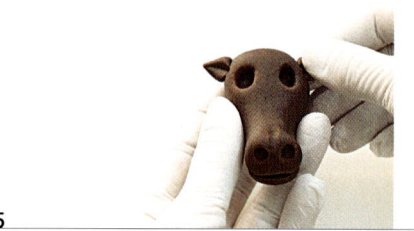

5
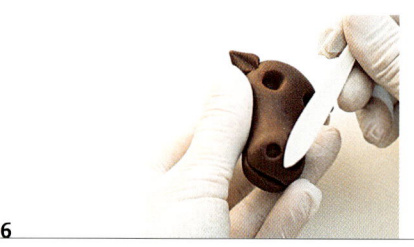

6

Die einzelnen Elemente des Stierkopfs

The elements making up the head of the bull

Kopf zwischen den Handballen birnenförmig modellieren

Make the head by modelling a basic pear shape with your hands

Maul mit dem Marzipanmesser einschneiden

Cut the mouth with a marzipan knife

Augenhöhlen mit dem Kugelmodellierholz einmodellieren

Use the modelling stick to fashion the eye sockets

Ohren ansetzen

Attach the ears

Nüstern mit dem Schiffchen deutlicher ausarbeiten

Work the shape

LION

Start the lion by making the body, cross the legs and make them hang over the edge of the boat. Model the head in the shape of a pear, cut the mouth at the bigger end and work into its proper shape. To make the mane, drape the yellow marzipan around the head in the shape of bananas and apply the texturing in wavy rays. Attach an extra ball for each eye socket, shape the eye brows and then model the ears and the tail and attach to the body. Apply some brown colour with the air brush, make the nose out of dark-brown marzipan and insert the tongue made from pink marzipan. Spray the eyes with decorating chocolate and make little indentations resembling stubby whiskers.

BULL

Model the bull from marzipan with a dark brown colouring. First shape the body starting from a pear-shaped piece and split the thinner end into quarters while holding it in your hand. Fashion the legs. For the head make another pear shape, insert a cut at the thinner end and model into the mouth. Push up the marzipan to make the nostrils and make holes as sockets for the eyes. Attach the ears with the modelling tool, make the horns out of light-coloured marzipan and apply to the forehead. Complete the bull by adding a yellow hair lock, a nose ring and the tongue. Spray the eyes with decorating chocolate, attach the head to the body and dress a read marzipan neck scarf around its neck. Don't forget the tail of the bull.

LÖWE

Für den Löwen zuerst den Körper herstellen, die Beine überschlagen aus dem Boot hängen lassen. Den Kopf birnenförmig modellieren, das Maul an der dicken Seite einschneiden und ausmodellieren. Für die Mähne das gelbe Marzipan bananenförmig um den Kopf legen, die Mähne strahlenförmig ausmodellieren. Die Augenhöhlen mit jeweils einer Extrakugel zu Augenbrauen formen und die Ohren und den Schwanz anmodellieren. Löwe mit dem Airbrush leicht braun schminken, dann die Nase aus dunkelbraunem Marzipan, die Zunge aus rosa Marzipan ansetzen. Die Augen mit Garnierschokolade spritzen, Bartstoppeln eindrücken.

STIER

Den Stier aus dunkelbraun gefärbtem Marzipan modellieren. Zuerst den Körper aus einer Birnenform modellieren und die schlankere Seite in der Hand liegend vierteln. Die Beine ausarbeiten. Den Kopf wiederum aus einer Birnenform modellieren, die schlankere Seite einschneiden und zum Maul formen. Die Nüstern hochschiebend formen und die Augenhöhlen eindrücken. Die Ohren mit dem Schiffchen ansetzen und die Hörner aus einem Stück hellem Marzipan auf der Stirn anbringen. Den Stier mit einer gelben Haarlocke, einem Nasenring und der Zunge vervollständigen. Die Augen mit Garnierschokolade spritzen, Kopf auf dem Körper befestigen und ein rotes Marzipanhalstuch anbringen. Den Schwanz des Stiers nicht vergessen.

PAPAGEI

Für den Papagei grün gefärbtes Marzipan birnenförmig modellieren, die dicke Seite zu den Schwanzfedern spitz zumodellieren, aus der dünneren Seite den Kopf herausarbeiten. Die Augenhöhlen durch zusätzliche Marzipankugeln verstärken und eindrücken. Die Flügel separat modellieren, ansetzen und den Schnabel sowie die Haarkrone aus orangefarbenem bzw. gelbem Marzipan anbringen. Die Augen mit Garnierschokolade spritzen. Den Papagei mit dem Airbrush leicht schminken.

FUCHS

Den Grundkörper aus rotbraunem Marzipan birnenförmig modellieren. Den Kopf ebenfalls aus einer Birnenform modellieren. Die Nase spitz zulaufen lassen, die Barthaare mit beiden Daumen seitlich flachdrücken und dann mit einer Schere einschneiden. Den Mund eindrücken und die Ohren mit den Fingerspitzen herausmodellieren. Die Augenhöhlen mit naturfarbenem Marzipan ansetzen, dann die Nasenspitze mit dunkelbraunem Marzipan anbringen und die Augen mit Garnierschokolade spritzen.

HUND

Den Kopf und den Körper birnenförmig modellieren. Eine rosa Marzipankugel als Mund einlegen und mit dem Messer anteilen. Die Ohren aus etwas größeren, tropfenförmigen Marzipanstückchen an den Kopf anmodellieren. Den Kopf des Hundes mit einer Nase aus braunem Marzipan, mit Augen aus Garnierschokolade und mit eingedrückten Bartstoppeln fertig stellen, auf den Körper setzen und einen Schwanz anbringen.

PARROT

To make the parrot, use green-coloured marzipan in the shape of a pear, model the thick end into the pointed tail feathers and work the head from the thinner end. Place additional marzipan balls on the head and push in the holes as sockets for the eyes. Model the wings separately and attach to the body, make the beak and the crown feathers from orange or yellow marzipan and attach to the head. Make the eyes with decorating chocolate. Use an air brush to apply some colour to the parrot.

FOX

Model the basic body in the shape of a pear using red-brown marzipan. Model the head also from a pear-shaped piece. Fashion the nose to a point, attach whiskers on the side and press flat and then cut with scissors. Push in a hole to make the mouth and model the ears using your fingers. Use natural-coloured marzipan to make the eye sockets, put on the point of the nose in dark-brown marzipan and then spray the eyes with decorating chocolate.

DOG

Make the head and the body starting from a basic pear shape. Insert a pink marzipan ball as mouth and split with a knife. Model the ears from slightly bigger drop-shaped marzipan pieces and attach to the head. Finish the head of the dog with a nose made from brown marzipan, eyes made from decorating chocolate and pressed in dimples to resemble short whiskers, add the head to the body and attach a tail.

CROCODILE

To make the crocodile start from a bright green marzipan ball and model it into a long wedge-shaped body. Fashion the thicker end into a head and cut in the mouth. Use the modelling stick to push up the nose holes, attach small balls of marzipan to shape the eye sockets, attach an additional marzipan roll on the back and work into shape with a knife. Attach the legs and spray the eyes with decorating chocolate.

GIRAFFE

Make the body of the giraffe from yellow marzipan – leave to dry on its side. To make the head, model a yellow marzipan ball into the shape of a pear, cut a mouth at the thin end, open the mouth slightly; use a modelling stick to push up the nostrils and shape a hole for the eyes. Use a knife to fashion the shape of the nose and then use the modelling tool to attach the ears on the side and the horns on top. Join the head and body together, use a gas torch to apply the patterns and finally add the eyes in decorating chocolate.

KROKODIL

Für das Krokodil kräftig grün gefärbtes Marzipan aus einer Kugel zu einem langen, keilförmigen Körper modellieren. Das dickere Ende zu einem Kopf ausformen und das Maul einschneiden. Die Nasenlöcher mit dem Kugelmodellierholz hochschieben, die Augenhöhlen durch eine Kugel Marzipan verstärkt einmodellieren, auf dem Rücken zusätzlich eine Marzipanrolle anbringen und mit dem Messer nachmodellieren. Die Beine ansetzen und die Augen mit Garnierschokolade spritzen.

GIRAFFE

Für die Giraffe den Körper aus gelbem Marzipan herstellen und liegend trocknen lassen. Für den Kopf eine gelbe Marzipankugel zur Birne modellieren, am dünnen Ende einen Mund einschneiden, leicht öffnen und mit einem kleinen Kugelmodellierholz die Nasenlöcher hoch formen und die Augen eindrücken. Mit einem Messer den Nasenrücken einmodellieren und mit dem Schiffchen die Ohren seitlich anbringen und die Hörner ansetzen. Kopf und Körper zusammensetzen, dann mit dem Gasbrenner die Maserung aufflämmen und zum Schluss die Augen mit Garnierschokolade spritzen

CHICKEN

ZUM GEBURTSTAG EINES FREUNDES KAM MIR DIE IDEE ZU DIESEM CHICKEN. AUCH KUNDEN KOMMEN HÄUFIG AUF AUSGEFALLENE IDEEN UND WÜNSCHE, DIE WIR BESTMÖGLICH IN MARZIPAN UMSETZEN. EIN BISSCHEN SPASS MUSS SEIN ...

THIS IDEA OF A CHICKEN CAME TO ME WHEN I PREPARED A BIRTHDAY TREAT FOR A FRIEND. CUSTOMERS OFTEN HAVE UNUSUAL IDEAS AND REQUESTS AND WE TRY OUR BEST TO EXPRESS THEM IN MARZIPAN. IT'S ALWAYS GOOD TO HAVE A LITTLE FUN ...

MAKING THE PARTS

Make a couverture base on a silicone Sushi mat, take off the sheet and apply some gold colouring. To make the chicken, start by modelling a basic pear-shaped body and use the round modelling stick to form the eye sockets at the thinner end of the body. Use red marzipan to make the comb and wattles, yellow marzipan to make the beak and then attach these to the body. Make the thighs and wings from pink marzipan, the shanks and claws from yellow marzipan and also attach these to the body. Leave to dry. Finally use decorating chocolate to apply the bikini and the eyes.

HERSTELLUNG

Eine Bodenplatte aus Kuvertüre von einer Silikon-Sushimatte abformen und dann angolden. Für das Chicken einen birnenförmigen Grundkörper modellieren, oben an der schlankeren Stelle die Augenhöhlen mit dem Rundholz eindrücken. Aus rotem Marzipan den Kamm und die Kieferlappen formen, den Schnabel aus gelbem Marzipan anfertigen und alles ansetzen. Die Oberschenkel und die Flügel aus rosa Marzipan, die Unterschenkel und die Krallen aus gelbem Marzipan modellieren und befestigen. Antrocknen lassen. Zum Schluss mit Garnierschokolade den Bikini und die Augen garnieren.

Einzelteile für den Grundkörper in den Stadien der Entstehung mit Schnabel, Kieferlappen und Kamm

The individual parts of the chicken in making, i.e. the basic body, beak, wattles and comb

1

Einzelteile für die Unterschenkel und die Krallen

The parts making up the shanks and claws

2

Einzelteile für die Oberschenkel und die Flügel

The parts making up the thighs and wings

3

HOCHZEIT, MUTTERTAG ODER VALENTINSTAG

WEDDINGS, MOTHERING SUNDAY, ST. VALENTINE

Ich bin immer offen für neue Wege, aber beim Marzipan bin ich eher klassisch. Meiner Meinung nach ist Marzipan eher etwas für Kinder, sie freuen sich mehr über lustige Figuren als über Designerfiguren. Für manche Anlässe kann es aber auch ganz anders aussehen ...

I am always open to new things but when it comes to marzipan I tend to stick to the classics. In my opinion marzipan is more for children because they have more fun with funny figures than with designer style items. But there are some occasions that buck the trend ...

MARZIPANHERZEN

Für das große Herz einen Ausstecher verwenden. Dazu neutrales Marzipan dick ausrollen, mit Folie belegen und mit der Folie ausstechen – so bekommt die Figur abgerundete Kanten. Rotes Marzipan dünn ausrollen, auf das ausgestochene Herz legen und vorsichtig damit einschlagen. Für die kleinen Herzen eine Kugel aus rotem Marzipan herstellen, die Kugel mittig auseinandermodellieren, dann beide Teile wieder zusammenklappen und mit dem Handballen herzförmig zusammenbringen. Das Herz zum Schluss leicht flach drücken.

MARZIPAN HEARTS

To make the large heart use a cutting shape. First roll out some neutral marzipan not too thin, place a foil over it and cut the shape through the foil – it will give the figure rounded edges. Roll out some red marzipan thinly, place onto the heart shape and use it to carefully wrap up the heart.
To make the small hearts, form a ball from red marzipan, cut into two equal parts, put the two parts together again and fashion between your hands into a heart shape. Finally, squeeze the heart to make it a bit flatter.

WEDDING COUPLE

First place the legs and shoes of the man directly onto the large heart followed by the skirt and shoes of the woman. Fit the respective upper bodies and use a straw to stabilise them. Model the hands of the man and arms of the woman separately and attach them to the bodies. To make the heads, form two balls, put on the hair and ears to the man's head. Attach the blossoms to the lap of the woman.

Use decorating chocolate to add the eyes and mouth, the woman is given a red marzipan mouth and the man a small red heart in addition.

PÄRCHEN

Zuerst Beine und Schuhe des Mannes, dann Rock und Schuhe der Frau direkt auf das große Herz modellieren. Die jeweiligen Oberkörper aufsetzen und mit einem Strohhalm stabilisieren. Hände des Mannes und Arme der Frau separat modellieren und ansetzen. Für die Köpfe Kugeln formen, die Haare ansetzen, beim Mann zusätzlich die Ohren. Die ausgestochenen Blüten im Schoß der Frau befestigen.

Mit Garnierschokolade die Augen und den Mund anbringen, die Frau bekommt zusätzlich noch einen roten Marzipanmund, der Mann ein kleines rotes Herz.

TWO-COLOURED ROSES
AND PATTERN FOIL LEAVES

Start the rose by making a rose bud on a supporting base, using red marzipan. Roll out some pink and red marzipan in the same thickness, place on top of each other and roll out again. Use a round cutting shape to cut out circles, flatten these circles at the edges and join up with the rose bud in the form of a blossom with a bud and several petals.

To make the leaves, roll out green marzipan and apply a pattern using a pattern foil. Use a leaf-shaped cutter to make the leaves, give them a slight twist and leave to dry for a while.

ZWEIFARBIGE ROSEN
UND STRUKTURFOLIENBLÄTTER

Für die Rosen zunächst eine Knospe aus rotem Marzipan auf einem stützenden Fuß formen. Hell- und dunkelrotes Marzipan in der gleichen Stärke ausrollen, übereinander legen und zusammen erneut ausrollen. Mit einem Ausstecher Kreise herstellen, diese Kreise an den Kanten ausdünnen und an der Knospe beginnend zu einer sich öffnenden Blüte zusammenfügen. Für die Blätter grünes Marzipan ausrollen und mit einer Strukturfolie ein Muster aufbringen. Mit einem Blattausstecher Blätter herstellen, diese leicht verdrehen und antrocknen lassen.

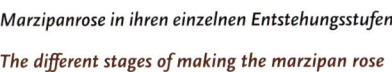

Marzipanrose in ihren einzelnen Entstehungsstufen
The different stages of making the marzipan rose

THE DOG PARLOUR

ICH LIEBE TIERE UND INSBESONDERE HUNDE. BEIM MODELLIEREN VON TIEREN BENÖTIGEN SIE VIEL GEFÜHL FÜR BEWEGUNG UND PROPORTIONEN. EIN BESUCH IM ZOO IST DER REINSTE ANATOMIEUNTERRICHT.

I LOVE ANIMALS AND IN PARTICULAR DOGS. WHEN MODELLING ANIMALS, YOU NEED A GOOD UNDERSTANDING OF MOVEMENT AND PROPORTIONS. YOU CAN LEARN A LOT ABOUT ANIMAL ANATOMY WHEN YOU GO TO THE ZOO.

THE BOY

To make the boy, start with the trousers using blue marzipan: shape a ball into a roll and insert a cut at one end with a knife. To make the upper part of the body, use red marzipan to form a ball, model the arms from the ball and squash the ball to resemble the flat shape of the upper body. Use a straw to connect the trousers with the sweater, add the roll neck and belt in brown marzipan. To make the head, form a ball in pink marzipan, attach the ears, the hair and the hat. Finally put on the eyes and the mouth with decorating chocolate.

JUNGE

Für den Jungen zuerst die Hose aus blauem Marzipan modellieren: Aus einer Kugel eine Rolle formen und mit dem Messer längs einkerben. Für den Oberkörper rotes Marzipan zu einer Kugel formen, die Arme aus der Kugel herausformen und den Oberkörper flach andrücken. Anschließend mit einem Strohhalm die Hose mit dem Pulli verbinden, den Rollkragen aufsetzen und dann den Gürtel aus braunem Marzipan anbringen. Für den Kopf eine Kugel aus rosa Marzipan modellieren, die Ohren, die Haare und die Mütze anbringen. Zuletzt die Augen und den Mund aus Garnierschokolade spritzen.

PUDEL AUF EINEM TISCH, SCHERE UND KAMM

Für den Pudel neutrales Marzipan birnen-förmig modellieren. Dann von der dickeren Seite nochmals eine Birne anmodellieren, so dass in der Mitte ein Körper mit zwei dünneren Enden entsteht. Das eine Birnen-ende ausgestreckt, das andere Birnenende abgewinkelt modellieren. Auf beiden Sei-ten Beine abteilen und die Pfoten eindrü-cken. Für das Pudelfell und den Schwanz Marzipan durch ein etwas grobmaschige-res Sieb drücken und anbringen. Für den Kopf Marzipan zu einer Birne modellieren für den Mund das schmale Ende einschnei-den, die eine Hälfte leicht zusammen-drücken, die andere Seite leicht einkerben und die Schnautzhaaransätze eindrücken. Die Augen eindrücken, dann wie beim Fell die Ohren modellieren und ansetzen. Den Kopf auf dem Rumpf anbringen und sobald er etwas angetrocknet ist, mit dem Airbrush weiß anschminken, die Fellpar-tien lila nachschminken. Die Augen aus Garnierschokolade spritzen. Den Tisch aus einem Block neutralem Marzipan schnei-den, dann aus dunkelbraun gefärbtem Marzipan die Tischbeine modellieren und anbringen. Für die Tischplatte eine mit einer Holzrelieffolie ausgerollte Marzipan-platte zurechtschneiden, trocknen und auf dem Block auflegen. Pudel auf den Tisch setzen, Schere und Kamm aus neutralem Marzipan modellieren, weiß schminken und zum Pudel legen.

POODLE ON A TABLE, SCISSORS AND COMB

To make the poodle, model some neutral marzipan into a pear shape. Then add an-other "pear" with the two thicker ends join-ing together so that both ends are thinner. Elongate one side of the pear and model the other side into an angled shape. Sep-arate out the legs on both sides and shape the paws. To make the coat and tail of the poodle, pass some marzipan through a wide-meshed sieve and then attach to the body. To make the head, shape some marzi-pan into a pear; insert a cut at the thinner end to make the mouth, squeeze one half together slightly and texture the other half to resemble the whiskers. Push in the holes for the eyes, model the ears like the coat and attach to the head. Fix the head to the body and as soon as it has dried out a bit, apply some white colouring with an air brush followed by purple for the fur parts. Add the eyes with decorating chocolate. Cut the table from a block of neutral mar-zipan, model the legs from dark-brown marzipan and attach. To make the table top, roll out some flat marzipan on a wood relief foil, cut to size, dry and then place onto the block. Place the poodle onto the table, model the scissors and comb from neutral marzipan, add white colouring and place next to the poodle.

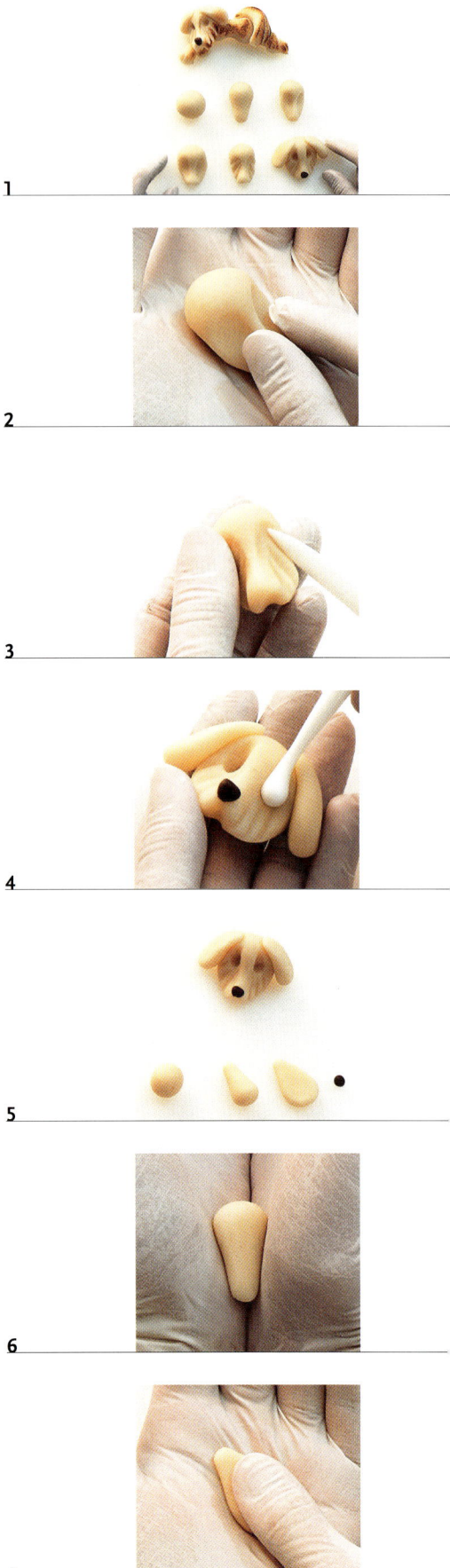

1

2

3

4

5

6

7

Einzelne Elemente des Hundekopfs

The elements of the dog's head

8

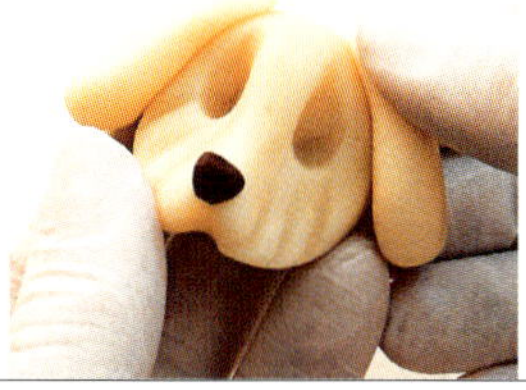

Ansetzen

Attach

Kopf modellieren

Modelling the head

9

Grundkörper Mischling

Basic body of mongrel

Bart modellieren

Modelling the whiskers

10

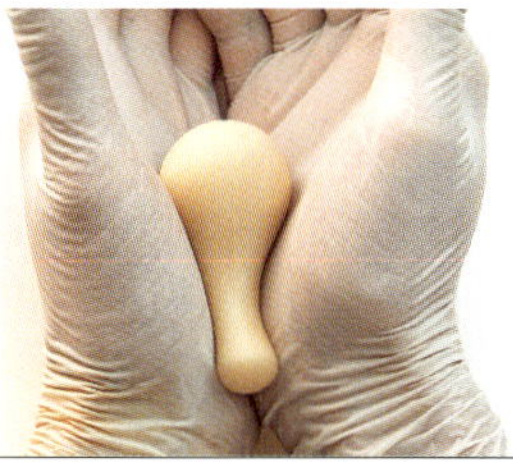

Grundkörper birnenförmig modellieren

Modelling the basic body in the shape of a pear

Augenhöhlen einmodellieren

Inserting the eye sockets

11

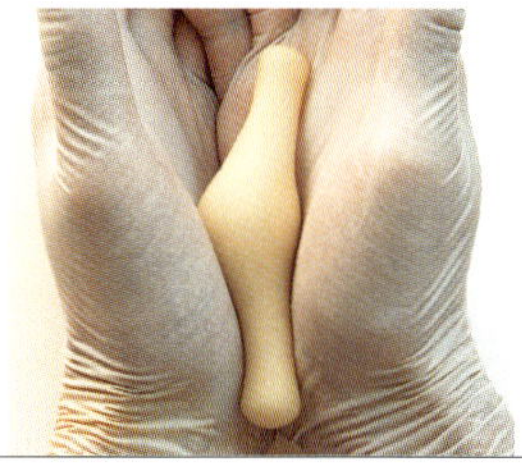

Anderes Ende des Grundkörpers birnenförmig modellieren

Modelling the other end of the basic body in the shape of a pear

Hundekopf mit Ohren und Nase

Dog's head with ears and nose

12

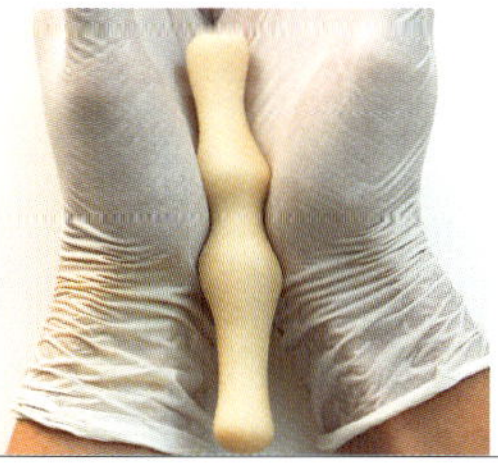

Grundkörper in der Mitte auseinander modellieren

Shaping the middle of the basic body

Eine Kugel zwischen den Handballen tropfenförmig modellieren

Place a ball between both hands and make the shape of a drop

13

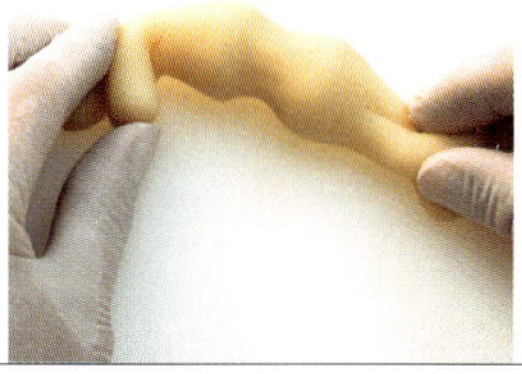

Geteilte Enden in der richtigen Körperhaltung als Beine legen

Split the ends, fashion into legs and arrange in the right position

Flach drücken

Press to flatten the shape

14

Einzelne Elemente des Schwanzes

The elements making up the tail

BULLI AUF DEM KISSEN

Für den Körper eine verlängerte Birne modellieren, die Vorderpfoten herausarbeiten, diese verlängerte Seite auseinander schneiden und zu einem sitzenden Hundekörper formen. Anschließend die Hinterpfoten aus zwei tropfenförmigen Marzipanstücken modellieren. Um die Halskrause herzustellen, rotes Marzipan zu einer Rolle formen, glatt ausrollen und gewellt zusammenlegen. (Mit dieser Technik kann man auch Nelken herstellen.) Für den Kopf eine Kugel zwischen beide Daumen legen, die runterhängenden Wangen und die Augenvertiefungen eindrücken. Mit einem Kugelmodellierholz die Augenhöhlen modellieren und die Ohren in Tropfenform anbringen. Das Maul und die Barthaare einmodellieren, aus gelben Marzipan die Krone und aus braunem Marzipan die Nase formen und beides am Kopf ansetzen. Die Augen aus Garnierschokolade spritzen. Das Kissen aus rotem Marzipan und die Bommelfransen aus gelbem Marzipan modellieren.

"BULLI" ON A CUSHION

To make the body, form a somewhat longer pear, fashion the front paws, cut this extended side apart and model into the body of a sitting dog. Now model the rear paws from two drop-shaped marzipan pieces. Make the toby collar by forming the marzipan into a roll, roll this flat and then drape in a wavy pattern. (This technique can also be used to produce carnations.) To make the head, place a ball between your two thumbs and form the drooping jowls and the indentations for the eyes. Use a modelling tool to make the eye sockets and attach the ears in the form of drops. Texture the mouth and whiskers, use yellow marzipan to make the crown and brown marzipan to shape the nose and attach both to the head. Add the eyes with decorating chocolate. Then form the cushion from red marzipan and attach the fringes made from yellow marzipan.

MISCHLING

Für den Mischling eine langgezogene Birne modellieren. Das andere Paar Beine von der Seite der Birne herausmodellieren und, wie beim Dackel, durchgeschnitten übereinander legen. Aus einem bananenförmigen Stück Marzipan den Schwanz modellieren und mit dem Schiffchen direkt an den Körper ansetzen. Den Kopf ähnlich wie beim Pudelkopf modellieren, nur dass die Seiten mit dem Schiffchen eingekerbt werden. Nach dem Zusammensetzen vorsichtig mit dem Gasbrenner abflämmen. Figur wieder abkühlen lassen, die Augen mit Garnierschokolade spritzen und die Nasenspitze mit braunem Marzipan ansetzen.

MONGREL

Start again with a somewhat elongated pear to make the mongrel. Fashion the other pair of legs from the side of the pear and cross over as for the dachshund. Use a banana-shaped piece of marzipan to model the tail and then use a modelling tool to attach it to the body. To make the head, proceed as for the poodle head except that the sides are given a surface texture with the modelling tool. Once you have joined the figure up you can use a gas torch to flame it carefully. Allow the figure to cool down again, add the eyes with decorating chocolate and the point of the nose in brown marzipan.

COCKER SPANIEL

Model the Cocker Spaniel from neutral marzipan, similar to "Bulli", with the tail made from dark-brown marzipan. For the head start with a pear shape but insert the eye sockets at the thin end and the mouth at the thick end. Fashion the ears in a long oval shape, make the nose out of dark-brown marzipan and attach both to the head. Fix the head to the body and spray the figure with brown cocoa butter. Fit the collar in coloured marzipan and add the eyes in decorating chocolate.

DACHSHUND

To make the dachshund, shape neutral marzipan into a roll, cut the ends apart, fashion into paws and cross them over. Model the head similar to the one for "Bulli" although the snout should be a bit more pointed and the mouth shaped from the centre upwards. Make the ears from slightly larger marzipan pieces and attach them to the side of the head. Don't forget the tail. As soon as the figure has dried somewhat, put into the freezer for a short while and then give a velvety coating with spray couverture. Add the eyes and nose with decorating chocolate.

BALLS AND BONES

Shape the bones from neutral marzipan and then apply some white colouring. To make the balls, make a red and a yellow ball, cut each into four sections and then put these together alternating the colours yellow/red. Finish off by adding a red dot at the top and bottom.

COCKERSPANIEL

Den Cockerspaniel ähnlich wie Bulli aus neutralem Marzipan modellieren und den Schwanz aus dunkelbraunem Marzipan modellieren. Dann den Kopf wieder in Birnenform modellieren, nur diesmal die Augen am dünneren Ende mit dem Kugel-modellierholz und das Maul an der dicken Seite formen. Die Ohren länglich oval, die Nase aus dunkelbraunem Marzipan modellieren und am Kopf anbringen. Dann den Kopf auf dem Körper fixieren und die Figur mit brauner Kakaobutter absprühen. Anschließend das Halsband aus gefärbtem Marzipan umlegen und die Augen mit Garnierschokolade spritzen.

DACKEL

Für den Dackel neutrales Marzipan zu einer Rolle formen, die Enden auseinander schneiden und als Pfoten übereinander schlagen. Den Kopf ähnlich wie bei Bulli modellieren, die Schnauze allerdings spitzer und das Maul von unten in der Mitte hochgeformt. Die Ohren aus etwas größeren, tropfenförmigen Marzipanstückchen anmodellieren und seitlich am Kopf anbringen. Den Schwanz nicht vergessen. Sobald die Figur etwas angetrocknet ist, leicht tiefkühlen und mit Sprühkuvertüre samtig ansprühen. Die Nase und die Augen aus Garnierschokolade spritzen.

BÄLLE UND KNOCHEN

Knochen aus neutralem Marzipan modellieren und später weiß ansprühen. Für die Bälle eine rote Kugel und eine gelbe Kugel modellieren, dann vierteln und abwechselnd gelb/rot zusammensetzen. Zum Schluss je einen roten Punkt oben und unten ansetzen.

HALLOWEEN

HALLOWEEN

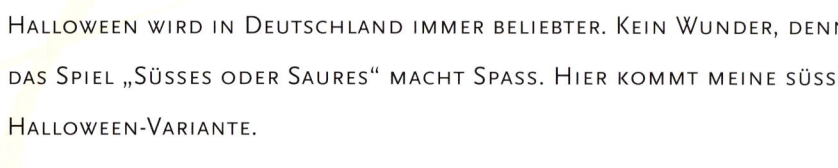

HALLOWEEN WIRD IN DEUTSCHLAND IMMER BELIEBTER. KEIN WUNDER, DENN DAS SPIEL „SÜSSES ODER SAURES" MACHT SPASS. HIER KOMMT MEINE SÜSSE HALLOWEEN-VARIANTE.

HALLOWEEN IS BECOMING MORE AND MORE POPULAR IN GERMANY, WHICH IS NO SURPRISE BECAUSE THE GAME "SWEET AND SOUR" IS GREAT FUN. BELOW IS MY SWEET HALLOWEEN VERSION.

GESPENST MIT KUGEL UND KETTE

Für das Gespenst mit Kakaopulver eingefärbtes Marzipan zu einer Birne modellieren. Weißes Marzipan dünn ausrollen und mit einem großen, runden Ausstecher einen Kreis ausstechen. Diesen in Falten über die Birne legen und dann am Kopf leicht andrücken.

Mit einer Lochtülle die Augen ausstechen und das weiße Marzipan im Inneren entfernen, gegebenenfalls mit dem Kugelmodellierholz die Augenhöhlen vertiefen. Mit dem Kugelmodellierholz aus weißem Marzipan den Mund anbringen. Für die Hände zuerst eine Kugel modellieren und zu einer Birne formen, dann das dünne Ende verlängern, umknicken und an beiden Seiten der Figur anbringen. Kugel und Kette nicht vergessen.

GHOST WITH BALL AND CHAIN

Colour some marzipan with cocoa powder and then make a pear shape to start the ghost. Roll out white marzipan, use a large, round cutter to cut out a circle. Drape this in folds over the pear and slightly indent at the head.

Use a round nozzle to cut out the eyes, taking the white marzipan out from the inside; you may want to make the eye sockets deeper by pushing in with a special modelling tool. Use the modelling tool again to attach the mouth from white marzipan. To make the hands, start with a ball and shape it into a pear, elongate the thin end, bend over and attach on both sides of the figure. Don't forget the ball and chain.

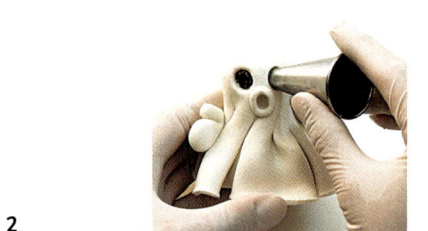

FLEDERMAUSVAMPIR

Für den Körper mit Kakaopulver eingefärbtes Marzipan verwenden. Zuerst eine
Birne und für die Flügel längliche, tropfen-
förmige Seitenteile modellieren und mit
dem dickeren Ende nach unten am birnenförmigen Körper anlegen. Für die Füße
Krallen modellieren und mit dem Kugelmodellierholz anbringen – den Bauchnabel nicht vergessen. Für den Kopf eine
Kugel modellieren und auch für die Ohren
zunächst Kugeln modellieren, diese dann
in der Handinnenfläche mit dem Daumen
anflachen, die dünnere Seite leicht zusam-
menknicken und seitlich am Kopf anbringen. Augenhöhlen, Nasenlöcher und Mund
mit dem spitzen Modellierholz einmodellieren. Kopf aufsetzen, den Umhang aus
rotem Marzipan dünn ausrollen und ausschneiden, dann anbringen und mit rotem
Marzipan die Blutstropfen an den Mund
dekorieren.
Abschließend mit Garnierschokolade Augen und Zähne aufspritzen.

BAT VAMPIRE

Colour some marzipan with cocoa powder
and use this to make the body. Start with
a pear shape, fashion oblong wings in the
shape of drops and attach them to the
pear-shaped body with the thin end uppermost. Model claws for the feet and attach
with the modelling tool; don't forget the
belly button. Make smaller balls for the
head and ears, make the balls for the ears
a bit flatter by pressing with your thumb
on the palm of your hand, fold the thinner
side together lightly and attach to the head.
Use a pointed modelling tool to make the
eye sockets, nostrils and mouth. Fix the
head, roll out some red marzipan and cut
out the shape of the cloak and attach it to
the body; decorate the mouth with some
drops of "blood" made from red marzipan.
Finish by adding the eyes and teeth with
decorating chocolate.

SPINNENETZE

Für die Spinnennetze temperierte Kuvertüre in Form eines Spinnennetzes auf glatt
gestrichenen Streuzucker garnieren. Sobald das Netz stabil ist, kann es verwendet
werden.

SPIDERS' WEBS

Dress some tempered couverture onto a
smooth level of sugar in the shape of a
spider's web. The web can be used as soon
as it has set.

Einzelteile des Gespenstes

Parts of the ghost

Augen mit einer Tülle ausstechen

Use a nozzle to cut out the eyes

PUMPKIN WITH WITCH'S HAT

Make the shape of a ball, make small insertions all round and use the modelling tool to fashion the nose. Make an indentation for the eye sockets with brows above, cut the mouth with a knife and leave to dry for a while. Spray the figure first with yellow colouring, then with orange colouring, model the branch and twines from green marzipan and arrange them on the figure. Make the witch's hat from cocoa marzipan. Start by making the shape of a cone with the point bent over a little. To make the brim, roll out some marzipan until quite thin, cut out a circle and attach the brim to the underside of the hat in a slightly wavy pattern. Use a knife to cut several small slots into the hat, attach the hat to the pumpkin and add the eyes in decorating chocolate.

KÜRBIS MIT HEXENHUT

Eine Kugel modellieren, rundherum Einkerbungen anbringen und mit dem Schiffchenmodellierholz die Nase formen. Die Augenhöhlen mit Augenwülsten sowie den Mund mit dem Messer einmodellieren und antrocknen lassen. Anschließend die Figur zuerst mit gelber Farbe, dann mit Orange ansprühen, den Stiel und die Ranken aus grünem Marzipan modellieren und anbringen. Den Hexenhut aus Kakaomarzipan modellieren. Hierzu zunächst eine leicht eingeknickte Spitze modellieren. Für die Krempe Marzipan dünn ausrollen, einen Kreis ausstechen und leicht gewellt an der Unterseite der Spitze anbringen. Den Hut anschließend mit dem Messer an verschiedenen Stellen leicht einkerben, auf dem Kürbis befestigen und dann mit Garnierschokolade die Augen aufspritzen.

AUTUMN LEAVES

Use a leaf-shaped cutter to cut out the leaves from thinly rolled-out marzipan. Give the leaves a slight twist and leave to dry a little before applying different colours with an air brush.

HERBSTBLÄTTER

Mit einem Blattausstecher dünn ausgerolltes Marzipan ausstechen. Die Blätter leicht verdrehen und antrocknen lassen, dann mit dem Airbrush in verschiedenen Farben einfärben.

CHOCOLATE BRANCHES

To make the chocolate branches, spread some cocoa powder until flat and draw thin branch lines with your finger. Dress the tempered couverture into the lines in a rough fashion and cover with cocoa powder. As soon as the couverture has set, add a little powder and use for decorating.

SCHOKOLADENÄSTE

Für die Schokoladenäste, Kakaopulver flach ausstreichen und mit dem Finger dünne Astlinien ziehen. Temperierte Kuvertüre etwas ungenau eingarnieren und mit Kakaopulver bedecken. Sobald die Kuvertüre stabil ist, leicht abpudern und zum Dekorieren verwenden.

HAPPY NEW YEAR

Zu Silvester und Neujahr kann man in Deutschland immer noch am besten Marzipanfiguren verkaufen – das ist zumindest in unserem Café so. Dies ist meine kleine Auswahl an Glücksbringern.

The best time to sell marzipan figures – at least in our café – is on New Year's Eve and New Year's Day. Here is my selection of lucky symbols.

CALENDAR

Roll out neutral marzipan, cut into a rectangular shape and leave to dry. Decorate one end with tempered couverture and apply the writing with decorating chocolate.

KALENDER

Neutrales Marzipan ausrollen, rechteckig zuschneiden und trocknen lassen. Ein Ende mit temperierter Kuvertüre absetzen und mit Garnierschokolade beschriften.

CLOVER LEAF

Use four green marzipan balls to form small hearts and join them up to a clover leaf. Press the eye sockets into the uppermost heart and add the eyes with decorating chocolate. Model nose, mouth and stalk and attach to the figure.

KLEEBLATT

Aus vier grünen Marzipankugeln kleine Herzen formen und zu einem Kleeblatt zusammenfügen. In das oberste Herzchen die Augenhöhlen eindrücken und dann die Augen mit Garnierschokolade einfügen. Abschließend Nase, Mund und Stiel anmodellieren.

SCHWEINCHEN

Rosa Marzipan zu einer Kugel modellieren, diese flach drücken. Für die Schnauze eine kleine Kugel abflachen, das Maul einschneiden, die untere Seite leicht zusammendrücken und die Nasenlöcher einmodellieren. Die beiden Teile verbinden und die modellierten Ohren ansetzen.

PIGLET

Make a ball out of pink marzipan and press it flat. Make the snout from a small flattened ball, cut the mouth, squeeze the lower jaw together a little and shape the nostrils. Join the two parts together, then make the ears and attach them.

GLÜCKSKÄFER

Rotes Marzipan zu einer Kugel modellieren und dann mit Garnierschokolade Kopf, Augen, Punkte und Trennlinie auf den Rücken aufbringen.

LADYBIRD

Make a ball out of red marzipan and use decorating chocolate to apply the head, eyes, dots and separating line on the back.

FLIEGENPILZE

Für den Stiel neutrales Marzipan birnenförmig modellieren, dann einen Mund aus hellrosa Marzipan und eine Nase aus rotem Marzipan anbringen. Außerdem die Augenhöhlen eindrücken. Für die Pilzhüte neutrales Marzipan zu einer Kugel formen, dann die Kugel in der Handinnenfläche mit dem großen Kugelmodellierholz aushöhlen. Trocknen lassen und mit dem Airbrush rot schminken. Mit weißer Garnierschokolade die Punkte anbringen, beide Teile zusammensetzen und die Augen mit Garnierschokolade aufspritzen.

TOADSTOOLS

To make the stem, model some neutral marzipan into a pear shape; add a mouth from pale pink marzipan and a nose from red marzipan. Push in the holes for the eye sockets. For the caps of the toadstools use neutral marzipan to shape a ball, hold the ball in one hand and hollow it out with a large round modelling tool. Leave to dry and apply red colour with an air brush. Use white decorating chocolate to apply the dots, join both parts together and use decorating chocolate to put on the eyes.

HUFEISEN

Für das Hufeisen neutrales Marzipan mit Kakao einfärben und zu einer Rolle formen. Nasen und Münder mit den Fingern modelllieren, dann Nasenlöcher, Augenhöhlen und Nagellöcher eindrücken. Nach dem Antrocknen leicht angolden. Zum Schluss die Augen mit Garnierschokolade anbringen.

HORSESHOE

Colour some neutral marzipan with cocoa and shape into a roll. Use your fingers to model the noses and mouths, then make indentations for the nostrils, eye sockets and nail holes. Once they have dried out, apply a little gold colour. Finally make the eyes with decorating chocolate.

verschiedene Gesichtsvarianten

Different face versions

verschiedene Gesichtsvarianten

Different face versions

CHIMNEYSWEEP

To make the chimneysweep shape some marzipan into a roll and cut at both ends in the centre. At one end, spread the two halves apart a little and fashion as legs, and at the other end fold back the arms at an angle to the body.

Allow to dry well and cover with tempered bitter couverture; before the couverture has fully set, attach all lucky symbols.

This method is well suited for stabilising large, thin or fragile figures or to make them more interesting and also longer-lasting.

To make the head, model some pink marzipan into a pear shape. Form the eye sockets with a modelling tool by pushing the material up, make the nose in three parts and ears and attach to the head.

Use cocoa marzipan to add the eye brows, a moustache and hair. Make his hat also from cocoa marzipan. First shape a ball into a slightly tapered roll, make the brim by rolling out brown marzipan thinly, cutting out the round centre and adding it to the hat; apply a little gold colouring to the edges.

Model the shoes from cocoa marzipan; place the basic body onto the shoes and then onto a couverture relief base. Use a straw to attach a neck and the head with hat. Finally make a scarf from a strip of yellow marzipan, cut the ends to make the fringe and drape the scarf around the chimneysweep's neck.

SCHORNSTEINFEGER

Für den Schornsteinfegerkörper neutrales Marzipan zu einer Rolle formen und an beiden Enden mittig einschneiden. Dann ein Ende als Beine leicht auseinander spreizen, das andere Ende als angewinkelte Arme umbiegen.

Gut durchtrocknen lassen und mit temperierter Bitterkuvertüre überziehen und noch bevor die Kuvertüre angezogen ist, alle Glücksbringer anbringen.

Diese Methode eignet sich gut, um große, dünne oder zerbrechliche Figuren zu stabilisieren, geschmacklich interessanter und auch haltbarer zu machen.

Für den Kopf rosa Marzipan birnenförmig modellieren. Die Augenhöhlen mit dem Kugelmodellierholz hochschiebend formen, dann die Nase dreiteilig sowie die Ohren separat anmodellieren.

Augenbrauen, Schnurrbart und Haare aus Kakaomarzipan ansetzen. Den Hut ebenfalls aus Kakaomarzipan herstellen. Dazu aus einer Kugel eine leicht konische Rolle formen und als Krempe das braune Marzipan dünn ausrollen, rund ausstechen, zusammensetzen und die Kanten leicht angolden.

Schuhe aus Kakaomarzipan modellieren, dann den Grundkörper erst auf die Schuhe, dann auf eine Kuvertüre-Reliefplatte setzen. Mit Hilfe eines Strohhalms einen Hals und den Kopf mit Hut anbringen. Zum Schluss einen Schal aus einem Streifen gelbem Marzipan herstellen, die Enden mit dem Messer ausfransen und um den Hals legen.

HOCHZEITSSCHWÄNE

WEDDING SWANS

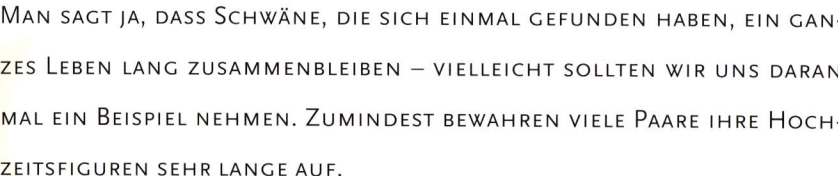

Man sagt ja, dass Schwäne, die sich einmal gefunden haben, ein ganzes Leben lang zusammenbleiben – vielleicht sollten wir uns daran mal ein Beispiel nehmen. Zumindest bewahren viele Paare ihre Hochzeitsfiguren sehr lange auf.

It is said that swans that have found each other as partners will stay together for life – perhaps we should learn a lesson from them. But at least many wedding couples keep their wedding figures for a very long time.

SCHWANENPAAR

Für den Schwan zuerst eine Kugel aus neutralem Marzipan formen. Diese zwischen den Handflächen so modellieren, dass auf einer Seite ein langer Hals mit einem kleinen Kopf entsteht und auf der anderen Seite ein spitzer, leicht nach oben gebogener Schwanz. Den Hals so an den Körper legen, dass ein schwimmender Schwan entsteht. Die Flügel aus flachgedrückten Tropfen modellieren, dann die Enden nach oben biegen, um dem Schwan eine elegante Form zu verleihen. Den Schnabel aus orangefarbenem und den Höcker aus kakaofarbenem Marzipan modellieren und anbringen. Die Figuren nach dem Trocknen anfrosten und mit dem Thermo-Airbrush mit weißer Kakaobutter samtig ansprühen. Achtung: Man sieht jeden Fingerabdruck! Schnabel und Höcker in der jeweiligen Farbe nachschminken und mit Garnierschokolade die Augen anbringen.

SWAN COUPLE

To make a swan, start by forming a ball from neutral marzipan. Model this between the palms of your hands to create a long neck with a small head on one side and a pointed tail that is slightly bent upwards on the other side. Arrange the neck so that it takes the shape of a swan on water. Fashion the wings from flattened drops, bend the ends upwards to give the swan its elegant shape. Model the beak from orange-coloured marzipan and use cocoa-coloured marzipan to form the knob on the beak. Freeze the figures after drying for a short while and then use a thermo airbrush to apply a velvety spray of white cocoa butter. Careful: each fingerprint will show. Apply extra colouring to the beak and knob in their respective colour and use decorating chocolate to put on the eyes.

Einzelne Elemente des Schwanes

The elements of the swan

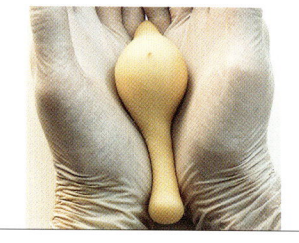

1

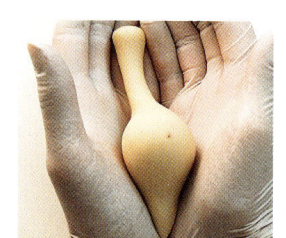

2

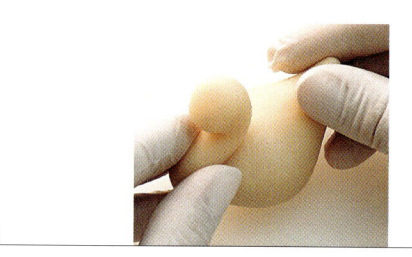

3

4

SEEROSEN AUF SEENPLATTE

Für die Platte blaues Marzipan ausrollen, in gewünschter Form ausstechen und mit umgedrehtem Ausstecher Wellen eindrücken, zum Schluss mit Blaumetallic-Farbe schminken.

Für die Seerosen mit einem Ausstecher zwei Blütenkränze ausstechen und mit einem Kugelmodellierholz in der Hand zusammenbringen. Kleine Kugeln formen, versilbern und dann in den Blütenkelch einsetzen. Die Blätter mit einem Spezial-Blattstempel, der beim Auswerfen das Blattmuster direkt aufbringt, ausstechen und mit metallicgrüner Farbe nachfärben. Einzelteile auf der Bodenplatte anbringen.

WATER LILIES ON A LAKE

To make the lake, roll out some blue marzipan, cut out the required shape and use the back of the cutting shape to make wave patterns; finally apply a coating of blue metallic colouring.

To make the water lilies, use cutters to cut out two blossom rings; join the two rings together in your hand with a modelling tool. Form small balls, apply silver colouring and put them into the centre of the blossom. Use a special leaf cutting device that applies the leaf pattern at the same time as cutting the leaf and cut out the leaves; apply metallic green colouring. Arrange all the parts on the base.

Schwanenhals modellieren

Modelling the swan's neck

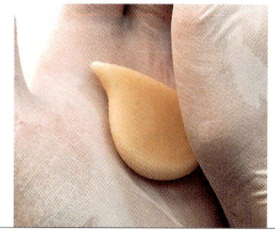

Flügelenden spitz zulaufen lassen

Let the ends of the wings come to a point

5

Schwanz modellieren

Modelling the swan's tail

Flügel tropfenförmig ausmodellieren

The wings have the shape of drops

6

Schwanenkörper in Form bringen

Shaping the body of the swan

Flügel flachdrücken

Flatten the wings

7

Für die Flügel eine Kugel formen

Forming a ball to make the wings

Angefrorene Figuren mit dem Thermo-Airbrush mit weißer Kakaobutter einfärben

Freeze the figures for a short while and then apply white cocoa butter with a thermo airbrush

8

CARNIVAL

KÖLN UND MAINZ SIND DIE HOCHBURGEN IN SACHEN KARNEVAL – ABER GEFEIERT WIRD ÜBERALL! DIESES BUNTE SPEKTAKEL LÄSST SICH WUNDERBAR IN MARZIPANFIGUREN UMSETZEN UND DER FANTASIE SIND DABEI KEINE GRENZEN GESETZT.

COLOGNE AND MAINZ ARE THE TRADITIONAL CENTRES OF CARNIVAL – BUT CARNIVAL PARTIES ARE COMMON IN MOST PLACES. THIS COLOURFUL EVENT LENDS ITSELF AS A THEME FOR MARZIPAN FIGURES AND THERE ARE NO LIMITS TO WHAT WE MIGHT DREAM UP.

CLOWN DOING HANDSTAND

Model the hands from pink marzipan, the shoes from cocoa marzipan and leave both to dry.
To make the head, form pink marzipan into a pear shape and insert the eye sockets at the smaller end.
Add the mouth in white and the large nose in red. Attach hair made from orange-coloured marzipan and a hat made from cocoa-coloured marzipan. Leave the parts to dry.

CLOWN IM HANDSTAND

Die Hände aus rosa Marzipan modellieren, die Schuhe aus Kakaomarzipan, beides trocknen lassen.
Für den Kopf rosa Marzipan zu einer Birne modellieren und am schmaleren Ende die Augenhöhlen eindrücken.
Den Mund in weiß und die große Nase in rot ansetzen. Haare aus orangefarbenem Marzipan und dann einen Hut aus kakaofarbenem Marzipan aufsetzen. Einzelteile trocknen lassen.

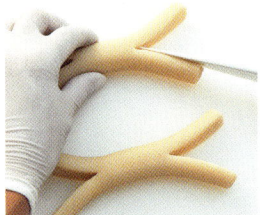

Beide Enden einer Marzipanrolle mittig trennen und leicht auseinanderspreizen

Cut a marzipan roll at the centre of each end and spread the two parts apart

1

Gut getrockneten Grundkörper mit temperierter Bitterkuvertüre überziehen

Allow the basic body to dry well and coat with tempered bitter couverture

2

CLOWNKÖRPER

Für den Clownkörper neutrales Marzipan zu einer Rolle formen, beide Enden mittig trennen und leicht auseinanderspreizen. Gut durchtrocknen lassen und mit temperierter Bitterkuvertüre überziehen. Noch bevor die Kuvertüre angezogen hat, die Hände, die Schuhe und den Kopf mit Hut anbringen. Diese Methode eignet sich gut, um große, dünne oder zerbrechliche Figuren zu stabilisieren, geschmacklich interessanter und auch haltbarer zu machen. Die fertiggestellte Figur mit Kuvertüre auf einer Kuvertüreplatte befestigen.

CLOWN'S BODY

To make the clown's body, shape some marzipan into a roll, cut at both ends in the centre and separate the parts slightly. Allow to dry well and coat with tempered bitter couverture. Before the couverture has set, attach the hands, shoes and the head with hat. This method is well suited for stabilising large, thin or fragile figures or to make them more interesting and also longer-lasting. Fix the finished figure with couverture on a couverture base.

OSTERN

EASTER

Ostern ist für mich ein besonderes Fest. In unserer Region gibt es zahlreiche Ostereiermärkte, bei denen ich immer etwas vorführe. Am allerliebsten mache ich dort für die Kinder die Marzipanfiguren einfach auf Zuruf – so entstehen immer die schönsten Figuren.

For me, Easter is quite a special occasion. In our region we have numerous Easter egg markets where I always do a demonstration show. What I like best is making marzipan figures for the children as they want them – this always leads to the prettiest figures.

HENNEN

Für die Henne neutrales Marzipan zu einer Birne formen, das dicke Ende spitz zulaufen lassen und, leicht flach gedrückt, zu einem Schwanz formen. Das andere Ende, je nach gewünschter Kopfstellung, in Form bringen und die Augen eindrücken. Einen gelben Schnabel sowie Kamm und Kieferlappen aus rotem Marzipan anbringen. Die Augen mit Garnierschokolade aufspritzen.

HENS

To make a hen, shape some neutral marzipan into a pear shape, model a point to the thick end and fashion into a tail, squashing it slightly flat. Fashion the other end to suit the position of the head as you want it and make indentations for the eyes. Attach a yellow beak, and comb and wattles in red marzipan. Add the eyes with decorating chocolate.

COCKEREL

For the cockerel I use a combined method: start by making the basic body from three chocolate half shells. Use two of the half shells to join up to an egg, place the third half shell on top of the egg with the open side upwards and melt together. As soon as both parts have set firmly, use a brush to dab the basic body with bitter couverture so that the surface is rough and the marzipan will stick better to it.

Use a piping bag with a special nozzle to pipe tempered and slightly set couverture onto baking paper in the shape of the feather coat and leave to set fully.

Use neutral marzipan to make the upper part of the cockerel's body. Start by modelling a pear shape, split the thicker end in half and attach to the base using the comb modelling tool; make indents for the eye sockets. Leave to dry superficially, then use an airbrush to spray yellow, red and orange colouring at the joint with the base, with the colours overlapping. Attach a beak, consisting of two parts made from yellow marzipan, and the comb and wattles in red marzipan.

Finally fix the tail and wing feathers with some couverture and use decorating chocolate to add the eyes.

HAHN

Der Hahn entsteht durch eine Mischtechnik: Zuerst einen Grundkörper aus drei Schokoladenhalbschalen herstellen. Dazu aus zwei Halbschalen ein Ei zusammensetzen, die dritte Halbschale anschmelzen und mit der Öffnung nach oben auf das Ei setzen. Sobald beide Teile fest angetrocknet sind, den Grundkörper mit Bitterkuvertüre und einem Pinsel abtupfen, so dass eine raue Oberfläche entsteht und das Marzipan später besser halten kann.

Anschließend aus temperierter, angestockter Kuvertüre und einer Spezialtülle das Federkleid in verschiedenen Größen auf Backpapier dressieren und dann erstarren lassen.

Für den Oberkörper des Hahns neutrales Marzipan verwenden. Dazu eine Birne modellieren, das dickere Ende halbieren, mit dem Kamm-Modellierholz am Unterbau anmodellieren und die Augenhöhlen eindrücken. Leicht antrocknen lassen und mit dem Airbrush am Übergang zum Unterbau einen Farbverlauf aus gelb, rot und orange aufsprühen. Einen zweiteiligen Schnabel aus gelbem Marzipan ansetzen sowie Kamm und Kieferlappen aus rotem Marzipan.

Zum Schluss mit Kuvertüre die Schwungfedern an Schwanz und Flügeln befestigen und die Augen mit Garnierschokolade anbringen.

GOLDENE OSTEREIER
AUF SCHOKOLADENREGAL

Die Eierschokoladenformen mit Kuvertüre ausgießen und nach dem Trocknen die Hälften zusammensetzen. Schokoladeneier leicht in den Händen anwärmen und in Goldpuder wälzen. Regal und Boden aus Bitterkuvertüre herstellen. Für das Gras grünes Marzipan durch ein grobes Sieb drücken.

OSTERHASE

Für den Körper eine Birne aus hellem Kakaomarzipan formen. Das dickere Ende nochmals birnenförmig ausarbeiten. Den dicken Mittelteil zu einer Hüfte modellieren, die beiden Enden jeweils mittig trennen, so dass Arme und Beine entstehen. In der gewünschten Form stabilisieren und antrocknen lassen. Bauchnabel und Pfoten leicht andeuten.

Für den Kopf zunächst aus einer Kugel einen Tropfen modellieren, dann mit den Zeigefingern den Tropfen mittig teilen. Den an der Oberseite entstandenen Kegel längs mit dem Messer halbieren und die Schnittflächen nach oben drehen. Schnittflächen mit dem Schiffchen eindrücken und ein Ohr nach vorne umklappen. An der Vorderseite Augenhöhlen eindrücken und Mund und Nase in rosa ansetzen. Dann einen Schnurrbart und eine Haarlocke aus gelbem Marzipan anbringen. Den Kopf ausreichend antrocknen lassen, auf den Körper setzen und mit einer Schleife den Übergang dekorieren. Die Augen mit Garnierschokolade aufbringen.

GOLDEN EASTER EGGS
ON A CHOCOLATE SHELF

Pour couverture into chocolate egg moulds and join together once dry. Warm the chocolate eggs slightly in your hands and then roll in gold powder. Make the shelves and base from bitter couverture. To make the grass, push some green marzipan through a course sieve.

EASTER BUNNY

To make the body, form a pear from pale cocoa marzipan. Shape the thick end so that it forms another pear shape. Model the thick middle part into the shape of a hip, split the two ends each into equal parts to fashion into arms and legs. Stabilise in the required shape and leave to dry. Mark the belly button and the paws with light scoring.

To make the head, start by modelling a drop from a ball and use your index fingers to separate the drop into two halves. Halve the cone on the upper side with a knife along the length of the cone and turn the cut faces upwards. Use the modelling tool to push in the cut faces and fold over one of the ears forwards. At the front, push in the eye sockets and attach the mouth and nose in pink. Then add the whiskers and a hair lock in yellow marzipan. Leave the head to dry sufficiently, place onto the body and decorate the joint with a bow. Add the eyes with decorating chocolate.

1

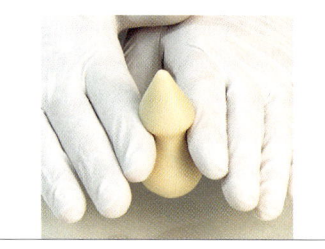

2

3

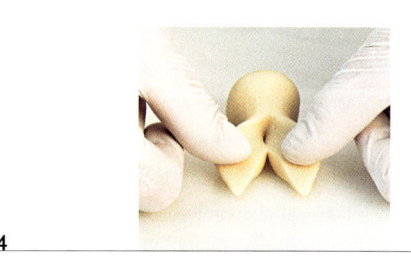

4

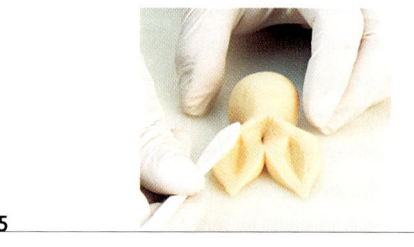

5

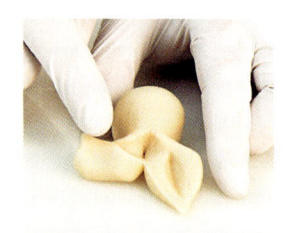

6

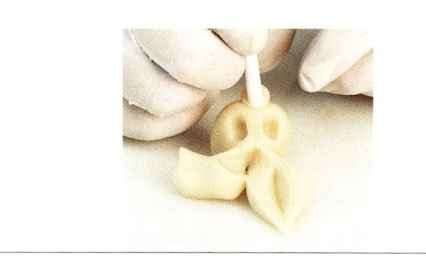

7

Mit den Handballen einen Tropfen aus einer Kugel modellieren

Take a ball into your hands and model into a drop shape

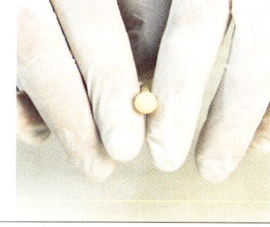

8

Schnurrbart zwischen den Fingern modellieren

Model the whiskers between your fingers

Den Tropfen mit den Zeigefingern mittig teilen

Use your index fingers to split the drop in the middle

9

Schnurrbart oberhalb des Mundes ansetzen

Attach the whiskers above the mouth

An der Oberseite entstandenen Kegel mit dem Messer längs halbieren

Cut the cone at the top with a knife along the shape

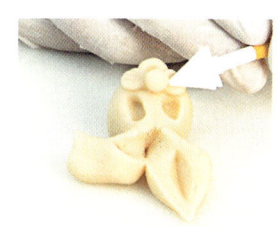

10

Kugelförmige Nase ansetzen und Schnurrbarthaare einritzen

Add a rounded nose and score to look like whiskers

Schnittflächen nach oben drehen

Turn the cut faces upwards

CHICKS HATCHING FROM THE EGG

KÜKEN AUS DER EIERSCHALE

First boil a genuine eggshell and dry in the oven.
To make the body, form a drop shape from yellow marzipan, squash the pointed end to make it flat for the tail and then bend it slightly upwards. Use a knife to score the end of the tail several times lightly, then mark the wings. To make the head, form a ball and push in the eye sockets. Make sure that the proportion of head to body is $^{1}/_{3}$ to $^{2}/_{3}$. Make the beak and comb from red marzipan and attach to the head. Add the eyes with decorating chocolate.

Zuerst eine echte Eierschale auskochen und im Ofen trocknen.
Für den Körper einen Tropfen aus gelbem Marzipan modellieren, dann das spitze Ende flachdrücken und das entstandene Schwänzchen leicht nach oben biegen. Das Schwanzende mit dem Messer mehrmals leicht einritzen, dann die Flügel anzeichnen. Für den Kopf eine Kugel formen und die Augenhöhlen eindrücken. Bitte darauf achten, dass das Verhältnis Kopf zu Körper $^{1}/_{3}$ zu $^{2}/_{3}$ beträgt. Schnabel und Kamm aus rotem Marzipan an den Kopf ansetzen. Die Augen mit Garnierschokolade anbringen.

Mit dem Schiffchen die Ohren ausmodellieren

Use a modelling tool to shape the ears

Ein ausmodelliertes Ohr nach vorne klappen

Bend one of the ears forwards

Augenhöhlen eindrücken, dann Mund ansetzen und ebenfalls eindrücken

Push in the eye sockets, put on the mouth and make another hole for the mouth

BIRTHDAY TIME

KINDERGEBURTSTAGE BIETEN EIN BREITES BETÄTIGUNGSFELD FÜR UNS KONDI-TOREN. KOSTENGÜNSTIG KANN MAN JEDEN KINDERWUNSCH ERFÜLLEN UND DA-MIT KINDERAUGEN ZUM LEUCHTEN BRINGEN. SIND DAS NICHT DIE SCHÖNSTEN SEITEN UNSERES BERUFS?

CHILDREN'S BIRTHDAYS OFFER PLENTY OF OPPORTUNITIES FOR US CONFEC-TIONERS. IT DOESN'T COST A LOT TO FULFIL ALL WISHES OF A CHILD AND MAKE THEIR EYES SHINE WITH DELIGHT. ARE THOSE NOT THE BEST MOMENTS OF OUR PROFESSION?

TEDDY BEAR

Model the body in one piece from a brown ball and use a modelling tool to score the shape of the paws. To make the head, form a ball, press it flat and attach another, smaller ball as the muzzle. Form the mouth from pink marzipan and shape the ears from two brown balls; attach both to the head. Add a small triangle as the nose and a hair lock in yellow marzipan. Add the eyes with decorating chocolate. Do not forget the white cloth.

TEDDYBÄR

Den Körper in einem Stück aus einer braunen Kugel modellieren und dann die Pfoten mit dem Modellierholz andeuten. Für den Kopf eine Kugel formen, diese flach drücken und eine zweite, kleinere Kugel als Schnauze ansetzen. Einen Mund aus rosa Marzipan und Ohren aus zwei eingedrückten braunen Kugeln herstellen und anbringen. Ein kleines, modelliertes Dreieck als Nase und eine Haartolle aus gelbem Marzipan auflegen. Die Augen mit Garnierschokolade aufspritzen. Das weiße Tuch nicht vergessen.

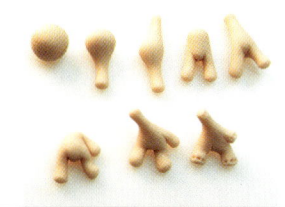

Eisenbahn auf Schienen und Blümchen

Zuerst die Balken für die Schienen herstellen. Dazu neutrales Marzipan etwa 3 Millimeter dick ausrollen und zu Balken zurechtschneiden, entweder mit Strukturfolie oder dem Modellierholz masern und abflämmen.

Aus einem Stück ausgerolltem Marzipan die Schienen ausschneiden, trocknen lassen, dann ansilbern und die Schienen mit den Balken arrangieren.

Für die kleinen Blümchen grünes Marzipan zu Tropfen modellieren und flach drücken, dann gelbes Marzipan für die Blüten zu dünnen Wülsten formen, flach drücken und zu einer Schnecke zusammenrollen. Als Blumensträußchen am Streckenrand arrangieren.

Für die Eisenbahn einen Unterbau herstellen, darauf eine dicke Rolle platzieren. Das Führerhaus hinten anstellen. Mit Schornsteinen und seitlich angebrachten Rädern ausdekorieren.

Das Gesicht der Lok aus einem Kreis modellieren, ebenfalls auflegen und die Augen mit Garnierschokolade anbringen. Fertige Figur mit Bronze anschminken.

Railway on rails and flowers

First make the sleepers for the rails. To do that roll out neutral marzipan to a thickness of 3 mm and cut into sleepers, apply the wood grain either with pattern foil or a modelling roll and then flame with a gas torch.

Cut the rails from a piece of rolled-out marzipan, leave to dry, apply silver colouring and then place the rails on the sleepers. To make the small flowers, shape some green marzipan into a drop shape and press flat, shape yellow marzipan for the blossoms into thin "sausages", press flat and roll up into a coil. Arrange as posies along the edge of the track.

To make the train, start with a base structure on which you place a thick roll. Cut the shape of the driver's cab and place behind the roll. Complete the locomotive with chimneys and wheels attached to the side. Use a cut-out circle to model the face of the locomotive, attach to the front and apply the eyes with decorating chocolate. Apply bronze colouring to the finished figure.

1
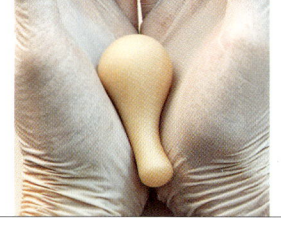

2
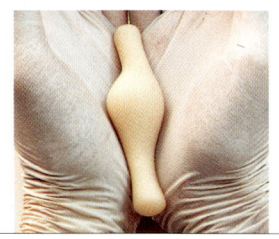

3
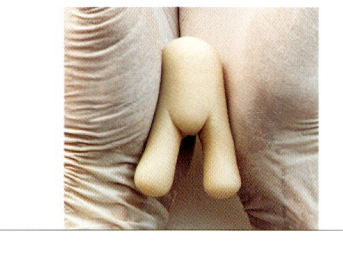

4
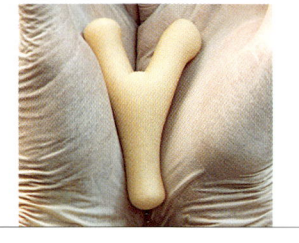

5

Himmelblauer Elefant

Den Elefantenkörper an einem Stück aus einer blauen Kugel modellieren, die Füße mit dem Kugelmodellierholz andeuten. Für den Kopf eine Kugel zur Birne formen, diese dann zum Rüssel verlängern. Die Ohren aus flach gedrückten Kugeln ansetzen, den Rüssel mit dem Kugelmodellierholz am vorderen Ende eindrücken und auch die Augenhöhlen damit vertiefen. Die Augen mit Garnierschokolade anbringen. Auch hier das weiße Tuch nicht vergessen.

Sky-blue elephant

Form the body of the elephant in one piece from a ball of blue marzipan and mark the shape of the feet with a modelling tool. To make the head model a ball into a pear shape and extend it to make the trunk. Add the ears from balls that you have pressed flat, use the modelling tool to push in a hole at the front of the trunk and to shape the eye sockets. Add the eyes with decorating chocolate. Again, remember the white cloth.

6
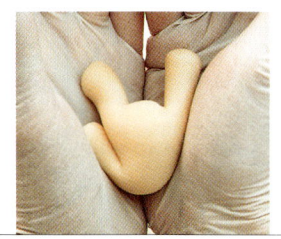

Einzelne Elemente des Elefantenkörpers

The elements making up the elephant's body

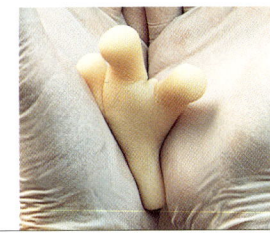

7

Auf die gleiche Weise den zweiten Arm ausarbeiten

Fashion the second arm in the same way

Eine Kugel zur Birne formen

Shape a ball into a pear

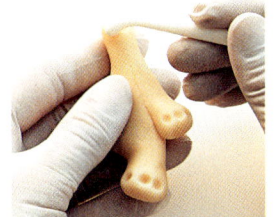

8

Fußnägel mit dem Modellierholz eindrücken

Use the modelling tool to mark the foot nails

Abgerundetes Ende ebenfalls länglich ausmodellieren

Extend the thicker end similar to the other end

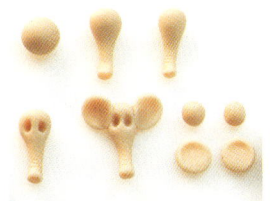

9

Einzelne Elemente des Elefantenkopfs

Elements making up the elephant's head

Längliche Enden als Beine umbiegen

Bend down the long ends to make the legs

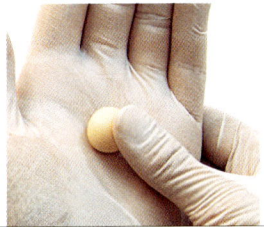

10

Kugeln für die Ohren mit Daumen flach drücken

Form the ears by pressing the marzipan balls flat with your thumb

Ersten Arm zwischen den Handflächen herausarbeiten

Fashion the first arm between the palms of your hand

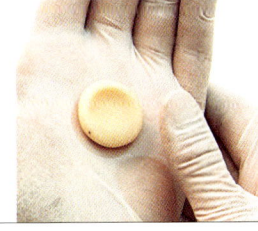

11

Ohren seitlich am Kopf anbringen

Attach the ears to the side of the head

Fertigen Arm umlegen

Arrange the completed arm

SCHNEEMANN

SNOWMAN

Leider gibt es bei uns in Deutschland seit ein paar Jahren nicht mehr so oft die Möglichkeit einen richtigen Schneemann zu bauen. Dabei gibt es doch für Kinder keine grössere Freude. Ich hoffe mein kleiner Schneemann kann das ein bisschen entschädigen.

Since a few years ago, we in Germany unfortunately no longer often get the chance of building a proper snowman. Which is a pity because there is not much that children like better. I hope my small snowman can compensate a little bit for the loss.

ZUCKEREIS

Für die Eisplatte Isomalt auflösen und leicht abgekühlt auf eine geölte Alufolie gießen. Nach dem Erkalten die Folie abziehen und das Zuckerblatt als Bodenplatte verwenden.

SUGAR ICE

To make the ice base, dissolve Isomalt, leave to cool a little and pour onto oiled aluminium foil. Once it has cooled down, the foil can be pulled off and the remaining sugar sheet can be used as the ice base.

SCHOKOLADENSCHNEEKRISTALLE

Für die Schneekristalle temperierte weiße Kuvertüre in Form eines Schneekristalls auf glatt gestrichenen, vorgezeichneten Streuzucker garnieren. Sobald die Kristalle stabil sind, kann man sie verwenden.

CHOCOLATE SNOW CRYSTALS

Make the snow crystals by piping tempered white couverture onto a smooth layer of sugar, with the shape of the snow crystal marked out. Use the crystals as soon as they are stable.

KLEINER SCHNEEMANN
MIT SCHLITTSCHUHEN

SMALL SNOWMAN
WITH SKATES

Für den Schneemann eine kleine Kugel helles Marzipan auf eine größere setzen, dann seitlich zwei Kugeln als Arme und Beine anbringen. Als Schuhe zwei abgeflachte Ovale mit Schlittschuhkufen aus Kakaomarzipan modellieren, ansetzen und die Kufen ansilbern. Als Kopf eine Birne modellieren und die Augenhöhlen eindrücken. Aus orangefarbenem Marzipan eine Karotte als Nase formen und im Gesicht befestigen. Ohrwärmer aus rotem Marzipan, Haare aus gelbem Marzipan und einen Hut aus kakaofarbenem Marzipan herstellen und ansetzen. Anschließend eine kleine Blüte auf den Hut dekorieren. Mund, Augen und Knöpfe aus Garnierschokolade anbringen.

Den Kopf auf den Körper setzen und einen roten Schal mit ausgefransten Enden umlegen.

Die Figur leicht anfrosten und mit weißer Kakaobutter von oben annebeln.

Build the snowman by placing a small ball of light-coloured marzipan onto a larger one, then add two balls on the sides for the extremities. To make the skates, use cocoa marzipan to model two flat oval shapes with skids; attach these to the body and apply silver colouring to the skids. To make the head, form a ball into a pear and push in the eye sockets. Use orange-coloured marzipan to make a carrot and then attach this as a nose in the face. Make the ear warmers from red marzipan, hair from yellow marzipan and a hat from cocoa-coloured marzipan and attach these to the head. Add a small flower to the hat. Put on the mouth, eyes and buttons with decorating chocolate.

Place the head onto the body and drape a red scarf with fringes around the neck. Freeze the figure for a short while and then apply a mist of white cocoa butter from above.

SILBERKUGELN

SILVER BALLS

Helles Marzipan zu Kugeln formen und in Silberpulver wälzen.

Shape light-coloured marzipan into balls and roll in silver powder.

Schneekristalle mit weißer Kuvertüre in vorgezeichneten Kristallzucker garnieren

Use white couverture to pipe the snow crystals onto the crystal shape marked in the sugar

VERGOLDETER FRÜCHTEKORB

GILDED FRUIT HAMPER

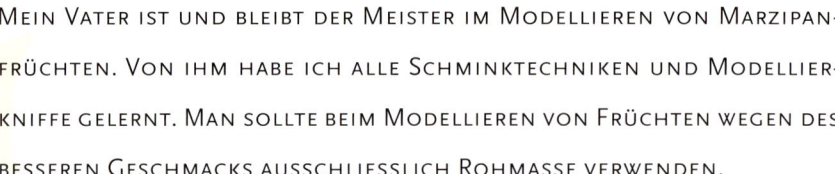

MEIN VATER IST UND BLEIBT DER MEISTER IM MODELLIEREN VON MARZIPAN-FRÜCHTEN. VON IHM HABE ICH ALLE SCHMINKTECHNIKEN UND MODELLIER-KNIFFE GELERNT. MAN SOLLTE BEIM MODELLIEREN VON FRÜCHTEN WEGEN DES BESSEREN GESCHMACKS AUSSCHLIESSLICH ROHMASSE VERWENDEN.

NOW AS BEFORE MY FATHER IS A MASTER IN MODELLING MARZIPAN FRUIT. ALL MY COLOURING METHODS AND MODELLING TRICKS I HAVE LEARNT FROM HIM. WHEN MODELLING FRUIT ONE SHOULD EXCLUSIVELY USE RAW MARZIPAN BECAUSE OF ITS BETTER TASTE.

FRÜCHTEKORB

Marzipan in der späteren Höhe des Korbes ausrollen. Mit einem Ring den Boden ausstechen. Anschließend einen Marzipanstreifen mit einem Spezialrollholz (Korbmuster) riefen. Marzipanstreifen als Seitenwände an den Boden anlegen und befestigen. Mit dem Wellenkneifer den Rand modellieren. Dazu den Kneifer immer wieder in Alkohol tauchen, um zu vermeiden, dass er am Marzipan festklebt. Den Korb antrocknen lassen und entweder mit einen Gasbrenner abflämmen oder, wie im Bild, mit Goldstaub angolden.

FRUIT HAMPER

Roll out some marzipan as wide as the hamper's intended height. Use a ring to cut out the base of the basket. Apply a basket weave pattern to the marzipan strip for the sides of the basket using a special pattern roll. Attach this strip to the base to make up the sides of the basket. Apply a wave pattern to the edge, using a wave crimping tool. When doing that, keep dipping the tool into alcohol in order to avoid it sticking to the marzipan. Leave the basket to dry on the surface and flame off with a gas torch or apply a dusting of gold dust as shown in the picture.

LEMON

Form a ball, with both ends coming to a slight point, and apply the surface texture using a studded modelling board. Use a small modelling tool to make an indentation at one end, put on the mouth and nose and make a slit with a knife for the eyes. Leave to dry, then apply a yellow colouring to the finished lemon; add a touch of green colouring towards the ends and use decorating chocolate to apply the spectacles.

ZITRONE

Eine Kugel modellieren, beide Enden leicht spitz zulaufen lassen und mit einem genoppten Modellierbrett (Senfbrett) die Oberfläche strukturieren. An einer Seite mit dem kleinen Kugelmodellierholz eine Vertiefung eindrücken, dann Mund und Nase anbringen und die Augen mit dem Messer einkerben. Trocknen lassen, anschließend fertige Zitrone zuerst gelb schminken, dann die spitzen Enden leicht grün auslaufen lassen und mit Garnierschokolade die Brille aufgarnieren.

PLUM

Form a marzipan ball, shaping both ends to a point so that the overall shape is oval; starting from one end use the small modelling tool to make an indentation and carry on from that to make a slight groove along the side of the fruit. Put on the mouth, nose and eyes with eyebrows. Leave to dry and then apply blue, black and finally metallic blue colouring. Use decorating chocolate to add the eyes and attach a stalk made from brown marzipan.

ZWETSCHGE

Eine Marzipankugel an beiden Enden leicht spitzoval modellieren, dann, vom einen Ende ausgehend, mit dem kleinen Kugelmodellierholz eine Vertiefung eindrücken und mit dem gleichen Modellierholz an der Seite eine Kerbe eindrücken. Mund, Nase sowie Augen mit Augenwülsten aufbringen. Trocknen lassen, dann mit blauer, schwarzer und zum Schluss mit metallicblauer Farbe schminken. Mit Garnierschokolade die Augen aufbringen und einen Stiel aus braunem Marzipan ansetzen.

CHERRIES

Shape the marzipan raw mixture into a heart shape and make a small indentation for the stalk, using the modelling tool. Put on the mouth and nose and make a slit for the eyes with a knife. Leave to dry, apply red metallic colouring and use decorating chocolate to add the eyes. For the stalks you can either use genuine dried cherry stalks, as in the picture, or buy artificial ones.

KIRSCHEN

Marzipanrohmasse leicht herzförmig ausmodellieren und mit dem kleinen Kugelmodellierholz eine Vertiefung für den Stiel formen. Dann Mund und Nase anbringen und die Augen mit dem Messer einkerben. Trocknen lassen, mit Rotmetallic-Farbe schminken und mit Garnierschokolade die Augen garnieren. Als Stiele entweder, wie im Bild, echte getrocknete Kirschstiele verwenden, ansonsten kann man auch künstliche kaufen.

1

2

3

4

ERDBEERE

Eine ovale Form modellieren, diese leicht abflachen, dann mit einem genoppten Modellierbrett (Senfbrett) die Oberfläche strukturieren. An einer Seite mit dem kleinen Kugelmodellierholz eine Vertiefung eindrücken, dann Mund und Nase anbringen. Die Augen mit dem gleichen Modellierholz einmodellieren. Trocknen lassen und die Frucht zuerst gelb, dann nur den Blütenansatz leicht grünlich und zum Schluss die komplette Frucht erdbeerrot schminken. Die Augen mit Garnierschokolade aufbringen. Grüne Blätter und eine kleine Blüte modellieren und am Blütenansatz anbringen.

STRAWBERRY

Model an oval shape, flatten it slightly and apply the surface texture using a studded modelling board. Use a small modelling tool to make an indentation at one end, then put on the mouth and nose. Use the same tool to shape the eyes.

Leave to dry, apply yellow colouring followed by a little green around the stalk area and finally colour the whole fruit in strawberry red. Add the eyes with decorating chocolate. Model green leaves and a small blossom and attach to the stalk area.

PFIRSICH

Marzipan zu einer Kugel modellieren und, von einem Ende ausgehend, mit dem kleinen Kugelmodellierholz eine Vertiefung eindrücken und mit dem gleichen Modellierholz an der gegenüberliegenden Seite eine Kerbe eindrücken. Mund und Nase anbringen, die Lippe jedoch erst nach dem Schminken anbringen. Vertiefungen für die Augen einmodellieren. Trocknen lassen, dann die Frucht zuerst gelb, dann die Seiten rot schminken. Anschließend mit Weizenpuder pudern. Die Augen mit Garnierschokolade aufspritzen und einen Stiel aus braunem Marzipan sowie die Lippe aus rosa Marzipan ansetzen.

PEACH

Form a marzipan ball and, starting from one end, use the small modelling tool to make an indentation and carry on with that tool to make a slight groove along the opposite side of the fruit. Put on the mouth and nose but wait with the lips until after the colouring. Make indentations for the eyes. Leave to dry; apply yellow colouring followed by red colouring to the sides. Apply a dusting of wheat powder. Use decorating chocolate to add the eyes and attach a stalk made from brown marzipan as well as the lip made from pink marzipan.

Einzelne Arbeitsschritte bei der Herstellung des Apfels

Production steps for making the apple

An den Enden grüne Farbe auftragen

Apply green colouring to the ends

Mit einem ausgefransten Pinsel rote Farbe aufnehmen, diese dann leicht abstreifen

Use a worn and scraggy brush to apply some red colouring in streaks

Apfel nach dem Antrocknen der vorher aufge-tragenen Farben leicht mit dem Pinsel abtupfen

Once the previous colouring has dried, use a brush to dab the apple lightly

BANANA

Model a piece of marzipan into a basic banana shape, with one end slightly pointed and the other end cut to an angular shape with a knife. Shape the mouth and attach the nose. Use the knife to make slits for the eyes. Leave to dry, then apply yellow colouring followed by a touch of green at the ends and some brown along the edges and the stalk end.

APPLE

Start with a marzipan ball that tapers slightly to one end. Use the small modelling tool to make an indentation for the stalk at the rounder end and another one at the blossom end. Make indentations for mouth and eyes but wait with the lips and nose until after the colouring. Leave to dry, then apply yellow food colouring followed by a touch of green at the ends; use a scraggy brush to put on bits of red colouring. Finally attach the lips and nose. Use decorating chocolate to add the eyes and attach a green leaf and a stalk made from brown marzipan.

ORANGE

Form a ball and apply surface texture using a studded modelling board. Use a small modelling tool to make an indentation for the stalk at one end. Put on the mouth and nose and make a slit for the eyes. Leave to dry and then apply yellow colouring followed by orange. Use decorating chocolate to add the eyes and attach a green leaf and a stalk.

BANANE

Marzipan zur länglichen Bananengrund-form modellieren, ein Ende leicht anspitzen, dem Stielansatz mit einem Messer eine eckige Form geben. Den Mund einmodellieren und die Nase anbringen. Die Augen mit dem Messer einkerben. Trocknen lassen, dann zuerst mit gelber Farbe schminken, danach die Enden leicht grün, die Kanten und den Stielansatz braun schminken.

APFEL

Eine Marzipankugel leicht konisch zulaufen lassen. Am runderen Ende mit dem kleinen Kugelmodellierholz eine Vertiefung für den Stiel eindrücken, am gegenüberliegenden Ende den Blütenansatz. Mund und Augen eindrücken, Lippen und Nase aber erst nach dem Schminken anbringen. Trocknen lassen, und zunächst mit gelber Farbe schminken, dann die Enden leicht grün färben und mit einem ausgefransten Pinsel rote Farbe auftupfen. Abschließend Lippen und Nase anbringen. Mit Garnierschokolade die Augen garnieren und ein grünes Blatt sowie einen Stiel aus braunem Marzipan ansetzen.

ORANGE

Eine Kugel modellieren, dann mit einem genoppten Modellierbrett (Senfbrett) die Oberfläche strukturieren. An einer Seite mit dem kleinen Kugelmodellierholz den Stielansatz eindrücken. Danach Mund und Nase anbringen und die Augen einkerben. Trocknen lassen und zuerst mit gelber Farbe, dann mit Orange schminken. Die Augen mit Garnierschokolade anbringen und ein grünes Blatt sowie einen Stielansatz anbringen.

SIEGFRIED'S DRAGON

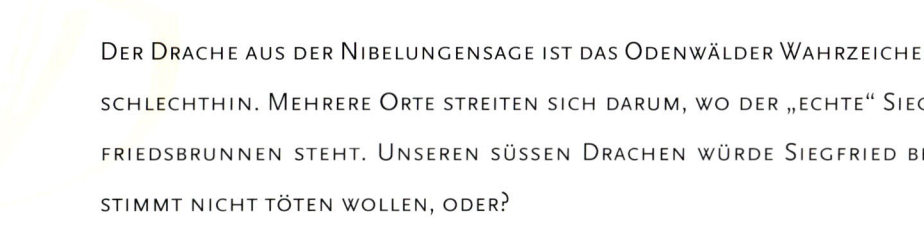

Der Drache aus der Nibelungensage ist das Odenwälder Wahrzeichen schlechthin. Mehrere Orte streiten sich darum, wo der „echte" Siegfriedsbrunnen steht. Unseren süssen Drachen würde Siegfried bestimmt nicht töten wollen, oder?

The dragon from the Nibelungen legend has become the main symbol for the Odenwald region. Several communities argue where the "genuine" Siegfried well is located. I can't imagine that Siegfried would have wanted to kill our sweet dragon, what do you think?

MAKING THE PARTS

Start by modelling the basic body, then use your fingers to fashion the spikes on its back and use the rounded modelling tool to make impressions resembling scales. To make the point of the tail, first form a ball, work it apart with the tips of your fingers, fold together and make a heart shape. Push flat and attach to the end of the tail.

To make the legs, shape the marzipan into cones, attach to the body and then shape the claws from the leg material using the small modelling tool.

HERSTELLUNG

Zuerst den Grundkörper modellieren, anschließend mit den Fingern die Rückenstacheln herausarbeiten und dann mit dem halbrunden Modellierholz die Schuppen eindrücken. Für die Schwanzspitze zuerst eine Kugel formen, mit den Fingerspitzen auseinander modellieren, zusammenklappen und zu einem Herz formen. Flachdrücken und am Schwanzende anbringen.

Für die Beine Marzipan zu einem Kegel modellieren, am Körper ansetzen und die Krallen mit dem kleinen Kugelmodellierholz anmodellieren.

Elemente für die Füße

Elements for the feet

1

6

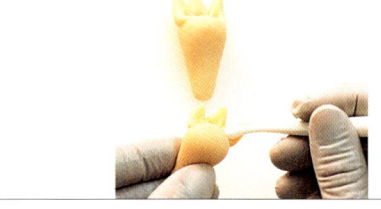

Krallen an den Fuß anmodellieren.

Fashioning the claws on the feet

2

7

Elemente für das herzförmige Schwanzende

Elements for the heart-shaped tip of the tail

3

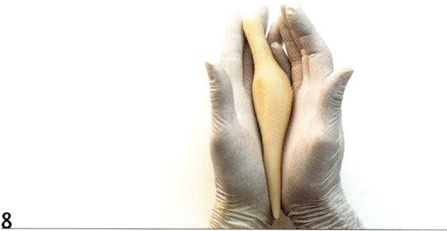

8

Flügel

Wings

4

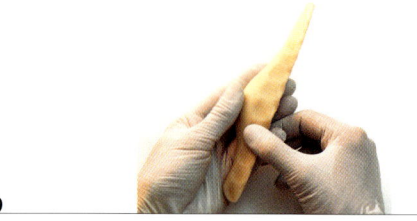

9

Elemente für den Grundkörper

Elements for the basic body

5

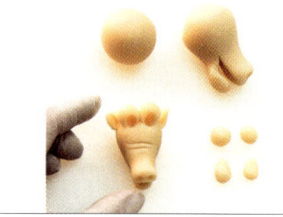

10

Kugel modellieren

Modelling a ball

Hals und Körper modellieren

Modelling the neck and body

Schwanz modellieren

Modelling the tail

Für die Flügel Marzipan zuerst zu Tropfen, dann flach modellieren und anschließend mit dem Modellierholz leicht gebogene Linien aufbringen. Die Flügel am Rücken anbringen, stabilisieren und über Nacht trocknen lassen.

For the wings, start shaping the marzipan into a drop shape, flatten and use the modelling tool to score with slightly bent lines. Attach the wings to the back, stabilise and leave to dry overnight.

Rückenzacken modellieren

Fashioning the jagged ridge line on the back

Für den Kopf eine Marzipankugel zu einer Birne modellieren, vom dünnen Ende her einschneiden und dann mit dem kleinen Kugelmodellierholz die Nasenlöcher hochschiebend formen. Das Maul leicht auseinanderklappen und ein Modellierholz wie einen Knochen quer hineinschieben, um den Unterkiefer stärker zu betonen.

To make the head, shape a marzipan ball into a pear, cut at the thin end and use the small modelling tool to push up the material to make the nostrils. Open the mouth slightly and push a modelling tool across the open mouth, like a bone, in order to emphasise the lower jaw.

Mit dem Messer den Nasenrücken modellieren, mit dem größeren Kugelmodellierholz die Marzipankugeln für die Augen und mit dem Schiffchen die Ohren seitlich anbringen.

Use a knife to model the ridge on the nose, use the larger rounded modelling tool to attach the marzipan balls as eyes and the spoon-type tool to attach the ears on the side of the head.

Elemente für den Kopf

Elements for the head

Nachdem alles stabil angetrocknet ist, den Kopf anbringen und mit dem Airbrush zuerst gelbe Farbe, dann grüne Farbe auftragen, dann leicht mit Silbermetallic-Farbe absprühen. Zum Schluss die Zunge und die Augen mit Garnierschokolade anbringen.

Once everything has dried well, attach the head to the body and apply first yellow and then green colouring with an airbrush, followed by a light spray with silver metallic colouring. Finally add the tongue and the eyes with decorating chocolate.

TAUFE

CHRISTENING

RELIGIÖSE FESTE SIND FÜR DEN KONDITOR MANCHMAL ETWAS SCHWIERIG UMZUSETZEN. ICH KANN MICH NOCH GUT AN MEINEN ITALIENISCHEN KOLLEGEN BEI EINER KONDITOREIKUNSTAUSSTELLUNG ERINNERN: ER SCHNITZTE DIE SCHÖNSTE FIGUR AUS KAKAOBUTTER, DIE ICH JEMALS GESEHEN HABE – ABER LEIDER HATTE DIE JURY EIN PROBLEM MIT DEM LEIDEN CHRISTI. ANDERS IST ES BEI DER TAUFE, DIESES FEST STEHT FÜR DAS LEBEN.

SOMETIMES IT CAN BE DIFFICULT FOR THE CONFECTIONER TO FIND THE RIGHT EXPRESSION FOR RELIGIOUS FESTIVITIES. I HAVE VIVID MEMORIES OF ONE OF MY ITALIAN COLLEAGUES AND HIS EXHIBIT IN AN ARTISTIC CONFECTIONERY EXHIBITION: HE HAD CARVED THE MOST BEAUTIFUL FIGURE FROM COCOA BUTTER THAT I HAVE EVER SEEN – BUT UNFORTUNATELY THE JURY HAD A PROBLEM WITH THE PASSION OF CHRIST. WITH CHRISTENINGS IT IS DIFFERENT, THEY ARE A CELEBRATION OF LIFE.

BABY

Je nach Geschlecht aus rosa oder himmelblauem Marzipan eine Bettdecke und ein Kissen herstellen und mit dem Messer über Kreuz einkerben. Für den Kopf eine rosa Kugel herstellen, die geschlossenen Augen, Nasenlöcher und Mund eindrücken. Seitlich die Ohren anbringen und an der Stirn eine Haartolle. Besonders gut kommt es bei der Taufgesellschaft an, wenn die Figur die Haarfarbe des Täuflings hat.

BABY

Depending on the sex of the baby, use pink or sky-blue marzipan to make a bed cover and pillow, using a knife to score the stitching in a crossways fashion. To make the head, start with a pink ball and push in the closed eyes, nostrils and mouth. Attach the ears on the side and a hair lock on the forehead. The baby figures are usually most popular if their hair is in the colour of the christened baby.

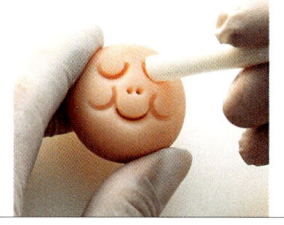

Augen in das Gesicht des Babys einmodellieren

Modelling the eyes of the baby

1

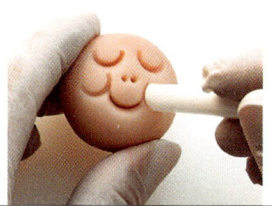

Mund mit Grübchen einmodellieren

Fashion the mouth with a dimple

2

STORCH

Für den Storch werden zwei verschiedene Farben verwendet, weiß für den Körper und orange für die Beine.

Zuerst eine lang gezogene Birne formen, an der dünneren Seite einen Hals mit Kopf modellieren. An der dickeren Seite orangefarbenes Marzipan ebenso lang ansetzen und mittig trennen, so dass zwei Beine entstehen, diese dann übereinander schlagen. Die Figur in einen kleinen Tortenring legen, einen Schnabel aus orangefarbenem Marzipan und einen Höcker aus kakaofarbenem Marzipan ansetzen. Das Baby einlegen, die Flügel aus einem weißen und einem kakaofarbenem Teil herstellen, anmodellieren und um das Baby gebogen trocknen lassen. Füße ausstechen, trocknen lassen und anbringen. Die Augen mit Garnierschokolade anbringen.

STORK

Use two different colours for the stork, white for the body and orange for the legs. Start by forming an elongated pear and modelling a neck and head from the thinner side. Add some orange-coloured marzipan of the same length at the thicker end and separate it into two equal parts to make the legs; cross the legs over. Place the figure into a small cake ring and attach a beak made from orange-coloured marzipan and a knob of cocoa-coloured marzipan. Insert the baby, make the wings from a white and cocoa-coloured part, attach to the bird, bend round the baby and leave to dry. Cut out the feet, leave to dry and attach to the body. Add the eyes with decorating chocolate.

MARZIPAN MOON AND CLOUDS

To make the clouds and the moon use cutting shapes. First roll out some neutral marzipan, about 1 cm thick, place a foil over it and cut the shapes through the foil – it will give the figures rounded edges. Fashion the face of the moon, leave to dry well and then place the figures with the top face onto the candy sugar, cover with foil and leave to candy for one or more days, depending on the sugar content desired. Remove the figures carefully from the candy bath, allow to drip-dry and apply colouring with an airbrush after fully drying them. Finish by adding the eyes with decorating chocolate.

To make the candy sugar, add 5 parts of sugar to 2 parts of water, bring to the boil and adjust to 74 °Brix.

MARZIPANMOND UND WOLKEN

Für die Wolken und den Mond Ausstecher verwenden. Dazu neutrales Marzipan etwa 1 Zentimeter dick ausrollen, mit Folie belegen und mit der Folie ausstechen – so bekommt die Figur abgerundete Kanten. Das Gesicht des Mondes nachmodellieren, gut trocknen lassen. Figuren dann mit der Oberseite auf den Kandierzucker legen, mit Folie bedecken und, je nach gewünschtem Kandierungsgrad, einen oder mehrere Tage kandieren lassen. Anschließend vorsichtig aus dem Kandierbad nehmen, abtropfen lassen und nach dem Abtrocknen mit dem Airbrush schminken. Abschließend Augen mit Garnierschokolade anbringen.

Für den Kandierzucker 5 Teile Zucker mit 2 Teilen Wasser zum Kochen bringen und auf 74 °Brix einstellen.

CHRISTMAS

WEIHNACHTEN OHNE MARZIPAN IST EINFACH UNVORSTELLBAR — ERST RECHT WENN MAN IN LÜBECK ZU GAST IST. ALS KIND MOCHTE ICH LANGE ZEIT KEIN MARZIPAN, DA ES MIR EINFACH IMMER ZU SÜSS WAR. ICH GLAUBE, DAS GEHT VIELEN MENSCHEN SO. ERST WENN MAN EINMAL RICHTIG GUTES MARZIPAN GEGESSEN HAT, KANN MAN VERSTEHEN, DASS DIES EINE GANZ BESONDERE SPEZIALITÄT IST.

CHRISTMAS WITHOUT MARZIPAN IS UNIMAGINABLE — ESPECIALLY WHEN YOU ARE SPENDING IT IN LÜBECK IN THE NORTH OF GERMANY. WHEN I WAS A CHILD, FOR A LONG TIME I DID NOT LIKE MARZIPAN BECAUSE I JUST FOUND IT TOO SWEET. I THINK MANY PEOPLE HAVE THE SAME EXPERIENCE. BUT WHEN YOU HAVE TASTED SOME REALLY GOOD MARZIPAN YOU WILL UNDERSTAND THAT IT IS SOMETHING VERY SPECIAL.

FATHER CHRISTMAS PART 1

Colour some marzipan and use it to make the body of the Father Christmas. Start by modelling a pear, then attach two extended drops as arms. Shape the hat with a bent top.

Use pink marzipan to form the head in a slightly oval shape; use the modelling tool to make the indentations for the eyes. Make small oval beads to insert as eyes, using the same modelling tool.

WEIHNACHTSMANN TEIL 1

Für den Körper des Weihnachtsmannes durchgefärbtes Marzipan verwenden. Zuerst eine Birne modellieren, dann zwei verlängerte Tropfen als Arme anbringen. Mütze mit gebogener Spitze modellieren. Der Kopf leicht oval aus rosa angewirktem Marzipan formen, mit dem Kugelmodellierholz Vertiefungen für die Augen eindrücken. Augen aus kleinen ovalen Kügelchen mit dem gleichen Modellierholz einlegen.

WEIHNACHTSMANN TEIL 2

Einen spitzen Bart aus naturfarbenem Marzipan modellieren und mit dem Schiffchen anbringen. Einen Mund aus rosa Marzipan sowie einen Oberlippenbart aus neutralem Marzipan anbringen, außerdem eine Nase aus dunklerem Rosa. Die Mütze aufsetzen und den Übergang mit einem Band aus neutralem Marzipan kaschieren. Den Kopf über Nacht in einem Tortenring trocknen lassen und mit einem Strohhalm am Körper anbringen.

FATHER CHRISTMAS PART 2

Model a pointed beard from natural-coloured marzipan and attach with the spoon-type tool. Attach a mouth made from pink marzipan as well as a moustache from neutral marzipan under a nose made from a darker shade of pink. Put the hat onto the head and hide the joint with a band of neutral marzipan. Leave the head to dry overnight in a cake ring and then attach to the body using a straw.

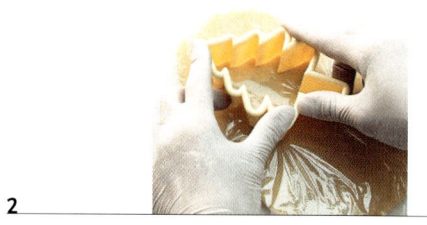

RUDOLF IN DER SCHNEEKUGEL

Für das Rentier zuerst eine Marzipankugel modellieren und mindestens einen Tag antrocknen lassen.
Für Kopf und Hufe Marzipan mit Kakaopulver braun einfärben. Hufe in Tropfenform modellieren und mit dem Schiffchen einkerben.
Für den Kopf ein Oval modellieren, an der Oberseite leicht mit den Zeigefingern eindrücken, das dickere Ende auseinanderschneiden und dann mit naturfarbenem Marzipan füllen. Mit dem Messer die Zahnreihen eindrücken, die Nasenlöcher mit dem Kugelmodellierholz hochschiebend modellieren und die Augenhöhlen eindrücken. Ohren modellieren, seitlich anbringen und ein Geweih aus zwei dunkelbraunen Wülsten anbringen. Zum Schluss eine gelbe Marzipantolle auf das Geweih setzen und eine rote Nase anbringen. Einzelteile trocknen lassen. Die Kugel in temperierter weißer Kuvertüre igeln und direkt Hufe und Kopf anbringen.

RUDOLF IN THE SNOWBALL

To make the reindeer, start with a marzipan ball and leave to dry for at least a day. Use cocoa powder to colour those parts making the head and hooves. Model the hooves in the shape of drops and insert the parting with the spoon-type modelling tool.
To make the head, model an oval shape, indent slightly at the top with your index fingers, insert a cut at the thicker end and fill this with natural-coloured marzipan. Use a knife to mark the texture of the teeth, use the modelling tool to press in the nostrils with an upwards movement and also the eye sockets. Model the ears, attach to the side of the head, make the antlers from two thin dark-brown rolls and attach. Finally, add a yellow marzipan quiff onto the antlers and attach a red nose. Leave the parts to dry. Use tempered white couverture to spike the ball and attach the hooves and head directly.

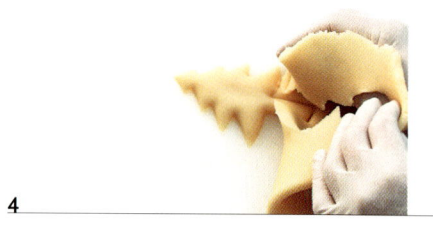

Marzipan 1 cm ausrollen und mit Folie abdecken

Roll out the marzipan, 1 cm thick, and cover with foil

Tannenbäume mit Folie bedeckt ausstechen

Use tree-shaped cutters to cut the shapes through the foil

Folie abziehen

Pull off the foil

Überschüssiges Marzipan entfernen

Remove any excess marzipan

Kandierter Marzipanbaum

Candied marzipan tree

PRESENTS

Form a number of balls from neutral marzipan and then use a small board to press these into the shape of dice. Leave to dry for a while and colour with metallic colouring; use decorating chocolate to apply the ribbons.

CANDIED CHRISTMAS TREES WITH METALLIC BAUBLES AND STAR

To make the Christmas trees, first roll out some neutral marzipan, about 1 cm thick, place a foil over it and cut out the shapes with a cutter in the shape of a Christmas tree. This gives the shapes rounded edges. Leave the Christmas trees to dry well and then place the figures with the top face onto the candy sugar, cover with foil and leave to candy for one or more days, depending on the sugar content desired. Carefully take the trees from the candy bath, leave to drip-dry and then a bit longer to dry off. To make the candy sugar, add 5 parts of sugar to 2 parts of water, bring to the boil and adjust to 74 °Brix.

Form small balls for the baubles, cut out small stars and colour both with metallic colouring; attach to the trees. Arrange and fix the trees and the other figures on a base slab.

GESCHENKE

Neutrales Marzipan zu Kugeln und dann mit einem kleinen Brett zu Würfeln formen. Antrocknen lassen und mit Metallicfarbe einfärben, dann mit Garnierschokolade die Bänder aufbringen.

KANDIERTE TANNENBÄUME MIT METALLICKUGELN UND STERN

Für die Tannenbäume neutrales Marzipan etwa einen Zentimeter dick ausrollen, mit Folie belegen und dann mit einem Tannenbaumausstecher ausstechen. So bekommt die Figur abgerundete Kanten.

Die Tannenbäume gut trocknen lassen, mit der Oberseite in Kandierzucker legen, mit Folie bedecken und, je nach gewünschtem Kandierungsgrad, einen oder mehrere Tage kandieren lassen. Anschließend vorsichtig aus dem Kandierbad nehmen, abtropfen und kurz antrocknen lassen. Für den Kandierzucker 5 Teile Zucker mit 2 Teilen Wasser zum Kochen bringen und auf 74 °Brix einstellen.

Kleine Kugeln formen, außerdem Sternchen ausstechen, beides mit Metallicfarbe einfärben und auf den Bäumchen anbringen. Die Bäume sowie die anderen Figuren auf einer Platte befestigen.

ACKNOWLEDGEMENTS

WHO TO THANK?

First of all my family. It is my family that gives me support and the motivation to face new challenges again and again.
Above all my two sons Leon and Mika – they are the engine, the foundation of life.

Then I would like to say a big thank you to my wife. She is the best mother in the world for our children and, apart from the many other tasks on her plate, she clears the path for my work, corrects and advises me and is the fuel in my engine. And often enough also the starter motor.

My sister is my advisor, just like my wife.
She takes care of our parental business and ensures that everything runs smoothly.

Then there are my parents without whom I would never have become a patissier and who have always backed me up and given support and encouragement in all my ventures.
My father, who has taken the brunt of the responsibility for the construction work we have undertaken in recent years, and my mother, who still is a stalwart support in the Café and, together with my sister, is a magician when it comes to packaging. In the bakery we often produce the most gorgeous creations but it is the packaging that crowns it all.

There are many other relations that I could mention and I certainly haven't forgotten, but a special thanks must go to my aunt Carla. She was simply there for us when we needed her.

Without any doubt, our members of staff have been terrific in being always willing to manifest those things that appear as ideas in my mind – so a big thank you goes to them as well.

In addition, I would like to thank by publishers, Matthaes Verlag, in particular Bruni Thiemeyer and Julia Bauer for their unwavering help and patience.

A very big thank you also goes to my favourite photographer and friend Matthias Hoffmann; without him my recipes would just be bits of paper with some writing.

From outside my family I would like to mention first of all my friend Mario Grazia. He is not only one of my former colleagues at Pregel and now travels the world as a consultant, he has always helped me with the preparations for the photo shoots.

Then there are the other members of my Pregel family: I would like to remember Patrizio Bedendo, Stefano Laghi, Paola Chiari and Dr. Raboni. During that time I have had the privilege of learning a lot. The only pity is that most of the friends have been scattered about the globe.

I should not forget all my friends and colleagues who I can always ask for advice and on whose help I can count.

A special thanks also goes to the delegates in my seminars around the world because without them and their questions I might not even have had some of the ideas in my creations.

Last but not least I would like to thank you, my respected readers. Without you, my ideas would never travel as far as they do. It is thanks to you that I can travel the world and yet also spend some time at home with my family.

And so I thank you also in the name of my family.

DANK DES AUTORS

WEM DANKEN?

Natürlich zuallererst meiner Familie. Sie ist es, die mir Halt gibt und die mich anspornt, mich immer neuen Herausforderungen zu stellen.
Allen voran meinen beiden Söhnen Leon und Mika, sie sind der Motor, der Lebensgrund.

Als nächstes möchte ich mich bei meiner Frau bedanken. Sie ist für unsere Kinder die beste Mutter der Welt und hält mir, neben den vielen anderen Aufgaben, den Rücken frei, korrigiert, berät und ist das Benzin in meinem Motor. Und oft genug meine Starthilfe.

Meine Schwester ist, genauso wie meine Frau, meine Beraterin. Sie kümmert sich um unser elterliches Geschäft und sorgt in allen Bereichen dafür, dass es rund läuft.

Dann sind da noch meine Eltern, ohne die ich nie Konditor geworden wäre, die immer hinter mir standen und mich in allem, was ich machen wollte, unterstützten und bestärkten.
Mein Vater, der mir den Rücken bei den Bauarbeiten der letzten Jahre frei gehalten hat und meine Mutter, die als Flaggschiff immer noch ihren Mann in unserem Café steht und mit meiner Schwester zusammen ein Verpackungswunder ist. In der Backstube machen wir oft die tollsten Sachen, aber erst die Verpackung setzt dem Ganzen die Krone auf.

Ich könnte noch viele andere Menschen aus meiner Verwandtschaft nennen, die ich bestimmt nicht vergessen habe, aber ganz besonders möchte ich meiner Tante Carla danken. Sie war einfach da, als wir sie brauchten.

Natürlich möchte ich auch all unseren Mitarbeitern danken, die immer kurzfristig die Dinge umsetzen müssen, die ich mir in den Kopf gesetzt habe.

Außerdem möchte ich mich bei meinem Verlag, dem Matthaes Verlag, bedanken, insbesondere bei Bruni Thiemeyer und Julia Bauer für ihre unermüdliche Hilfe und Geduld.

Ein großer Dank geht auch an meinen Lieblingsfotografen und Freund Matthias Hoffmann. Ohne ihn wären meine Rezepte nur Zettel mit Buchstaben.

An externen Familienmitgliedern möchte ich dieses Mal zuallererst meinen Freund Mario Grazia nennen. Er ist nicht nur einer meiner früheren Kollegen bei Pregel und reist heute als Berater durch die ganze Welt, er war auch immer als Hilfe bei den Vorbereitungen für die Fotos dabei.

Auch die restlichen Mitglieder meiner Pregel-Familie, Patrizio Bedendo, Stefano Laghi, Paola Chiari und Dr. Raboni möchte ich an dieser Stelle nicht vergessen. Ich habe in dieser Zeit viel lernen dürfen. Schade, dass die meisten mittlerweile in alle Winde verstreut sind.

Nicht zu vergessen auch all meine Freunde und Kollegen, die ich immer um Rat fragen kann und auf deren Hilfe ich bauen kann.

Danken möchte ich auch besonders meinen Schülern in den Seminaren auf der ganzen Welt, denn ohne sie und ihre Fragen würde ich vielleicht auf die eine oder andere Idee gar nicht erst kommen.

Nicht zuletzt möchte ich Ihnen, meinen sehr verehrten Lesern, danken. Ohne Sie kommen meine Ideen nicht um die ganze Erde. Nur durch Sie kann ich in der ganzen Welt unterwegs sein und doch öfters einmal zu Hause bei meiner Familie bleiben.

Danke, auch im Namen meiner Familie.

BERND SIEFERT...

... und seine Familie

... and his family

Bernd Siefert, Jahrgang 1967 ist Konditor und Patissier aus Passion. Viele seiner süßen Versuchungen wurden mit „Gold" gekürt, Titel wie „Konditor des Jahres", „Vize-Weltcup-Sieger" sowie „Weltmeister der Konditoren" sind dem Weltenbummler mit Wurzeln im Odenwald verliehen worden. Wenn Filmstars, Modezaren oder Scheichs exquisite Desserts wünschen, ist Bernd Siefert gefragt. Aber auch Rundfunk und Fernsehen klopfen regelmäßig an.

Berater für exklusive Marken der süßen Branche, Referent an Fachschulen, Foodstylist, Trainer der Nationalmannschaft der Köche sowie Betreiber des familieneigenen Cafés sind nur ein kleiner Auszug seiner vielfältigen Betätigungen.

Mehr über Bernd Siefert und sein Seminarangebot finden Sie unter: www.bernd-siefert.de und www.cafesiefert.de.

Born in 1967, Bernd Siefert is a pastry chef and confectioner by passion. Many of his sweet temptations have gained gold awards. This globetrotter, with his roots in the Odenwald region of Germany, has won titles such as German Champion, World Cup Vice-Champion, as well as World Pastry Champion. When film stars, fashion gurus and sheikhs call for exquisite desserts, they often ask for Bernd Siefert. Other regular callers are broadcasting and television companies.

Consultant for exclusive brands in the sweets industry, lecturer at Further Education colleges, food stylist, cook's national team coach as well as manager of his own family-owned café: these are just a few of his many attributes.

More about Bernd Siefert and his seminars: www.bernd-siefert.de and www.cafesiefert.de.

MATTHIAS HOFFMANN

Die Arbeiten von Matthias Hoffmann, Food-Fotograf mit langjähriger Erfahrung, wurden vielfach ausgezeichnet. Neben Industrie und Werbung arbeitet er regelmäßig für Zeitschriften- und Buchverlage.

www.hoffman-fotodesign.de

Matthias Hoffmann, a food photographer with many years of experience, was awarded several prizes for his work. Besides industry and advertising agencies, he is working for book and magazine publishers on a regular basis.

www.hoffman-fotodesign.de

IMPRESSUM

ISBN 978-3-87515-105-3

1. Auflage 2008

Alle Rechte vorbehalten.

Nachdruck, auch auszugsweise, sowie Verbreitung durch Fernsehen, Film und Funk, durch Fotokopie, Tonträger oder Datenverarbeitungsanlagen jeder Art nur mit schriftlicher Genehmigung des Verlags gestattet.

Übersetzung: DDDienst, Gerlingen
Fotografie: Matthias Hoffmann, Delmenhorst
Grafische Gestaltung und Satz: Atelier Krohmer, Dettingen/Erms
Redaktion: Redaktionsbüro Bluthard, Stuttgart

© 2008 Matthaes Verlag GmbH, Stuttgart

IMPRINT

ISBN 978-3-87515-105-3

1st edition 2008

All rights reserved.

Any reproduction, also parts, as well as distribution via television, film and radio broadcasting, by making photocopies, by audio devices or data processing systems of any kind are permitted only with the expressed permission of the publishers.

Translation: DDDienst, Gerlingen
Photography: Matthias Hoffmann, Delmenhorst
Graphic Design and Typography: Atelier Krohmer, Dettingen/Erms
Redaktion: Redaktionsbüro Bluthard, Stuttgart

© 2008 Matthaes Verlag GmbH, Stuttgart